The Color of Liberty

Edited by Sue Peabody and Tyler Stovall

The Color of Liberty

HISTORIES OF RACE IN FRANCE

Duke University Press   Durham and London

2003

#51519592

Contents

3
Colonial and Global Perspectives

4
Race and the Postcolonial City

Acknowledgments

We first met in 1996, during a panel about integrating race into the teaching of French history, held at the annual meeting of the Western Society for French History. Both of us had been working on the topic for several years and had often felt that our concerns definitely lay outside the mainstream of our profession. Yet our modest panel was packed with colleagues interested to learn about our ideas, and about the history of race in France as a whole. That panel marked the true inception of this book. Over the last twenty-five years, questions of racial difference have become ever more salient in the cultural and political life of contemporary France, most recently in Jean-Marie Le Pen's impressive showing in the May 2002 presidential elections. At the same time, a number of scholars, especially graduate students and younger professors, have begun to investigate the historical roots of this phenomenon in France, critically interrogating traditional notions of French color blindness, French national identity, and the relationship between metropole and overseas empire. This edited volume represents some of the best of this new research, and we hope it will prompt reflection on the nature of French history and of race in general.

Many people deserve thanks for helping to make *The Color of Liberty* a reality. First and foremost, we would like to thank our contributors for their stimulating scholarship and their seemingly endless patience. All responded to our editorial suggestions promptly and with appreciation, and many suggested other individuals who should be included in this project. We feel honored to have been able to bring together their work in this volume. We would also like to express our gratitude to the people at Duke University Press who had faith in this book project and who transformed it from a series of papers into an integrated text. Our editor, Valerie Milholland, encouraged our belief in the importance of this project and made sure to keep it moving on schedule. In particular, editorial assistant Miriam L. Angress walked us through the process of getting a publication contract and then producing the final text. Our thanks go also to the anonymous readers at Duke University Press, who made important suggestions about the shape of the project in general, and whose support was vital in making it happen. In addition, we are very grateful to Leigh Anne Couch and Petra Dreiser for their fine editorial work.

We would also like to thank a variety of individuals at our respective universities, Washington State University, Vancouver, the University of California, Santa Cruz, and the University of California, Berkeley, for their support and encouragement. Roger Schlesinger, chair of the history department at Washington State University, helped us in a variety of ways, notably in suggesting *The Color of Liberty* for the title. Candace Freiwald, of Stevenson College, and Meg Lilienthal, of the history department at UC Santa Cruz, helped prepare parts of the manuscript and coordinated contacts between the editors and contributors. Shari Clevenger, of humanities and liberal arts, WSUV, assisted in the preparation of the manuscript. Professor Peter Sahlins, of UC Berkeley, was particularly encouraging and made a number of useful suggestions. Candice Goucher, chair of liberal arts at WSUV, and a scholar of Caribbean history in her own right, offered financial and moral support at a critical juncture in the project. The France-Berkeley Fund at UC Berkeley provided funding support.

Finally, we are indebted to our families for their support, encouragement, and tolerance. Our partners, Scott Hewitt and Denise Herd, put up with numerous telephone calls, not to mention the travel necessary to complete the project. Our children, Miles, Louise, and Justin (two of whom were born during this process), showed an admirable appreciation for the nuances of French history. Above all, we would like to thank each other for making the rigors of compiling an edited volume both intellectually stimulating and personally enriching.

Foreword

In the fall of 1970, I entered the fifth grade in the public schools of Marseille, in France, where I grew up. At the same time, continuing inflows of non-European immigrants were creating a new ethnic and cultural pluralism in the suburbs. Whether from former colonies in North Africa, Southeast Asia, or sub-Saharan Africa, the visibly nonwhite population was growing so fast that Marseille began to assume a substantially different face than that of the prewar era. Although such a large scale of immigration was not unusual in the region, the ethnic and social origin of the migrants provoked intense political conflict and sometimes violent resistance, and it was impossible for a ten-year-old pupil of Caribbean descent, whose main preoccupations were soccer and the ever-tragic fortunes of his beloved Olympique de Marseilles, to avoid confronting the meaning of such turmoil. My parents told me, although I do not remember the incident, that one day I went back home very anxious because at school I had trouble writing an assigned essay on the question, "What does it mean to be French for you?" I surely knew, even if at ten I would hardly have expressed it in this way, that French identity was formed around notions of shared culture, territory, and language, all organized by the state, understood as an expression of the sovereign people. At the same time, I certainly knew by intuition that race did matter in daily experience of life, that the color of a French citizen could make him not quite French, that although color-blind in theory, the French idea of the nation had been racially coded in practice. This was likely the main reason for my anxiety. What could being French possibly have meant to me? Little surprise that years later, I was given the opportunity to turn what would have been a sort of existential crisis into a scientific questioning about identity, culture, citizenship, and race in a comparative perspective.

It is fortunate that scholars on both sides of the Atlantic have begun to investigate the historical and contemporary meanings of race in France. Contrary to deep-rooted academic views and popular opinion, racial thinking in France has its own original history. Recently, social scientists have shown how under certain conditions, the universalistic idea of the nation became in fact inter-twined with culture and heritage as part of the definition of French-ness, creating a contradiction between global and particularistic perspectives on citizenship and social membership. Thus they have turned their attention to the plasticity of race, pointing to the ar-bitrariness of racial categorization and illuminating how race be-came a social marker throughout France's history, while never being officially endorsed as such. From the 1789 revolution to the colo-nial era, from the Third Republic to the Vichy regime, from the Fifth Republic up to now, many authors have already shed some light on the so far hidden sides of the French "color-blind" model, which appears far more an ideal than an empirical reality.

From this perspective, the collection of essays remarkably se-lected by Tyler Stovall and Sue Peabody, makes for a timely contri-bution to this rich new interdisciplinary scholarship by bringing together some of the very best groundbreaking recent research on the history of race in France. Collectively, the essays assembled tend to unveil, from a specific but complementary angle, some of the critical tensions between the ideal and practice in the making of modern France, generating a dynamic that has challenged both. Traced over almost four centuries, the concept of race is no longer presented as the outcome of France's difficult adjustment to post-imperial order. Race, as a socially constructed category, if not as a practical device for policy implementation, appears deeply rooted in the particularities of French history — despite the continuing of-ficial denial of this fact. Indeed, race did not happen by accident in the last quarter of France's twentieth century. In that respect, the book's broader purpose is to explain the odd configuration of French racial politics over time, namely the combination of *grand moments*, celebrated as great successes (1789 — the universal Dec-laration of the Rights of Man, 1804 — the Code Civil, 1870 — republican legislative acts, 1905 — the separation of church and state, etc.), with great failures (the persistent exclusion of colonial subjects from the status of citizen, the permanence of socioracial inequalities between full and equal citizens by law, anti-Semitism under the Vichy regime, the constant interplay of ethnic consid-eration in French policy of nationality, and the possibly growing racial hostility). How can both occur simultaneously? Why this particular combination of successes and failures? How come the former have been so much trumpeted, while the latter so far have remained silenced? This is a good set of questions, and *The Color of*

Liberty tackles it with accuracy and significant empirical raw materials. Despite the fact that each essay stands alone, collectively they show perfectly how the historiography of race constitutes an intimate part of modern France. Anyone interested in French studies and in contemporary dilemmas surrounding issues of equality, cultural diversity, and the practice of citizenship should no longer ignore how a thoughtful historical approach on race matters can deepen our understanding of both French political ideals and public policy. The analysis of the challenge of color blindness as a core element of the French universalistic idea of nation and, in turn, the practical impact of race throughout France's modern history will certainly be recognized as a *passage obligé* for any scholarship on France. The present collection is well-researched, conceptually original, and full of new insights. It also provides well grounded, sometimes provocative views, which anyone concerned about the relationship between race, identity, citizenship, and social membership must come to terms with. Beyond academia, it will also be sure to invite controversy, especially once translated into French.

For many reasons, which have to do with the weakening of the social fabric in France, race as a concept has never been so much present in the society at large as it has in the past twenty-five years — even if it still remains somehow hidden. The "race-neutral" approach happens no longer to prove as effective as it was once presumed to have been in ensuring every citizen full and equal rights, regardless of origin, race, or religion. If not in theory, there is in practice growing evidence of the racial factor's recognition. Why, then, is France still so reluctant to change official policy? Why does the state keep on rejecting officially what it increasingly accepts in practice? These two questions lead to a third one: how does race change politics and, reciprocally, how does politics change race? These three questions come together in the lucid and stimulating readings provided by *The Color of Liberty*.

Last but not least, this book is about history and power. It deals with the many ways in which power operates in the making and recording of history, and it rejects both the naïve proposition that we are prisoners of our past and the pernicious suggestion that history is whatever we make of it. Thus to tell the story of race in modern France is to reconsider the crucial issue of membership, of exclusion and inclusion, namely to deal with the recurrent question piercing my youth — what does it mean to be French? It also means attending to its even more compelling corollary: what can we do to reconcile France's official self-representation (i.e., Frenchness) with the extraordinary anthropological diversity of the country's population? By raising such issues of intense dispute, the contributors to *The Color of Liberty* have definitively met the challenge that Michel-Rolph Trouillot evoked so forcefully in his acclaimed book, *Silencing the Past*: "The ultimate mark of power may be its invisibility, the ultimate challenge, the exposition of its roots."

FRED CONSTANT
Université Senghor, Alexandria, Egypt

Sue Peabody and Tyler Stovall

Introduction

Race, France, Histories

Recently a colleague approached one of us to discuss a roadblock encountered in a faculty committee formed to encourage racial diversity on campus. Members of the committee, all of whom could be described as "progressive" in their politics, had reached an impasse in the wording of the statement they were crafting on diversity. Two members were arguing to alter the now almost sacred litany of identity categories — gender, ethnicity, sexual orientation, religion, ability, age, and so on — to exclude the category *race* because, they argued, it had no scientific basis. Other committee members argued for the importance of preserving the overt specification of race because, regardless of its scientific merit, the word held social and political meaning.

Disputes over the meaning of the word *race* are both scholarly and political. Used first as a legal and practical category of discrimination in American history, *race* has also served as a rallying point for the civil rights, anti-imperialist, and antiapartheid movements, becoming enshrined in American affirmative action policies. Now, just as genetic research has destabilized the concept's claims to scientific legitimacy, a conservative political movement in the United States threatens to undermine affirmative action policies aimed at redressing racial discrimination. Attacked from both sides, the legitimacy of racial discourse appears significantly undermined. Yet, as nearly any person of color will affirm, discrimination and fear based on physical markers of difference continue to thrive in everyday American praxis.

Racial thinking in France has a parallel and yet unique history. Many Americans have the impression that the French suffer no — or at least minimal — racial bias. This reflects certain moments in French history: French fur trappers' alliances with Native American women as compared with Puritan disdain for miscegenation; French imperial citizenship policies versus those of the British;

the reception of African American soldiers during World War II or American performers of the jazz age. Yet as historical research has shown, under certain conditions the French have relied on racial barriers to preserve a notion of national purity. And, if anything, the problem of racial disharmony worsens as France continues to adjust to a postimperial order.

Indeed, the plasticity of race becomes clearest when the concept is traced over a long temporal trajectory. Over the three centuries detailed in the essays included here, the French nation itself, along with the meaning of race, was very much in flux. In the centuries leading up to the revolution of 1789, France was not entirely integrated into "France" yet, either linguistically or culturally. Until the eighteenth century, religion served as a far more important marker of inclusion or exclusion than national or racial boundaries, culminating in Louis XIV's revocation of the Edict of Nantes in 1685. With relatively few foreigners, particularly non-Europeans (for example, there were no more than about 4,000 blacks living among the 25 million French at the time of the revolution), human diversity was generally imagined more in terms of various "nations" rather than races. For many French people in the eighteenth and nineteenth centuries, questions of race centered around the distinction between Franks and Gauls, dating back to the origins of French national identity. This was a key theme of Jacques Barzun's *The French Race* (1932).[1] Questions of social class also frequently assumed a racialized character, as an analysis of Arthur de Gobineau's *Essai sur l'inégalité des races humaines* (1884) makes clear.[2] Moreover, Parisians and other city dwellers often deemed French peasants savages and uncivilized, at times blurring the distinctions between countryside and colonies.

The transformation of France's most economically productive colony, Saint-Domingue, into independent Haiti, Napoleonic expansion in Europe, and lurches between monarchical and republican governmental forms assured that racial and minority issues intrigued the intelligentsia during the first half of the nineteenth century, but they apparently drew little popular attention within the Hexagon. National education led to a greater homogenization of French culture within, while the new imperial impulse of the later nineteenth and early twentieth centuries ensured more points of contact between, and redefinitions of, "French" and "other." Anti-Semitism, present to greater and lesser degrees since the crusades, erupted violently in the late nineteenth century as well, gradually assuming a more racialized character in the years between the Dreyfus Affair and the Holocaust. After World War II, the vast immigration of colonial nationals created a hitherto unexperienced degree of cultural and ethnic pluralism, from which French society is still reeling today.

If the social, political, and geographical contexts within which racial thinking emerged have changed, so, too, has the concept of race itself. As anyone who has ever attempted to study the origins, permutations, and practical experiences of race has discovered, the idea of race — at first so apparently omnipresent and obvious — is actually quite supple. Race appears as a means to subordinate a conquered or enslaved people; race is used as an exclusionary tool to limit access to privilege (though so, too, are other categories, including religion, language, class, etc.); race is reappropriated culturally as a principle of resistance to denigration, as in the early-twentieth-century *nègritude* movement; and race exists as a scientific discourse with an internal intellectual genealogy, quite independent of — though also intersecting with — social relations. With a subject as plastic as race, approaches to analyzing it are quite varied.

This book has been assembled with the intention of contributing to the historiographies of both race and modern France. The current historical literature dealing with questions of race is of course enormous and quite sophisticated. Most of it, especially that written in English, tends to focus on the history of the United States and, to a lesser extent, on colonial societies in the Americas, Africa, and Asia. Although some anthropologists and literary scholars have begun to devote significant attention to the problems of postcolonial Europe, few historians have as yet systematically addressed questions of race there. France in particular offers a useful point of comparison for those whose experience with questions of race has been primarily American. It resembles the United States not only in its level of socioeconomic development, but also in possessing a strong universalist tradition in its politics and culture, as well as persistent contradictions between republican ideology and racially discriminatory practices. Yet the question of race in France also differs significantly from its American manifestations, in particular with regard to the size of nonwhite populations and the role played by the overseas empire. The French case thus provides an excellent reference for all those interested in developing a transnational, global perspective on the history of race.

For example, French racism is often contrasted with that of Britain, Germany, and the United States as being less "hard" or biological. That is, French racism is based on conformity or assimilation to French cultural norms, and thus does not constitute "racism" at all. But, as some black citizens of Guadeloupe argued in a recent public debate on French and American racisms, this insistence on conformity to metropolitan norms carries with it humiliations and the annihilation of cultural heritages, thus causing similar psychological damage to its citizens that the "harder" racisms abroad instill. The French universal curriculum for secondary students makes no mention of slavery or race, thereby making them appear irrelevant to the lives of some of the poorest residents of former French colonies. To many of these black French citizens, the American "multicultural" model of education appears enviable.

The portrait of French racial thinking that emerges from the essays in this book is much more nuanced. In general, the articles reject any opposition between biological and cultural racism, insisting, as Fogarty and Osborne have put it, that "French racial attitudes in general were and remain based on a mixture of biological and cultural factors" (206). There is also a strong emphasis on the concept of racial hierarchies, contrasting with the implicit bipolarism that still shapes much American thinking on questions of race. From Pierre H. Boulle's discussion of racial categorization in the seventeenth century to Michael G. Vann's consideration of such hierarchies in colonial Indochina two centuries later, French assessments of the foreign are gauged according to a universal of perfection that is Frenchness. In addition, the role of politics assumes center stage in many of these essays, so that racial thinking appears not just a matter of prejudice and ignorance, but rather a question of ideology. In particular, the contradiction between republican universalism and racial particularism has prompted a reconsideration of the history of both ideas in France.

The most striking characteristic of French racial thinking, and the one that most distinguishes it from the American example, is the relationship between the metropole and the colonies. Whereas relatively little of the historical literature on race in the United States deals with questions of empire, virtually all of the essays in this collection address either life in the French colonies or the experience of peoples of colonial origin in metropolitan France. A clear lesson of this book, therefore, is that one cannot understand questions of race in France without taking the colonial experience into consideration.

Yet we have chosen not to regard this book as a study in colonial history, or a comparative history of race in France and its colonies, rejecting the erroneous position that they constitute two distinct units. Instead, following the lead of Gary Wilder, we regard metropole and empire as a whole composed of continually interacting parts, and we consider race one of the most important of those interactions. The central role of colonial history in French racial thinking underscores the importance of considering race in global as well as national terms. Just as the history of French colonialism is both national and global, so does the study of race in France involve both the traditions of the Hexagon and interchanges between the French and peoples throughout the world.

At the same time, this book offers an important resource for those interested in the history of modern France. Many scholars in France have been curiously resistant to any discussion of race as a factor in national life, instead emphasizing the universalist character of French identity as a result of the French Revolution. For example, when William B. Cohen's landmark study *The French Encounter with Africans* (1980) appeared in French translation in 1982, it was sharply attacked for applying American racial categories to France.[3] Although some French historians have begun exploring the nation's history of immigration, they have usually ignored racial questions in their studies. The fact that racial tension has constituted a major issue in French public life during the last twenty years has failed to shake this widespread attachment to a color-blind perspective. This volume argues, on the contrary, that race has been a significant factor in French life over the past three centuries; it is not something that suddenly happened in France with the rise of the so-called second-generation immigrants of the 1980s. Moreover, we suggest that an analysis of race can help illuminate broader aspects of French history, such as the nature of universalism and citizenship, questions of gender and difference, and the role of cities in national life.

The essays in this collection have been assembled for the variety of their approaches as well as their range — chronological and geographical–of subject. The book is divided into four parts. Part 1, "Race: The Evolution of an Idea," explores the origins of the concept of race in French thought and the ways in which that idea changed over time. The essays in this section all deal with early modern France, reflecting the tendency of French historiography to look toward the Enlightenment and the development of overseas exploration and trade as the locus classicus of the origins of race as an idea. Part 2, "Representations of the Other," addresses the various ways in which French writers, artists, and business people conceived of and portrayed those groups seen as racially distinct from the French themselves. Ranging from the revolutionary period to the contemporary era, the essays in this section look at representations of racial difference, as well as that based on religion and gender, to cast new light on French conceptions of their own national identity. Part 3, "Colonial and Global Perspectives," picks up on a theme already established earlier—the international dimensions of French racial thinking—and investigates it in greater detail. Common to all the essays in this section is an analysis of the ways in which French ideas about race were either shaped by overseas encounters or, in turn, helped shape racial perspectives in other parts of the world. The essays consider both relations between the French metropole and empire as well as interactions between France and the United States. In Part 4, "Race and the Postcolonial City," the book concentrates on the urban experience, which in France (as elsewhere) has often proven central to racial encounters. The four essays in this final section consider the impact of peoples of color on life in Paris and Marseille during the late nineteenth and twentieth centuries. They consider both French discourses about race and the experiences of nonwhites, demonstrating how questions of racial difference have contributed to the shaping of the French city in the modern era.

Despite the fact that each essay was composed in relative isolation from the others, readers will discover certain continuities in the casting, props, and staging of the modern racial dramas. Eighteenth- and nineteenth-century racial theorists, including Bougainvilliers, Buffon, Grégoire, and Broca, help to establish some continuity among essays by Boulle, Sepinwall, and Blanckaert. Blanckaert focuses sustained attention on the eighteenth- and nineteenth-century anthropological theory about racial hybridism, or miscegenation, while Fogarty and Osborne briefly touch on this theme as it applied to disease immunity studied by colonial doctors in the field. Hale's essay on racial imagery and commercial trademarks provides an interesting context for Auslander and Holt's discussion of representations of blacks in collectible objects. Blaise Diagne, who makes a cameo appearance in Fogarty and Osborne, makes the central subject of Conklin's study. Franz Fanon's theories of racial politics are the subject of two quite different perspectives by Wilder and

McEnnerney. Thus, though each essay stands alone, being read alongside one another enriches all.

As stimulating and wide-ranging as these essays are, the collection is by no means exhaustive. Some of the gaps in the collection suggest many promising avenues for future research. For example, the process by which France's internal unification and homogenization in the nineteenth century interacted with overseas imperialism has not been sufficiently studied. Nor has the treatment of French religious minorities over the centuries (Jews, Protestants, Muslims) been analyzed comparatively with regard to ideas about race. Finally, one glimpses the importance of military service in claims to racial equality in France, as in the United States; much more can be learned by analyzing the relationship between military induction, race, citizenship, and gender.

No doubt readers will discover for themselves many more themes and omissions in the collection. We hope that by providing a model of French history which critically examines the tradition of French universalism, as well as one which approaches the metropole and the colonies not as separate entities but rather as parts of a unified political and cultural formation, this collection will help spur other historical investigations of the place of race and racial difference in French life.

Notes

1 Jacques Barzun, *The French Race: Theories of Its Origins and Their Social and Political Implications Prior to the Revolution* (New York: Columbia University Press, 1932).
2 Joseph Arthur, comte de Gobineau, *Essai sur l'inégalité des races humaines* (1884; Paris: Firmin-Didort, 1922).
3 William B. Cohen, *The French Encounter with Africans: White Response to Blacks, 1530–1880* (Bloomington: Indiana University Press, 1980).

1

Race: The Evolution of an Idea

Pierre H. Boulle

François Bernier and the Origins of

the Modern Concept of Race

In 1684, the journal of the French Academy of Sciences, the *Journal des sçavans*, published an anonymous article entitled "A New Division of the Earth, according to the Different Species or Races of Men Who Inhabit It."[1] This short piece, correctly ascribed to François Bernier (1620–88), has been cited as the first presentation of the modern concept of race, but it is usually mentioned as a mere curiosity.[2] When studying the origins of modern racial thinking in France, more stress is placed either on the early-eighteenth-century theorist of noble race, Count Henri de Boulainvilliers (1658–1722), who has been called one of the "true ancestors of racism,"[3] or on the natural scientist Georges-Louis Leclerc de Buffon (1707–88). Indeed, few are those who have bothered to study Bernier's text.[4]

And yet Bernier was not an insignificant personage. He had been the student and friend of the libertine philosopher Pierre Gassend *dit* Gassendi (1592–1655).[5] A medical doctor, he was best known for his travels to Southeast Asia, which he visited from 1655 to 1667, and the account he published of his eight-year residence in Agra as a practicing physician at the court of the Mogul ruler, Aurengzeb.[6] While in Agra, he corresponded with various French deskbound érudits and on his return reported on India to the French government.[7] He also earned a reputation as a philosopher in his own right with his *Abrégé de la philosophie de Gassendi* (1674), published as a defense of his old master and recognized, at least in its vastly enlarged revised edition (1682), as more than a mere replication of the latter's ideas.[8] Although the "New Division of the Earth" is characteristic of the writing of Paris salons, to which Bernier, on his return from the east, became a welcomed participant under the nickname of Bernier-Mogol,[9] it deserves some attention. But first, what did race mean at the time Bernier wrote?

The Meaning of Race in Bernier's Time

The term *race* entered French usage in the late fifteenth century, probably with the many other contemporary borrowings from the Italian (*razza*). Used first to define the qualities sought in breeding animals for the hunt or for warfare, *race* was quickly applied to humans supposed to possess similarly valuable inherited qualities. The term was first applied to the king and his ascendants with whom he shared the peculiar attributes of the monarch. Thus the Capetians were deemed the third race of kings, following the Merovingians and the Carolingians. By the 1550s, usage had been extended by analogy to other old families within the nobility, the *noblesse de race*, differentiating them from both the new nobles and the "vulgar."[10] In short, the term was first associated simply with lineage, rather than with fixed, physically defined differentiations between broad human groups, as it is today.

Yet *race* was never an entirely value-free concept. At the time of the term's introduction into French, the nobility came under severe stress owing to the rise of new men into the army and the requirement of new skills for state offices. *Race* replaced more neutral terms describing noble lineage, such as *maison* (household) or *famille*, precisely because it distinguished between good breeding and the absence of breeding. Gentility and other traits inherited through birth came to differentiate *gentilshommes* (that is, the well-bred) from mere nobles, who could be manufactured by the king.[11] From the first, therefore, the term focused on natural—what we would now call biological—differences and placed great value on the possession of inherited character traits.

Unlike the modern advocates of race, however, noble theorists of the sixteenth century did not see such qualities as fixed or inevitable. Not only was there a real sentiment that the nobility could degenerate, but most thinkers believed that new nobles, after three or four generations, could shed their "vulgar" origins. Furthermore, the transmission of noble qualities had as much to do with familial training as with natural inheritance. Indeed, good breeding was not only a matter of proper parentage, but also of an appropriate education, and even of the proper diet.[12] Race, then, in the sixteenth-century context, remained narrowly defined as direct lineage and had none of the generic connotations of its modern counterpart. Even the much vaunted Frankish origins of the nobility, used to differentiate *gentilshommes* from *roturiers* by right of conquest, did not imply a common biological origin of the nobility, since the Franks were regarded not so much as a tribe than as a group of free warriors, unconnected by blood.[13]

Little movement appears to have occurred from these positions until Bernier's time.[14] Indeed, as late as the early eighteenth century, Boulainvilliers retained much of the sixteenth-century vision. The Franks, from whose greatness the nobility had, according to him, declined to its current sorry state, were no more racially unified than they had been perceived one hundred years earlier. Indeed, in Boulainvilliers's view, the Franks, decimated by wars, had soon been joined by some of the worthier Gauls, with whom they intermarried, and later by other northern peoples who "earned . . . the right to bear the name of French," so that these "various peoples," originally distinguished by separate "mores, languages, and customs . . . in the fullness of time became a single nation."[15] Furthermore, repeated use of *race* and *blood* notwithstanding, Boulainvilliers placed as much emphasis on education and diet as sixteenth-century theorists.[16] It was not inherited physical or mental attributes which counted, but the placing of an individual in a family with a long history of noble deeds. True nobility, he argued, "consists in a *tradition* of virtue, glory, honor, sentiments for dignity and good."[17] This is why he so valued genealogical studies, which encouraged emulation by educating nobles through the examples of a particular set of distinguished ancestors and which discouraged them from shaming these ancestors by ignoble conduct. In short, and perhaps most significantly, Boulainvilliers differed from modern racial thinkers in continuing to equate races with families, each of which possessed its own peculiar qualities and characteristics.[18]

The "Nouvelle Division de la Terre"

Bernier's 1684 article proposes an entirely different approach to races, which he there defines as broad human categories characterized by distinct physical traits. The article begins thus:

> Until now, geographers have divided the earth only by the different countries and regions which are found there. What I have noted about men during my long and frequent voyages gave me the idea of dividing it differently. For, even though men almost always differ from each other in the external form of the body and principally the face, according to the various regions of the earth they inhabit,

so that those who have traveled extensively can often without error distinguish by these features each nation in particular, I have noticed that there are mostly four or five species or races of men so noticeably different from each other that they can serve as a justifiable basis for a new division of the earth.[19]

Bernier's first race includes the peoples of Europe, "leaving aside a part of Muscovy"; it also includes those living in a broad band of territory extending from the Mediterranean coast of Africa to parts of Borneo, via Arabia, Persia, India, and Siam. This first race is left undefined, except for the absence in "ourselves" of the features defining the other three races: the Africans, the Asians, and the Samoeds of Lapland. What characterizes each of these three is a combination of physical features and skin color, though the latter, in order to play a role, must be a fixed attribute, as in Africa, where "blackness . . . is an essential feature of theirs . . . not caused by the sun's hot rays, as is usually thought, since, if an African couple is transported to a cold country, their children and all their descendants will be no less black than they, until they marry white women." On the other hand, "even though the Egyptians . . . and the Indians are quite black or, rather, swarthy, this color is only accidental, resulting from their exposure to the sun, since those who protect themselves and are not required to expose themselves as often as the common people, are no darker than many Spaniards."

More significant are other, essential features. In addition to the color black, Africans have thick lips, flat noses, woolly hair, and an oily skin. Although Asians are "truly white," they have flat noses, piglike eyes, and practically no beard. The worst are the Samoeds, though Bernier admits that "I have only seen two of them, in Danzig": "They are small and short [de petits courtaux], with thick legs, large shoulders, a short neck, and a face that I can only describe as drawn-out [je ne sçay comment tiré en long], quite frightful and which seems to derive from the bear . . . they are ugly animals."

The categories are broad, and Bernier recognizes that many groups within each race diverge somewhat from the norm: "It is true that most [East] Indians differ somewhat from us in the shape of their face and in their color, which leans toward the yellow, but this does not seem sufficient reason to make them into a separate specie; otherwise, we would have to turn the Spaniards into one as well, and the Germans into another, and so on for some other European peoples." It is precisely for this reason that he finally rejects the idea that the Native Americans form a fifth race. Despite the fact that "they are, in truth, olive-skinned for the most part, and their face is shaped differently from ours," he considers them part of the first race, that of the Europeans.

Bernier's perception of race is somewhat idiosyncratic, apparently having much to do with personal canons of aesthetics, especially related to the type of women he found attractive.[20] It differs in some details from the categorization of human races, notably on the basis of color, which marks anthropological discourse from the eighteenth century onward.[21] His description of Asians as "truly white" with piglike eyes (*des petits yeux de porc*) is drawn from his encounter with Tartars in India rather than with other more typical groups, such as the Chinese, whom he apparently did not know.[22] Indeed, it is worth recalling that he assimilated yellow-skinned south Asians with the race of Europeans, as he did also Native Americans. This last association, however, may have resulted from his readings about Amerindians from New France, usually described in that period as resembling Europeans.[23] In any event, Bernier's view of the *Américains* is consistent with depictions, both iconographic and literary, found in popular collections of voyages available to contemporaries.[24] On the other hand, Bernier's affirmation that differences in the coloring of East Indians stem purely from exposure to the elements is surprising. Not only is it wrong—in failing to take into account the vast mixture of human types in India, resulting over time from invasions by northern peoples and their assimilation into Indian society[25]—it also contradicts his own remarks concerning color prejudice and marriage practices in Mogul India in his earlier travel accounts, where he notes that newcomers seek to find brides from Kashmir, "so as to have children who will be whiter than the Indians, and can pass for true Moguls."[26]

It remains that Bernier's use of the term *race* fundamentally differs from its original meaning in discourse concerning the nobility. Not only does the "New Division of the Earth" extend the concept to mankind in general, but it also focuses, as modern racial distinctions do, on fixed physical features. Of particular note is the distinction made between inherent skin pigmentation and that which results from exposure to the elements. Of equal importance is Bernier's insistence that the transmission of characteristics by inheritance predominates over environmental or cultural determinants. This constitutes a startling departure from contemporary beliefs, which Bernier himself seems to have shared when, in an earlier text, he argued that members of the Mogul elite in India, over three or four generations, "have taken the brown face and the slow humor of the country."[27] Indeed, in this respect, he is more "modern" than Buffon, who posited a hierarchy of races according to climate. Each race had degenerated from the white European norm, found in its perfection in temperate Europe. The further the distance north or south from this region was the habitat, the more debased were the inhabitants.[28]

Even though Bernier's description of the races does not openly suggest a hierarchy, the very ranking, from "we Europeans" to the Samoeds suggests a gradation of values. That this was not entirely unconscious is shown not only by the likening of the latter to "ugly animals," but by the description of some Venuslike African slave women he encountered in Moka as exceptions among a people with "ugly faces," characterized by "those thick lips and that squashed nose." Indeed, Bernier's use of *races* and *species* as synonymous terms places a huge distance between the Europeans and the others.

Influences on Bernier

Three particular influences may be suggested as significant for the development of Bernier's ideas. The first relates to his youthful libertine contacts; the second, to his medical training; the third, to his travels. To these should be added the French intellectual context of the 1670s and 1680s, notably within the Parisian aristocratic circles which Bernier joined on his return from the east.

As a young man, Bernier had obtained a privileged position within libertine circles, that group of intellectuals who, in the first half of the seventeenth century, contested orthodox thinking. As I have noted, Bernier was the student and close companion of Pierre Gassendi, from the mid-1640s to the latter's death in 1655. Gassendi, by then a professor at the Collège Royal, was one of the major figures of the libertine movement, an innovator considered at the time "the equal of Descartes, if not his superior."[29] His libertinism consisted of a systematic refusal of authority in all but theology. All other realms — philosophy, physics, natural sciences, and the like — were to be studied through experience and observation. A thorough materialist in all these fields, Gassendi took a keen if eclectic interest in all aspects of nature.[30] From his nearly two decades of close contact with Gassendi, Bernier must have learned a habit of inquisitiveness unshackled by preconceptions, a habit reflected in his observations on the Mogul Empire and, later in life, in his *Abrégé*, which questions even his master's own ideas.

On the surface, Bernier's medical education at Montpellier would appear to have confirmed these tendencies. The medical faculty at Montpellier was the great rival of the Paris school, and many considered it as the more "modern" of the two. Montpellier was the first to modify the traditional curriculum by the inclusion of nonclassical authorities like Vesalius, Paracelsus, and Ambroise Paré; it also emphasized observation and anatomical studies, as well as providing students with information on pharmacology based on a *jardin des plantes* it had created.[31] However, the mid-seventeenth century, during which Bernier was a student, seems to have been a less than distinguished period in Montpellier. The regent professors, who previously had been selected in open competition, had become royal appointees, so that patronage rather than talent characterized most of them. The exception may have been Lazare Rivière, who held the chair of surgery and pharmacology from 1622 until his death in 1655 and who authored a number of respected works, notable for their emphasis on observation. More typical was the dean of the faculty, Siméon Courtaud, whose sole notable publication was a defense of the privileges of Montpellier against its Parisian rival, written in such bad Latin and filled with such errors that the Paris doctors had an easy time drowning the attack in laughter.[32]

Additionally, Bernier's stay at Montpellier was very short. He registered for the *baccalauréat* on 5 May 1652 and defended his doctoral dissertation less than four months later, on 22 August.[33] Such quick student careers were not uncommon at the time and are explained by the growing competition among medical schools, which led Montpellier to waive residency and practicum requirements for nonlocal students.[34] It is unclear where Bernier previously obtained the theoretical knowledge required for his examinations — perhaps in Paris, auditing lectures while serving as Gassendi's secretary[35] — but it wasn't at Montpellier prior to his registration, for he traveled in Poland during 1648–49 and returned leisurely through Italy. In April 1652, he was with Gassendi in Digne, observing an eclipse, and throughout 1651 and 1652 Bernier busily wrote a defense of his master against Jean-Baptiste Morin, Gassendi's colleague at the Collège Royal.[36] To be fair, Bernier, while in Montpellier, at least had the time to recognize the quality of a fellow student, Jean Pecquet, and to befriend this noted experimentalist.[37] Nonetheless, it may be his subsequent practice of medicine, rather than the study of the discipline, which provided Bernier with an interest in and a knowledge of the natural sciences, especially as they concerned mankind.[38]

Of equal significance, obviously, are his travels during which he visited Egypt, the Arabian Peninsula, and northern India. Not only did he have the opportunity to observe firsthand some non-Europeans, but, in the seventeenth century, these regions housed, as the "New Division of the Earth" suggests, a veritable mosaic of human types. Perhaps most significant was his residence in India, where he became familiar with the Indian and even the Mogul attention to biological purity and color.[39]

The Contemporary Context

France's learned community had changed somewhat when Bernier returned from India. For one thing, a new theory was being propounded concerning the reproduction of human life.[40] Earlier authorities had split between the Aristotelians, who ascribed to males the sole reproductive role and to women simply the task of nurturing the embryo, and advocates of the Galenic thesis, which posited that life was the result of the conjoining of male and female semen, sex being determined by whether the male semen was dominant or not. Now, following William Harvey's study of animal reproductive organs (De generatione animalium, 1651), the new fad was for "ovism," the belief that female humans produced eggs later fertilized by male semen. Such a theory was based only on similitude with the rest of the animal kingdom, for no one had yet seen a human ovum (or, for that matter, understood exactly the role of semen). If few scientists still believed, with Aristotle, that the mating of individuals from two separate species would result in a perfectly formed copy of the male, it remained that the form of the fetus was viewed as tentative and fragile until birth. Female imagination, in particular, continued to be viewed as a potential cause of malformations. One positive aspect of the renewed discussion created by ovism was an even greater interest in anatomical studies. Demonstrations were conducted in Paris and attended by a varied public, including some of the fashionable elite. It is likely that Bernier attended such demonstrations.[41]

At the same time, Paracelsus's polygenetic concepts saw a revival.

Biblical studies influenced by libertine thought, notably by Isaac La Peyrère (1597–1676), and the new biological observations, notably by the Italian anatomist Marcello Malpighi (1628–94), conjoined to suggest that physical differences existed from creation and that, consequently, different human groups had separate geneses. While not openly adopting these views, Bernier replicated the belief of his master, Gassendi, that physical traits are preprogrammed in the individual.[42] While Bernier was writing his "New Division of the Earth," scientific thinking was clearly in the process of shifting from a system of evidence based on analogies to one supported by fixed laws of nature and, in the case of the natural sciences, from a view of forms as well-nigh accidental, or at least molded by all sorts of external forces, to a belief in the permanence of species.

Such a hardening of thoughts about the transmission of inherited characteristics spread beyond the scientific community. It is worth noting, for instance, that polygenesis is closely linked to eighteenth-century racist thought, notably in Voltaire.[43] Its growing popularity in the second half of the seventeenth century coincides with the generalization of black slavery, linked to the contemporary spread of the sugar plantation system.[44] Not surprisingly, this distancing of Africans from Europeans finds its way even into contemporary salon literature, as in a letter from a galant, accompanying the gift to a lady of "the two ugliest animals that it [Africa] has produced . . . the stupidest of Moors and the most mischievous [*malicieux*] of monkeys," in which Fontenelle suggests in an obvious sexual double entendre that what capacity to reason the African possesses, he obtained from "the long practice" he's had of the monkey.[45]

The major treaty on the nobility of the period, La Roque's *Traité de noblesse* (1678), also took a position that represented a significant hardening of the race concept. Not only did La Roque conceive of old and new nobilities as different "species," but he was categorical where sixteenth-century thinkers had hesitated as to the effect of a dishonorable or derogating individual on lineage: "An individual who possesses the type of nobility called natural and of the blood cannot ever alienate it, since the original essence remains even in those condemned [for crimes] and passes on to their children." If nobility was incommutable, a "character that nature has imprinted in the person" of the noble, then its decline could only occur through "the stain [*des taches*]" of misalliance with "a vulgar [*vile*] and abject individual," a process La Roque likened to prostitution.[46] At the same time, the nobility began adopting an attitude toward the lower classes tinged with racial and color connotations, satirized in the often-quoted La Bruyère portrait of dark-skinned peasants, toiling like animals in the fields.[47]

Bernier's Significance

Given these new attitudes toward non-Europeans and the lower classes, one would expect that Bernier's article received a good deal of attention and that advocates of the natural inferiority of others would take up his categorization. The opposite seems to have happened. Further references to race in the *Journal des sçavans* tend to ignore his "New Division" and dictionaries continued to equate race to lineage.[48] Similarly, as we have seen, natural scientists in the eighteenth century continued to follow other paradigms in their analyses of human traits, even if, in the long run, these paradigms led to conclusions similar to those of Bernier. I have not found, either, any reference to Bernier among the increasingly racist colonial tracts that began to appear in defense of slavery during the eighteenth century.[49] In short, Bernier-Mogol remained a man of the salons. He was not a *maître à penser* and founded no school of thought.

This requires some explanation. It may be that precisely Bernier's connection with the Parisian salon society impeded the broad circulation of his thought. Indeed, the rather precious style of the "New Division" interferes somewhat with the seriousness of its message. Besides, while the *Journal des sçavans* remained an influential source of information on scientific thought for the cultivated elite of France, its most important and recognized contributions were its reviews of published works, not the odd pieces it published. Original as it may be, Bernier's piece, therefore, may best be regarded as reflective of the shift in thought that occurred in the second half of the seventeenth century, a shift that prepared, in the next century, the emergence of a racial discourse.

Notes

The author wishes to thank the various institutions that contributed financially to this research: McGill University, the Social Science and Humanities Research Council of Canada, the John Carter

Brown Library (Providence, Rhode Island), and the Newberry Library (Chicago).

1 This is my translation, as is the case for all other French material in this essay. The full title is "Nouvelle Division De La Terre, par les differentes Especes ou Races d'hommes qui l'habitent, envoyée par un fameux voyageur à M. l'Abbé de la **** à peu prés en ces termes." It appears as the lead article in the *Journal des sçavans* issue of 24 April 1684, 133–40. The title is slightly modified in the reprinted edition of the *Journal des sçavans pour l'année M.DC.XXXIV* (Amsterdam, 1685), 148–55.

2 See, for instance, Léon Poliakov, *Le mythe aryen: Essai sur les sources du racisme et des nationalismes* (Paris: Calman-Lévy, 1971), 138; William B. Cohen, *The French Encounter with Africans: White Response to Blacks, 1550–1880* (Bloomington: Indiana University Press, 1980), 8. Neither author does more than cite the article.

3 Léon Poliakov, *Histoire de l'antisémitisme*, 4 vols. (Paris: Calman-Lévy, 1966), 3:145.

4 One exception is Sue Peabody, in her Ph.D. dissertation, " 'There Are No Slaves in France': Law, Culture, and Society in Early Modern France, 1685–1789" (University of Iowa, 1989), 128–34. The passage is dropped from the published version, entitled *There Are No Slaves in France: The Political Culture of Race and Slavery in the Ancien Régime* (New York: Oxford University Press, 1996).

5 On the early life of Bernier and his relationship with Gassendi, see René Pintard, *Le libertinage érudit dans la première moitié du XVIIe siècle*, new ed. (1943; Geneva: Boivin, 1983), 328–29, 384–86, 409–12.

6 François Bernier, *Histoire de la dernière révolution des estats du grand Mogol* (1670); and Bernier, *Suite des memoires du Sieur Bernier sur l'Empire du grand Mogol* (1671). The two went through various editions, not only in France, but also in England, before being published together as *Voyages de François Bernier . . . contenant la description des etats du grand Mogol* (1679). I have consulted the *Histoire* in its two-volume new edition (Paris, 1681), the *Suite* as vol. 2 of the *Voyages* in the two-volume new revised edition (Amsterdam, 1723). Passages used below will be cited from these two editions.

7 See these letters and reports in the 1723 edition of his *Voyages*.

8 See the review of the revised edition in *Journal des sçavans*, 24 July 1684, 241–44, which focuses on the originality of Bernier's revisions.

9 Maurice Besson, *L'influence coloniale sur le décor de la vie française* (Paris: Agence economique des coloniel, 1944), 25.

10 For a useful summary of the meaning of race in sixteenth-century

French, see Arlette Jouanna, *L'idée de race en France au XVIe siècle et au début du XVIIe*, rev. ed., 2 vols. (Montpellier: Universitè Paul Valery, 1981), 2:723–31. See also the *Dictionnaire historique de la langue française*, 1st ed., s.v. "race," which proposes the Italian *razza* as only one of the corruptions of the Latin *generatio* from which the French term may have originated.

11 The distinction is made in 1583 by René de Sanzay in his unpublished "L'origine, dignité, et debvoir du prince," quoted in Manfred Orlea, *La noblesse aux états généraux de 1576 et de 1588: Etude politique et sociale* (Paris: Presses Universitaires de France, 1980), 145. It is already inferred in Sébastien Champier, *Le fondement et origine des tiltres de noblesse* (Paris, 1544), n.p. See also Noël Du Fail, *Les baliverneries et les contes d'Eutrapel*, ed. E. Courbet, 2 vols. (1585; Paris, 1894), 1:283, 2:127. *Gentil/gentle* derives from the Greek *genos* and the Latin *gens* (family); it is etymologically linked to *gene, generation*, and *generous*, a fact already noted in the sixteenth century. See François de l'Alouette, *Traité des nobles et des vertus dont ils sont formés* (Paris, 1577), vols. 20–21.

12 Among other expressions of degeneration and the acquisition of gentility over generations, see Pierre de Sainct-Julien de Balleure, *Meslanges historiques* (Lyon, 1588), 293, 554. On education and diet, see Florentin Thierriat de Lochepierre, *Trois traictez, sçavoir: 1. De la noblesse de race; 2. De la noblesse civile; 3. Des immunitez des ignobles* (Paris, 1606), 255, where the perfect noble is described as "né d'une bonne et ancienne Race, et bien nourry et enseigné."

13 George Huppert, *The Idea of Perfect History: Historical Erudition and Historical Philosophy in Renaissance France* (Urbana: University of Illinois Press, 1970), 81.

14 Ellery Schalk notwithstanding. His *From Valor to Pedigree: Ideas of Nobility in France in the Sixteenth and Seventeenth Centuries* (Princeton, N.J., Princeton University Press, 1986), claims that a major shift in the nobility's self-image occurred in the early seventeenth century, when lineage replaced older rationales for the class's preeminence (see especially his chapter 6). However, the texts he cites offer no new idea and often contain older explanations, so that it is, at best, a matter of a slight and very gradual shift in emphasis.

15 Henri de Boulainvilliers, "Dissertation sur la noblesse françoise servant de préface aux mémoires de la maison de Croï et de Boulainviller," written between 1701 and 1709 and revised by Boulainvilliers until his death in 1722, quoted here from the Angoulême manuscript published by André Devyver in the appendix to *Le Sang épuré: Les préjugés de race chez les gentilshommes français de l'ancien régime, 1560–1720* (Brussels: Editions de l'Universitè de Bruxelles, 1973), 501–48; see 519 and 506–7 for the quoted passages.

16 On education, Henri de Boulainvilliers, "Idées d'un système général d'éducation," 1700, in *Oeuvres philosophiques*, ed. Renée Simon, 2 vols. (The Hague: M. Nijoff, 1973–75), 2:134–42; on food, linked, however, to the quality of semen, Boulainvilliers, "Idée d'un système général de la nature," 1683, in ibid., 2:171.

17 Henri de Boulainvilliers, "Memoire sur la noblesse," n.d., quoted from Devyver, *Le sang épuré*, 548; emphasis added.

18 This interpretation of Boulainvilliers owes much to the revisionist article of Harold A. Ellis, "Genealogy, History, and the Aristocratic Reaction in Early Eighteenth-Century France: The Case of Henri de Boulainvilliers," *Journal of Modern History* 8 (1986): 414–51.

19 All the quotes in this section are taken from the *Journal des sçavans*'s article, cited above.

20 Nearly half of the article is devoted to the women he encountered in his travels, stressing the beauty of certain of them, notably those of Kashmir and the Lahore region.

21 W. F. Bynum, E. J. Browne, and Roy Porter, eds., *Dictionary of the History of Science* (Princeton, N.J.: Princeton University Press, 1981), 356–57, s.v. "race."

22 The physical description of the Tartars is found in the "Lettre au Mesme [M. de Merveilles], ecrite à Kachemire . . .," 1664, published in Bernier, Voyages, 2:281. We know that Bernier actually met Tartars from his description of an Uzbek embassy to Agra, in his *Histoire*, 2:5–6. It is thanks to the 1664 letter, principally, that the authorship of the "Nouvelle Division de la Terre" can be assured, for a number of phrases in the latter coincide word for word with it. Other parallels are found in his *Histoire*, 2:35, and *Voyages*, 2:331.

23 Physical descriptions in the accounts of contemporary travelers are rarely precise and focus principally on similarities with the Europeans, or at least with the healthier ones. Color is usually noted as "bazanez" or "olivastre," but due to exposure to the weather and the application of oils and paints. On this, see Masarah Van Eyck, " 'We Shall Be One People': Early Modern French Perceptions of the Amerindian Body" (Ph.D. diss., McGill University, 2001), ch. 2, notably pages 62–63. Such descriptions, including Bernier's own, are opposed to a tradition dating from classical antiquity, which depicted wild men as naked, hairy cannibals. The tradition was still applied to Native Americans not only in Antoine Furetière, *Dictionnaire universel . . .*, 3 vols. (The Hague, 1690), s.v. "sauvage," but as late as the third edition of its successor, the *Dictionnaire universel françois et latin . . . vulgairement appellé Dictionnaire de Trévoux*, 5 vols. (Paris, 1732).

24 As for instance in André Thevet, *La cosmographie universelle* (Paris, 1575), or in the various voyages to America edited by the de Bry

family until the middle of the seventeenth century, where Native Americans are depicted as classical figures. See also the literary description of the Tupinambas in the equally popular Jean de Léry, *Histoire d'un voyage fait en la terre du Bresil, autrement dite Amerique* (La Rochelle, 1578; at least five other editions until 1644), 108–10, which compares them to Europeans, ascribes what physical differences exist to their cultural practices, and likens their "couleur naturelle" to that of the Spaniards, in almost the same words as those Bernier uses to describe the color of Egyptians and East Indians. Such descriptions prevailed despite more realistic depictions, as for instance the remarkable portraits, obviously drawn from life, of three Tupinambas baptized in Paris, in Claude d'Abbeville, *Histoire de la mission des pères Capucins en l'Isle de Maragnan* (Paris, 1614), vols. 361, 363, and 364. On this last point, see Svetlana Alpers, *The Art of Describing: Dutch Art in the Seventeenth Century* (Chicago: University of Chicago Press, 1983), 163–64.

25 On this and the perpetuation of these distinctions through endogamous caste practices, see especially André Béteille, *Castes: Old and New: Essays in Social Structure and Social Stratification* (Bombay: Asia Publishing House, 1969).

26 "Lettre au Mesme [M. de Merveilles]," in Bernier, *Voyages*, 2:281.

27 "Lettre à Monseigneur de Colbert," 1669, in Bernier, *Histoire*, 2:145.

28 Buffon, like Bernier, identified both Africans and the Samoeds as the furthest from European perfection. The views are found in Georges Louis Leclerc, comte de Buffon, *Histoire naturelle, générale et particulière*, 29 vols. (Paris, 1749–88), and especially "De l'homme" and "Variétés dans l'espèce humaine," published earlier. On Buffon's theories, see Michèle Duchet, *Anthropologie et histoire au siècle des lumières: Buffon, Voltaire, Rousseau, Helvétius, Diderot* (Paris: I. Maspero, 1971), 229–80.

29 Olivier René Bloch, *La Philosophie de Gassendi: Nominalisme, matérialisme et métaphysique* (The Hague: M. Nijoff, 1971), xiii.

30 See ibid., and especially ch. 2, 30–76, on Gassendi's "liberté philosophique." Bloch notes the limits of Gassendi's daring, which render him eclectic and unsystematic, and he concludes that "il apparaît sans conteste comme un penseur moderne . . . mais non sans doute comme un penseur d'avant-garde," like Descartes (75). In that, however, Bloch judges Gassendi to be "la règle" for his time, and Descartes "l'exception" (487).

31 On the Montpellier faculty in the seventeenth century, see Jean Astruc, *Mémoires pour servir à l'histoire de la faculté de médecine de Montpellier* (Paris, 1767); Louis Dulieu, *La médecine à Montpellier,*

vol. 3, *L'époque classique* (Avignon: Presses Universelles, 1979–88); Hubert Bonnet, *La faculté de médecine de Montpellier: Huit siècles d'histoire et d'éclat* (Montpellier: Sauramps Medical, 1992), 61–72. On medical education in general, see Laurence Brockliss and Colin Jones, *The Medical World of Early Modern France* (Oxford: Clarendon, 1997), 188–98; also Jacques Roger, *Les sciences de la vie dans la pensée française du XVIIIe siècle: La génération des animaux de Descartes à l'Encyclopédie* (Paris: A. Colin, 1971), 7–48; and L. Dulieu, "Médecine," in *Histoire générale des sciences*, vol. 2, *La science moderne* (de 1450 à 1800), ed. René Taton (Paris: Presses Universitaires de France, 1978), 378–422. The first two raise doubts about how innovative teaching was, even in Montpellier.

32 Astruc, *Mémoires*, 263. On the various professors at the time of Bernier's studies, see ibid., 258–67. Dulieu, *La médecine à Montpellier*, 3:325ff., notes also the presence of an excellent anatomical demonstrator, Jean Nissolles.

33 In between, he obtained his *baccalauréat* on 22 May and his *licence* on 8 August, see Dulieu, *La médecine à Montpellier*, 828.

34 Brockliss and Jones note that this was done without lowering standards, for outsiders "under[went] exactly the same oral examinations and sustain[ed] the same public dissertations as local students." Nonetheless, Montpellier and other institutions which followed the practice—all save Paris—thus served essentially as "examination boards" for past theoretical learning, rather than genuine teaching faculties (*Medical World*, 195–96). No doubt this policy and the economy it implied explain the large number of Montpellier graduates in the mid-seventeenth century: over 25 percent of French doctorates in the 1650s, when Bernier was in attendance, against less than 5 percent for Paris (ibid., 199, table 3a). Dulieu's biographical dictionary of Montpellier students, in *La médecine à Montpellier*, vol. 3, part 2, demonstrates that Bernier's case was not unusual.

35 Astruc, who mentions Bernier among Montpellier's notable graduates, states that he did "de bonnes études" (*Mémoires*, 385).

36 This defense, *Anatomia ridiculi muris* (Paris, 1651), followed by *Favilla ridiculi muris* (Paris, 1654), on which he appears to have been busy in the spring of 1652, was Bernier's introduction to the French literary public. For his travels between 1648 and 1652, see Pintard, *Le libertinage érudit*, 384–85.

37 On Pecquet's student career at Montpellier (nearly as brief as Bernier's, from 5 July 1651, to 23 March 1652), see Dulieu, *La médecine à Montpellier*, 3:959–60; on his significance, see Roger, who compares him to Descartes and Pascal (*Les sciences de la vie*, 7). On Bernier's (and Gassendi's) appreciation of Pecquet's "belles décou-

vertes," see Joseph Bougerel, *Vie de Pierre Gassendi, prévôt de l'Eglise de Digne et professeur de mathématique au Collège royal* (1737; Geneva: Slatkine Reprints, 1970), 356–57.

38 See Pintard's comments about the medical profession, in *Le libertinage érudit*, 79–80; also Roger, who notes that, despite the lack of innovations in medical faculties, it was medical practitioners who were at the forefront of seventeenth-century advances in biology and, especially, in the understanding of reproduction (*Les sciences de la vie*, 169).

39 See notably his "Lettre à Monseigneur de Colbert," 2:145–46.

40 The following passage, on biological theories, is drawn from E. Guyénot, "Biologie humaine et animale," in Taton, *La Science moderne*, 355–77; Roger, *Les sciences de la vie*, parts 1 and 2, especially 49–97, 205–24, and 334–53; François Jacob, *La logique du vivant: Une histoire de l'hérédité* (Paris: Gallimard, 1976), 27–86; Maryanne Cline Horowitz, "The 'Science' of Embryology before the Discovery of the Ovum," in *Connecting Spheres: Women in the Western World, 1500 to the Present*, ed. Marilyn J. Boxer and Jean H. Quataert (New York: Oxford University Press, 1987), 86–94; David N. Livingstone, *The Preadamite Theory and the Marriage of Science and Religion* ([Philadelphia]: American Philosophical Society, 1992), 5–11.

41 At any rate, one of his salon acquaintances, Madame de la Sablière, did. On this and on the general fad for anatomical dissection, see Roger, *Les sciences de la vie*, 181. The relationship between Madame de la Sablière and Bernier is demonstrated by the two-part article, "Extrait de diverses pièces envoyées pour étreines par Mr. Bernier à Madame de la Sabliere," published in the *Journal des sçavans*, 7 and 14 June 1688, 17–32, and 33–37, respectively.

42 For Gassendi's relation to the biological debate, and Bernier's in the *Abrégé*, see Roger, *Les sciences de la vie*, 135–40, 345, 463.

43 Duchet, *Anthropologie et histoire*, ch. 2, notably 285–98.

44 The Code Noir, which enshrined the status of black slaves in the French West Indies, was promulgated less than a year after the publication of Bernier's article. One clearly did not cause the other, but the "coincidence" is nonetheless striking.

45 Bernard le Bovier de Fontenelle, "Lettres galantes de M. le chevalier d'Her***," 1683, in *Oeuvres diverses*, vol. 5 (Paris, 1715), 130–31. Fontenelle, too, shares a belief in preexisting biological forms (Roger, *Les sciences de la vie*, 345–48).

46 Gilles-André de La Roque, *Traité de noblesse, de ses différentes espèces, de son origine* (1678); various passages cited from eighteenth-century editions of the work by Devyver, *Le sang épuré*, 164, 183, 202–3. But see Ellis, "Genealogy," 429.

47 Found in the fourth edition of *Les caractères ou les moeurs de ce*

siècle (1689), reprinted in Jean de La Bruyère, *Oeuvres complètes*, ed. Julien Benda (Paris: Gallimard , 1951), 333. That this constitutes a satire of upper-class attitudes is argued by Maurice Lange, *La Bruyère: Critique des conditions et des institutions sociales* (1909; Geneva: Slatkine reproductions, 1970), 202–3.

48 On the *Journal des sçavans*, see Peabody's dissertation, " 'There Are No Slaves in France,' " 135–44; for dictionaries, see Furetière, *Dictionnaire universel*, s.v. "race." The article "Genre" seems indeed to reject specifically the categorization offered by Bernier: "On dit particulierement le *genre* humain, pour signifier tous les hommes, quoy qu'il n'y ait sous luy que des individus, & point d'espèces differentes." Here again, the concepts are repeated (in the case of *genre*, word for word) in the third edition of the *Dictionnaire de Trévoux*.

49 I have studied this discourse for the end of the century in " 'In Defense of Slavery': Eighteenth-Century Opposition to Abolition and the Origins of a Racist Ideology in France," in *History from Below: Studies in Popular Protest and Popular Ideology in Honour of George Rudé*, ed. Frederick Krantz (Montreal: Concordia University, 1985), 221–24 (new ed. [Oxford: B. Blackwell, 1988], 219–46). A subsequent look at the origins of this discourse has revealed no obvious reference to Bernier.

Alyssa Goldstein Sepinwall

Eliminating Race, Eliminating Difference

Blacks, Jews, and the Abbé Grégoire

The abbé Henri-Baptiste Grégoire—priest, French revolutionary, abolitionist, and scholar—has often been called the "friend of men of all colors" and a liberator of the world's oppressed. Indeed, from his entrance on the French political and intellectual scene in 1788 until his death in 1831, Grégoire attacked prejudices directed toward Jews, people of African descent, and other oppressed groups throughout the world. Where nineteenth-century French Jews hailed him as the father of their emancipation, Haitians praised him as the "new Las Casas," an heir to the sixteenth-century Spanish friar who had insisted that the Indians were human and should not be enslaved.[1]

The French government gave official sanction to this notion of Grégoire as a precursor of modern antiracism when it inaugurated him into the Panthéon during the bicentennial of the French Revolution in 1989. In an effort to highlight France as the source of modern ideas of human equality, Grégoire's remains were accompanied along the rue Soufflot by women from the Senegalese island of Gorée, representing with their emancipated bodies the fruit of Grégoire's campaigns against slavery. Recalling Grégoire's abolitionist efforts and referring to a moment when "1789 is reborn in Prague in 1989, in Berlin in 1989, in Moscow, Budapest, Sofia, Santiago, [and] Beijing in 1989," culture minister Jack Lang declared it necessary to recall Grégoire's words: " 'The only governments which are in accordance with the rights of peoples are those founded on equality and liberty.' "[2]

In comparison with many of his contemporaries, Grégoire's ideas about race and slavery were in fact quite radical. Nevertheless, we would read him anachronistically if we interpreted his ideas about race as early versions of modern multiculturalism. Rather than seeing cultural and racial differences as values to be celebrated, Grégoire saw them as obstacles to social progress. This essay will thus explore the nuances of Grégoire's thought about race. On the one hand, Grégoire was a staunch abolitionist, who gloried in attacking slave-owners and holders of racialist ideas, whether inside France or across the Atlantic. He also was one of the strongest defenders of Jews in France against those who said they inherently and permanently differed from Christians. On the other hand, however, Grégoire's vision for ending racial prejudice depended on a process of homogenization—both cultural and biological. His opposition to racial prejudice was in fact rooted in his larger goal of bringing all of mankind into the Catholic Church.[3]

Battling Racial Prejudice during the Revolution

From Grégoire's earliest years in French public life, ending prejudice constituted a high priority for him. He would first gain prominence through his defense of French Jews: in 1785, he entered (and in 1788 shared the prize in) an essay contest sponsored by the Academy of Metz on alleviating the Jewish plight. Where other intellectuals had declared that Jews were a separate species of humans, corrupt and unregenerable, Grégoire declared such a perspective absurd. For him, Jews were not essentially different from other humans, but only seemed that way because of the degrading conditions to which they had been subject: "Any people placed in the same circumstances as the Hebrews . . . would become just like them." Jews and Christians were "children of the same father," he argued, who lacked "any pretext for the hatred of [their] brothers."[4]

Later, as a member of the national assembly, Grégoire was one of the strongest and earliest supporters of the idea of giving Jews citizenship. He tried to push for this issue in the earliest months of the revolution and published a *Motion en faveur des Juifs* when other deputies refused to place the topic on the assembly's agenda.[5] Throughout his life, Grégoire would maintain good relations with Jewish leaders for his defenses of them against anti-Jewish attacks.

Jews were not the only group Grégoire sought to defend. Though he had once condemned philanthropists more concerned with slaves "two thousand leagues distant" than Jews at home, Grégoire soon saw parallels between their cause and that of the Jews and became one of the assembly's most infamous opponents of the white colons and their supporters in France. After mixed-race property holders (*gens de couleur*) from Saint-Domingue complained that the colons were excluding them from the colonial assemblies held in December 1789, Grégoire denounced the "aristocracy of color." Skin color, he declared, was an arbitrary social distinction that kept the "human family" from unification. It was outrageous, he charged, that people of mixed race were not only prohibited from voting, but were also legally prevented from even eating together with whites in certain areas. He asked his fellow deputies to place themselves in the shoes of the *gens de couleur*: "Imagine that on the banks of the Gambia, your white skin attracted the insults of blacks. With what vehemence you would denounce this injustice!"[6] Along with other members of the Société des Amis des Noirs, he urged his colleagues in the assembly—and other priests—to use their standing to denounce racial prejudice.[7] Even as his rhetoric proved too radical for the majority of the assembly, and Grégoire found himself attacked as a troublemaker by the colons and their allies,[8] he continued his efforts to eradicate the legal and social prejudices that kept people of color separated from whites.

Grégoire's desire to grant immediate citizenship during the revolution to people of mixed race did not extend to slaves. While invoking the universalism of the Declaration of the Rights of Man in favor of the *gens de couleur* in May 1791, he stated that black slaves did not yet merit rights. Their cause "has nothing in common with that of the [free] mulattoes. . . . One must not rush into anything . . . and give complete political rights to men who do not know all their duties. This would be putting a sword in the hands of the furious." At a time when deputies worried that slaves might break out in revolt, just as some *gens de couleur* had begun to do, one of his arguments in favor of the *gens de couleur* was that they could help whites "contain the slaves."[9] Slaves were not yet at a point, he felt, where they could understand the idea of rights and duties; it would therefore be dangerous to include them in a democratic nation, one in which all citizens needed to be civic-minded.

Nevertheless, Grégoire shuddered at the injustices of slavery and hoped it could one day end. Already in 1789, he began to advocate ending the slave trade, as a first step toward a gradual abolition of slavery. Yet he could not even persuade the Société des Amis des Noirs to support such a radical move.[10]

Grégoire and Slavery in the Postrevolutionary Years

Any hesitation Grégoire might have had during the revolution about the immediate abolition of slavery disappeared later in his life, especially after the national convention's 1794 decree abolishing slavery as an affront to republican principles. From that time until his death, Grégoire showed himself a staunch abolitionist, an intractable foe of slave-owners and slave traders. His activities in this realm became especially pronounced in the years after Napoléon's reimposition of slavery in the French colonies. Through published writings and in correspondence with intellectuals around the world, Grégoire spoke out against slavery's evils, whether in the French empire or in other New World empires and nations that relied on slavery.

Grégoire's most important antislavery work was his 1808 classic *De la littérature des nègres*. At a time when censorship laws prevented direct criticism of Napoleonic policies, Grégoire's work (masquerading as a literary history) set out to destroy the ideological foundations of slavery by proving that people of African descent were capable of the same intellectual achievements — and had the same moral capacities — as whites. By recounting the biographies of exceptional men and women of African descent, Grégoire aimed to prove that people of color could show great intellectual achievement if only the world would encourage their talents instead of repressing them. He made clear that his reflections extended not only to blacks, but also to other oppressed groups throughout the world, including "the untouchables of Asia," "Jews of all colors," and Irish Catholics.[11]

De la littérature had, in many ways, been inspired not only by Napoléon's reimposition of slavery, but also by Thomas Jefferson. Grégoire admired Jefferson and Americans in general; at a time of reactionary repression in Europe, the United States seemed to many French radicals the world's best hope for the future of republicanism. Grégoire had been incensed, however, by Jefferson's comments in *Notes on the State of Virginia*, to the effect that blacks were naturally and irrevocably incapable of the same intellectual achievements and moral sentiments as whites.[12] Grégoire also considered it a scandal that the young republic had not only failed to abolish, but had in fact *enshrined* slavery into its constitution through the three-fifths compromise (which counted blacks as three-fifths of a person for purposes of taxation and representation, but did not free those enslaved and did not allow free blacks to vote).

Though he praised the Virginian in the preface for his work against the slave trade, Grégoire attacked the view of Jefferson and others that blacks were naturally inferior intellectually. Grégoire countered the idea of separate racial origins with a biblically inspired argument that all human beings belonged to a single species: "Who would dare . . . deny that all humans are variations on a single type, and who would claim that some of them are incapable of attaining civilization?" Only historical events—particularly the brutality of slavery—had degraded blacks. Any logical person, he thundered, must recognize that the injustice of whites, rather than any innate defect, had made blacks seem inferior: "What sentiments of dignity, of self-respect, can possibly exist in beings treated like beasts . . . ? What can become of individuals degraded below the level of brutes, overloaded with work, covered with rags, devoured with hunger, and torn by the bloody whip of their overseer for the slightest fault?" Answering the many counterarguments against his position, Grégoire declared, "Those claiming the superiority of whites are none other than whites defending their own interests."[13] Grégoire's criticism of Jefferson did not remain implicit; he rebuked the Virginian by name numerous times.[14]

In these years of Napoléon's reign, and after the Bourbons' return to power, Grégoire worked closely with French and British abolitionists to first achieve a ban on the slave trade and then to get it enforced. Nevertheless, Grégoire found those in power much less interested in issues of slavery than his revolutionary contemporaries had been. To Grégoire, the United States, which unlike France was still a republic, thus remained Grégoire's best hope for advancing the abolitionist cause.[15]

In addition to his efforts on the continent, Grégoire therefore worked directly with Americans to end slavery and wipe out the scourge of racism. In 1800, he published an *Apologie de Barthélemy de Las-Casas*, aimed at improving the reputation of the Spanish defender of the Indians, and sent it to several American intellectuals. He corresponded with numerous abolitionist societies in the New World, such as that headquartered in Philadelphia, and with men like Gulian Verplanck, an abolitionist who presided over the New York Historical Society. Verplanck, for his part, would praise Grégoire as "the champion of toleration against bigotry" and "the friend of the oppressed."[16] Leading American libraries ordered copies of Grégoire's books on racial issues.[17]

Nevertheless, Grégoire's American efforts also proved discouraging. By the 1820s, Grégoire fretted that abolitionism was making little headway in the United States and that racial prejudice remained as strong as ever. Indeed, to him, racial prejudice was as bad — if not worse — in the American republic of that time than in any European colony. In 1826, Grégoire lamented: "Skin color prejudice exists in its most extreme degree in the French, Dutch, and British colonies, and especially in the United States." He denounced the contradiction between Americans' claiming their own liberty as a result of natural law, but refusing to extend this liberty to their slaves.[18]

Still, though Grégoire felt frustrated about the impact of his antislavery views on the United States during his life, his ideas helped inspire a new generation of abolitionists there in the nineteenth century and a new generation of civil rights leaders in the twentieth century.[19] Where the American civil rights leader Guichard Parris called him the "father of Negro literary and biographical history" in 1937, the Caribbean intellectual Aimé Césaire would refer to Grégoire in 1950 as "the first scientific refuter of racism."[20]

Toward Cultural and Physical Homogeneity

Given the modern resonance of his attacks on racial prejudice and his reputation as being the "father" of several modern ideas, Grégoire might thus seem a precursor of modern-day multiculturalism. Looking more closely at his ideas, however, makes clear that his opposition to racial prejudice was founded on the premise that oppressed groups, once they had escaped their oppression, would abandon their cultural — and even racial — particularity.

Indeed, Grégoire had indicated in his first efforts at writing about Jews that his main goal in improving their status was to facilitate their voluntary conversion. The problem with punishing the Jews, he suggested, was that it only made them more reluctant to adopt Christianity. Noting that "persecuting a religion is a sure means of making it even dearer to its adherents," he had argued that "complete religious liberty accorded to them is a great contribution to reforming them, and I dare say, to converting them." "If we encourage the Jews," he added, "they will insensibly adopt our way of thinking and acting, our laws, our customs, and our morals." Though Grégoire sincerely denounced forced conversions, he had no problem with requiring Jews to attend mandatory lectures on

Eliminating Race, Eliminating Difference 33

Christianity: "Obliging the Jews to instruct themselves, is not forcing them to convert."[21] This voluntary conversion was especially important to the Catholic priest because the Messiah would not come without it. The return of the Jews to Israel and their conversion were, for him, necessary precursors to Jesus' return.[22]

Similarly, Grégoire saw his work with blacks as steps toward bringing them into European culture and Christianity. For example, before the 1794 abolition, Grégoire appealed to the *gens de couleur* to spread Christianity among their own slaves; becoming Christian, he suggested, constituted a necessary component of the preparation that would allow slaves to learn how they could conduct themselves as free men and women.[23] From 1815 to 1827, he would be very involved with Haitians, an involvement that both reflected his admiration for their republicanism and his desire that they become more fully Christian. In these years, Grégoire criticized the depravity of fashionable European society, but he ultimately saw European and Christian models of "civilization" as the only avenues for Haitians and others outside Europe to achieve social progress.[24]

For Grégoire, Christianity also provided the means for bringing the world together. In a series of essays on oppressed groups throughout the world, from the indigenous peoples of the Americas to untouchables in India, Grégoire suggested that conversion (or "return") to Catholicism provided the answer for their troubles. Alluding to the benefits that could accrue to Indians as a result of their increased contact with Europeans, Grégoire asserted that "Christianity would allow Indians to take advantage of the secret of their powers and their rights. It would allow them to develop their intellectual faculties." The more a people was persecuted, he suggested, the more it needed Christianity: "Though Christianity is suited to all centuries, regions, and conditions, it is especially suited to the needs of oppressed groups [*malheureux*], because it offers consolations for all types of calamities." If all men adopted it, humans could recover the "unity of the human family" suggested by Genesis.[25]

Yet cultural and religious differences were not all he sought to eliminate with regard to Jews, blacks, and other nonwhite groups throughout the world. Indeed, Grégoire also made clear from this first essay on the Jews in 1788 that religion was not the only thing that marked them off as different from their fellow citizens. Using a synthesis of ideas borrowed from Johann Kaspar Lavater and from eighteenth-century natural history (especially Buffon), Grégoire painted a picture of a degenerate Jewish physical constitution. Jews' dietary practices had served to make them weak: the kosher laws, with their prohibition on eating the least trace of blood, he argued, had deprived them of vital nutrients. Moreover, "their women are constantly enervated by a sedentary life, as are most of their men." Because many of them were peddlers, rather than field-workers, he remarked, "they never have the vigorous arms of our cultivators." Moreover, Grégoire hinted, Jews were sexually degenerate, with a high propensity toward "solitary libertinage"; he also suggested that "Jewish women would be strongly subject to nymphomania" if they did not marry early.[26]

Though Grégoire had attacked contemporaries who portrayed Jews as having *permanent* biological differences, Grégoire thus did not object to the idea that they had *existing* (and, hopefully, correctable) biological differences. Far from disagreeing with those who talked of Jews' physical differences, Grégoire cited with pride a discussion he had with Lavater, a renowned eighteenth-century scholar considered an expert on physiognomy: "The philosopher Lavater, who can be considered a virtual legislator in pronouncing on physiognomy, told me that he had observed that, in general, they have a pallid face, hooked nose, sunken-in eyes, prominent chin, and strongly pronounced muscles constricting the mouth. I congratulate myself on seeing the moral consequences that he deduced from this coinciding with what I argued in the last chapter."[27] Grégoire clearly agreed with Lavater's assessment and believed the moral failings of the Jews stemmed from their physical deficiencies.

If Jews were currently physically degenerate, though, what could be done to improve them and make them like others, thus preempting the arguments of Christians whose anti-Jewish sentiments prevented them from seeing Jews as "children of the same father" as they? Drawing on natural history and the idea of crossbreeding species to improve them, Grégoire proposed an idea which would later reappear in his discussions of blacks: the "crossing of the races" through intermarriage as a corrective to Jews' "inbreeding" via intrareligious marriage. This "race-crossing" through intermarriage would prove essential for curing their weaknesses and regenerating them physically. He opined that "marriages between blood relations do not perfect the species" and that "crossbreeding within species causes races to degenerate [*abâtardit les races*]." This inbreeding, he argued, had "operated the physical degradation of the Parsis in the Orient and the Jews everywhere." Intermarriage would also facilitate Jews' cultural assimilation and conversion by establishing intimate links between them and Christians. He hoped that products of mixed marriages would be raised Catholic: "Allowing marriages to be contracted between Christians and Jews would establish a new point of contact [between them]. We cannot multiply these enough."[28]

Intermarriage remained an important theme of his in the early nineteenth century in regards to blacks, particularly when he advised Haitians about the best ways to create a stable, Christian, harmonious society, in which the divisions wrought by slavery could be healed. Interracial marriage, he argued, was a crucial means for bringing blacks and whites together: "Relations of blood can establish habitual relations between them." The new mixed race, he alleged, would be better than blacks or whites had been on their own. Echoing the ideas of Buffon about animals and plants, he asserted: "All the physiologists attest that the crossed races are together more robust."[29]

Mixed marriage also formed an essential part of Grégoire's idea of reuniting people throughout the world. In addition to helping smooth Jewish-Christian and white-black relations, he saw it as a solution to tensions between Greeks and Turks, French Catholics and Protestants, and Europeans and indigenous peoples in India.[30] As he noted in an essay on the influence of Christianity in India, mixed marriages between European men and Hindu women could play a key role in bringing Western culture and Christianity to Asia.[31]

Throughout the course of his life, Grégoire fought a remarkable fight to end prejudice of all kinds. Courting ridicule from his contemporaries, Grégoire asserted the basic equality of all humans, no matter how socially despised some of them may have been. Yet we need to recognize that as the French Jewish writer Rabi noted in 1962, "Grégoire was a missionary, and a missionary in three senses: of the Revolution, of the French language, and of the Church. A missionary, of course, is a person who, while showing a true and active sympathy for the individuals who compose the group to which his mission is aimed, evinces a fundamental contempt for their cultural and spiritual heritage."[32] Grégoire deeply wanted to aid Jews, blacks, and other oppressed groups, but not in a way that would reinforce their "clinging to" cultural practices he viewed as backward, wrongheaded, or heretical. He also longed to "help" them shed their physical degradation by combining their blood with those of white Christians. The ideal society Grégoire envisioned would have no more prejudice. But neither would it have cultural or racial difference. Through cultural regeneration and mixed marriage, the world could become a harmonious and homogenous "universal human family"—whose culture and values would be that of French Catholic republicans.

Grégoire's legacy in regard to difference—as that of the revolution itself—is therefore complicated. As Jack Lang indicated at the Panthéon in 1989, Grégoire was a pioneer of modern antiracism. Yet Lang also omitted something: Grégoire could function as a symbol not only for antiracism, but also for the contradictions of French universalism. For even as the abbé had advocated the inclusion of all peoples in the universal human family, he had also strengthened the idea that nonwhites and non-Catholics remained backward and in need of "regeneration" to "elevate themselves" to the level of white, Catholic Frenchmen. From the colonial "civilizing mission" to the chador affair of the 1980s, this paradigm would underlie the French approach to managing cultural difference—an approach that welcomed vast populations into the "French family" even as it demanded the erasure of their differences.[33]

Notes

1　For fuller information on Grégoire's activities and writings and on these issues' historiography, see my "Regenerating France, Regenerating the World: The Abbé Grégoire and the French Revolution, 1750–1831" (Ph.D. diss., Stanford University, 1998).

2　Jack Lang, "Hommage solemnel à Condorcet, l'abbé Grégoire et Monge au Panthéon. Mardi 12 décembre 1989. Eléments du discours de Jack Lang, Ministre de la Culture, de la Communication, des Grands Travaux et du Bicentenaire," copy donated by Lang to Conservatoire National des Arts et Métiers (CNAM, Bibliothèque du CNAM, B1659, 2, 4, 19, and 21–22); this and all unmarked translations are mine. See also Steven Laurence Kaplan, *Farewell, Revolution: Disputed Legacies: France, 1789/1989* (Ithaca, N.Y.: Cornell University Press, 1995), 341–42.

3　This in fact paralleled some of Las Casas's motivations. See Bartolomé de las Casas, *In Defense of the Indians: The Defense of the Most Reverend Lord, Don Fray Bartolomé de Las Casas, of the Order of Preachers, Late Bishop of Chiapa, against the Persecutors and Slanderers of the Peoples of the New World Discovered across the Sea,* ed. and trans. Stafford Poole (1552; DeKalb: Northern Illinois University Press, 1992).

4 Henri Grégoire, *Essai sur la régénération physique, morale et politique des Juifs,* ed. Rita Hermon-Belot (1789; Paris: Flammarion, 1988), 117, 67, 177.

5 Henri Grégoire, *Motion en faveur des Juifs* (Paris: Belin, 1789).

6 Ibid., 43.

7 *Archives Parlementaires de 1787 à 1860,* 1st series (Paris: Librairie administrative de Paul Dupont, 1879–1913), 10:362 (3 December 1789); this publication will henceforth be referred to as *AP. AP,* 12:383 (28 March 1790); *AP,* 26:70 (14 May 1791); Henri Grégoire, *Mémoire en faveur des gens de couleur ou sang-mélés de St.-Domingue et des autres isles françoises de l'Amérique, adressé à l'assemblée nationale* (Paris: Belin, 1789), 8, 21, 46. In a response to Grégoire, one pamphlet writer asserted that Grégoire was misinformed and that there were no laws blocking people of different races from dining together. See G. Legal, *Observations sur tout ce qui concerne les colonies d'Amérique, notamment celle de Saint-Domingue. No. 1: Réponse à un mémoire de M. Grégoire en faveur des gens de couleur des colonies* (Paris: n.p., [1790]), 19.

8 See, for example, Legal, *Observations*; Charles de Chabanon, *Dénonciation de M. l'abbé Grégoire et de sa lettre du 8 juin 1791 adressée aux citoyens de couleur et nègres libres de Saint-Domingue* (Paris: De l'imprimerie de la Feuille du Jour, 1791); and the national assembly debates at *AP,* 10:362 (3 December 1789) and *AP,* 27:231 (14 June 1791). For an excellent summary of these debates and of opposition to Grégoire, see David Geggus, "Racial Equality, Slavery, and Colonial Secession during the Constituent Assembly," *American Historical Review* 94 (1989): 1290–1308.

9 *AP,* 25:737–42 (11 May 1791); Grégoire, *Mémoire en faveur des gens de couleur,* 38, 51 n. 24. On the impact in the assembly of the rebellion led by Vincent Ogé, see Geggus, "Racial Equality," 1302.

10 See Marcel Dorigny, "The Abbé Grégoire and the Société des Amis des Noirs," trans. Jeremy D. Popkin, in *The Abbé Grégoire and His World,* ed. Jeremy D. Popkin and Richard H. Popkin (Dordrecht, Netherlands: Kluwer Academic Publishers, 2000), 30–31.

11 Henri Grégoire, *De la littérature des nègres, ou, Recherches sur leurs facultés intellectuelles, leurs qualités morales et leur littérature, suivies de notices sur la vie et les ouvrages des nègres qui sont dis-*

tingués dans les sciences, les lettres, et les arts (Paris: Maradan, 1808), 87.

12 Thomas Jefferson, *Notes on the State of Virginia* (New York: Harper and Row, 1964), 133.

13 Grégoire, *De la littérature des nègres*, 14, 44–45, 35. On the biblical bases of Grégoire's defense of the common origins of the entire human species, see Alyssa Goldstein Sepinwall, "Exporting the Revolution: Grégoire, Haiti, and the Colonial Laboratory," in Popkin and Popkin, *The Abbé Grégoire and His World*, 54. On secular arguments in the eighteenth century about the multiple origins of races, see Michèle Duchet's classic study *Anthropologie et histoire au siècle des lumières: Buffon, Voltaire, Rousseau, Helvétius, Diderot* (Paris: F. Maspero, 1971), especially section 2.2 on Voltaire.

14 Duchet, *Anthropologie et histoire au siècle des lumières*, 36, 150, 255–56, 260.

15 On the abolitionist efforts of Grégoire and other Frenchmen during these years, see Ruth F. Necheles, *The Abbé Grégoire, 1787–1831: The Odyssey of an Egalitarian* (Westport, Conn.: Greenwood, 1971), chap. 6; and Lawrence C. Jennings, *French Anti-slavery: The Movement for the Abolition of Slavery in France, 1802–1848* (New York: Cambridge University Press, 2000), especially 6–8.

16 Gulian C. Verplanck, *An Anniversary Discourse: Delivered before the New York Historical Society, December 7, 1818* (New York: James Eastburn, 1818), 15.

17 For example, the Library Company of Philadelphia, the leading subscription library in the early republic, purchased a number of Grégoire's writings, including his 1790 *Lettre aux philantropes sur les malheurs, les droits et les réclamations des gens de couleur de Saint-Domingue, et des autres îles françoises de l'Amérique* and a 1791 English translation of his *Essai sur la régénération morale, physique, et politique des Juifs*. Both were owned by the time the library printed its 1807 catalog, and, according to chief reference librarian Philip Lapansky, were probably acquired soon after publication. It is not clear when the Library Company acquired its two copies of *De la littérature*.

18 Henri Grégoire, *De la noblesse de la peau ou, De préjugé des blancs contre la couleur des Africains et celle de leurs descendants noirs et sang-mêlés* (Paris: Baudouin, 1826), 23–24.

19 See, for nineteenth-century examples, Charles Sumner, "The Abbé Grégoire, 1808," in *Prophetic Voices Concerning America: A Monograph* (Boston: Lee and Shephard, 1874), 151–54; and the discussion in Jean-François Brière, introduction to *On the Cultural Achievements of Negroes*, by Henri Grégoire, ed. Thomas Cassirer

and Brière (Amherst: University of Massachusetts Press, 1996), xlv–xlvi.

20 Guichard Parris to Duraciné Vaval, 12 January 1937, Guichard Parris Papers (MG 31), box 1, folder "Grégoire — Correspondence," Schomburg Center for Research in Black Culture, New York; and Aimé Césaire, "Discours d'inauguration de la place de l'abbé Grégoire: Fort-de-France — 28 décembre 1950," in Oeuvres complètes ([Fort-de-France]: Editions Desormeaux, 1976), 422.

21 Grégoire, Essai sur la régénération, 62, 134, 138, 148–49.

22 On this aspect of Grégoire's thinking, see Paul Grunebaum-Ballin, "Grégoire convertisseur? Ou la croyance au 'Retour d'Israël,'" Revue des études juives 1, 1/2 (1962): 388; and Rita Hermon-Belot, "L'abbé Grégoire et la conversion des Juifs," in Les Juifs et la Révolution française: Histoire et mentalités, ed. Mireille Hadas-Lebel and Evelyne Oliel-Grausz (Louvain: E. Peeters, 1992), 22.

23 Henri Grégoire, Lettre aux citoyens de couleur et nègres libres de Saint-Domingue, et des autres isles françoises de l'Amérique (Paris: De l'imprimerie du Patriote françois, 1791), 12–13.

24 On Grégoire's Haitian involvements, see Sepinwall, "Exporting the Revolution," 41–69.

25 See Sepinwall, "Regenerating France, Regenerating the World," 344–45, 336.

26 Grégoire, Essai sur la régénération, 75, 77–78, 65.

27 Ibid., 72.

28 Ibid., 74, 157. For a parallel discussion of intermarriage in Grégoire's thinking, see Jean-Loup Amselle, Vers un multiculturalisme français: L'empire de la coutume (Paris: Aubier, 1996), 57.

29 Grégoire, Considérations sur le mariage, 14–15.

30 See Archives départementales de Loir-et-Cher, F592, folder 4; and "Questions religieuses," Arsénal Ms., 15049/140, Bibliothèque de l'Arsenal, Paris.

31 See Sepinwall, "Regenerating France, Regenerating the World," 294.

32 Rabi [Wladimir Rabinowitch], Anatomie du Judaisme français (Paris: Editions de Minuit, 1962), 14, building on an earlier formulation by a young French Zionist named Méïr Leviah in "L'abbé Grégoire contre la synagogue," Chalom: Revue juive mensuelle 10, 58 (1931): 5. On Grégoire's language politics, see especially Michel de Certeau, Dominique Julia, and Jacques Revel, Une politique de la langue: La Révolution française et les patois: L'enquête de Grégoire (Paris: Gallimard, 1975); and David A. Bell, "Lingua Populi, Lingua Dei: Language, Religion, and the Origins of French Revolutionary Nationalism," American Historical Review 100, 5 (1995): 1403–37.

33 In the colonial context, I am referring here only to the doctrine of assimilation, and not that of association. See Raymond F. Betts, As-

similation and Association in French Colonial Theory, 1890–1914 (New York: Columbia University Press, 1961). On the "civilizing mission," see Alice L. Conklin, *A Mission to Civilize: The Republican Idea of Empire in France and West Africa, 1895–1930* (Stanford, Calif.: Stanford University Press, 1997).

Claude Blanckaert

Of Monstrous Métis?

Hybridity, Fear of Miscegenation, and

Patriotism from Buffon to Paul Broca

In July 1907, the Société d'Anthropologie de Paris created a "Permanent Commission for the Study of Métis," with the aim of resolving one of "the most grave and, at the same time, most obscure" problems in the science of man. The commissioners lamented the absence of an understanding of "the fecundity of miscegenous relations, and of the physical, intellectual, and moral aptitudes of their offspring, the métis, except for isolated, incomplete, and often biased observations, or general estimations without empirical foundations."[1]

Following the Société d'Anthropologie's well established procedures, the commission prepared a questionnaire for colonial functionaries, administrators, doctors, and teachers.[2] A panel of prominent anthropologists, including Georges Hervé and Paul Rivet, took as their starting point for the 1908 "questionnaire on the métis" the presumed distances between "purely and clearly different" races. The survey, whose implicit framework reflected the waning influence of polygenist theorists, obliged French imperial travelers to take observations on the diverse ethnic crossbreedings they encountered overseas. The observers were, to avoid conceptual contamination, invited to "abstain absolutely from any general or theoretical estimation." Rather, members of the commission would rely on the impartiality of fieldwork to gather evidence of the métis' levels of intelligence and personal "value," from health to the investigation of criminality or "sexual morality." While today the questionnaire's fundamental assumptions reek of base prejudice, in 1908 such a project went unchallenged on these grounds. As a sign of the times, even the opponents of antimiscegenation prejudice had to conform to the conceptual framework prepared for them by the anthropological commission.[3]

The question of human crossbreeding retained its supposed importance through the first few decades of the twentieth century.[4] It profited, moreover, from a kind of critical secular interest. In its two constituent elements — Are métis viable or not? Do they inherit the best "qualities" from their parents, or are they a vehicle of degeneration? — the "problem" of the métis, and particularly of the mulattoes, belongs to the long history of colonial domination. Its political, judicial, and literary expression is reflected in both the self-serving racist character of proslavery ideologues as well as in the inherent contradiction of the most philanthropical partisans, who sought to reclaim equality of nature for the *sang mêlé* with his or her white, civilized father — to the scorn of their double inheritance.[5] But the "phantasm of the hybrids," founded on the transgression of endogamic rules,[6] also participates in a parallel naturalist tradition distinct from the aggressive propaganda of the planters of overseas possessions. This tradition arises from an anthropology that claims to articulate all the elements of a fixed economy of nature, altogether a relationship to a world created by God, a relationship to the other and to the self. The determination of species (or of "race") is the pivot of it. For this reason, one should not read into the developments of the natural history of the métis, from Buffon to Georges Hervé, a simple mechanical transposition of colonial events; this tradition grows at its own internal rhythm. Which is, of course, not to deny that at certain important moments in the politics of slavery, proponents of one side or another appropriate the argument more or less opportunistically.[7]

As early as the eighteenth century, the status of the métis was already the object of the most peremptory controversies, splitting the partisans of the unity of man, the monogenists, from the doctrinaires of the plural origins of the human races, the polygenists.[8] The monogenists saw in the vitality of the métis the sign of the unity of races, these being no more than geographical or climatic varieties, in accordance with the cosmopolitanism of man. But the polygenists, identifying races with Linnean species, suspected even the viability of the "hybrids" of races, as they were called. This question, the scientific treatment of which was already rich with political implications before 1850, took a nationalist and defensive Pan-Latinist turn with the diffusion of the ideas of Gobineau and the American ethnological school. In this regard, the middle of the nineteenth century appears as the most significant period. For if, as the 1908 questionnaire indicates, the "problem" persists and will be updated, it appears that the fundamental arguments were forged between 1830 and 1859, the latter the date of publication for Paul Broca's famous *Recherches sur l'hybridité animale en général et sur l'hybridité humaine en particulier*. All these formed the constitutive disputes of the natural history of man, which for a long time gave a wide range of opinion to the biological and ontological status of the métis. It consisted of, as Georges Papillault recalled around the time of the second Congrès Universel des Races, knowing whether or not the great human groups constituted *species* in the Linnean sense of the word.[9]

"The Large and Unique Family of Our Human Genus"

For the majority of the nineteenth-century monogenists, the foundation of species did not reside in the outward resemblance of forms but, more important, in the physiological criterion of the continuing fecundity of the métis. This "mixiological" criterion was old and knew diverse variations from John Ray to Réaumur. But it was especially Buffon, in 1749, who popularized it in this form: "One must see as belonging to the same species that which by means of copulation perpetuates itself and preserves the similarity of this species, and as different species those which, by the same means, cannot produce anything together."[10] It followed from this definition and the principle that there was nothing constant or common between their "races" but the conformity of internal organization that permitted them to "all produce together," that dogs comprised "only a single and same species."[11] By contrast, the horse and the donkey, despite their similarity, participated in "the grace of creation." They were, by their original production, two separate types that could not be "joined"; from their coupling resulted only "vitiated and infertile" mules. These could not "found a family of new generations."[12] From this characterization of species, Buffon deduced that the "varieties" in the human species were only the contingent, "ordinary," and, moreover, reversible result of "degeneration," in turn due to the influence of climate and food.[13] The best proof of the primordial unity of men resided in the capacity that they manifested to "unite themselves in the common stem." Skin color, size, hair texture, or the "manners of peoples" could vary, while the "germ" was the same:[14]

If the Negro and the white could not reproduce together, if even their offspring remained infertile, if the mulatto was truly a mule, there would then be two quite distinct species; the Negro would be to man what the donkey is to a horse: or rather, if the white was a man, the Negro would no longer be a man; he would be a distinct animal, like the monkey, and we would be right to think that the white and the Negro would not have had a common origin. But even this supposition is given lie to by fact; and since all men can have intercourse and reproduce together, all men come from the same stock and are of the same family.[15]

By consecrating the principle of interfecundity as the "most fixed point that we have in natural history," Buffon delivered to his successors a "stipulative" — soon to be classical — definition of species.[16]

It was still necessary that in its restrictive usage, the definition of species so promulgated did not encounter empirical contradiction. In contrast to the naturalists of the nineteenth century, Buffon never questioned the vitality of the mixed populations in the human genus. But he soon demonstrated the fragility of the criterion of species by pursuing and reporting on some experiments of fecund and enduring hybridity between the dog and the wolf, the goat and the sheep, and diverse species of birds.[17] In 1776, he denounced, in the name of "experience and reason," the "prejudice," the "very great error," by which hybrid animals — the "mules" according to the generic term of the era — were vitiated and sterile. So the first censure of the system on which the monogenist doctrine reposed emanated from Buffon himself. The director of the Jardin du Roi now regretted that the use of the word *mule* had been generalized incorrectly to apply to all hybrids and that the verified lack of fecundity of the mule had been arbitrarily extended to all quadrupeds and birds, even to plants, of "mixed" species.[18] For him, none of these mixed creatures were "absolutely infertile"; "all, on the contrary, could reproduce, and there is only a difference of degree."[19] From this time forward, Buffon recognized that certain hybrids derogated from the order of creation and could procreate, that their capacity for reproduction was measured by the "number of correspondences [*convenances*] or incongruities [*disconvenances*]," and therefore that in general "the relationship of species is one of these profound mysteries of nature that man will not be about to fathom except by means of repeated, long, and difficult experiments."[20]

In this way Buffon left to posterity a series of solutions and a series of problems. For example, in his celebrated article on the "Varieties of the Human Species" of 1749, he explained that intermixture between human types, such as the "coarse" Tartar with Georgians and Circassians, could yield an improvement on at least the first of them.[21] Monogenist currents in the nineteenth century would take up this notion of regeneration through intermixture. However, fertile hybridity, expanded on by Buffon in later texts, threatened at its core the same absolute criterion of species, the principle of continuity of reproduction. The fact that congeneric species, like the dog and the wolf, or the camel and the dromedary, could successfully reproduce, undermined the core physiological criterion of species. Without ever drawing a direct equivalence between the mulatto and a mule, as the polygenists did, some monogenists presented the objection and remained unconvinced. Johann Friedrich Blumenbach or James Cowles Prichard, taken as representative examples, affirmed that the determination of the unity of the human species by continuous fecundity was neither sure nor sufficient, that the criterion was difficult to apply, and that the physical and moral analogy of all men would have to be decisive in all controversial cases.[22] However, the Buffonian criterion benefited from an almost unanimous accord after 1830, when the quarrel between the monogenists and the polygenists increased in intensity and converged on the status of racial crossbreedings. Contrary to true métis, which perpetuated themselves indefinitely, the hybrids of distinct species, it was said, would not reproduce beyond two or three generations inter se: "Never would the crossbreeding of species yield an *intermediate species*."[23] At best, hybrids maintained their ability to reunite, by reverse mixing, with one of their nonadulterous parental species.[24] From which came this new specification: "*Continuous fecundity yields species; limited fecundity yields genus*."[25]

Around 1850, the monogenists, denying that hybrids might found a family in spite of verified examples,[26] put forward three propositions that would all become the subject of bitter debates:

1. The differences that separate men are extremely nuanced. The "races" appear to pass gradually from one to another as soon as one takes count of all the human varieties, and not simply the two "extremes," the blacks and the whites.[27]

2. The events of colonization that bring together the most alien peoples prove the complete fecundity of human métis, as evidenced in the colonial taxonomies of intermixture, such as the Griquas

issued from Hottentots and Dutch, Cafusos from South Americans mixed with African negroes, Papuas, and the like.[28]

3. The mixing of races, far from being disastrous, is in fact advantageous, as though the métis inherit the best qualities from their parents.[29] Crossbreeding was perceived, moreover, as one of the most assured means of rehabilitation, of "renovation," indeed even redemption, of races declared "degraded."

The praise of miscegenation, already present in the Buffonian oeuvre, became a kind of dogmatic postulate, which allowed for the conciliation of a *virtual* equality of the races alongside their *actual* inequality, as this passage by Michel-Hyacinthe Deschamps illustrates:

> The *regeneration* of the *human species,* or the return of all the colored races to the white type, is possible by suppressing the odious prejudice, by means of perpetual crossbreeding of the *métis* with the primordial, now European, white race. The natives of an island, a country, of a vast colony would be whitened. Negroes would not have to be *born slaves,* our *inferior brothers*; they are our equals in the order of creation; they have a right — as we do — to the sun, to liberty, and to the banquet of life.[30]

This theme traversed the half-century. Both proslavery partisans and abolitionists, such as Julien Virey, Bénédict Morel, and Étienne Serres, anticipated Armand de Quatrefages and bestowed on iniquitous practices the guarantee of the most noble ethics of nature.[31] In a similar vein, the diplomat Reiset, a member of the Société Ethnologique de Paris and delegate to Guadeloupe, believed that the black race would achieve civilization through intermarriage with whites.[32] Regeneration through miscegenation offered those who subscribed to a progressive philosophy of history a sign of humanity reconciled in the complementarity of its ethnic elements.

In an era when scientific schools' positions were founded on tenuous but significant indices, the partisans of monogenism justified their rallying to the Buffonian thesis by the natural, regular, and infinite generation of type. Continuity — the heredity of physical abilities and generative capacity — ratified species. The common ancestry of all men revealed itself in the "beauty and vigor" of the métis.[33]

Here again, Buffon served as guide. Buffon thought that the unity of species would have to be judged by the parity or correspondence of sexual instincts. Animals revealed their nature by their behavior (*naturel*). Though capable of reproducing together, the dog and the wolf, for example, did not couple with one another spontaneously. It was necessary to overcome their resistance by artificial means and denaturing education. Buffon took from this the opinion that they consisted of two separate species and that some animals "completely alike in form, but completely different in disposition" could not have a common origin.[34] This restrictive clause, known today as an "ethological criterion" of a species, was popularized by Georges Cuvier in his celebrated *Discours sur les révolutions du globe*: "Nature also takes care to prevent the alteration of species, which could result in their mixture, by the mutual aversion that she has given to them."[35] But people often transgressed social interdictions opposing interracial liaisons. An "immense number of métis," born of clandestine unions, prospered in the colonies. Their vitality seemed "the most obvious proof that the mixing of human races resulted from a penchant that the laws of nature do not disavow."[36] In this way, the monogenists criticized the rank prejudice of proslavery advocates who knowingly called on a kind of physiological discontinuity between the different "species of man" to justify their domination and to protect, at the same time, their "superior" blood.

Nevertheless, by around 1850, the monogenists had assumed a defensive posture. The Buffonian criterion of continuous intraspecies fecundity was under attack by numerous polygenists. They did not all speak with the same voice, but each denounced the petitio principii and the religious dogmatism of their adversaries. Several fields of controversy would develop around a common point of departure: the knowledge of whether the human races constituted true biological species, sharing the three major attributes of resemblance, filiation, and stability.[37] In addition to their polemical promotion of the morphological criterion of species, the polygenists posed three technical questions that would decide the outcome of the quarrel in the half-century to come: (1) Are métis really viable? (2) Are true hybrids sterile? (3) Do crossbreedings contribute to the progress of humanity or to its decadence?

The Métis: Monster of Human Nature

The polygenists' first challenge bore on the monogenists' least contested evidentiary assertion. Was it truly verified that individuals born of the mixing of the most "extreme" races, according to the popular wisdom of the day, were both vital and fertile inter se, something commonly associated with the offspring of intraspecies couplings? For many polygenists, the answer was indisputable: according to travelers, nature did not like mulattoes and mixed bloods; some likened this mixed race to a "sewer."[38] Polygenists held that without the colonial oppression of populations of color, without the debauchery and the abuse of prerogatives, racial types would ordinarily remain reciprocally exclusive because a powerful brake, which could be called the ethnocentric ideal of race, was added to the already extant barrier of heredity. This was a decree of nature especially promoted by Honoré Jacquinot, member of the second circumnavigatory expedition of Dumont D'Urville: "The Negro appears hideous to each European, in the same way that our paleness will be regarded with disdain by the black man. For coupling to take place between these two species, there must necessarily be a perversion of the generative impulse." Jacquinot incriminated this "shameful exploitation" of one part of humanity by another, without which these mixings would "not or only rarely exist"; a métis, he explained, is "an abnormal, monstrous being, which persists under the influence of the conditions that presided at his creation, but which must necessarily become extinct when the same conditions disappear."[39]

Let us decipher this verdict. For Jacquinot, who claimed to be "the first to signal this sterility of the métis of the human species,"[40] it was not the mulattoes who reproduced among themselves in the Antilles; it was the political circumstances that reproduced the conditions of their reproduction. His travel companion, the surgeon and botanist Jacques-Bernard Hombron, published the same denials. Far from eulogizing the beauty of the métis, he even judged "beyond doubt that, the lower the mixed species are in the human series, the less the métis, which is the result of their union, participates in the physical and moral qualities of the most beautiful of the two authors."[41] Further, Hombron doubted the fecundity of their descendents without renewal by alliance with either of the original parental branches.

As a matter of fact, the theoreticians of the metropoles could mobilize the Buffonian criteria and return them contentiously against the monogenetic problematic. On the one hand, the polygenists had great esteem for these "men's repugnance to join together with individuals of other races," which they interpreted as a primitive instinct preventing the intermixture of peoples. On the other hand, they refused to admit the reality of mixed races. There was only a "great probability" that the union of métis would not succeed in continuous reproduction without resorting to mating with someone belonging to one of the original, "pure" races.[42] This is why, originally, a number of polygenists would contradict neither the "mixophobic" argument nor the definition of species based on the criteria of unlimited fecundity. Since these old ideas contained all the possibilities of subversive usage, they contented themselves with demonstrating the plurality of species in the human genus. In other words, the mulatto to them constituted a sterile "mule" or an infertile in the following generation.

This extreme thesis, reproducing in inverse symmetry the major assertion of the Prichardian monogenists, was published, after Jacquinot, by Robert Knox, an anatomist from Edinburgh whose university career was shattered following a criminal trial in 1830. A nihilist and a political radical, Knox abhorred slavery in all its forms. But his doctrines on the inferiority of the black races served the most conservative political interests, and he later became the intellectual guide to James Hunt, the racist founder of the Anthropological Society of London.[43] Knox published his masterwork, *The Races of Men*, in 1850, in it affirming that the laws of heredity, rigidly assigned to all living forms, opposed the perpetuation of mulattoes as an intermediate type: "Nature produces no mules; no hybrids, neither in man nor animals. When they accidentally appear they soon cease to be, for they are either non-productive, or one or the other of the pure breeds speedily predominates, and the weaker disappears."[44] According to Knox, mulattoes were "monstrous." Because they violated the laws of species and lived in an unstable, confused, contradictory identity, they seemed incapable of sustaining their autonomous existence beyond two or three generations. Their children came to die at a young age, offering the least resistance to environmental attacks: "In a mulatto I examined the nerves of all the limbs were a good third less than in a person of any pure race, fair or dark."[45] Field observers and doctors residing in slave states gave testimony to support this proposition. The fruit of adultery, scorned by nature and society, miscegenation provoked the imbalance of vital forces regulating the course of species. Mulattoes took from their double origin their feeble fertility and their "poor constitution."[46] Such assertions did not long remain isolated. Led by Samuel George Morton, the American school of ethnology catalogued the physical and moral forms of degeneration striking mulattoes. Apologist of the so-called sacred institutions of the southern states, the Mobile, Alabama, doctor Josiah Nott set out the balance sheet of his nosographic observations in 1842: disavowed by nature, human hybrids died young; they withstood fatigue less than their progenitors; mulatto women had a delicate constitution, subject to miscarriages; their children followed this degenerative propensity. Nott justified his conclusions as supported by over fifty years' residence in South Carolina and Alabama.[47]

Copied and compiled, such apparently irrecusable statements appeared to overwhelm completely the monogenetic theses regarding the universality of reproduction among the human races. One adherent, for example, noted that in Peru, Nicaragua, and other Latin American countries the Zambos born of "Indians" and negroes recapitulated all of the imperfections of their parents, without inheriting any of their virtues.[48] On other points of the globe, the presumed absence of métis born of Europeans and indigenous people again signaled a nullifying vice for the assimilation of the races:

> It is remarkable that, although a great number of Europeans live today in the same countries as the Andaman Islanders, the existence of hybrids resulting from their union are never mentioned any more. This circumstance is perhaps due to the fact that the difference between these two extremities of the human series renders the procreation of hybrids more difficult.[49]

The first polygenist syntheses relative to these questions appeared at the end of the 1850s. The defenders of racial purity agreed that the vitality of the métis, and therefore the affinity of species of their antecedents, were related to the harmony of the forces from which they resulted. If their directions diverged without combination, the métis would be imperfect, anomalous, and bastard, incapable of settling its own type. From this fact, a mixed race could never "have but a subjective, ephemeral existence." It derived from a hybridological law, thus enunciated: "A mean type cannot exist by itself, but only by the condition of being maintained by the two creative types."[50]

From 1858 onward, the polygenist doctor Paul Broca published his *Memoirs on Hybridity* [*Mémoires sur l'hybridité*] in regular installments of the *Journal de physiologie de l'homme et des animaux.*

An adversary of Prichard, Broca exercised his talents of freethinking pamphleteer against the physiological criteria of species consecrated by the monogenists. He saw there one of those "paradoxical conceptions that science, on its last legs, gives birth to when she finds herself in the grips of dogmas."[51] Broca prevented himself from issuing any absolute judgment on the sterility of hybrids, but he concluded — "until better informed" — that the study of the phenomenon of miscegenation was "far from being favorable to the doctrine of the monogenists."[52] He noted with approval, however, the observations of Nott and Morton.[53] Taking as an axiom that "with few exceptions, the results of mixings are increasingly more defective in proportion to the distance between the species,"[54] it appeared probable that the "imperfection of the products" explained the rarity of the métis born from the Anglo-Saxons' "concubinage" with Australian or Tasmanian women. Broca balanced his judgment: without question, certain human mixings between proximate "races" were viable. But there were definitely degrees of "mongrelism" (métivité), according to the generic neologism of Isidore Geoffroy Saint-Hilaire. The more inferior of them, the one that physiological suitability rendered "uncertain the fecundity of the first mixing," was observed "precisely there where the mixings are the most disparate, between one of the most elevated races and the two most inferior races of humanity."[55]

Broca had neither the competence of the traveler nor that of the colonial doctor. His anti-Prichardian dissertation was not original but it appeared, in the French context, as a skillful and documented synthesis. Having exhausted the didactic tradition attached to Buffon by following his logic, he induced that, in any case, the criterion of interfecundity proved the plurality of human species. However, Broca was wary of the generalities published by Jacquinot and Knox. Latecomers, the generation of despisers of miscegenation, seemed to willfully ignore the phenomena of fertile hybridity. However, it remained possible to reevaluate the validity of the Buffonian criterion by opposing it with authenticated and well-known examples of perfectly viable mixed animals. If two distinct species like the dog and the wolf produced by their coupling a mongrel that engendered a line of a permanent mixed type, that proved that marriages contracted between human races would not be valuable as a test of the unity of origin. They would return to a class of more general hybridological phenomena which no natural law guaranteed, but which experience alone established:

From the fecund métis that the White and the Negro produce together, and that by diverse combinations one could bring back the
descendents issued from their mixing to one of the two sources, one
has concluded that they had identical origin! However the ability
to produce fecund métis is not a proof that the father and mother
are of identical species. The Goat and the Ewe, the Wolf and our
Dogs, the Linnet and the Canary which are very distinct species,
give rise by their union to beings capable of reproducing themselves forever: but the Horse and the Donkey, though so similar in
appearance, only result in Mules, which are ordinarily infertile.
While, in the same genus, one frequently finds similar species that
do not fecundate with one another, or of which the adulterous
union only yields sterile products; one finds enough dissimilar ones
the hybrids of which prosper, bear fruit, and sometimes become the
progenitors of ever reproduced races.[56]

Thus empirical observation began to undermine Buffon's criterion
of species.

Sexual Similitude and Hybridity

Before the revolution of 1848, few polygenists doubted the vitality
of human hybrids. They spoke of them rarely and positively. In his
celebrated zoological essay on mankind, *L'homme,* Jean-Baptiste
Bory de Saint-Vincent, one of the most influential polygenists of the
Restoration, noted that "the peoples issued from diverse races have
been, for such a long time, as though tumbled upon one another,
and so intermingled, that the definitive boundaries have in part
disappeared; what has happened to them is what occurred for the
diverse species of domestic Animals that, from the points of their
departure, Men have driven together as though to submit them to
the causes of degradation to which they themselves were liable."[57]
The teacher and friend of Paul Broca, Pierre-Nicolas Gerdy, similarly postulated in 1832 that the human genus, originally composed
of distinct species, had mixed in all directions to the point that no
present nation was "pure of any foreign blood." Gerdy thought that
it was vain to reconstitute primordial humanity, incessantly mixed:
"The earth is covered with mixed or secondary species." And
adding to this confusion, the mixing of peoples had, for him, the
virtue of often yielding "métis more beautiful than either of the two
species from which they were descended." Gerdy did not believe in

Of Monstrous Métis? 53

racial essentialism. He kept his distance from authors who popularized the system of races and described the primordial species without taking into account their historical transformations.[58] In any case, the classical formulation of species, based on descent, lost its nomological pertinence: "For the métis, being different in nature from the species of either parent, [this criterion] cannot be appropriate to hybrid individuals." The monogenists were therefore not well-founded in constructing their doctrine on this sort of hypothesis.

In the nineteenth century, a complete phalange of polygenists, who did not share the verdicts of Jacquinot or Knox, went on to register numerous examples of the crossing of species that produced viable and prolific hybrids in all classes of animals. It is useless to make a list of them here; they can be found in the literature of the times. But it remains important to study the evolution of the disciplinary field and the subsequent development of the debate on the métis. If one could verify that primitive species were alterable by generation, that an infinite number of accidental types preserved their mixed character "until perpetuity," as did the métis of the Europeans with the Mongol and negro "species," or that, on the contrary, the intermixture engendered a sort of undecipherable ethnic chaos, then the classificatory objective of anthropologists became unrealizable.[59] Gerdy had already established this. Consequently, the problem remained, even if the discovery of an increasing number of fecund animal hybrids served the polemic of the polygenists. The question of the biological limits of generation was renewed. In other words, "In the middle of the innumerable mixings that invasions, conquests, and colonizing have occasioned among men, can one flatter oneself that there still exist today any examples of primitive races?"[60]

The law of the hybrids was henceforth completely indexed on this rationalization. The impulse came from North America, where the interethnic contacts assumed the violent form of the massive oppression of a class of human beings judged inferior. In 1847, Samuel George Morton published an inventory of animal or vegetable species producing fertile métis.[61] By multiplying the range of examples, he obliterated the classic objection of the monogenists, such as James Cowles Prichard, who justified the order of nature by the mutual aversion of individuals belonging to separate species. Morton noted that—apart from any condition of husbandry or breeding—hybrids formed spontaneously in nature. In the same way, he argued, domesticity could override this "natural repugnance." It finally appeared as a "law of nature" that species' ability to produce fertile métis paralleled their aptitude for domestication. Morton did not explain this relationship. He merely emphasized the existence of a manifest rapport between the propensity of species to submit to man and their capacity to engender a mixed lineage. Due to the fact that man was not destined to live in a state of nature — that he even seemed, in the opinion of Blumenbach, "the most perfect of all domestic animals"[62] — the diverse human species or races had to join again under this common law. Morton added that the reciprocal "repugnance" to disparate marriages was observed in humans as well as in animals. But he did not deem the obstacle invincible. Slavery on one hand, the promiscuity of domesticated animals on the other, depraved the sexual instinct by favoring illegitimate unions. Thence came these anti-Buffonian and anti-Prichardian conclusions, often reproduced:

1. A latent power of hybridity exists in many animals in the wild state, in which state, also, hybrids are sometimes produced.
2. Hybridity also occurs not only among different species, but among different genera; and the crossbreeds have been prolific in both cases.
3. Domestication does not cause this faculty, but merely evolves it.
4. The capacity for fertile hybridity, *coeteribus paribus*, exists in animals in proportion to their aptitude for domesticity and cultivation.
5. Since various different species of animals are capable of producing together a prolific hybrid offspring, hybridity ceases to be a test of specific affiliation.
6. Consequently, the mere fact that the several races of mankind produce with each other, a more or less fertile progeny, constitutes, in itself, no proof of the unity of the human species.[63]

Translated and discussed in France, Morton's theses made an impression.[64] The criterion of interfecundity, guarantee of the unity of man, perished with their diffusion. Morton's success, which might astonish the modern reader, derived not only from his technical reasoning. First, Morton had established his international scientific reputation by two of his preceding works, *Crania Americana* (1839) and *Crania Aegyptiaca* (1844), and he was counted among the three most famous anthropologists of the half-century, along with Blumenbach and Prichard. His voice therefore had to be heard. In addition, he was intervening in a crucial debate where pro- and antislavery partisans clashed. The latter held that the unity of all men since Adam was proved by the ability of blacks to have a prolific progeny with whites. Morton had just reestablished, in favor of the colonial planters, that this condition, were it fulfilled, would not decide the question of origin. Were the fox and the dog to intermix, one could ask, "would that be enough for them to be of the same species?" to possess the same instincts and be equal in regard to creation?[65]

In the end, the polygenists had, in a general manner, resurrected the Great Chain of Being, denounced by Cuvier and Blumenbach. They explained that nature privileged transitions, acting by nuances. In this way, the black man had been placed closest to the ape, as a linking joint, an interpolation between animal and the white man. Consequently, it was normal and conformed to the march of nature that the phenomena of hybridity, far from being uniform, obeyed the same movement, from the sterile mule to the fertile métis. In 1848, Pierre Bérard, one of Paul Broca's professors at the Faculté de Médecine de Paris, attempted a synthesis of the contradictory information on the degrees of hybridity.[66]

In the same period, Morton also proposed a hybridological series taking sexual disparities or affinities into account. His tripartite division enumerated degrees of fertility: "Remote species" did not produce hybrids; "allied species" produced a sterile descent inter se; "proximate species" yielded a fertile descent.[67] Morton knew and cited the works of Jacquinot, Hombron, and Knox in other publications. But there is little doubt that, for him, the examples of sterility between "extreme" human races obeyed the same mechanisms and the same logic as the sterility observed on other occasions among animals. Like Bérard, Morton insisted on the regular gradation of the physiological phenomena of hybridization; both posed, as the principle of their demonstration, the hypothesis of indefinitely fertile intrageneric crossings.[68] Josiah Nott took up these distinctions after Morton's death in 1851 in one of the most influential chapters of the collective work, *Types of Mankind*.[69] He, like Morton, believed that human species belonged to the group of close or proximate species, with the following restrictions, which Broca would retain a few years later: "Nevertheless, some are perfectly prolific; while others are imperfectly so — possessing a tendency to become extinct when their hybrids are bred together." And so were, in their forced relation, the crossings between the white and black races.[70] In this way the monogenists' double allegations could be refuted:

not only did some species of the best-identified zoological genera maintain the capacity to produce prosperous bastards, but there continued to exist, in the human group, obscure disharmonies condemning the mixed blood of the first generation.

That such a discourse obeyed a colonial logic is incontestable. But the observations offered by travelers, naturalists, and doctors were also embedded in a general scientific problematic. Just prior to Gregor Mendel's experimental program of hybridization, begun in 1856, the years 1820 to 1850 represented, in effect, a golden age of hybridology.[71] During this period, zoologists and horticulturists, certainly unaware of the great anthropological quarrels, undertook numerous experiments of cross-fertilization in an attempt to penetrate the secrets of nature. The meeting of these two preoccupations conferred both a validity and a topical interest on the polygenists' hypotheses. Broca became convinced of their soundness in the autumn of 1857, when he was presented with some specimens of leporides, the supposed issue of a pairing of hare and rabbit. At Angoulême, the leporide producer assured Broca that seven prolific generations had been obtained. Broca never doubted the experimental protocol put in place by the breeders and lent his backing to a rapidly disputed "biological myth."[72] This anecdotal circumstance, tirelessly recalled by historians of French anthropology, must not make us forget the essential. A reader of the American polygenists, Broca combated the authors of the Prichardian school, who saw in interfecundity the touchstone of species. The leporides constituted the occasion to engage in an ideological battle rather than the catalyst of tensions that traversed the field of racial studies.

Broca's *Memoirs on Hybridity*, published between 1858 and 1860, and the point of departure for his anthropological career, contain nothing truly original. For the historian, they nevertheless represent the best up-to-date synthesis of polygenist hybridology and, if you will, the gems of the previous literature. To break through resistance, Broca had to carry the critical dossier of his predecessors further. He tried to offer a vision of the general mechanisms of reproduction of mixed species and characterized, through serial divisions, the physiological links of diverse human groups. Broca would give the name *homoeogénésie* (sexual similitude) to the functional analogy that permitted fertilization between two distinct species. All along his career, Broca made gradualism a heuristic principle for evaluating the respective situation of the races with regard to one another. But his study of the phenomena of hybridity also shows that he saw there to exist an a priori framework for the expression of a philosophy of the continuity of nature. In the *Memoirs*, Broca described four categories or stages of hybridity, distinguished by intrinsic fertility of first-generation crossbreeds.

> 1. *Sterile Hybridity*: Métis of the first generation are completely infertile between themselves, or with either parental type, and consequently unable to reproduce either direct descendents or métis of second generation.
>
> 2. *Dysgenesic Hybridity*: Métis of the first generation are almost completely sterile;
>
> a) They are sterile inter se, issuing no direct descendents.
>
> b) They can, sometimes, but rarely and with difficulty, reproduce when backcrossed with one or the other of the parent species. The métis of second generation, born of this second pairing, are infertile.
>
> 3. *Partially Fertile Hybridity*: Métis of the first generation possess a partial fecundity.
>
> a) They are rarely or never fertile between themselves, and when they produce direct descendents, these have only a diminishing fertility, inevitably exhausted after several generations.
>
> b) They reproduce easily with parents of at least one of the two species. The métis of the second generation, born of this second pairing, are fertile, as well as their descendents, whether amongst themselves, with the métis of the first generation, with the nearest pure species, or with the intermediate métis that result from these diverse couplings.
>
> 4. *Eugenesic Hybridity*: Métis of the first generation are completely fertile.
>
> a) They are fertile inter se and their direct descendents are equally so.
>
> b) They interbreed easily and indistinctly with parents of the two species; the métis of the second generation, themselves and their descendents, are, by turn, indefinitely fertile, whether between themselves or with métis of any degree that result from the mixture of the two original species.[73]

This abstract typology allowed for the integration of hybridological knowledge accumulated by zoological science during the first half of the nineteenth century. It created at the same time a decisive opening in the field of polygenist anthropology. Broca wanted to bypass, or destroy, the biased positions of the theoreticians of uniformly fecund racial mixing (in the first place, the Prichardians) and of those nostalgic for a bygone era where purity of blood symbolized moral purity (the followers of Gobineau). Both schools laid themselves open to criticism in that they based their rejection of a durable and prolific hybridity on the dogma of the fixity of species.

However, on this question of species, Broca was, like the mature Buffon, won over to nominalism. According to him, nature had a creative power unknown to nomenclators.[74] The perfect *homoeo-génésie* between the dog and the wolf, the hare and the rabbit, of certain "Caucasian" human races confirmed the perfect vitality of intermediate new races, realizing, in practice, a stable physiological balance. The dysgenesic métis, such as the mule, did not contribute directly to the transformation of species. The products of the second generation, issued from an alliance with one of the original stocks, in effect, seemed abortive or atonic, and, in any case, unfruitful. But this was not the case for "partially fertile" hybrids (*paragénésiques*) which, recovering their fecundity by backcrossing with one of their parent races, could acquire a "physical or moral validity" sufficient for creating a durable race, near to the original one, but with different characteristics. From this fact, the constancy of types founded on the sterility of hybrids became a particular — which is to say relative — mode of the relations maintained between the species in the state of nature.[75] Broca added that the phenomena of spontaneous "reversion" to one of the primitive lines were hypothetical and not verified through experimentation.[76] Broca therefore believed he offered the proof that nature did not recognize specific boundaries and that it proceeded, in all operations, by the gradation of its effects. No hybridological *law* existed, if this word implied uniformity of action of a unique process inevitably attached to the marriages of races, without consideration of their capabilities for miscegenation. In return, it was possible to empirically observe a distribution of the affinities of races, ranging from perfect reciprocal fertility through to a misalliance, such that the existence of métis of the first generation, and a fortiori of the second generation, was increasingly doubtful.

It was not enough to attack Buffon and his successors. Broca went on to expose the errors or paralogisms of the polygenist Gerdy and his emulators: "Let us prevent ourselves from imitating the paradoxical reasoning of our adversaries and, from the fact that the crossbreedings of *certain* human races are eugenesic [i.e., perfectly fertile], let us not conclude *a priori* that *all* other crossbreedings must necessarily be so."[77] All distinctions effected, Broca thought that the diverse European races were eugenesic without restriction.

Of Monstrous Métis? 59

It also appeared to him that the union of a white man and a "negress" was indisputably fertile while that of the "negro" and a white woman was "very often sterile!" This thesis, borrowed from Etienne Serres, professor of anthropology at the Paris Muséum National d'Histoire Naturelle and taken up very often in the years 1840 to 1850, offered an example of unilateral hybridity in human crossbreeding.[78] Finally, notwithstanding the censure of ancient or modern accounts that had neither the consensus of voyagers nor decisive statistics, Broca admitted that certain human hybridizations seemed partially fertile (*paragénésiques*) or even infertile (*dysgénésiques*). The feeble viability of Dutch and Malay métis in Java, or the offspring of Germans and Ethiopians were examples of the first case. The rarity of métis between whites and Hottentots, Australians, or Tasmanians gave credence to a "zoological distance" still greater between the extreme races of the "human series."

Having made the division between established facts and the assertions of "armchair philosophers" who cast aspersions on the ugliness or the "dirtiness of indigenous women," Broca concluded that nothing could curb the "lubricity of the Europeans," except—precisely—the physiological antipathy between disparate human types. The unity of man must therefore be challenged and "the great human family" of the monogenists be opposed by the verdict of the natural sciences showing that, in the genus *Homo*, there were "very diverse degrees of reproductive power."[79]

Broca was one of the most active propagandists of this theoretical antihumanism founded on certain insuperable barriers of the human species. Because they encountered widespread interest, his *Memoirs on Hybridity* had international reverberations. Translated into English under the auspices of the Anthropological Society of London in 1864, the *Mémoires* won a notoriety unequaled by any of the parallel and concurrent studies published by Armand de Quatrefages.[80] Broca's research logically inscribed itself in the long run of the polygenist paradigm. It gave first to anthropology, then to eugenics, some soon-to-be classic concepts for interpreting the products of racial crossbreeding.[81] At the same time, Broca destroyed the mixiological criterion of species, without completely leaving behind the field of possibilities opened by Buffon in his reflections on hybrids. He named "sexual similitude" what his predecessor called "correspondences" or "incongruities," and he was contented, as was Buffon, to identify by a word an unresolved problem. This dilatory solution left the field open to investigations solicited by the

Instructions générales pour les recherches anthropologiques à faire sur le vivant [General instructions for anthropological research to be conducted on live subjects], the first field manual edited by Broca for the use of travelers, twelve pages of which were devoted to "crossbreedings and half-breeds."[82] Above all, during the 1850s, it followed the determining requirements of national and doubtlessly patriotic order in Broca's political activities.

"The Fatherland Is Not in Danger"

When the Comte de Gobineau's ardent pages on the fading of the Aryan race's last remains appeared in 1853–55, they received, if not the anthropologists' esteem, at least their attention. Gobineau affirmed that man was presently and already in decline, that his future, traced in a "horrifying spectacle of ethnic anarchy," would end in the fatal degeneration of which many "human herds" announced the outcome. In his *Essai sur l'inégalité des races humaines*, Gobineau articulated three theses formally in agreement with the knowledge of the polygenist anthropologists: 1) Groups that remained the most pure enjoyed a relative superiority; 2) in the crossing of unequal races, the "lesser" are elevated and the "greater" are abased by the same measure; 3) "a side effect of indefinite mixtures is to reduce the population to lesser and lesser numbers."[83]

In the southern states, the Gobineauian prophecy was well received. As early as 1854, the physician Josiah Nott wrote that many countries of Europe were already inhabited by "*dark*-skinned races," blended from Berber and African blood. He cited Spanish, Italian, and Portuguese as the most adulterated, but the population of France was also "tainted with bad elements."[84] In this way, mediocrity, depreciation, and sterility became indices of a predestined, predictable end.

In part, Broca's "Recherches sur l'hybridité" responded to this new challenge. Having attacked the progressive view of the monogenists, Broca sought to relieve the French people from the accusation of degeneration formulated in Gobineau-influenced circles. To the extent that the French carried the "seal of hybridity," it was necessary to combat a new kind of fetishism celebrating racial purity and to invalidate this "alarming proposition that any mixed race cannot persist in humanity."[85] The stakes were high. Anthropology came in its hour "to furnish its stone to this national edifice."[86]

At the opening of the meetings of the Société d'Anthropologie de Paris in 1859, Broca gave a reading of his first great inquiry into the ethnology of France. Two old, contrasting Gallic races, the Kimris — tall and blonde — and the Celts — short and dark — formed the ethnic base of the French population. These two roots, already well known to anthropologists by the works of Amédée Thierry and William Edwards, were irregularly distributed on the national soil, with the Kimric influence predominating between the Seine and the Rhine, while the Celtic imprint remained preponderant in Brittany and south of the Loire. Broca was persuaded, as were most polygenists, that the Gallic races constituted biological species and that, by virtue of their repeated unions, the greater part of the French people bore the instability of characteristics peculiar to hybrids. Moreover, these ethnic elements, already heterogeneous at birth, intermingled repeatedly with the Germans, the Romans, and other Mediterranean races. Bowing to general prejudice, Broca evaded all mention of the African influence of the Berbers on the present composition of the French nation. For him, Nott's "dark" pseudoraces belonged to the dark-haired Celtic branch and the Basques, while a "beautiful tint, more white than brown," represented an isolate of the "Aquitaine race." Protected from miscegenation by the barrier of the Pyrenees, the Basques paradoxically came to be considered "as one of the most pure, and perhaps the most pure, of the Caucasian races."[87] In spite of this tormented genealogy, the details of which are omitted here but which made research of ethnic origins "one of the most complicated problems of our science," Broca affirmed that the French nation was well and good. So good that Knox's supposed hybridological law condemning métis was nothing but an abusive generalization which did not take into account the innocuousness of eugenesic mixtures.[88] "The pure representatives of the primitive races are a very small minority there, and yet this hybrid people, far from falling into decadence — following the theory of Gobineau, far from presenting a declining fecundity — following the theories of several other authors, grows every day in intelligence, prosperity, and numeric force!"[89]

It would certainly be excessive to conclude that Broca undertook this long study on hybrids in order to challenge the harbingers of the end of the civilized world. However, two elements should be taken into account here. First, Broca's hybridological series and the theory of sexual affinities, formulated in 1859, permitted both the restoration of a genetic distance between "superior" and "inferior" races as well as the salvation of the integrity of a biologically homogenous "Caucasian" type.

At the same time, the followers of Gobineau believed that political instability was a symptom of the mixed races' biological decadence. For them, the social body lost all unity by the ethnic anarchy of its constituents and became ungovernable if not under the yoke of a despotic government: "*Dark*-skinned races, history attests, are only fit for military governments. It is the unique rule genial to their physical nature; they are unhappy without it, even now, at Paris."[90] Broca, an opponent of the empire—his democratic convictions forged during his participation in the republican clubs of 1848[91]— came to react violently to the "calumnies" propagated by Knox, Gobineau, and Nott. To counter them, it sufficed to demonstrate that no physical or moral degeneration struck the nation and that the "benefits of social regeneration that we owe to the Revolution" could be found in the notable prolongation of the French life span and the ascendant demographic march of the population. Thus, as Broca would state more than once, "we can sleep peacefully: the fatherland is not in danger."[92] This apology for a mixed race took, in the context, a nationalist turn, even a Pan-Latinist defense. For Broca, the fall of the Roman Empire or the regression of Spanish civilization doubtlessly had many other historical and social reasons than the "disparate hymens" invoked by the followers of Gobineau. In this way, by an unexpected dialectical reversal, the eugenesic hybridity of the French, which attested first to their plural, heterogeneous origins, was called on to confirm their fundamental present political identity. The people of France manifested a fusionist state by the convergence of racial elements, the complementarity of creative tendencies, and constitutive energies. Broca incidentally took advantage of a key idea of his doctrinal adversaries, the monogenists, to serve his own patriotic ideal. By a circular argument, he hoped to use natural history to verify and plant the seeds of a republican political history.

Retrospectively, we know the tenor of prejudice that fundamentally underwrote all of this specious research—from both monogenist and polygenist ends of the spectrum. We understand the petitio principii and its inanity: the métis, in effect, exists only for those who profess the so-called system of pure race. This idea certainly had scientific validity in the framework of the classificatory projects undertaken by naturalists at the beginning of the nineteenth century.[93] But with the diffusion of the doctrines of evolution, assigning to man generations without number, the postulate of fixed and original races would necessarily lose its relevance and utility. It endured, nevertheless, despite Darwin and Lamarck, as an inert but paradoxically active element in the heart of the anthropological paradigm well into the early twentieth century.

Notes

The author heartily thanks Sue Peabody for her translation of this article and for her valuable editorial suggestions.

1 "Questionnaire sur les métis," *Bulletins et mémoires de la Société d'Anthropologie de Paris* 9 (1908): 688; Filippo M. Zerilli, "Il 'Questionnaire sur les métis' della Société d'Anthropologie de Paris (1908)," *La ricerca folklorica* 32 (1995): 95–104.

2 Claude Blanckaert, "Le 'manuel opératoire' de la raciologie: Les instructions aux voyageurs de la Société d'Anthropologie de Paris (1860–1885)," in *Le terrain des sciences humaines: Instructions et enquêtes, XVIIIe–XXe siècle*, ed. Blanckaert (Paris: Editions L'Harmattan, 1996), 139–73.

3 See, for example, Auguste Bonifacy, "Les métis franco-tonkinois," *Bulletins et mémoires de la Société d'Anthropologie de Paris* 1 (1910): 607–42.

4 See George W. Stocking, *Race, Culture, and Evolution: Essays in the History of Anthropology* (Chicago: University of Chicago Press, 1982), 48ff.; Gérard Lemaine and Benjamin Matalon, *Hommes supérieurs, hommes inférieurs? La controverse sur l'hérédité de l'intelligence* (Paris: A. Colin, 1985), 59 sq.; Pierre-André Taguieff, *La force du préjugé: Essai sur le racisme et ses doubles* (Paris: Editions La Découverte, 1987), chap. 9; Taguieff, "La bataille des sangs," in *Des sciences contre l'homme*, ed. Claude Blanckaert (Paris: Autrement, 1993), 1:144–67; Filippo M. Zerilli, "Il dibattito sul meticciato: *Biologico e sociale* nell' antropologia francese del primo novecento," *Archivio per l'antropologia e la etnologia* 125 (1995): 237–73.

5 Louis Sala-Molins, *Le code noir, ou Le calvaire de Canaan* (Paris: Presses Universitaires de France, 1987), 264ff.; Léon-François Hoffmann, *Le nègre romantique: Personnage littéraire et obsession collective* (Paris: Payot, 1973), 231.

6 Léon Poliakov, "Le fantasme des êtres hybrides et la hiérarchie des races aux XVIIIe et XIXe siècles," in *Hommes et Bêtes: Entretiens sur le racisme*, ed. Poliakov (Paris: Mouton, 1975), 167–81.

7 For example, Yves Benot, *La démence coloniale sous Napoléon* (Paris: La Découverte, 1992), chap. 7; Claude Blanckaert, "L'es-

clavage des noirs et l'ethnographie américaine: Le point de vue de Paul Broca en 1858," in *Nature, Histoire, Société: Essais en hommage à Jacques Roger*, ed. Blanckaert, Jean-Louis Fischer, and Roselyne Rey (Paris: Klincksieck, 1995), 391–417; Luc Forest, "De l'abolitionnisme à l'esclavagisme? Les implications des anthropologues dans le débat sur l'esclavage des noirs aux États-Unis (1840–1870)," *Revue française d'histoire d'outre-mer* 85 (1998): 85–102; Martin Staum, "Paris Ethnology and the 'Perfectibility of Races,'" *Canadian Journal of History/Annales canadiennes d'histoire* 35 (2000): 453–72; and Staum, "The Paris Geographical Society Constructs the Other, 1821–1850," *Journal of Historical Geography* 26, 2 (2000): 222–38.

8 Claude Blanckaert, "Monogénisme et polygénisme," in *Dictionnaire du darwinisme et de l'évolution*, ed. Patrick Tort (Paris: Presses Universitaires de France, 1996), 3:3021–37.

9 Georges Hervé, "Enquête sur les croisements ethniques," *Revue anthropologique* 22 (1912): 337.

10 Georges Louis Leclerc de Buffon, *Oeuvres philosophiques*, ed. Jean Piveteau, with Maurice Fréchet and Charles Bruneau (Paris: Presses Universitaires de France, 1954), 236.

11 Georges Louis Leclerc de Buffon, *Oeuvres complètes de Buffon,* ed. Frédéric Cuvier (Paris: F. D. Pillot, 1829–32), 14:238.

12 Ibid., 14:99 ff.

13 Phillip R. Sloan, "The Idea of Racial Degeneracy in Buffon's *Histoire Naturelle*," in *Racism in the Eighteenth Century*, ed. Harold E. Pagliaro (Cleveland, Ohio: Cleveland Press of Case Western Reserve, 1973), 293–321.

14 Buffon, *Oeuvres philosophiques*, 394.

15 Buffon, *Oeuvres complètes*, 14:110.

16 See Carl G. Hempel, *Eléments d'épistémologie*, trans. B. Saint-Sernin (Paris: A. Colin, 1972), 134.

17 Buffon, *Oeuvres complètes*, 14:285–333, 18:311–33. See Jacques Roger, *Buffon: Un philosophe au Jardin du Roi* (Paris: Fayard, 1989), chap. 19.

18 Or relative lack of fecundity. Buffon in effect wrote in his article "Des mulets" (1776) that in hot countries "the he-mule can engender" and "the she-mule can produce." He admitted, however, that such cases were rare and that the mules' infertility, "though not absolute, can nevertheless be regarded as positive" (Buffon, *Oeuvres complètes*, 18:325–27).

19 Ibid., 18:328–29.

20 Ibid., 18:345.

21 Georges Louis Leclerc de Buffon, *De l'homme* (Paris: F. Maspuo, 1971), 255.

22 Johann Friedrich Blumenbach, *Manuel d'histoire naturelle*, trans. S. Artaud (Metz: Chez Collignon, 1803), 1:30–31; Blumenbach, *De l'unité du genre humain et de ses variétés*, trans. F. Chardel (Paris: Allut, 1804), 104; James Cowles Prichard, *Researches into the Physical History of Mankind*, 4th ed. (London: Sherwood, Gilbert, and Piper, 1841), 1:138ff.

23 Pierre Flourens, *Cours de physiologie comparée: De l'ontologie, o Etude des êtres: Leçons professées au Muséum d'histoire naturelle, recueillies et rédigées par Ch. Roux* (Paris: Hachette, 1856), 16; see also Flourens, *Histoire des travaux et des idées de Buffon*, 2d. ed. (Paris: Hachette, 1850), 168.

24 Prichard, *Researches*, 1:144.

25 Flourens, *Cours de physiologie comparée*, 8.

26 See Isidore Geoffroy Saint-Hilaire, *Histoire naturelle générale des règnes organiques principalement étudiée chez l'homme et les animaux* (Paris: V. Masson, 1854–62), 3; Jean-Louis Fischer, "L'hybridologie et la zootaxie du siècle des Lumières à *l'Origine des espèces*," *Revue de synthèse* 101–102 (1981): 47–72.

27 See, for example, Filippo de Filippi, *Le déluge de Noé*, trans. A. Pommier (Paris, 1858), 68–69.

28 James Cowles Prichard, *The Natural History of Man: Comprising Inquiries into the Modifying Influence of Physical and Moral Agencies on the Different Tribes of the Human Family*, 3d. ed. (London: H. Ballière, 1848), section 5. See also, for example, Buffon, *De l'homme*, 352–53; Blumenbach, *De l'unité du genre humain*, 162ff.; Julien-Joseph Virey, *Histoire naturelle du genre humain*, new ed. (Paris: Crochard, 1824), 2:186–91; Louis-François Jéhan de Saint-Clavien, *Dictionnaire d'anthropologie, ou Histoire naturelle de l'homme et des races humaines* (Paris: J. P. Migne, 1853), 378–79; Alfred Maury, *La terre et l'homme, ou Aperçu historique de géologie, de géographie et d'ethnologie générales* (Paris: Hachette, 1857), 396–97.

29 As, for example, in Etienne-Renaud-Augustin Serres, "Rapport sur les résultats scientifiques du voyage de circumnavigation de l'Astrolabe et de la Zélée: Première partie: Anthropologie," *Comptes rendus des séances de l'Académie des Sciences* 13, 13 (1841): 648.

30 Michel-Hyacinthe Deschamps, *Etudes des races humaines: Méthode naturelle d'ethnologie* (Paris, 1857–59), 135.

31 Julien-Joseph Virey, "Homme," in *Nouveau dictionnaire d'histoire naturelle appliquée aux arts*, new ed. (Paris: Deterville, 1817), 15:101; Virey, *Histoire naturelle du genre humain*, new ed. (Paris: Crochard, 1824), 1:298–99, 2:193–94; Bénédict-Auguste Morel, *Traité des dégénérescences physiques, intellectuelles et morales de l'espèce humaine et des causes qui produisent ces variétés maladives*

(Paris: H. Baillère, 1857), 497ff., 511ff.; Armand de Quatrefages, "La Floride," *Revue des deux mondes* (1 March 1843), 758; "Rapport sur l'ouvrage de M. de Gobineau, intitulé 'Essai sur l'inégalité des races humaines,'" *Bulletin de la Société de géographie* 13 (1857): 204, 210; "Discussion sur le croisement des races," *Bulletins de la Société d'Anthropologie de Paris* 1 (1860): 199; Armand de Quatrefages, *Rapport sur les progrès de l'anthropologie* (Paris: Imprimerie nationale, 1867), 490–93. For Etienne Serres, see Claude Blanckaert, "La création de la chaire d'anthropologie du muséum dans son contexte institutionnel et intellectuel (1832–1855)" in *Le muséum au premier siècle de son histoire*, ed. Blanckaert et al. (Paris: Editions du Muséum national d'histoire naturelle, 1997), 111–12.

32 *Bulletin de la Société ethnologique de Paris* 2 (1847): 93–94.

33 Eusèbe de Salles, *Histoire générale des races humaines ou philosophie ethnographique* (Paris, 1849), 274.

34 Buffon, *Oeuvres complètes*, 14:252–58.

35 Georges Cuvier, *Discours sur les révolutions du globe* (1812; Paris, 1885), 148; see also Pierre Flourens, *Cours sur la génération, l'ovologie, et l'embryologie fait au Muséum d'histoire naturelle en 1836 [. . .] recueilli et publié par M. Deschamps* (Paris: Librairie medicale de Triuquart, 1836), 14; and Prichard, *Researches*, 1:143.

36 Dominique A. Godron, *De l'espèce et des races dans les êtres organisés et spécialement de l'unité de l'espèce humaine*, 2d ed. (1859; Paris: J. B. Baillère et fils, 1872), 2:360.

37 Claude Blanckaert, "Réflexions sur la détermination de l'espèce en Anthropologie (XVIIIe-XIXe siècles)," in *Documents pour l'histoire du vocabulaire scientifique* (Paris: Institut national de la langue française, 1982), 43–80.

38 See Michèle Duchet, "Racisme et sexualité au XVIIIe siècle," in *Ni juif ni grec: Entretiens sur le racisme*, ed. Léon Poliakov (Paris: Mouton, 1978), 136–37.

39 Honoré Jacquinot, "Considérations générales sur l'anthropologie," in *Voyage au pôle Sud et dans l'Océanie sur les corvettes l'Astrolabe et la Zélée*, ed. Jules-Sebastien-Cesar Dumont d'Urville (Paris: Gide, 1846), *Zoologie*: 2:91–92.

40 Since the end of the eighteenth century, some historians of Jamaica, like Edward Long, had asserted the physiological incapacity of whites and blacks to produce fully fertile hybrids. See Nancy Stepan, *The Idea of Race in Science: Great Britain 1800–1960* (London: Macmillan, 1982), 29; and Paul Broca, "Recherches sur l'hybridité animale en général et sur l'hybridité humaine en particulier considérées dans leurs rapports avec la question de la pluralité des espèces humaines," in *Mémoires d'anthropologie* (Paris: C. Reinwald, 1871), 3:530.

41 Jacques-Bernard Hombron, "De l'homme dans ses rapports avec la création," in Dumont d'Urville, *Voyage au pôle Sud et dans l'Océanie*, 1:275.

42 Emile Blanchard, "Texte de l'anthropologie," in Dumont d'Urville, *Voyage au pôle Sud et dans l'Océanie*, 33–35.

43 Evelleen Richards, "The 'Moral Anatomy' of Robert Knox," *Journal of the History of Biology* 22 (1989): 373–436.

44 Robert Knox, *The Races of Men: A Fragment* (Philadelphia: Lea and Blanchard, 1850), 65–66.

45 Ibid., 88–89, 163–64.

46 Blanchard, "Texte de l'anthropologie," 35.

47 Josiah C. Nott, "Hybridity of Animals, Viewed in Connection with the Natural History of Mankind," in *Types of Mankind: Or, Ethnological Researches Based upon the Ancient Monuments, Paintings, Sculptures, and Crania of Races, and upon Their Natural Geographical, Philological, and Biblical History*, ed. Nott and George R. Gliddon (Philadelphia: Lippincott, Grambo, 1854), 373; see Reginald Horsman, *Josiah Nott of Mobile: Southerner, Physician, and Racial Theorist* (Baton Rouge: Louisiana State University Press, 1987), chap. 4.

48 Jean-Christian-Marc Boudin, *Traité de géographie et de statistique médicales et des maladies endémiques* (Paris: J. B. Baillère, 1857), 2:219–20.

49 Jean-Baptiste d'Omalius D'Halloy, "Des races humaines, ou Eléments d'ethnographie," in *Dictionnaire d'ethnographie moderne, ou Recueil de notions sur les moeurs, usages et caractères des peuples existants sur la terre par M. X.xxx.* (Paris: J. P. Migne, 1853), chap. 7.

50 Georges Pouchet, *De la pluralité des races humaines: Essai anthropologique* (Paris: 1858), chap. 7.

51 Broca, "Recherches sur l'hybridité," 411.

52 Ibid., 521.

53 Ibid., 525.

54 Ibid., 538.

55 Ibid., 558.

56 Jean-Baptiste Bory de Saint-Vincent, *L'homme (Homo): Essai zoologique sur le genre humain*, 3d. ed. (Paris: Rey et Gravier, 1836), 1:68–69.

57 Ibid., 2:135–36.

58 Pierre-Nicolas Gerdy, *Physiologie médicale didactique et critique* (Paris, 1832), 1:285 ff.

59 See Antoine Desmoulins, *Histoire naturelle des races humaines du nord-est de l'Europe, de l'Asie boréale et orientale, et de l'Afrique australe* (Paris: Mequiguon-Marvis, 1826): 194–97.

60 Pierre Bérard, *Cours de physiologie fait à la faculté de médecine de Paris* (Paris: Labe, 1848), 1:465.

61 See William Ragan Stanton, *The Leopard's Spots: Scientific Attitudes toward Race in America, 1815–59* (1960; Chicago: University of Chicago Press, 1982), 113 ff.

62 Johann Friedrich Blumenbach, "Contributions to the Natural History," 1811, in *The Anthropological Treatises of Johann Friedrich Blumenbach*, ed. and trans. Thomas Bendyshe (London: Longman, Green, Longman, Roberts, and Green, 1865), 293–94.

63 Samuel George Morton, "Hybridity in Animals and Plants Considered in Reference to the Question of the Unity of the Human Species," *American Journal of Science and Arts* 3 (1847): 23.

64 Samuel George Morton, "Sur l'hybridité chez les animaux, considérée par rapport à la question de l'unité de l'espèce humaine," *Nouvelles annales des voyages et des sciences géographiques* 1 (1848): 122–26.

65 Ibid., 123 (French editor commentary).

66 Bérard, *Cours de physiologie*, 1:463–64.

67 Samuel George Morton, "Some Remarks on the Value of the Word Species in Zoology," *Proceedings of the Academy of Natural Sciences of Philadelphia* 5 (1852): 82. See Stanton, *Leopard's Spots*, 137, 227 n. 4.

68 Samuel George Morton, "Notes on Hybridity," *Charleston Medical Journal and Review* (1850): 145–52, and (1851): 1–8.

69 Nott, "Hybridity of Animals," 376.

70 Ibid., 397–98.

71 Robert Olby, *Origins of Mendelism*, 2d ed. (Chicago: University of Chicago Press, 1985).

72 Jean-Louis Fischer, "Espèce et hybrides: A propos des léporides," in *Histoire du concept d'espèce dans les sciences de la vie* (Paris: Editions de la Ffondation Singer-Polignac, 1987), 253–68.

73 Broca, "Recherches sur l'hybridité," 431–32.

74 Claude Blanckaert, " 'L'anthropologie personnifiée': Paul Broca et la biologie du genre humain," preface to Broca, *Mémoires d'anthropologie*, new edition (Paris, 1989), esp. xxvii–xxix.

75 Broca, "Recherches sur l'hybridité," 434 ff.

76 Ibid., 438 ff.

77 Ibid., 517.

78 Blanckaert, "Création de la chaire d'anthropologie," 111–12; Broca, "Recherches sur l'hybridité," 521 ff.

79 Broca, "Recherches sur l'hybridité," 538 ff.; and Broca, "Discussion sur le croisement des races humaines," *Bulletins de la Société d'Anthropologie de Paris* 1 (1860): 249–62.

80 Armand de Quatrefages, *Unité de l'espèce humaine* (Paris: Hachette,

1861). It is also worth mentioning an important work by Theodor Waitz, *Anthropologie der Naturvölker*, the first volume (1859) of which was translated in 1863 for the library of the Anthropological Society of London. In one of the first chapters (part 1, section 3), Waitz, who was a monogenist, pointed out the polygenists' dilemma: They absolutely refused the possibility that environmental forces had the capacity to make variations in humanity. They therefore invoked mixed breeding as the primary agent for the transformation of peoples, while denying the unlimited vitality of the métis (Theodor Waitz, *Introduction to Anthropology* [1863; New York: AMS Press, 1975], 190).

81 Eugène Dally, introduction to *De la place de l'homme dans la nature*, by Thomas Henry Huxley (Paris: J. B. Baillière et fils, 1868), 73 ff.; Paul Topinard, *L'anthropologie*, 2d ed. (Paris: Schleicher, 1877), 382–83; Fernand Delisle, "Hybridité," in *Dictionnaire des sciences anthropologiques*, ed. Bertillon et al. (Paris: O. Doin, n.d. [1881–89]), 585.

82 Paul Broca, *Instructions générales pour les recherches anthropologiques à faire sur le vivant*, 2d ed. (Paris: G. Masson, 1879), 202–14.

83 Arthur de Gobineau, "Conclusion Generale" in *Essai sur l'inégalité des races humaines* (1853–55; Paris: P. Belfond, 1967).

84 Nott, *Types of Mankind*, 405. See also 373–74.

85 Broca, "Recherches sur l'hybridité," 507.

86 Paul Broca, "Recherches sur l'ethnologie de la France," *Mémoires de la Société d'Anthropologie de Paris* 1 (1860–63): 2.

87 Ibid., 19.

88 Broca, *Mémoires d'Anthropologie*, 474. See also Broca, "Recherches sur l'ethnologie de la France," *Bulletins de la Société d'Anthropologie de Paris*, 1 (1860): 6–15; and Broca, "Recherches sur l'hybridité," 515.

89 Broca, "Recherches sur l'hybridité," 515.

90 Nott, "Hybridity of Animals," 404–5.

91 Claude Blanckaert, "La crise de l'anthropométrie: Des arts anthropotechniques aux dérives militantes (1860–1920)," in *Les politiques de l'anthropologie: Discours et pratiques en France (1860–1940)*, ed. Blanckaert (Paris: C'Harmattan, 2001), 101 ff.

92 Paul Broca, "Sur la prétendue dégénerescence de la population française," (1867) in Broca, *Mémoires d'anthropologie*, 1:497.

93 Claude Blanckaert, "On the Origins of French Ethnology: William Edwards and the Doctrine of Race," in *Bones, Bodies, Behavior: Essays on Biological Anthropology*, ed. George W. Stocking (Madison: University of Wisconsin Press, 1988), 18–55.

2

Representations of the Other

John Garrigus

Race, Gender, and Virtue in Haiti's

Failed Foundational Fiction

La mulâtre comme il y a peu de blanches (1803)

The independence of Haiti from France in 1804 rested as much on a cultural transformation as on the invincibility of France's former slaves. In 1801, after ten years of brutal conflict, what had been France's most profitable slave colony had become an autonomous, French-speaking New World republic, governed by former bondsmen and their descendants. That year the black general Toussaint Louverture named himself governor for life under a constitution that made few concessions to French oversight. Toussaint Louverture did not create an independent Haiti. As governor, he remained ostentatiously faithful to French religion and culture, urging white investors to return and imposing plantation discipline on former slaves. Nevertheless, in 1802, a massive French expedition removed him to a French prison and tried to reimpose slavery. This attempt to revoke the liberty purchased by a decade of revolution provoked a bitter war that eventually led to the unthinkable — a formal proclamation on 1 January 1804 by the leaders of the "native" army, announcing the independence of Haiti, a new American nation, black and indigenous.

In spite of the denunciations of French "barbarism" that accompanied Haiti's birth, the new nation's relationship to its former master remained confused. The Enlightenment that had helped inspire Caribbean and European opponents of slavery had also reified the categories *black* and *mulatto* that would continue to divide Haiti long after emancipation. Moreover, Haiti's leaders were following French and North American revolutionary examples based in very different social and cultural contexts. Not only had 90 percent of Saint-Domingue's inhabitants been brutally enslaved, but many of them had recently arrived from various African homelands.

The obstacles to building a self-consciously black nation from what had been France's "Pearl of the Antilles" are highlighted by a novel published anonymously in Paris in 1803, the year Haiti won its independence. The text, entitled *La mulâtre comme il y a peu de blanches*, is an epistolary romance that could be described as the first Haitian novel.[1] It would be far more accurate, however, to label it a failed foundational fiction, the blueprint for a society never established.[2] This romance was part of the postrevolutionary re-cast(e)ing of brown and black women from sycophantic courtesans and vile slaves to virtuous wives and loving mothers. Such representations suggested that colonial society conformed to the gendered division of public life found in postrevolutionary France and the United States and made it possible to imagine Saint-Domingue as an orderly — and perhaps even independent — American nation. Although it represents a road *not* taken, the text sheds important light on the official national ideology Haiti ultimately adopted — and the social tensions concealed by that model.

The residents of French Saint-Domingue did not develop a coherent racial ideology until the middle of the eighteenth century. By this time, the colony had such a large and wealthy free population of mixed ancestry that the simple idea of "white over black" was not enough to ensure social hierarchy. The new racial concepts that emerged in Saint-Domingue after 1763, therefore, used gender stereotypes to separate whites from free people of African-European descent.[3] *La mulâtre* was written to reject this gendered racism and establish the possibility of a virtuous Caribbean republic.

The roots of French racial ideology in Saint-Domingue stretch back to the 1640s, when France first claimed this territory. At that time, the western coast of Hispaniola was a frontier region, inhabited by pirates, hunters, and tobacco farmers. The few black slaves these buccaneers owned worked alongside indentured servants from Europe. The colony's European population was overwhelmingly male, and these masters considered the children they had with slave women to be free. The territory offered numerous opportunities for these free persons and their descendants. Ten times larger in area than Martinique and Guadeloupe combined, Saint-Domingue's mountainous interior was largely undeveloped until the 1770s. Though Saint-Domingue's residents knew both slavery and freedom, because of these conditions social categories within the free population remained notoriously fluid well into the eighteenth century.[4]

It was only after 1720 that this buccaneer lair began to emerge as a plantation giant. Racial categories became more important as slavery grew, though they remained inexact compared to later standards. Free blacks and mulattoes founded separate militia companies from whites in the 1720s, realizing they would otherwise never become officers. Royal administrators tried to control colonists' slave manumissions. Yet in this sparsely populated colony, French governors could barely enforce laws in the major port towns. Versailles disapproved when colonists married the descendants of slaves, but it never outlawed these unions in Saint-Domingue, though it did on other French islands. Similarly, the crown never restricted the value of property Dominguan whites could give to free people of color. By 1750, therefore, the colony had a number of free, propertied families known locally to have African ancestry, but officially classified as "white."[5]

In 1763, however, a new colonial era dawned in French America as Versailles attempted to reform what remained of its New World empire after the Seven Years' War. A flood of lesser bureaucrats, charged with bringing order to colonial society, crossed the Atlantic. They were accompanied by a tide of economic immigrants hoping to become wealthy planters. The ministry dissolved the unpopular colonial militia and relaxed its commercial regulations in hopes of increasing colonial loyalty. The end of the war also brought a quickening of the slave trade, which tripled in volume in the next twenty years.[6]

New populations and government initiatives spurred the colonial elite to a new self-consciousness. This process was heavily influenced by the European events Jürgen Habermas has labeled "the emergence of the public sphere."[7] In France, the expanding legal and underground press supplied more and more readers with a wider variety of texts. The same phenomenon occurred in Saint-Domingue, which received its first permanent printing works in 1763. By the 1780s, the colony was producing its own newspapers, legal, political, and technical pamphlets, and colonial book collections compared to those of France's legal and academic milieus. Booming Atlantic port cities like Bordeaux and Nantes built new plazas, markets, and promenades. In Saint-Domingue, too, after 1763, the colonial government reconfigured port towns, constructing new fountains, administrative buildings, and public gardens. In both colony and metropolis the upper and upper-middle classes founded Masonic lodges, theaters, and associations of amateur scientists.[8]

This public sphere was as much an intellectual as a sociological development. By the middle of the eighteenth century, the notion of "public opinion" had become an integral part of French — and French colonial — political rhetoric. By the 1750s, French royal judges regularly published their objections to royal policies, and an underground literature amplified their opposition.[9] Accused of tyranny, royal ministers presented their counterarguments in the press. Both groups appealed to the ideal of rational, civic-minded public discussion, immune to the selfish interests of royal favorites or ambitious judges.[10]

A conflict between "despotic" administrators and "defiant" magistrates also defined public discourse in Saint-Domingue, flaring into outright revolt in 1769.[11] The colony's two judicial councils fought the military governors appointed by Versailles, especially after a newly activist breed of governor tried to reestablish mandatory militia service in 1765. Inspired by French rhetoric, colonial judges denounced the tyranny of royal officials. In 1769, they appealed to the colonial public to resist the reimposition of the militia, but this revolt failed. The defeat convinced elite colonial reformers that Saint-Domingue lacked "public spirit." Their fellow colonists suffered military rule because they were too engaged in selfish private interests to see a larger common good.[12]

In the 1770s, Creole magistrates joined forces with royal officials to purify an emerging colonial public that both sides agreed was corrupt. In France, a number of critics of the state used misogynist stereotypes to explain royal despotism. Their rhetoric described courtesans like the Marquise de Pompadour as effeminizing Louis XV, warping court life with their selfish passion and narcissism. These writers contrasted the benefits of public discussion with the private influence of these unnaturally powerful women.[13] Drawing on Montesquieu and especially Rousseau, those writers who worried about the corrupting influence of women on the French state created a gendered vision of the opposition between "despotism" and "liberty." Evoking classical republican imagery, Rousseau imagined a civic world of virtuous men, complemented by a domestic sphere where women would fulfill their natural roles as mothers and wives.[14] Jacques-Louis David's 1785 *Oath of the Horatii*, where a band of brothers prepares to battle Rome's enemies while heavily draped women passively weep in what is almost another room, powerfully illustrated this gendered political ideal.[15]

In Saint-Domingue, a stylized misogyny drawing on these sources became even more central to elite discussions of the public than in France, for after 1763 colonial legislators incorporated such gender stereotypes into a new scientific racism. Inspired by contemporary French discourse, colonial elites blamed Saint-Domingue's lack of public spirit on the pernicious influence of people of color. They described free men and women of mixed ancestry using the same terms metropolitan writers employed to portray courtly decadence. While writers celebrated the colony's new parks, markets, and theaters, for example, the women of color who flocked to these public spaces disturbed them. For Moreau de Saint-Méry, a Creole judge, amateur scientist, and persistent critic of colonial incivility, the elaborately dressed mulatto women in the streets indicated an "excess of civilization." He contrasted their spectacle with the more "innocent pleasures" of male camaraderie in the colony's new Masonic lodges.[16]

Almost all Frenchmen who came to make their fortune in Saint-Domingue took women of color as concubines. As colonial elites adopted the notion of a rational civic-minded colonial public, they grew alarmed at the power these brown and black women had over white men. Despite new taxes and official sanctions, colonists continued to free their favorite slave women and mixed race children. They persisted in endowing these mistresses and children with land, slaves, and, for some, European educations. In other French colonies, governors and judges had been able to limit such practices, which they described as dangerous to the white public. Saint-Domingue's colonists seemed not to care.[17]

Many writers concluded that mulatto women corrupted white men with highly developed sexual skills. No account of Saint-Domingue in the 1770s or 1780s was complete without a description of these tropical temptresses. According to the Swiss traveler Girod-Chantrans, "These women, naturally more lascivious than European women, flattered by their control over white men, have collected and preserved all the sensual pleasures [voluptés] they are capable of. La jouissance has become for them an object of study, a specialized and necessary skill [used] with worn-out or depraved lovers, who simple nature can no longer delight."[18] For the Baron de Wimpffen, "these Priestesses of an American Venus . . . have made sensual pleasure [la volupté] a kind of mechanical skill and have taken it to the highest perfection. Next to them Aretino is a prudish school boy. . . . They combine the explosiveness of saltpeter with an exuberance of desire, that, scorning all, drives them to pursue, acquire, and devour pleasure, like a blazing fire consumes its fuel."[19]

These descriptions emphasized both nature and depravity. The Caribbean climate and African ancestry explained the sexual energy of brown women, but their mastery of the sexual arts was what Moreau de Saint-Méry, or Rousseau, might call "an excess of civilization." These Caribbean courtesans were the equivalent of Versailles's Pompadour or Polignac, sapping the strength and virtue of planters and merchants.

The emphasis on free women of color as a source of colonial corruption—both in public and private spaces—formed part of a newly biological conception of colonial society. Moreau de Saint-Méry, an advocate of a virtuous national colonial public, constructed an elaborate racial calculus in the late 1780s that was reinforced by stereotypes of "effeminate" corruption.[20] As influenced by the social theories of Montesquieu and Rousseau as by Buffon's natural history, Moreau described persons of mixed African and European "blood" as unstable hybrids, physically and morally degenerate. Mulatto men were beardless, sensual, and foppish, less strong than Africans and not as intelligent as whites. For Moreau, the archetype of this racial group so enslaved by appetites and ambitions was the *mulâtresse*, not the *mulâtre*.[21] Though couched in biological terms, Moreau's racial ideology leaned heavily on the gendered political rhetoric of those hoping to regenerate the French monarchy.

This synthesis of Enlightenment biology and sociology reveals the ideas behind Saint-Domingue's new racial laws. After the failed militia revolt, Saint-Domingue's judges worked with royal officials to purify the colony's new public spaces. In the 1770s, colonial lawmakers barred men of color from all militia commissions, government jobs, and the white sections of churches and theaters. Free people of color were forbidden to wear swords, drive coaches, or wear certain types of clothing.[22] At the same time, legal officials began to apply the racial labels *mulatto* and *quadroon* to colonial families that had long been considered "white." In some colonial parishes, as these new definitions were applied in the late 1770s and 1780s, census figures for the free population of color rose dramatically, while "white" numbers dropped correspondingly.[23]

Because nearly one hundred years of frontier society had produced so many people of mixed race, including propertied, French-educated families, simply degrading African descent did not suffice to establish a coherent white community. "Effeminizing" people of mixed ancestry created a stark division between white and colored. At the same time, these misogynist images excused the behavior of white colonists. As colonial elites grew frustrated with military rule, they attributed the absence of a principled, patriotic colonial opposition to the corruption of colonial mores by degenerate women and men of color. Barring this vice-ridden class from white society offered hope for reforming white civic spirit.

Use of such stereotypes to articulate an emerging white Creole consciousness was not unique to colonial Saint-Domingue. In Cuba, for example, in the 1830s and 1840s, white elites began to develop a "highly sexualized and racialized discourse on national culture" in the midst of a booming sugar economy supported by massive slave imports. This literature focused on the aggressively sensual *mulatta*, most famously in Cirilio Villaverde's 1839 story "Cecilia Valdés," later expanded into a novel. For Villaverde as for Moreau de Saint-Méry, women of color were much more threatening to the social order than their male counterparts.[24]

In Saint-Domingue, however, the French Revolution allowed free men of color to challenge this vision. After 1769, they became the foot soldiers of the Dominguan militia white colonists hated.[25] In France, the events of 1789 established the male citizen soldier as a new political ideal. Free men of color built their political strategy around this masculine image. They appeared before the national assembly in revolutionary Paris, presenting themselves as virile, virtuous husbands and fathers, as natural men, abused by a corrupt colonial society and abandoned by white fathers and brothers.[26]

This argument became all but irrefutable in 1791 when Saint-Domingue's slaves launched the revolt that became the Haitian Revolution. Free men of color proved central to France's campaign against the rebels, though many colonial whites refused to accept them in full revolutionary fraternity. In Martinique, rioting colonists reportedly castrated a twelve-year-old mulatto boy after men of color paraded under the tricolor.[27] Conservative planters became counterrevolutionaries in 1794, when France, unable to defeat its former slaves, officially emancipated them. By 1798, black and brown generals ruled Saint-Domingue as French republicans defending liberty and fraternity.

The emergence of first brown and then black men into full French citizenship was marked by an attention to gender as well as to color.

As Betsey Colwill's analysis of Louis Pierre Dufay's 4 February 1794 pro-emancipation speech to the convention points out, for Dufay "former slaves earned the status of citizens when they insisted on the rights of their sex . . . freemen appeared as republican husbands and fathers who claimed their children as personal 'property' and represented their wives as patriotic helpmeets and model mothers."[28] In 1797, Anne-Louis Girodet, a student of David, painted Jean-Baptiste Mars Belley, a Senegalese who had risen from Caribbean slavery to become a military leader and one of Saint-Domingue's first black delegates to Paris. Because prerevolutionary racism had not effeminized African men as it had men of mixed descent, but denied their intelligence, Girodet's portrayal of Mars Belley as an ultramasculine black patriot in tight military pants was perhaps not as radical a leap as his portrayal of the delegate's impressive cranium, explicitly compared to a bust of the abolitionist Abbé Raynal.[29]

At about the same time, the revolutionary press began reconfiguring the stereotype of the black woman. In 1794, an engraving by Fougea translated David's *Oath of the Horatii* into the Caribbean. As in the 1785 painting, the printed image is starkly divided into a vigorous male world of public action and an interior feminine space filled with emotion. A black father and his precociously virile son move toward the door with their weapon, while in another, heavily draped plane, a woman lets a second child fall from her breast as she weeps. The theme of natural black motherhood was developed with more attention in another print of the same vintage.

This conversion of slaves into virile soldiers and devoted mothers did not mark a complete reversal of slave-era racial imagery. Moreau de Saint-Méry and other prerevolutionary writers had portrayed blacks in natural terms to stress the artificiality of mulattoes. African slaves were heedless and indolent, but passionate and strong. Moreau suggested "the advantage that nature, or the use of palm wine, has given to negroes over other men in that which constitutes the physical agent of love." He insisted on the overwhelming power of maternal love in black women, though dissolute *mulâtresses* feared the sacrifices of motherhood.[30]

Reimagining the social role of Saint-Domingue's mixed-race women was a far greater challenge to slave-era gender stereotypes than these only partially revised images of virile black soldiers and devoted mothers. In 1803, the author of *La mulâtre* attacked the cliché of corrupt feminine sexuality that had delineated the colonial public sphere. This work dismantled prerevolutionary conventions from its very title, which mixes the feminine article *la* with the masculine form *mulâtre* instead of *mulâtresse* to make the point that the novel's heroine was as virtuous as any brown soldier-citizen or white woman. The subtitle extends this comparison to include white women and black men : *La mulâtre comme il y a beaucoup de blanches, ouvrage pouvant faire suite au "Nègre comme il y a peu de blancs."*[31]

Not only do these words suggest the hollowness of gender and racial distinctions, but by comparing itself to Joseph LaVallée's 1789 novel *Le nègre comme il y a peu de blancs*, the text further establishes its place in the history of revolutionary abolitionism. Like most black literary heroes of this era, however, LaVallée's hero Itanako was an African, enslaved in the French Caribbean, who ultimately returned home.[32] LaVallée had designed his book to rehabilitate the image of blacks, describing it as less a novel than "the story of a national character." *La mulâtre* is also about national character, but it goes a step further by describing a French American society in which republican values have extinguished racism.

La mulâtre is an early representative of what Doris Sommer has called "foundational fictions" or "national romances," historical novels written in newly independent nineteenth-century Latin America about "star-crossed lovers who represent particular regions, races, parties, economic interests and the like." Like these later, more successful texts, *La mulâtre* uses racial mixture as a metaphor for "national consolidation," equates personal with public virtue, and appeals to nature against political and social authorities. Yet while many of these national novels in the Spanish-speaking Caribbean, like Cuba's *Cecilia Valdés* (1839) or the Dominican Republic's *Enriquillo* by Manuel de Jesus Galvan (1882), are essentially anti-mulatto, *La mulâtre* strives to legitimate mulatto power by redefining *mulâtresse* from "tropical temptress" to "republican companion." The publication of *La mulâtre* the year before Haitian independence shows Saint-Domingue's mulatto class preparing for political power.[33]

Can the text be considered "the first Haitian novel," a distinction most scholars award to Emeric Bergeaud's *Stella* (1858)?[34] Though published in Paris, *La mulâtre* focuses on colonial society, advocating a new relationship between Saint-Domingue and France. Perhaps because of its place of publication, recent surveys of francophone Caribbean literature do not discuss the work and only Léon-François Hoffmann's *Le nègre romantique* gives it even a passing mention.[35]

Indeed, the reasons *La mulâtre* is not properly "Haitian" go beyond place of publication and acknowledgment in the literary tradition. Bergeaud's *Stella* tells the story of two half-brothers named Romulus and Rémus, one mulatto and the other black, raising the central problem of the social divisions in independent Haiti. *La mulâtre* avoids this issue almost entirely, instead refuting white prejudice against people of mixed ancestry. Obsessed with the debates of the colonial era, *La mulâtre* envisioned a "mulatto solution" to the revolution. Superseded by political events almost as soon as it was published, the novel constitutes a failure that nevertheless says much about Haiti's emerging national identity. As discussed below, the image of the brokenhearted *mulâtresse* and the virtuous American "native" remain part of "the fictions necessary to the myth of the Haitian nation."[36]

The novel was published at a moment when Saint-Domingue was in fact emerging as a largely autonomous French province, governed by black and brown men. As early as 1796, the mulatto general André Rigaud virtually ruled the colony's southern peninsula as an independent republic after having driven out an invading English army. To the north, Toussaint Louverture, who had led his rebel slave troops from an alliance with the Spanish to a coalition with the French republican forces in 1794, followed Rigaud's double strategy of loyalty to the republic, while using local allies and ethnic tensions to drive out political rivals. In 1797, the French revolutionary directory named Toussaint Louverture *général en chef*, and later that year he succeeded in forcing the revolutionary commissioner Sonthonax to return to France. The following year saw the departure, similarly arranged by Toussaint Louverture, of the French general Hédouville. By August 1800, Toussaint Louverture's armies had conquered Rigaud's southern province. Exploiting, as his rivals had, the social and cultural tensions between propertied mulattoes who had never been slaves and the black soldiers who could now claim equal citizenship, Toussaint Louverture purged the colonial government of many of Rigaud's partisans. In 1801 he published a new constitution for Saint-Domingue that named him "governor-general for life," making him, in effect, the autonomous ruler of a distant French province.[37]

Though Toussaint Louverture based his rule on plantation exports and French culture, Bonaparte deposed him after the Peace of Amiens brought temporary peace to Europe in 1801. Toussaint Louverture's numerous enemies were more than willing to help the French—at first. The massive expedition of 1802 included many of the mulatto leaders Toussaint Louverture had expelled, and those in the colony who resented the governor's personal power rallied to the French.[38] It was at this decisive moment that the anonymous author of *La mulâtre* published the romance, broadly adapting the plot and philosophical message of Rousseau's *La nouvelle Héloise* (1764) to prerevolutionary Saint-Domingue.

Set in the colony's northern province in the mid-1770s, the text purports to be the correspondence of Sylvain, a white man, and Mimi, a French-educated free woman of color. After more than five hundred pages, the book ends shortly after the death of the two lovers. Like Rousseau's Julie, Mimi "lets social convention triumph over natural inclination," but through her death achieves "victory for a higher form of nature."[39]

The attributes of *La mulâtre*'s central characters are based on post-1763 critiques of colonial mores. Sylvain, whose name has the same association with *forest* in French as in English, hews closely to Moreau de Saint-Méry's description of the "imperious, lively, and fickle character" of the white Creole elite. "The Creole, losing sight of everything that does not satisfy his baser inclinations, scorning all that is not marked for pleasure, surrenders himself to these forces. Passionate for dance, music, celebrations, and anything that engages and sustains his folly, he seems to live only for sensuality."[40] A successful planter who abandoned a promising military career, Sylvain is widely respected for his compassion, learning, and talent, but he is also known for seducing women of color. He lives with Fany, a beautiful free black woman he describes as his first true love, and their children, to whom Sylvain is devoted. Nevertheless, for two years he pursues Mimi.

If Sylvain represents the instinctive natural passion of the white Creole, Mimi, whose name suggests "kiss" or "caress," incarnates virtue based in reason. Though so beautiful that Sylvain falls instantly in love, she is not a stereotypical *mulâtresse*. Their relationship remains entirely epistolary and platonic until the end of the novel. Despite Sylvain's persistent efforts, Mimi will not become his mistress because she believes he will eventually betray her, as he has Fany. In the novel's recreation of slave-era Saint-Domingue, interracial marriage is illegal, so it provides no solution.[41] Like Latin American writers several decades later, the author of *La mulâtre* emphasizes the heroine's principles and highlights the need for a new state by linking legal prejudice to the tension between erotic and platonic love.[42]

Sylvain attributes Mimi's reluctance to her excessive concern with public opinion; he urges her instead to heed nature, the source of true virtue (2:120, 2:130). His challenge evokes the stereotype of the artificial *mulâtresse* as a public woman, but Mimi's response turns the image inside out. She connects her concern for social convention with what, by 1803, had become the core ideals of the French Revolution, all the while proclaiming a Creole patriotism. Denouncing the "barbarous prejudice" that denies her a respectable marriage, she writes: "Children of the same *patrie*, we are deprived of its tenderness and blessings" (1:207).Though she agrees that justice should never prohibit nature's best instincts, Mimi expresses her loyalty to that *patrie* in Rousseauean terms:

> Ultimately social opinion overrides nature, through unjust but inevitable laws that force [individuals] to sacrifice their desires to the general will. Now, since this general will is called *Patrie*, obedience to its laws is the highest virtue. According to this principle, which is based if not in reason then at least in necessity and therefore in prudence, your doctrine would seem to all the world to lead to licentiousness, which is why I cannot adopt it, although I love you whole-heartedly. Not only do I love you, but I would have you love and respect me, and you would not do so if I freed myself from my duties. (2:140–41)

Mimi contains her desire out of respect for a social order that she recognizes as flawed. Civic virtue triumphs over private pleasure, though her sacrifice, appropriately, is veiled in domesticity. She never identifies their shared *patrie* by name, leaving both France and Saint-Domingue as candidates.

As the novel ends, the reversal of colonial stereotypes comes to its logical conclusion. Sylvain protests that his love is pure and natural, but he cannot control his ardor and surprises Mimi alone one night. She dies of grief ten days after their passionate encounter, and Sylvain commits suicide. Mimi's death after losing her virginity proves that virtue was her life; like Rousseau's Julie, she represents neither nature nor the corrupt civilization she inhabits, but an ideal society. Just before killing himself, Sylvain describes to a friend the lesson he, and the reader, are to take from *La mulâtre*: "Invincible power of virtue! It has more power than all the sentiments . . . even more than love itself! It took Mimi to teach me this" (2:292).

Though her character is designed to refute the gendered racism of the late slave period, Mimi echoes the political complaints of the prerevolutionary colonial elite about the lack of a virtuous public in Saint-Domingue. When Sylvain uses his connections to help her mother in a lawsuit, Mimi describes the military court as "a dark and despotic tribunal," too susceptible to personal influence (2:187). Prerevolutionary white colonists blamed governmental corruption on the private indulgence of men controlled by lascivious women of color. But Mimi portrays colonial institutions contributing to free colored vice. Since there was no impartial justice, "How could we not be corrupted? How could girls of color not throw themselves into the arms of white men, as they have?" (2:189).

Despite this political critique, Mimi does not blame Saint-Domingue's military governors for racial prejudice. Instead she identifies this as the creation of a self-conscious, but flawed, public sphere:

> Where and when did this odious prejudice emerge? In public only. . . . It scarcely existed between individuals, which proves that the whites need to band together and have each other's support to dare show [this prejudice.] Each white, as an individual, treats women of color with respect and familiarity. But once assembled, either to act or to command, they become proud despots, imperious tyrants. (2:253)

Like many antislavery texts of the period, *La mulâtre* traces the corruption of Dominguan mores to the unnatural powers of slavery. Mimi observes that "white women are glad to have a lover in a place where men have so much power over slaves! Women of color are so proud to capture one of those who affect such scorn for their class . . . . From this is born the lack of confidence in the virtue of these persons and from this lack of confidence, a lack of attachment" (1:212). Later she criticizes Sylvain's treatment of his manservant and proclaims that slavery degrades all men (2:258).

Yet *La mulâtre*'s abolitionism is muted, for its primary concern is to portray Mimi's sensitivity. The lovers' servants carry their letters back and forth, using subterfuges that both Sylvain and Mimi admire, but only once does a slave speak, when Sylvain quotes Mimi's black woman Fédalie to clarify a misunderstanding. The citation allows him to contrast the pidgin of this "detestable" and "perfidious" slave with the elevated sentiments that he and Mimi share. The white man writes, "I leave you to imagine the impression [Fédalie's creole words made] on a heart as passionate [as my own]" (2:112), but he extols Mimi's ability to express her feelings "in the most tender and persuasive terms" (2:123). Indeed, he is so impressed with her letters that he shows them to a friend, who pronounces Mimi's prose more elevated and compelling than Sylvain's (1:118–19).

Mimi's French education separates her not only from her slaves, but also from other *mulâtresses*. She was returning from her studies in Europe when she and Sylvain first met, and from his earliest letters he praises "your style, your delicacy, the elevation and nobility of your sentiments" (1:22). He scorns the free men of color who court her, claiming they only know love as a physical act. Mimi's education, he informs her, has refined her spirit to the point that she can know true happiness. Nevertheless, he pushes her to consummate their natural love, without the "artificial bonds" of marriage (2:10–11). Mimi agrees that schooling has allowed her to appreciate the platonic pleasures of their relationship, but it also gives her the strength to follow society's laws, even when they contravene nature (2:40). In other words, French culture sustains her feminine virtue.

In attacking the colonial idea that women of mixed European and African descent were sexual corrupters, *La mulâtre* completes the cycle of revolutionary redemption first activated by men of mixed ancestry. Representing Saint-Domingue as capable of producing its own virtuous republican wives and daughters, the novel attempts to include Saint-Domingue in the Atlantic revolution that had created new public spaces for educated, propertied men and new domestic roles for bourgeois women in the United States and France.[43]

Of course, Mimi's chaste and literate domesticity was accessible only to those with the wealth and education she possessed. *La mulâtre* never suggests that women like the despised Fédalie might someday have that schooling. This blindness to the challenges presented by the end of slavery demonstrates that *La mulâtre* is more a failed foundational fiction than a statement of new Haitian identity. Though the romance of Mimi and Sylvain suggests that postrevolutionary Saint-Domingue could be self-governing, it also reflects the tensions of 1789, when mulatto claims to citizenship sparked the long revolutionary conflict.

Bonaparte's attempt to reimpose slavery in 1802 doomed the

novel's anachronistic social vision, at least as a public ideology, for the next twenty-five years. Black field-workers were the first to oppose the French expedition, and their sacrifices proved central to the eventual victory of Toussaint Louverture's successor Dessalines in late 1803. Most prominent mulattoes eventually left the French and joined the anticolonial army; some had long been allied with ex-slave forces. French treachery in 1802 revealed that a society built around the union of a brown "Mimi" and a white "Sylvain" would mean slavery for most of Saint-Domingue's residents.

The mostly unforeseen revolution of 1802–3 required a new ideology, one that described a warrior nation, not an unnamed *patrie* shared with white planters. In December 1803, the heir to Toussaint Louverture's power, Jean-Jacques Dessalines, assigned Charéron, one of his mulatto secretaries, to write a declaration of independence for official proclamation on 1 January 1804. The document he produced, long vanished, was inspired by the U.S. Declaration of Independence and written in the language of law and philosophy, like Mimi's fictional missives to Sylvain.[44] Dessalines, aware of the importance of creating a broad social coalition against an angry France, rejected this text. Instead, he entrusted the task to Félix Boisrond-Tonnerre, the French-educated scion of a propertied family whose mulatto grandfather had been identified by a royal notary as a white man in 1764.[45] Though he had more in common with the fictional Mimi than with his patron Dessalines, who had hired him only six months earlier, Boisrond-Tonnerre caught the general's ear by exclaiming, famously, that the declaration should be written " 'with a white man's skin for parchment, his skull for an inkstand, his blood for ink, and a bayonet for a quill.' "[46]

According to the text Boisrond-Tonnerre delivered publicly on 1 January 1804, Haiti was not the mixture of Africa and Europe, it was the creation of "natives" who rejected colonial slavery. Although a majority of the officers who signed the document were of mixed race, Boisrond-Tonnerre's declaration established the Americanness of the new nation without raising the troubling question of racial and cultural mixture, too identified with mulattoes and their divided loyalties.[47] Instead, Haitians were "natives," heirs of the sixteenth-century Tainos who died rather than accept Spanish slavery. Like its counterparts elsewhere in Latin America, the Haitian elite laid claim to the tradition of indigenous struggle against colonization in an attempt to mask its own ambiguous and conflicting relationships to French power.[48]

The French—a "barbaric people," "vultures," and "bloodthirsty tigers"—would have no place in the new society, just as Dessalines ripped the white from the tricolor to create a flag for the new nation. The constitution of 1805 identified all Haitians as "black" and issued a standing invitation to Amerindians and blacks fleeing slavery to become citizens of Haiti.[49]

The legacy of 1803, a year that produced both *La mulâtre* and the defeat of proslavery forces, was the definition of mulattoism once again as corrupt and even foreign. Repeated French attempts after 1804 to negotiate Haitian subjection and slavery in return for mulatto citizenship strengthened this stereotype. Henri Christophe, Dessalines's dark-skinned successor, who constructed an authoritarian kingdom in the northern part of the country, ordered the assassination of over a thousand mulatto men, women, and children in 1812, even as he attempted to impose European culture and create a court inspired by the British monarchy. The mixed-race writers and officials of Christophe's court published texts defending "black" Haiti.[50]

Ironically, the mulatto general Alexandre Pétion, who established a republic south of Christophe's kingdom, was far more accepting of peasant culture and less devoted to imposing marriage, Christianity, and plantation discipline on the population. Rather than adopt the bourgeois social virtues *La mulâtre* extolled, the same advocated by contemporary U.S. and French writers, Pétion never married, had a daughter with the woman with whom he lived openly, and extended official recognition to children born out of wedlock. Perhaps there was little need to build a republican cult of domesticity—to divide into male and female spheres—in a society where class and culture so divided men. In fact, foreign observers described Pétion's republic as every bit as oligarchic as Christophe's kingdom was autocratic. Pétion's cultural policy stemmed in part from a concern about the potentially divisive power of race at a moment when French counterrevolution was still possible. He made it a point to include black generals in the oligarchy and welcomed refugees from Christophe's plantation regime.[51]

Pétion's attention to racial balance was highlighted by the policies of his successor Boyer, who, after 1820, also ruled what had been Christophe's kingdom. Though Boyer denounced color prejudice, foreign visitors perceived a strong government bias against black Haitians, and under him the national political and military elite was much lighter-skinned than ever before. In 1825, Boyer signed a peace treaty with France that ended Haiti's diplomatic isolation and with it the fears of invasion that had weighed on Christophe and Pétion. Tellingly in these conditions, for the first time since the publication of *La mulâtre,* a self-conscious mulatto ideology emerged. Though they identified themselves as black, vigorously defending the black national identity inaugurated at independence, these light-skinned historians and essayists shared with the author of *La mulâtre* an obsession with colonial-era racial discrimination. Racism more than slavery, they maintained, had defined the unjust prerevolutionary society. Moreover, despite their self-proclaimed blackness, they argued for the advantages of racial and cultural mixture, opposing voodoo and other neo-African cultural expressions developing in rural Haiti in favor of France's "civilizing" influence. As in the failed foundational fiction of 1803, this literary elite, including pioneering historians like Thomas Madiou, Beaubrun Ardouin, and Beauvais Lespinasse, accepted as "natural" that Haiti would be led by those with superior French educations.[52]

As this summary suggests, the ideas expressed in *La mulâtre* did not disappear in 1804. Just as the novel's mulatto ideology surfaced publicly again in the 1830s and 1840s, the figure of Mimi lives on, a cultural archetype with perhaps no direct connection to this early-nineteenth-century text. In her work on Haitian religion, historical consciousness, and twentieth-century literature, Joan Dayan describes the prominent voodoo spirit or *loa* known as Erzulie Fréda as "a pale mulatto [woman], voluptuous, richly dressed, and always speaking French, . . . both virgin and Venus."[53] In creating Mimi, who combines European sophistication with indigenous virtue and sorrow with sexuality, the author of *La mulâtre* evoked an unsettling political and cultural image. The figure of the amorous but brokenhearted *mulâtresse* may express the way Haiti's independence was built on racial, cultural, and gendered separations. At any rate, in modern Haiti Erzulie has escaped the oblivion that awaited the failed romance of a mulatto Saint-Domingue.

Notes

1 Anne Leighton found this text in the French National Archives, overseas section, in Aix-en-Provence, and my understanding of it has been much shaped by discussions with her. The archive's catalog identifies its copy as part of Moreau de Saint-Méry's library. I have

been unable to find other copies of the novel in the computer catalogs of major U.S. or French research libraries. All subsequent references will be given parenthetically in the text.

2 The exception may be the short-lived republic ruled by the mulatto general André Rigaud in 1810 on Haiti's southern peninsula.

3 See John D. Garrigus, "Redrawing the Colour Line: Gender and the Social Construction of Race in Pre-revolutionary Haiti," *Journal of Caribbean History* 30 (1996): 28–50.

4 On the problem of smuggling and social order, see Charles Frostin, "La piraterie américaine des années 1720, vue de Saint-Domingue (répression, environnement et recrutement)," *Cahiers d'histoire* 25, 2 (1980): 177–210; and Pierre Pluchon, *Le premier empire colonial: Des origines à la Restauration* (Paris: Fayard, 1991), 370–82. The classic study of racial attitudes in Saint-Domingue is Yvan Debbasch, *Couleur et liberté: Le jeu du critère ethnique dans un ordre juridique esclavagiste* (Paris : Dalloz, 1967).

5 John D. Garrigus, "Blue and Brown: Contraband Indigo and the Rise of a Free Colored Planter Class in French Saint-Domingue," *The Americas* 50 (1993): 233–63; and Garrigus, "Color, Class, and Identity on the Eve of the Haitian Revolution: Saint-Domingue's Free Colored Elite as *Colons américains*," *Slavery and Abolition* 17 (1996): 20–43.

6 Pluchon, *Le premier empire*, 239, 415, 586; and Charles Frostin, "Les colons de Saint-Domingue et la métropole," *Revue historique* 482 (1967): 381–414.

7 Jürgen Habermas, *The Structural Transformation of the Public Sphere: An Inquiry into a Category of Bourgeois Society*, trans. Thomas Berger (Cambridge, Mass.: MIT Press, 1989); my interpretation relies heavily on Joan B. Landes, *Women and the Public Sphere in the Age of the French Revolution* (Ithaca, N.Y.: Cornell University Press, 1988).

8 James E. McClellan III, *Colonialism and Science: Saint Domingue in the Old Regime* (Baltimore: Johns Hopkins University Press, 1992), 75, 78–81, 94–96, 102, 106–8; Jean Fouchard, *Plaisirs de Saint-Domingue: Notes sur sa vie sociale, littéraire et artistique* (Port-au-Prince: Imprimerie de l'Etat, 1955), 36, 111; M. L. E. Moreau de Saint-Méry, *Description topographique, physique, civile, politique et historique de la partie française de l'isle Saint Domingue*, ed. Blanche Maurel and Etienne Taillemite (Paris: C.Guerin, 1984), 361, 879–83, 1099; and Elisabeth Escalle and Mariel Gouyon Guillaume, *Francs-Maçons des loges françaises "aux Amériques," 1750–1850: Contribution à l'étude de la société créole* (Paris, 1993).

9 Marisa Linton, "The Rhetoric of Virtue and the *Parlements*, 1770–1775," *French History* 9, 2 (1995): 189; Dale K. Van Kley, "New

Wine in Old Wineskins: Continuity and Rupture in the Pamphlet Debate of the French Prerevolution, 1787–1789," *French Historical Studies* 17, 2 (1991): 454–55.

10 Keith Michael Baker, *Inventing the French Revolution: Essays on French Political Culture in the Eighteenth Century* (New York: Cambridge University Press, 1990), 171–72.

11 See Charles Frostin, *Les révoltes blanches à Saint-Domingue aux XVIIe et XVIIIe siècles (Haïti avant 1789)* (Paris: l'Ecole, 1975), 297–341.

12 "Reflexions sur la position actuelle de St Domingue," 1785, AN Col. F³ 192, Archives Nationales, Paris.

13 Baker, *Inventing the French Revolution*, 198.

14 See Carol Blum, *Rousseau and the Republic of Virtue: The Language of Politics in the French Revolution* (Ithaca, N.Y.: Cornell University Press, 1986), 124–25; and Landes, *Women and the Public Sphere*, 70–76.

15 This is the argument presented in Landes, *Women and the Public Sphere*. It is further developed by the contributors to Lynn Hunt, ed., *Eroticism and the Body Politic* (Baltimore: Johns Hopkins University Press, 1991), especially Sarah Maza, "The Diamond Necklace Affair Revisited (1785–1786): The Case of the Missing Queen," 65–69.

16 Moreau de Saint-Méry, *Description*, 316, 361–62, 885, 1054, 1055.

17 Debbasch, *Couleur et liberté*, 21–105.

18 Justin Girod-Chantrans, *Voyage d'un Suisse dans les colonies d'Amérique*, ed. Pierre Pluchon (Paris: Tallandier, 1980), 152; this and all unmarked translations are my own.

19 Quoted in Pierre Pluchon, *Nègres et juifs au XVIIIe siècle: Le racisme au siècle des Lumières* (Paris: Tallandier, 1984), 286.

20 Although he did not publish the work until 1797, Moreau insisted in his preface that he had stopped writing the *Description* in 1789. Although the revolutionary decade had changed a number of his ideas, he maintained that his only change was to remove some material, recovered by later editors, that might be offensive to individuals "already punished by public misfortunes." *Description*, 5, 10.

21 Moreau de Saint-Méry, *Description*, 103–11, especially 104.

22 M. L. E. Moreau de Saint-Méry, *Loix et constitutions des colonies françaises de l'Amérique sous le vente* (Paris: Quillau, Méquignon Jeune, 1784–90), 4:225, 229, 342, 412, 466, 495; 5:384–85, 823; AN Col. F³243, 341; Col. F³273, 119; AN Col. F³91, 115; AN Col. F³189, decree of 2 June 1780.

23 Garrigus, "Blue and Brown," 260.

24 The quote comes from Vera M. Kutzinski, *Sugar's Secrets: Race and the Erotics of Cuban Nationalism* (Charlottesville: University Press of Virginia, 1993), 4–7, 21–22; Arlene Díaz, " 'Necesidad hizo parir

mulatas': Liberalismo, nacionalidad e ideas sobre las mujeres en la Cuba del siglo XIX," in *Género, familia y mentalidades en América Latina*, ed. Pilar Gonzalbo Aizpuru (Dan Juan: Editorial de la Universidad de Puerto Rico, 1997), 209, 223, 226.

25 John D. Garrigus, "Catalyst or Catastrophe? Saint-Domingue's Free Men of Color and the Savannah Expedition, 1779–1782," *Review/Revista Interamericana* 22 (1992): 109–25.

26 Monique Pouliquen, ed. *Doléances des peuples coloniaux à l'assemblée nationale constituante, 1789–1790* (Paris: Archives Nationales, 1989), 149–50; *Précis sur les gémissements des sang-mêlés dans les colonies françoises* (Paris, 1789), 7; Abbé Grégoire, *Lettre aux philantropes, sur les malheurs . . . des gens de couleur de Saint-Domingue* (Paris: Belin, 1790).

27 M. L. E. Moreau de Saint-Méry, *Considérations présentées aux vrais amis du repos et du bonheur de la France, à l'occasion des nouveaux mouvements de quelques soi-disant Amis-des-noirs* (Paris, 1791), 24.

28 Elizabeth Colwill, "Sex, Savagery, and Slavery in the Shaping of the French Body Politic," *From the Royal to the Republican Body: Incorporating the Political in Seventeenth- and Eighteenth-Century France*, ed. Sara E. Melzer and Kathryn Norberg (Berkeley: University of California Press, 1998), 212.

29 Thomas Crow, *Emulation: Making Artists for Revolutionary France* (New Haven, Conn.: Yale University Press, 1995), 225, 227; Srinivas Aravamudan, "Trop(icaliz)ing the Enlightenment," *Diacritics: A Review of Contemporary Criticism* 23, 3 (1993): 46–68.

30 Moreau de Saint-Méry, *Description*, 47, 58, 60–61, 107.

31 In English, the title reads, *La Mulâtre Like Many White Women, a Book in the Tradition of "The Negro Like Few White Men."*

32 See Léon-François Hoffmann, *Le nègre romantique: Personnage littéraire et obsession collective* (Paris: Payot, 1973), 87–88; Joseph LaVellée, *Le negre comme il y a peu de blancs* (Paris: Chez Maradan, 1789).

33 Doris Sommer, "Love and Country: Allegorical Romance in Latin America," in *Reading World Literature: Theory, History, Practice*, ed. Sarah Lawall (Austin: University of Texas Press, 1994), 178, 180–81, 186; and Sommer, "Irresistible Romance: The Foundational Fictions of Latin America," in *Nation and Narration*, ed. Homi K. Bhabha (London: Routledge, 1990), 79–82.

34 Léon-François Hoffmann, *Haïti: Couleurs, croyance, créole* (Haiti: Henri Deschamps, 1990), 83.

35 Hoffmann, *Le nègre romantique*, 235. Other works consulted include Hoffmann, *Littérature d'Haïti: Histoire littéraire de la francophonie* (Vauves: Collection Universités Francophones, 1995); Régis

Antoine, *Les écrivains français et les Antilles: Des premiers pères blancs aux surréalistes noirs* (Paris: Maisonneuve et Larose, 1978); Patrick Chamoiseau and Raphaël Confiant, *Lettres créoles: Tracées antillaises et continentales de la littérature: Haïti, Guadeloupe, Martinique, Guyane, 1635–1975* (Paris: Hatier, 1991); Roger Toumson and Charles Porset, eds., *La période révolutionnaire aux Antilles dans la littératures caribéennes francophone, anglophone et hispanophone* (Martinique: GRELCA, 1987). More usually, the book does not appear in standard reference works on French literature of this period, for example, Alexandre Cioranescu, *Bibliographie de la littérature française du dix-huitième siècle* (Paris: Editions du Centre national de la recherche scientifique, 1969–70) and its nineteenth-century equivalent. Nor is it mentioned in Antoine-Alexandre Barbier, *Dictionnaire des ouvrages anonymes* (Paris: Paul Daffis, 1895), nor in Yves Giraud and Anne-Marie Clin-Lalande, *Nouvelle bibliographie du roman épistolaire en France: Des origines à 1842* (Fribourg, Switzerland: Editions Universitaires, 1995).

36 Joan Dayan, "Erzulie: A Woman's History of Haiti," *Research in African Literatures* 25, 2 (1994): 19.

37 Pierre Pluchon, *Toussaint Louverture: Un révolutionnaire noir d'Ancien Régime* (Paris: Fayard, 1989), 129, 173, 256, 288.

38 Thomas Madiou, *Histoire d'Haïti*, (1847–48; Port-au-Prince: Henri Deschamps, 1988–91), 2:180; Claude B. Auguste and Marcel B. Auguste, *L'expédition Leclerc, 1801–1803* (Port-au-Prince: Henri Deschamps, 1985), 108.

39 Robert Darnton, "A Star Is Born," *New York Review of Books* (27 October 1988), 85.

40 Moreau de Saint-Méry, *Description*, 37–38.

41 In fact, such unions accounted for one-fifth of all religious unions throughout the eighteenth century. Jacques Houdaille, "Trois paroisses de Saint-Domingue au XVIIIe siècle," *Population* 18 (1963): 100.

42 See Sommer, "Love and Country," 191–92.

43 Ruth Bloch, "The Gendered Meanings of Virtue in Revolutionary America," *Signs* 13, 1 (1987): 37–58.

44 David Nicholls, *From Dessalines to Duvalier: Race, Colour, and National Independence in Haiti* (London: Macmillan, 1996), 36; Madiou, *Histoire d'Haïti*, 3:144–45.

45 Garrigus, "Color, Class, and Identity," 34.

46 Quoted in Madiou, *Histoire d'Haïti*, 3:145.

47 David P. Geggus, "The Naming of Haiti," *New West Indian Guide/Nieuwe West-Indische Gids* 71, 1 and 2 (1997): 45. Geggus establishes the contemporary sources for this self-consciously indigenous and historical name, probably chosen by Dessalines's mulatto secretaries.

48 Julie Skurski, "The Ambiguities of Authenticity in Latin America: *Doña Barbara* and the Construction of National Identity," *Poetics Today* 15 (1994): 611–12.

49 Hoffman, *Haïti: Couleurs*, 79; Nicholls, *From Dessalines to Duvalier*, 33; David Nicholls, "Haiti: Race, Slavery, and Independence (1804–1825)," in *Slavery and Other Forms of Unfree Labour*, ed. Léonie J. Archer (London: Routledge, 1988), 266.

50 Madiou, *Histoire d'Haïti*, 5:154–63; David Nicholls, "Pompée-Valentin Vastey: Royalist and Revolutionary," *Revista de historia de America* 109 (1990): 141.

51 Madiou, *Histoire d'Haïti*, 4:81, 5:209.

52 Nicholls, *Dessalines to Duvalier*, 89–101.

53 Joan Dayan, "Caribbean Cannibals and Whores," *Raritan: A Quarterly Review* 9, 2 (1989): 45.

Laurent Dubois

Inscribing Race in the

Revolutionary French Antilles

In 1794, the French national convention decreed slavery abolished
in all France's colonies and all men of all colors French citizens. The
new order emerged out of a complex series of struggles during the
early 1790s and had its foundation in the alliance between republican administrators and insurgent slaves. Such alliances, which came
into existence most dramatically in Saint-Domingue in 1793, signaled a remarkable transformation in the political and social order,
and in the meaning of race, in the colonies. Slaves, previously denied
the most basic of human rights, were not only freed but became, in
the language of republican administrators and the deputies who
spoke in the national convention, the true, loyal republican citizens
of the colonies. The white planters previously at the summit of the
social order, some of whom had turned to France's enemies in the
hope of preserving slavery, found themselves in political exile from
a republic that saw them as traitors—and often enough in literal
exile from a Saint-Domingue wracked with violent conflict. The
abolition of slavery in 1794 constituted a stunning victory for the
slave insurgents of the French Caribbean, and in its extent and
speed must be considered one of the most striking political reversals
in history.

The dramatic move from slavery to freedom, from a society fundamentally based on the maintenance of a racial hierarchy to one in
principle based on a deracialized citizenship, posed major juridical
and political challenges for administrators and citizens on both
sides of the Atlantic. Unlike the gradual emancipations set in motion in North America in the preceding decades, this transformation
took place in slave societies populated by a majority of slaves (in
Saint-Domingue by a majority of African-born slaves), and it took
place with no administered period of transition or any apprentice-
ship of the kind later instituted in the course of British emancipation. Wherever the French republican regime was instituted in the

Caribbean, all slaves were decreed free. No road map existed for such a transformation, and it fell to local administrators to negotiate and manage the situation in the face of pressures from the metropole and local planters for continued plantation production, in the midst of a worldwide military struggle with the British, and in a struggle with ex-slaves who had their own ideas about what freedom should mean. In the years before 1794, the issue of racial identification, and its place in political representation, had already been debated fiercely on both sides of the Atlantic through struggles over the rights of free *gens de couleur*. The ending of slavery, however, posed new and complex questions about what juridical and political traces would be given to race. To what extent could the racial terminology that had been central to the functioning of the slave society be maintained? How were administrators to oversee the encounter between a world saturated with racial hierarchy and a new political project based on racial equality? How was this principle of racial equality to be balanced with the economic exigencies, when any maintenance of plantation production would depend on the maintenance of a racialized order of labor?[1]

As I have argued elsewhere, in the French Caribbean during the 1790s, administrators developed a form of "Republican racism," which justified and enforced new kinds of racial exclusion through arguments about the incapacity of recently freed slaves to be full citizens and which maintained a racialized labor regime. In this respect, the story of these regimes represents an early example of the broader process through which the contradictions and failures of emancipation led to new forms of racial exclusion. These forms of racial exclusion, themselves premised on and responses to projects of racial equality, have functioned with durable effectiveness in the democracies of the Americas.[2]

Emancipation nevertheless profoundly shifted the political and juridical significance of race in the French Caribbean. This essay explores the particular ways in which the inscription of race took place in postemancipation Guadeloupe and makes some comparisons to the different situation in Saint-Domingue during the same period. By examining the presence of race in a variety of documents, but most specifically in *état civil* registers of births and deaths and censuses, I seek to highlight both how the meaning of race changed through emancipation and how forms of racial identification and hierarchy were maintained in the midst of a regime in principle based on racial equality.

How can slavery and racism be made to disappear? In an oblique way, the brief debate that preceded the 1794 abolition of slavery brought up this lingering issue when it was argued that the term *slavery* should not be allowed to soil the registers of the national convention. The abbé Grégoire, one of the most radical antislavery figures in France, riposted with the prevailing argument that if slavery was not named specifically, it could not be made to disappear. In the preceding years, the opposite approach had been taken in several cases with regard to the problem of racial discrimination. In the wake of the massive insurrection in Saint-Domingue in 1791, as whites scrambled to form alliances with *gens de couleur* as a bulwark against the insurgents, a "Concordat" signed between representatives of the two groups proposed the erasure of racial distinctions such as *le nommé, Nègre libre, mulâtre libre, quarteron libre, citoyens de couleur*, so that all citizens would be referred to with the terms previously used only for whites. Two years later, in Guadeloupe, the governor Collot drew up a law that decreed that terms such as *citoyen noveau, citoyen de couleur*, "and others which mark the distinction between free men," were to be eliminated in all public speeches and laws, in favor of the undivided denomination of *citizen*. The damaging effects of racial discrimination were to be neutralized through the elimination of any trace of racial distinction in the new political language of citizenship. This approach to ending racial distinctions was in essence that taken in Guadeloupe by one notary, Elie Dupuch, who consistently avoided the use of racial markers in the acts he drew up after emancipation. In a 1799 act of the wedding between two ex-slaves, for instance, which involved white and *gens de couleur* soldiers as well, Dupuch used no racial ascriptions. He also provided his services to these former slaves for free. This probably constituted the expression of an ideological stance—Dupuch was a committed republican and defender of emancipation throughout the 1790s.[3]

Ultimately, however, the more prevailing tendency in postemancipation Guadeloupe was to maintain the use of racial categories, though in ways influenced by the arrival of emancipation. Legal documentation in the colonies had always depended on the normalcy of whiteness. It was those who deviated from this normalcy—whether freed people of African descent or slaves—who had their races noted in documents. The arrival of emancipation briefly undermined the white privilege of racelessness. In 1794, a mission of French republicans carrying the decree of emancipation attacked Guadeloupe, held at the time by British troops. As their conquest of the island progressed, in areas still under the control of the British, local officials there sporadically introduced a new form of racial categorization—that of *European*. The use of this term continued for about two weeks and then faded, although it appeared sporadically in other contexts during the following years. It had its analog in the term *blanc*—"white"—used in a few *état civil* documents in 1796–97. For *gens de couleur*, who had been free before 1794, the arrival of emancipation meant both the forceful institutionalization of a political equality they had struggled for during the early 1790s and the end of the legal difference that had distinguished them from the mass of slaves. Some individuals developed ways of naming themselves based not on race but on their particular history of emancipation—they described themselves as "free before the decree." Occasionally, the term *ancien libre*—"previously free"—was also used. The use of such new terms, while fairly isolated, suggests how the advent of an order of racial equality posed challenges for those who had been free in the preexisting society and wanted to maintain some of the associated privileges, and to the documentary forms they had used, pushing local officials to experiment with new kinds of racial ascriptions.[4]

For the majority of the population of Guadeloupe, the ex-slaves, emancipation meant access to the forms of documentation from which they had previously been excluded. Ex-slaves took advantage of this new right. Approximately 70 percent of the 177 births in the Basse-Terre *état civil* register of 1796–97, for instance, seem to have involved ex-slaves, and roughly half of the acts in the registers of deaths did during the same period. In most of these cases, ex-slaves were described as *noir*—"black"—but there were a significant number of exceptions. In the birth register, for instance, only 66 percent of the acts involved the use of racial ascriptions at all, 54 percent of them using the term *noir* and another 11 percent the term *de couleur*, with a smattering of other racial terms such as *câpresse*.[5]

What determined who was raced and who was not? In many ways, the pre-emancipation practices remained in force, as whites were predominantly placed in the documents without racial ascriptions, while the majority of ex-slaves and others of African descent were described according to their race. There was, of course, a significant change in terminology, since *noir* completely replaced the use of *nègre*, which had been consistent in legal documents in the colony before emancipation. Although it is not possible to track a precise and consistent correlation between the use of these terms and the political positions of those who used them, in general republican defenders of emancipation tended to use the term *noir*. As a term based on color, and which was divested of some of the broader connotations of *nègre*, the term *noir* provided a way of naming race while accepting the rupture with the past of slavery.[6]

It is also significant, however, that in a reasonable number of cases, ex-slaves received the privilege of racelessness in the documents. How did they gain this privilege? Those ex-slaves not described as *noir* were most often soldiers in the republican army, which rapidly recruited ex-slaves as part of the French effort to fight the British in the Eastern Caribbean, or else individuals who worked for the local administration. In contrast, plantation laborers were consistently described as *noir*. The use of racial terminology was also linked to gender. In early 1795, the first individuals described as *noir* in a series of documents involving ex-slave soldiers were women still living on plantations. When the soldier Cazimir married Marie-Noël, with other soldiers as witnesses, all those present were ex-slaves, but only Marie-Noël was marked racially when she was described as a "Citoyenne Noire." During the same period, when the ex-slave Anastazie married the soldier Pierre Louis Labiche, a soldier recently arrived from metropolitan France, the only person among the interracial group described according to her race was Anastazie's mother, the "Citoyenne Noire" Marie. These acts allowed male ex-slaves to escape a racial ascription due to the privilege of military service, while highlighting the racial difference of certain women.[7]

Who determined the deployment of racial ascriptions? This is a difficult question to answer. On the one hand, those who drew up the registers may have chosen to make distinctions between different classes of ex-slaves they saw presented before them. At the same time, the requests of republican soldiers and others not described according to race might have also played a role. Among those who actively participated in drawing up the *état civil* were several individuals of African descent. The twenty-eight-year-old Joseph Gérard, for instance, was a "municipal officer" who oversaw the drawing up of acts in the *état civil*. Gérard participated as a witness in a large number of wedding, birth, and death acts, many of which involved ex-slaves consistently described as "noir." Like other "new citizens" who had positions as "guards of the municipality" and who were in a few cases described as either *noir* or *de couleur*, his race almost always went unmentioned. That in contrast the plantation laborers who presented themselves to Gérard and other local officials were consistently described as *noir* suggests that racelessness remained essentially the privilege of those — all of them men — who held positions of value in the republican hierarchy.[8]

A series of fascinating "baptisms" that took place between 1797 and 1799 can perhaps give us additional insight into the agency of various individuals, notably plantation laborers, in the creation of *état civil* documents and the development of new forms of racial terminology. In 1795, the recently married Sophie Mondésir and Fabien Bellair, a twenty-two-year-old policeman in Basse-Terre, presented to the municipal officer of Basse-Terre "a little girl who is a native of Guinea and who has recently arrived in this colony." Acting just as those who presented recently born children did in the other birth declarations contained in the register, they gave her a new name — Zaide. No other acts of this kind appeared in the next years, but in 1797 and 1798, they became almost standard as forty-six new arrivals from Africa were given French names, by managers of plantations in a small number of cases, but more often by a variety of ex-slaves who were soldiers, *cultivateurs*, or residents of Basse-Terre. These new arrivals were men and women captured on slave ships by French corsairs, and brought to Guadeloupe as free men and women. (British documents recorded 817 slaves captured and brought to Guadeloupe in 1795 alone, and another 750 during the next four years.) Once on the island, these individuals, now free, had been placed on specific plantations by the government, where they served as *cultivateurs*.[9]

Before emancipation, there was a practice among some planters in the French Caribbean of placing newly arrived African slaves under the tutelage of more experienced slaves as a way of integrating them into the community and the daily functioning of plantation labor. The *parrains* — "godparents" — were often chosen because they originated from the same African "nation" as the new arrivals and could therefore speak their language. This supervision would continue until the godparents oversaw the baptism of the new slave by the local clergy, during which they would receive a new, French name. The masters who organized this godparenting did so as a way of facilitating the transformation of the slave into an efficient and healthy laboring machine. The relationship between the godparents and the African slave, and the practices they used to welcome and integrate the new arrival into the community, certainly involved a broader form of integration into life in the new community.[10]

The renamings of the revolutionary period constituted a continuation as well as a transformation of this tradition. Rather than a baptism in the church, the granting of the new name took place in front of a republican administrator. Although in most cases those who gave the "African citizens" their new names hailed from the plantations where the latter had been placed, there were several cases in which the events brought together people drawn from other plantations or from the town of Basse-Terre. In such cases, a community that stretched beyond the plantation took on the responsibility of integrating the new arrival. The godparenting practiced in slavery had probably similarly involved broader networks of family and friends, but with emancipation this involvement was facilitated — and openly registered. The existence of such mixed groups around the new African arrivals suggests that the plantation managers were not the driving force behind the creation of the *état civil* acts. The plantation *cultivateurs* and town dwellers who brought the Africans into Basse-Terre understood the important legal implications of this ritual. Registered alongside births in the colony, the renamings they carried out simultaneously signaled a rebirth and a naturalization. The African, liberated from enslavement by the French, was officially incorporated into the population of those born on the island.

The terminology used in these acts also suggests an understanding of their social and political importance. In most of the acts from 1796 and 1797, terms such as *nouveau citoyen* or *citoyenne nouvelle* (new male citizen or new female citizen) were used with the description "from the coast." This descriptor was used in these and many other *état civil* acts to refer to those who had come to the island from the coast of Africa. In a few cases, other terms were used: "citoyen africain" and "jeune citoyenne africaine." The use of this terminology was significant. Rather than using race as a marker for identity, it used origin. In so doing, it collapsed the considerable diversity certainly represented by these arrivals into a birthplace called *Africa*, a word that took on a particular meaning in the Americas.[11]

The fact that the new African arrivals were given a French name — rather than receive citizenship through the declaration of the existing African name — suggests the existence of a complex set of practices surrounding the integration of the African-born into the communities of colonial Guadeloupe. Perhaps this marked the expression of a rejection of African identity among those who participated in the renaming. Alternatively, it might have constituted an acknowledgment of the social and legal value of a French name, which could have been used as an official name even as the original African name was used in other contexts. Interestingly, the granting of French names to African arrivals coexisted during this period with the incorporation of some African names, as well as family histories that included the names of parents left behind in Africa, in some *état civil* documents.[12]

The republican administration in Guadeloupe, meanwhile, embarked on its own effort to define and categorize the population according to race — from above. Victor Hugues initiated a massive census project that depended on the explicit categorization of the island's population according to race. Already in the old regime, the control of the movement of slaves among plantations and between plantations and towns formed a central concern in the colony's administration. After emancipation, the entire functioning of Hugues's regime, in its attempt to force *cultivateurs* to stay on their plantations, depended on the repression of one of the key assertions of freedom available to the ex-slaves: movement. But freedom transformed the terms of surveillance, since it was a different matter to police slaves than it was to policemen and -women who, at least in principle, were free citizens. The exigencies of the administration of freedom led Hugues to embark, in 1796–97, on a massive project of documenting the population of the island. In place of the plantation registers of the previous decades, islandwide censuses were completed, listing names, ages, races, and professions by commune.

In metropolitan France before the revolution, lists of *noirs* had been drawn up in connection with the issuing of *cartouches* (identity cards) as part of the attempt to control the movement and the growth of this group, but such detailed lists did not exist in the colonies themselves. Emancipation, however, created the need for more sophisticated forms of documentation, as the proclamations of the republican commissioners Polverel and Sonthonax in Saint-Domingue made clear in the first colonial emancipations in 1793. Article 4 of Sonthonax's 5 May 1793 statement, which prepared the call for general emancipation, ordered all property owners and plantation managers to give to the military commanders a list of "all free men, all slaves of all ages and sexes that make up their house, plantation, or workshop, by names, surnames, and ages." The attempt to control the population of plantation laborers in Saint-Domingue constituted a continual concern for the administrators who succeeded Sonthonax, notably Toussaint Louverture himself. In the late 1790s, Toussaint Louverture was particularly concerned with rebuilding the plantation economy in order to produce commodities for export, notably as a way of purchasing provisions for the colony and weapons and ammunition for his army. In this context, he perfected the system, based on the policies of Sonthonax and similar to that of Hugues in Guadeloupe, which required plantation laborers to continue working on the plantations. He ultimately enforced this order to a large extent by placing those plantations left behind or confiscated from white émigrés under the control of officers from his army. Most of these officers were themselves of African descent, and many in fact were ex-slaves, so that the system of control was based less on the maintenance of a racial hierarchy than on the assertion of new forms of social power. At the same time, of course, conflicts between *gens de couleur* and slaves, notably in the south, took on racial overtones in Saint-Domingue.[13]

The situation was quite different in Guadeloupe, an island run throughout the late 1790s by white administrators from the metropole. There, race proved central to the creation of a rigorous post-emancipation project of documentation. On the first day of the Republican Years 5 and 6 (1796 and 1797), each commune in Guadeloupe delivered a complete list of all its inhabitants. The census used three categories to divide the free population of Guadeloupe: black, red, or white. The invention of the category *red*, which was meant in principle to include those of African descent who had been free before 1794, made for an interesting choice that perhaps sought to mark the return of racial difference within a different, national exigency. The roots of this term's selection remain unclear, and nowhere in the archives is this choice explained. It seems likely, however, that the use of these three categories was tied to the tricolor flag that had appeared both in Saint-Domingue and in Paris during the course of 1793. This flag pictured three soldiers — white, *de couleur*, and black — over the three colors of the republican flag. From this symbol, which articulated racial equality even as it represented racial difference, Hugues and his administration could well have drawn the symbolic terms necessary for the creation of a census that brought together the entire population of the island in one document, while maintaining the separation between the races as a practical way of identifying, and controlling, the labor necessary for the nation.[14]

How were people categorized as black, white, and red? The classification of people into racial categories for the purposes of the census seems to have been the result both of self-ascription and of the decisions made by the census-makers, but in the absence of more detailed information about the drawing up of the censuses, it is difficult to determine which of these held greater importance. The attribution of racial ascriptions took shape within a complex web of social, economic, and phenotypical determinations. In the case of the attribution of the term *rouge*, phenotypical determinations seem to have been more important than social rank, since there were many individuals described as *rouge* who were plantation laborers, and many individuals who had been free before 1794 and who were property owners or artisans who were described as *noir*. But social relations may still have played an important role in determining who was put in what category, since on many of the smaller plantations run by *rouges*, the laborers were all described as *noirs*. There were also several cases in which individuals described as either *blanc* or *noir* in other contexts appeared as *rouge* in the censuses, a fact which highlights the contingent nature of racial marking both before and after emancipation.[15]

In postemancipation Guadeloupe, the inscription of race had a variety of functions. Even as plantation laborers used their right to documentation, they were distinguished by the use of racial ascriptions from the smaller number of ex-slaves who worked for the republican administration or served as soldiers. At the same time, the actions of some plantation laborers in giving new names to those they described, at least in some cases as "African citizens," transformed the form of racial ascription from one of color to one of origin. Meanwhile, the administration itself used racial categories in its effort to document and control the ex-slaves of the island as part of its broader project of limiting the impact of emancipation on the production of plantation commodities.

Despite the racial egalitarianism of the 1794 decree of emancipation, the naming of race remained of central importance in the French Caribbean. But its meaning had shifted in important ways. In some contexts, racial terminology was avoided entirely in an effort to truly put into practice a regime of racial equality. At the same time, racial ascriptions were used to fix certain individuals in the new order in certain roles. Still, the particular ways race was inscribed into the documents in postemancipation Guadeloupe differed profoundly from what had come before — and what, in the case of Guadeloupe, would come again. This is perhaps best illustrated by the bitter conclusion of the story of Guadeloupe's "African citizens." The mark of citizenship so powerfully asserted in 1797 would ultimately be reversed for these new arrivals baptized into the republic. In 1802, as French troops defeated insurgents on the island and began reconstructing slavery, those plantation managers or owners who had received *cultivateurs* on their plantations "from the captures" were invited to come and register them as slaves. Once again, these men and women found themselves in front of the local officials of Basse-Terre to be described and registered, but instead of being documented as citizens, they were documented as objects, given prices, and identified according to particular African ethnicities. Their place of origin was described according to the old categories of slave traders, and their bodies and the marks they carried — either from rituals of scarification or from the scars of brutality in the Americas — were described in detail. They were no longer "from the coast of Africa," and they were certainly no longer "African citizens." They were enslaved, as they would have been had they never had the fortune to land on an island of emancipation a few years before.[16]

Notes

1 On the debates surrounding *gens de couleur*, see David Geggus, "Racial Equality, Slavery, and Colonial Secession during the Constituent Assembly," *American Historical Review* 94, 5 (1989): 1290–1308; and Yves Bénot, *La Révolution française et la fin des colonies: Essai* (Paris: Editions La Découverte, 1989). On the broader history of race in the French Antilles, the classic and still unsurpassed study is Yvan Debbasch, *Couleur et liberté: Le jeu de critère ethnique dans un ordre juridique esclavagiste* (Paris: Dalloz, 1967).

2 I use the term *Republican racism* in "'The Price of Liberty': Victor Hugues and the Administration of Freedom in Guadeloupe, 1794–1798," *William and Mary Quarterly* 56, 2 (1999): 363–92. On the link between emancipation and racial exclusion, a central work is Thomas C. Holt, *The Problem of Freedom: Race, Labor, and Politics in Jamaica and Britain, 1832–1938* (Baltimore: Johns Hopkins University Press, 1992); see also Frederick Cooper, Thomas C. Holt, and Rebecca J. Scott, *Beyond Slavery: Explorations in Race, Labor, and*

Citizenship in Postemancipation Societies (Chapel Hill: University of North Carolina Press, 2000).

3 M. J. Mavidal and M. E. Laurent, eds., *Archives parlementaires de 1787 à 1860, première série (1787–1799)* (Paris: Centre National de Recherche Scientifique, 1962), 84:276–85; "Concordat, ou, Traité de paix entre les citoyens blancs et les citoyens de couleur des quatorze paroisses de la Province de l'Ouest de la partie française de Saint-Domingue," 19 October 1791, Bibliothèque Nationale, Paris; "Extrait des régistres . . . Commission Générale et Extraordinaire," 5 September 1793, Archives Nationales D^{XXV}, Paris, 123, 973. I have connected these debates of the early 1790s to broader traditions of French antiracism in "Republican Racism and Anti-racism: A Caribbean Genealogy," *French Politics, Culture, and Society* 18, 3 (2000): 5–17; on Dupuch, see Notariat Guadeloupe, Dupuch 902, 23 Prairial An 7, 11 June 1799, Archives Nationales — Section Outre-Mer (hereafter ANSOM); and Marcel Dorigny and Bernard Gainot, *La Société des Amis des Noirs, 1788–1799: Contribution à l'histoire de l'abolition de l'esclavage* (Paris: UNESCO, 1998), 344. All unmarked translations are mine.

4 For the term *European*, see EC Basse-Terre 5, cahier 5, 51–60, 28 July–12 August 1794, ANSOM; for the use of the term *blanc*, see the register of deaths in EC Basse-Terre 9 and EC Basse-Terre 7, #27, ANSOM; for examples of the use of the term *free before the decree*, see EC Basse-Terre 6, #26, #29, and #34, and EC Basse-Terre 10, #332, both in ANSOM; for *ancien libre*, see the "Etat nominatif . . . Baillif," dernier jour complémentaire, An 4, 21 September 1796, G1 500, #4, ANSOM.

5 EC Basse-Terre 8, "Naissances An 4," ANSOM; on the deceased, which include a total of 502 entries, see EC Basse-Terre 9, "Décès An 3" and "Décès An 4," and EC Basse-Terre 10, "Décès An 4," ANSOM.

6 A thorough study of the particular political symbolism involved in the use of the term *noir* versus *nègre* during the revolution still needs to be done; an initial study is Serge Daget's "Les mots eslave, nègre, noir, et les jugements de valeur sur la traite nègrière dans la littérature abolitionniste française de 1770 à 1845," *Revue française d'histoire d'outre-mer* 60, 221 (1973): 511–48.

7 See EC Basse-Terre 6, 6 Ventôse An 3, 24 February 1795, and #30, 6 Germinal An 3, 26 March 1795, both in ANSOM.

8 Usually Gérard was not given a racial ascription, but twice he was described as a *noir*; among many examples of his appearance as a witness, see EC Basse-Terre 6, #38 and #54, ANSOM. For his description as a *noir*, see EC Basse-Terre 6, #33 and EC Basse-Terre 8, #105, ANSOM. For the "guards," see EC Basse-Terre 7, #10; EC Basse-Terre

7, #11; and EC Basse-Terre 9, #15, #16, #22, #27, #41, #48, #57, all in ANSOM.

9 The act, from March 1795, is in EC Basse-Terre 7, #68, ANSOM. The process of the distribution of the captured slaves is documented in the register C⁷ᴬ 81, ANSOM; for the numbers of slaves captured as recorded in British documents, see David Eltis et al., *The Trans-Atlantic Slave Trade: A Database on CD-Rom* (Cambridge: Cambridge University Press, 1999).

10 Gabriel Debien, *Les esclaves aux Antilles françaises (XVIIè–XVIIIè siècle)* (Basse-Terre, Guadeloupe: Société d'Histoire de la Guadeloupe, 1974), 72–74, 258–59; and Howard Justin Sosis, "The Colonial Environment and Religion in Haiti: An Introduction to the Black Slave Cults in Eighteenth-Century Saint-Domingue" (Ph.D. diss., Columbia University, 1971), 159–60. On Catholic clergy and the baptism of slaves in the French Caribbean, see Sue Peabody, "'A Dangerous Zeal': Catholic Missions to Slaves in the French Antilles, 1635–1800," *French Historical Studies* 25, 1 (2002): 53–90.

11 See the acts from December 1796 in EC Basse-Terre 10, #19, #20, #38, #44, #50, #128, and #129, and EC Basse-Terre 11, #122, all in ANSOM.

12 See Anne Pérotin-Dumon, *La ville aux îles, la ville dans l'île: Basse-Terre et Pointe-à-Pitre, Guadeloupe, 1650–1820* (Paris: Kharthala, 2000), 704; on the coexistence of different names within slavery, see Debien, *Les esclaves*, 71–73.

13 On metropolitan France, see Sue Peabody, *"There Are No Slaves in France": The Political Culture of Race and Slavery in the Ancien Régime* (New York: Oxford University Press, 1996), 72–87; for Sonthonax, see Gabriel Debien, "Documents: Aux origines de l'abolition de l'esclavage," *Revue d'histoire des colonies* 36, 1 (1er trimestre 1949): 24–55, and 36, 2 (2ème trimestre 1949): 35–43, 348–423; on Toussaint Louverture's regime, see Mats Lundahl, "Toussaint L'Ouverture and the War Economy of Saint-Domingue, 1796–1802," *Slavery and Abolition* 6, 2 (1985): 122–38. See also more generally Carolyn E. Fick, *The Making of Haiti: The Saint-Domingue Revolution from Below* (Knoxville: University of Tennessee Press, 1990).

14 I discuss the flag in "'The Price of Liberty,'" 363.

15 "Etat Nominatif . . . Basse-Terre," G¹ 500, #5, ANSOM; "Etat nominatif . . . de Trois-Rivières," 1 Vendémiaire An 5, 22 September 1796, G¹ 502, #2, ANSOM.

16 See C⁷ᴬ 81, 22 Frimaire An 11, 13 December 1802, ANSOM.

Patricia M. E. Lorcin

Sex, Gender, and Race in the Colonial

Novels of Elissa Rhaïs and Lucienne Favre

In examining women and gender in the European colonies, a number of studies have focused on woman as a colonial trope, a negative
image for endorsing a positive colonial identity.[1] Others have explored the semantics of imperialism: rape, penetration, violation, all
gendered representations of the way in which the colonizing power
exercised its will over the colonized terrain.[2] In examining the
works of Elissa Rhäis and Lucienne Favre, two authors writing in
the interwar period in Algeria, this essay will build on these approaches, but it will focus on the way these women's novels responded to cultural developments in France and sociopolitical
events on both sides of the Mediterranean.

The subject of the indigenous woman and her plight had always
interested the French, principally as a facile way of highlighting the
differences between the two cultures, but the interwar period saw a
marked increase in this interest. Not only did women make for a hot
topic, but women were also asserting themselves on the Algerian
literary scene in an unprecedented way.[3] Rhaïs and Favre were involved in this development on both levels: first, as part of the emerging wave of female writers in Algeria and, second, as writers focusing on women as a subject. But here the likeness ends. Although
both women wrote about Algeria, focusing extensively on women
and their lives and passions, they approached the subject matter in
dissimilar ways. Rhaïs wrote sentimental tales that today would be
classed as *romans de bibliothèque de gare*. In spite of this genre, her
stories were published in the *Revue des deux mondes*, the *Revue
bleue*, the *Revue de Paris*, and the *Revue hebdomadaire*. In 1951, a
poem by Michel Carré, based on one of Rhaïs's novellas, *Kerkeb*,
was presented at the Paris opera set to the music of Samuel Rousseau.[4] Her prose was evocative, descriptive, and romantic. To her
contemporaries, she was an "authentic" voice of "exoticism."[5] As
one reviewer put it: "If ever there were doubts as to whether medi-

ocre adventures could charm and move merely by accentuating the primitive aspects of humanity, Elissa Rhaïs dispels them."[6] In contrast, Favre employed the style of realism. "She may overdo . . . the exclamation marks," a reviewer remarked, "but she never sounds false."[7] Her understanding of women was considered "profound," yet as a writer she had none of "the intellectual traditions of her sex," so was able to convey human emotion with perfect measure.[8]

Rhaïs and Favre represented two strains of colonial literature, the merits of which were extensively debated in the early twenties. On the one hand, there was the tradition of exoticism associated with Pierre Loti, on the other, the "new" colonial realism. Marius-Ary Leblond formalized the debate in a work entitled *Après l'exotisme de Loti: Le roman colonial.*[9] Realism, the two men declared, was indispensable for the colonial writer wishing to convey authoritatively exotic characters and decors to a European public.[10] Rhaïs dissociated herself from Loti, declaring that unlike him, she intended to portray the life of Algerians realistically, a disclaimer the French public seemed to accept. As we shall see, her work and identity were remarkably "exotic," raising questions as to public perceptions of her.[11] Both Rhäis and Favre, therefore, were seen accurately to portray important aspects of colonial society.

The establishment responded to the women positively. Favre received the Prix Corrard de la Société des Gens de Lettres for *L'homme derrière le mur* (1927), the Grand Prix Littéraire de l'Algérie in 1931 (shared with Jeanne Faure-Sardet) for the ensemble of her work, and was nominated for the Prix Femina for her novel *Bab-el-Oued* (1926), although she did not receive the requisite number of votes to get the prize.[12] According to the romanticized biography by Paul Tabet, Rhaïs was considered for membership in the Légion d'Honneur, although the nomination was withdrawn at the last minute.[13] The Légion d'Honneur does not constitute a literary prize as such, but rather an acknowledgment of services rendered to the state. Tabet, in his footnoteless text, quotes a handwritten letter from the minister of education declaring that the nomination rewarded "the quality of her work and the worthiness of her life."[14] Emily Apter, in her article on Rhaïs, states that the nomination was made because her novels stimulated the tourist trade and thus contributed to the invaluable political function of enhancing the " 'civilizing mission,' " although she provides no substantiation of her source for this statement.[15] That Rhaïs inadvertently served the civilizing mission is evident, but Apter's extrapolation ignores the fact that it was Louis Bertrand, one of the founders of the *algérianiste* movement and eventual member of the Académie Française, who first introduced her to the editor of the *Revue des deux mondes*, René Doumic (also a member of the Académie), and thus to the French public.[16] Within months of Bertrand's recommendation, Rhaïs had signed a five-year contract with the publishing house Plon, which continued to publish her work throughout the twenties. Leading newspapers, journals, and reviews were equally quick to try and obtain her collaboration.[17] In spite of a few detractors, Rhaïs soon joined the literary mainstream.[18]

Assuming a Literary Identity

When Elissa Rhäis signed her contract with Plon in 1919, the publishing house issued a communiqué saying that she was a French-educated Muslim who had emerged from a harem and started to write.[19] In fact, she was not Muslim but Jewish and had never lived in an Arab harem.[20] Her acceptance of a Muslim identity, or her collusion with Plon in presenting herself in a more marketable form, was a conscious decision. The nature of this step takes on an added significance given the existing tensions between the Arab and Jewish communities in Algeria, which flared up sporadically.[21] French anti-Semitism may also have constituted a relevant factor, although it had not yet reached the strident proportions of the thirties.

In contrast to Rhaïs, there is less to be said about Favre. There was no "exotic" dimension, real or fictional, to her background. The daughter of an artisan, she was born in Paris in 1896. At one time a factory worker, she immigrated to Algeria, marrying a doctor there.[22] When and why she went to Algeria remains unknown, although the publication of her first Algerian novel in 1925 would suggest she did so in her early to mid-twenties. Her contemporaries judged Favre to be "independent" and "fearless"; a true and dependable friend, who threw herself wholeheartedly into life and conformed to "a man's image of camaraderie."[23] In short, she was "one of the boys." Her modest background stimulated empathy for members of the lower strata of society, and she was at her best when writing about their milieu. Her literary debut was greatly assisted by Colette, who introduced her in France and gave her continuing support.[24] By 1929, four years after the publication of Favre's first novel, one reviewer opined that, undisputedly, she had the potential to become one of the leading female writers of her time.[25]

On the one hand, therefore, we have Elissa Rhaïs, an author who, in assuming a *nom de plume*, takes on a new identity: ethnic, religious, and social. She makes the leap over the troubled terrain of the ethnoreligious conflict present in Algeria at the time without apparent hesitation. Indeed, she appears to revel in her Arab/Muslim identity, enjoying the caftans, the djellabas, and other "exotic" apparel, in which she receives her guests at her home at boulevard Raspail, where she soon becomes "the darling" of the Parisian literary world.[26] The only concession she makes to her Jewish origins lies in the subject matter of her novels, a few of which are focused on the Jewish community and many of which include references to the triangular antagonisms of the settlers, the Jews, and the Muslims. The air of mystery with which she surrounds herself panders not only to her readers' appetite for oriental exoticism, but also to the male image of the mysterious woman as eminently desirable.

On the other hand, we have Lucienne Favre, a no-frills realist with a passion for life, who managed to ascend the social ladder in Algeria both socially and professionally. Like Rhaïs, the concession she makes to her origins resides in her subject matter, which deals with the socially deprived, the working classes, and the struggle to rise above one's circumstantial handicaps. Unlike Rhaïs, however, she provides her readers with a quasi-anthropological approach to her topics, presenting them, and by extension herself, with "honesty." Her "sharp, often brutal, observation was coupled with great humanity. She had a flair for the right phrase."[27] Hers was not an escapist literature, emotional and hence "feminine." To be sure, there was plenty of passion, but it was in the sober tones associated with a "masculine" style.

The differences of approach and personal identity of these two women prove important in so far as their contemporaries perceived both writers to be in tune with the realities of women's lives and to ably and accurately describe the society in which they lived. In a review of Rhaïs's first novel, *Saada, la Marocaine*, Firmin Roz declared that her "documentary precision . . . was not part of a premeditated plan," but due to the fact she was "heir to those Arab storytellers who pour out their tales like water from an inclined vase."[28] She had learned her art listening to stories at her mother's knee, thus "she had been schooled in a fine tradition before becoming a French writer."[29] The reviewer goes on to say that the only other time he had felt such a direct contact with African life was when reading Bertrand's *Le sang des races*.[30] The comparison proves significant in view of the fact that Bertrand was an important literary figure and champion of the settlers. Rhaïs constituted the foil to Bertrand, providing what was lacking in his work: an "insider's" view of indigenous society and, above all, its women.

Like Rhaïs, Favre was deemed to understand and convey the essence of "a woman's heart."[31] Her realism unveiled the "mysteries" of the colony's female world. Her insider's vision was, however, somewhat different. Among the literary trends connected with colonial literature, one existed that saw the Algerian production as regionalist, "laying claim to (French) identity/(Algerian) specificity in relation to metropolitan France," and, as Marcel Berger emphasized in the *Revue des deux mondes* in 1929, "the regionalist novel [was] . . . primarily a documentary novel."[32] Favre, a metropolitan French woman and author living in Algeria, personified this trend and was well placed to convey the ambiguities of Algeria's insider-outsider status. Like Rhaïs, she chose to do so focusing for the most part, but not exclusively, on women.

The Sociopolitical Setting to the Novels

Uncertainty and unrest characterized the interwar period in France and Algeria. In France, the cultural and social angst was caused by the realization that the pre–World War I world had evaporated for good and that trying to recapture it was an exercise in futility. The war disrupted accepted gender relations and, as Mary Louise Roberts has shown, gender and its perception proved central to France's "cultural self-representation as well as to its organization of identity and power" in the twenties.[33] Unrest and violence marked the following decade as fascism emerged on the European political scene. The political scandals and street fighting of the thirties deepened existing French anxieties, polarized society politically and, in some circles, gave rise to fears of civil war. The response was to decry modernity and lament the erosion of traditional values.

Algeria, too, had its quota of unrest and anxiety. Muslim Algerians had fought alongside the French during the war, had given their lives, but they had not been compensated in the measure they deserved; equality in the trenches did not translate into equality at home. The 1920–26 Rif war, following on the heals of World War I, reminded the settlers that they could not take for granted colonial tranquility. This war was the most powerful volley in North Africa against a colonizing power until the struggles for independence. Although the combined Spanish and French armies subdued Abd-el-Krim, putting an end to the short-lived "Republic of the Rif," its impact rippled throughout North Africa. Also at this time, North African nationalism began to emerge, highlighting the so-called indigenous question. Reforms proposed in France, particularly in regard to citizenship, were rejected by the colonial lobby, which remained intransigent in its relations to the Muslims.[34] Settler society was by now entrenched in Algeria, but cultural ambiguities and social anxieties constituted ever-present features of colonial life. In different ways, the novels of Rhaïs and Favre marked a reaction to these circumstances.

For the Love of France: Rhaïs and Erotic Colonialism

Spanning a period of twenty years from 1919 onward, Rhaïs published twelve volumes of fiction (ten novels and five novellas) and had short stories included in two works of collected fiction. In one of these she appeared alongside Luigi Pirandello.[35] Her most blatantly symbolic work was *La riffaine*, published in 1929. It is the tale of M'silla, a beautiful but rebellious (hence implicitly less socially desirable) woman from the Rif mountains, and her subjugation by the pasha El Hadj Mohand, who is a "total convert to the French cause" and "knows that the union with France, and the collaboration of the indigenous population with the Europeans will produce a grandiose oeuvre."[36] The symbolism of the plot, with the leading characters representing the Rif and France, needs no further explanation. But the tale is of interest for its graphic descriptions of violence and its titillating sexuality. The combination of violence and eroticism, which threads its way through the book, makes it a powerfully suggestive tale. The violence is both social and sexual. In one scene, M'silla, who has witnessed the war in the Rif, continues to dream of the struggle and of the chief, Mokhtar the Victorious, "who fights like a tiger . . . his face transfigured with hatred . . . crushing the hesitant; [with] blood gushing from heads; skulls cracked open; brains crushed and splattered on the rocks, and M'silla in the thick of the battle jumping from shoulder to shoulder,

Novels of Elissa Rhaïs and Lucienne Favre 113

encouraging the carnage" (87). In another scene, the Riffaine tells the hated pasha how she sexually enticed one of the lieutenants he had sent against Abd-el-Krim, only to cut off his genitals at the last minute (62). The juxtaposition of sex and violence occurs frequently throughout the book. While it is meant to portray what the French officer in the book describes as "the curious nature of the Orientals, in whom charm and delicacy can be allied with violence and cruelty" (119), Rhaïs presents it in such a way as to mute its impact. As in all her denouements, love subdues violence; the submissive woman calms the aggression of man; the rebellious woman is calmed by the love of man.

With regard to sexuality, it is inevitably in the harem, that focus of so much orientalist erotic imagery, that Rhaïs develops it most explicitly. Early on, Rhaïs details the role of Khotba, the "masterful" female attendant of the harem: "She knew the art of preparing concubines for love . . . she knew how to massage their flesh with sweet-smelling vapors, to make them up, perfume them, dress them. She knew how to extract a virgin from a hot bath, all soft and giddy with desire, veil her, and offer her to the pasha" (52). The harem was full of such beauties, eagerly awaiting their turn, "tossing on their couches, their bodies protected by gauzelike silk, [which if] torn, revealed a black star shining in between two resplendent thighs" (53). This passage, of which I have quoted only a brief extract here, contains undertones of lesbian desire that augment the titillating quality of the heterosexual harem imagery. The recalcitrant M'silla is subjected to the same treatment:

> Already a horde of negresses assail her, leading her over the hot tiles, placing her on the massage table. These unspeakable [*immonde*] beings take hold of her body, twist her hair, massage her all over with oil, unguents, perfumes . . . while stringed instruments play music of voluptuous passion. An hour later, the Riffaine emerges from the bath, languorous, breathless, excited, ready for love. Ready to give herself even to her enemy. Half-naked under her veils, she is taken to Sid El Bacha. (89)

This passage is immediately followed by a vivid description of torture, as the pasha fantasizes about how to curb this rebellious woman. His desire for her naturally prevents him from acting out his sadistic musing.

In the final passages of the book, when M'silla has been vanquished, a member of the pasha's entourage questions him as to why he has accepted this "criminal" into his harem. He replies: "The repentant soul is worth more than the saint" (132). M'silla then advances toward him, "dazzling him with her beauty, arms open, her body trembling under the blue veils, her head crowned with a royal diadem." She has been elevated to the rank of "favorite" (132). The theme of the rebellious woman, subdued by love, is a recurring one in Rhaïs's work. Kerkeb, heroine of the novella of the same name and another of Rhaïs's defiant women, has her comeuppance in much the same way as M'silla.[37] Like most of Rhaïs's work, *La riffaine* and *Kerkeb* contain descriptive passages that assault the senses. Love stories in an exotically erotic setting, to be sure, but charged with a definite message.

If rebellion against gender taboos eventually works out in the heroine's favor, the defiance of racial taboos does not. In *La fille des pachas* (1922), the heroine Zoulika is married off to an old but wealthy man. She falls in love with Hubert, an army officer who she believes is a French Christian. Hubert is in fact a Jew, but he keeps it a secret, for he knows that while Muslims were "indifferent to Christians, they hated the Jews."[38] When the tryst is discovered, the officer is beheaded, and Zoulika is condemned to death for adultery. Before the execution of the sentence, Zoulika pleads for Hubert's life, and as she is about to be led away herself, she discovers for the first time that he is a Jew. Blinded by rage at the deception, and insulted that she had been linked to a Jew rather than a Christian, she recoils in horror. "Come [do your work quickly]," she tells the executioner, "I do not want to live, for I would no longer be a Muslim."[39] In fact, this is a misrepresentation that serves the colonial message. In strict Muslim practice, a Muslim woman is considered defiled if she marries any non-Muslim, and punished accordingly.

Animosity between Jews and Arabs and between Jews and the French appears regularly in Rhaïs's work, reflecting reality in both France and Algeria. Tensions between French and Arabs, on the other hand, are glossed over or, when they do occur, are usually resolved, creating the illusion of relative harmony. Rhaïs paid lip service to the French ideology of equality by introducing the concept at appropriate places. In *Le mariage de Hanifa*, the teacher from France, Mademoiselle Mathieu "with her kind, French generosity," tells her class of mixed "races": "We are all equals, my dears."[40] In the situational content of the novels, however, Rhaïs is clear about the social hierarchy. The civilizing mission of the French is endorsed through the allegiance of many of her leading Arab characters to the French cause.[41] They counterbalance the grumblings of her lesser characters against French occupation.

In reading Rhaïs's work today, the most obvious question is not, why was she so popular, but why was she so popular in the circles she was? Although the passages quoted above come across better in French than in English, no stretch of the imagination can elevate them into the realm of good literature.[42] Yet some of the best literary journals of her day published her works, and such literary personalities as Colette, Mallarmé, and Morand supported her. In the first instance, her attraction, particularly to the literati, was as an exotic addition to the literary scene: a female Arab storyteller who spoke to the world "truthfully" about herself and her people.[43] Secondly, for all the orientalism, Rhaïs was considered by her contemporaries to portray the customs of the indigenous population "as realistically as was possible for a child of the Orient."[44] While this condescending assessment is closer to French conceptions of Arab reality than it is to reality itself, it nonetheless does indicate one motive for encouraging Rhaïs, namely showing the world what a French-educated indigenous woman was capable of. But there was more to it than colonial politics. In a throwaway line at the end of a 1920 article on Rhaïs, Lucien Maury declares: "Is not the Orient of the Orientals, in another form, but with the same anxieties, the obsessive image of the modern and universal social question?"[45] This rhetorical question is much nearer the mark.

Rhaïs's tales of violence and love represented symbolic interpretations of the social upheavals going on both in France and in Algeria. War had created new opportunities for women. Not only had they realized their possible capabilities outside the private sphere, but they also began rebelling against the idea of having to return to their former existence. In her dream of battle, M'silla is at the center of the fray. She, too, participates to the full, but she eventually returns to the more acceptable role of subordinate (albeit as the favorite). This, then, constitutes the leitmotiv of so much of Rhaïs's work. Her novels, for all the passion, had the reassuring quality of order reestablished out of chaos: The woman's place was in the home (harem). Disrupted gender relations, the result of woman rearing her rebellious head, for whatever reason — and the novels provide a variety — were resolved to the advantage of the established order. The message, for all its oriental trappings, embodied the universal one of separate spheres. Rhaïs provided a reassuring panacea for a world where matters of gender seemed to have been stood on their heads.

In the more specific context of Algeria, which had only suffered the ravages of war at a distance and whose social problems were connected to establishing a modus vivendi of race rather than to the social disruptions of war, a different spin emerged. Rhaïs endorsed the separation of the "races": Arabs, Jews, and French could possibly live side by side in relative harmony, but intermarriage remained unthinkable. A practicing Muslim could not marry a member of another religion without serious consequences. By putting the onus of this refusal to intermarry on the Arabs rather than on the French settlers, she obscured French refusal to accept the Arabs on a par with themselves. Rhaïs in no way examined the limits of French tolerance. Nor did she look into the reality of the problematic relations between the settlers and the indigenous population. Harmony was possible if the established order was maintained. The Algerian-born journalist and author Jules Roy summed it up best in an article entitled "Le mythe d'une Algérie heureuse," which appeared in *Le Monde* in 1982: "She was marvelously old-fashioned," he wrote, "she incarnated the myth of Algeria as a happy place, irreplaceable in our hearts."[46]

It was the ambiguities inherent in Rhaïs's literary personality and work that made her so attractive. Firstly, there was the innovation of a francophone Muslim woman writer. Secondly, if her prose left something to be desired, her graphic descriptions of sex and violence differed refreshingly in their capacity to shock. What made them acceptable and popular was the fact she was describing a culture that was "other." Thirdly, her message remained intrinsically conservative. She thus provided the wherewithal in her work and approach to appeal to a range of literary and political interests.

Favre and the Art of Colonial Realism

Favre's consideration of colonial society had none of the exotic delivery of Rhaïs's. Although she was from France, and therefore had not grown up in Algeria, she felt she knew Muslim Algerians well enough to be able to write from their perspective. Two of her most popular novels, *Mille et un jours: Mourad* (1944) and *Orientale*

1930 (1930), are written in the first person.[47] Of her fourteen works, five had women as their central characters, and three were representations, fictional or descriptive, of the Casbah, the Muslim and oldest quarter of Algiers.[48] For all its realism, Favre's work remains ambiguous. All her works on Algeria bring out the hostility between the Arabs (and Berbers) and the settlers, as well as the tensions between the French from France and the settlers. Although it is often done in an oblique fashion, she raises the social and economic problems faced by the Muslim population.[49] This suggests a liberal outlook and empathy with the indigenous population, which Favre undoubtedly felt, having grown up among the less privileged in France. This sense of liberalism, however, is counteracted by the fact that her plots are relatively conservative and, for all their apparent exposure of the ill-treatment of the Muslim, are not free of the type of stereotyping associated with colonial narratives.

Orientale 1930 is the fictional autobiography of a female servant, or Fathma, as women servants were collectively called.[50] This choice of name for the central figure suggests that Fathma represents Muslim women. In the opening pages of the book, Fathma explains that she will tell her story to her mistress "who is as wise as a *marabouta*," adding, "only a woman is capable of understanding another woman's truth."[51] In a symbolically significant passage, she notes: "A photograph of me veiled will appear on the cover with her name underneath. Thus, nobody will know who I am or be able to shame me. She will split her earnings with me. I think she will do so honestly because she is a real Frenchwoman from France" (10). Both women, French author and Arab "heroine," appear on the cover, but not on equal terms. The Arab woman is anonymous, hidden from view, unidentifiable beyond the ethnic category of Arab, in much the same way as the Muslim population is effaced by settler marginalization. While the contents of the book will counteract the anonymity of the cover, by unveiling the Arab woman's life, it will be done in the presence of a French woman from France, not one from Algeria. That this symbolic passage comes so early in the book, underscores both the social hierarchy of the colony with the "true" French in the most esteemed position and demonstrates the self-imposed distance of the French from the settlers or *pieds-noirs*, a distance the latter resented.

The first chapter of the book, which deals with Fathma's reminiscences of her early life, opens with the memory of a beating at the hands of her brothers, accompanied by an ineffectual remonstrance by her mother, who was "secretly proud of their strength" (14). This passage also serves a dual purpose. It introduces the concept of violence as endemic to Arab life, and it underlines the subordination of Muslim women. Subordinate not only in the gender hierarchy and to the whims of their menfolk, but also to European women who, as developments in the novel will demonstrate, are better respected by Arab men (242). Favre thus clearly defines the colonial hierarchy of both race and gender at the outset. This theme is reintroduced in all her Algerian novels.

The position of the French at the top of the social hierarchy, above settlers from other Mediterranean countries, the *neo-Français* (as Favre calls them),[52] and, of course, above the Arabs, is endowed with a morality that makes their position unassailable. In *Bab-el-Oued*, a novel about the social ascendance of a poor Spanish emigrant woman, aptly named Ascension, the heroine spends a part of her life living with a Frenchman she nursed to health during the First World War. Unlike his Spanish counterparts, we are told, he is affable, has a sense of fun, gets drunk in moderation, only occasionally beats his wife, and allows her to take part in family deliberations. His consideration of her sets her up as an equal and differentiates her from Spanish women who crouch in corners with the servants: "What a gallant girl, to have landed herself a Frenchman."[53]

To this image of the French as more refined and equitable, Favre added that of the French as educators, or civilizers. In *Mille et un jours: Mourad*, Mourad explains how his friend Charles, "a real Frenchman from France," has refined him by teaching him proper social behavior (inter alia, not to blow his nose on his fingers) and how to be conciliatory toward the Christians (135). Similarly, in *Orientale 1930*, the French woman Marie, who marries one of Fathma's relatives in an unusual fictional account of intermarriage, teaches the Arab women of the household more sophisticated domestic arts as well as introducing them to French culture through storytelling and accounts of life in France (219–22). The paternalism (or maternalism) of these passages responds to the prevalent belief at the time in the uncouth mores and childlike characteristics of colonized peoples.

Furthermore, in the passage underlining the Muslim need to develop more conciliatory attitudes toward the Christians, Favre shifts the onus of Arab-French tension from the actuality of colonial domination to the realm of religious intolerance, the volatility and preventability of which many perceived to be beyond rational control. Favre further reinforces the Muslims' position at the bottom of a morally defined hierarchy in a description of the 1934 Constantine pogrom. Mourad explains that while nearly all residents of Algeria were anti-Semitic, "the French and the neo-French content themselves with shaming the Jews with regularity, [but] the Muslims are quick to take direct action, without prior warning or provocation" (*Mourad*, 401). The stereotype of the Muslims as intrinsically violent and less able to contain their hatred than the other groups of Algerian society is presented through the observation of Mourad, himself a Muslim. This literary device reinforces the idea while appearing to distance the author. Similarly, in *Orientale 1930*, Marie enchants the female members of her Arab family with fairy tales, and Fathma states that she likes Blue Beard best, "for it could as easily have happened in our society" (232). The image of Blue Beard is reintroduced in *Dans la Casbah*, where Favre, describing the stalls where "women's robes swung from the ceiling swathed in the scent of amber, musk, cinnamon, and cloves" compares them to "embalmed bodies, hanging in the cavern of some Oriental Blue Beard."[54] Again the reference, descriptive and juxtaposed to the pleasures of aromatic spices, remains an indirect one, but it serves to reinforce images of violence and exoticism as intrinsic to the indigenous Orient, or "other."

The social hierarchy of race, so closely linked to culture, was upheld by both sides. Settlers and Muslims frowned on crossing the interracial divide through intermarriage. As Favre has one of her characters say: "Race, like the nurturing mother; inevitably one returns to its fold" (*Orientale 1930*, 96). In *Dans la Casbah*, Omar laments the fact he cannot marry the sister of one of his non-Muslim schoolmates: "What Algerian (settler) would be as liberal as a Frenchman and give his daughter to a *bicot*, however cultivated or well-off he might be?" (20).[55] Favre does emphasize the Muslim reluctance to marry out of their faith, but unlike Rhaïs, she often links it to retrograde ideas maintained by women. In *Orientale 1930*, the working-class Marie marries Ahmed while he is working in France. On returning to Algeria, Marie at first gets on admirably with her new extended family. When Ahmed starts to drink, however, she berates him severely, which shocks the Muslim women. They resent the fact Ahmed does not reprimand her as he would an Arab woman: "It is true that when one of our race marries a Christian, he always respects her more; he treats her like a caïd's daughter, even if she is poor" (242). Eventually Ahmed is persuaded to leave the family home and set up in a French-style house with Marie, where they "will no longer be surrounded by old women, who are set against progress and union between races" (265).

The themes of women as essentially conservative and the reluctance of Muslim men to see their women emancipated (westernized) are developed in a variety of ways. In *Mourad*, of the four young women the hero is linked to romantically during the novel, his first wife, Yamina, is ignorant, destructive, and retrograde, refusing contact with Mourad's French friends, the education Mourad offers her, and disrupting his life as a teacher. When she dies and he remarries, it is to his young ward, a virgin in whom he has found "perfect submission and absolute innocence" (393). Of the two emancipated women in his life, one (Baya) is a courtesan and the other (Zina) provokes impotence in him (368). In *Bab-el-Oued*, although Ascension is ambitious enough to want to improve her social lot, she nonetheless believes, "like all Latins, that a woman's role is to maintain order at home" (96). Love provides the defining feature of woman's life as well as her strength: "Woman is a matrix; body and soul. She is made to reproduce [the man] who has penetrated her, has marked her profoundly. . . . before being in love, Ascension was already a force; in love Ascension is a power determined to triumph by any means" (224). Woman draws her strength from man.

Although French women in Favre's colonial novels are substantially more liberated than Muslim or neo-French women, in Favre's only non-Algerian novel, *La noce* (1929), the heroine's entrapment in patriarchal structures is little better than that of her Muslim counterparts. The arranged marriage of the heroine, Dominique, is threatened when she falls in love at her nuptials with one of the guests. Throughout the novel, her illicit love counterbalances Dominique's sense of familial and social duty. When her lover is killed, she loses her will to live and dies. The novel is set in pre–World War I France in a stultifying milieu of the provincial middle classes. While Favre is certainly attempting to critique the values of prewar France by recounting the tragedy of a woman caught between her social obligations and her love, the choices she provides Dominique with remain male-defined. The present-day reader cannot help speculating why Favre, considered so independent by her contemporaries, chose to create a singularly dependent heroine in her only novel situated in France. Was there perhaps a reluctance to join the mainstream of feminist criticism by openly espousing the concept of the "new woman," or was it a class-based reluctance to endorse what she perceived as essentially middle-class gains for women? The content of her novels would suggest the latter.[56] With the exception of *La noce*, which stands as a critique of a certain middle class, all her novels concern the lower strata of society. She obviously feels most at home when dealing with the struggles of working-class men and women and describing the slights, obstacles, and deprivations of their lives. In this harsh world of well-defined hierarchies and economic struggle, *la femme moderne* found herself relegated to the backseat.

Even sexuality is muted in tone, with none of the exotic eroticism of Rhaïs's work. Favre's Algerian novels underscore the stereotypes of Arab sexuality. Mourad's highly developed libido is the thread that runs throughout the novel and binds its disparate parts together. His womanizing stands in contrast to the stable marriage of his French friend, Charles, suggesting the polarity between Arab polygamy and French monogamy. Mourad's sexuality and attitudes to women, and his eventual drifting away from his friend Charles, underscores the colonial image of the Muslim, however educated he may be, as irreconcilably different from the French. Favre's women are sexually conservative, with any adventurous exploits being clandestine or ill matched.[57]

It is only when dealing with prostitution that Favre is more explicit. Her three works on the Casbah, a privileged site of exoticism and sexuality in the colonial narrative, deal with the subject. Favre's focus, however, comes through the lens of working women and social hierarchy. Prostitution, as one of her characters explains, is a "social service" and a job like any other. In the demimonde of the Casbah, the women living and working there "have a highly developed sense of hierarchical values and racial difference" (*Dans la Casbah*, 9).[58] The shop girls disdain the girls from the bordellos, who in turn look down on indigenous girls (*filles*, in the sense of "prostitutes"). Only in exceptional cases will they unite to defend one of their own against an injustice which might one day happen to them (103).[59] Any eroticism Favre conjures up is connected to their milieu. In her description of the Rues-aux-Filles, it is the Casbah that is eroticized and not the girls: "Rue-aux-Filles in the Casbah. . . . More seductive than the girls themselves. . . . One is bewitched, possessed by the atmosphere, overcome by desire exacerbated by the heat, the music, the colors, the laughter, . . . The females [*femelles*] are there to assuage this collective fury. . . . We take them, in the end, these insipid tarts [*garces*], to be free of this possessive rage" (128). "Parce qu'," the passage ends, "on ne peut pas pétrir cette muraille, pénétrer ce parfum, jouir dans cette vasque." This sentence, flat and virtually incomprehensible if translated into English, is erotically suggestive in French. The Casbah, thus described, symbolizes the social distance between the men and the prostitutes, but, more importantly, the inability of the French (and néo-French) to enter into the realm of the local population, that is to say the realm of Islam. For Favre, therefore, sexuality is another way of explicating the cultural divide between the colonizing power and its less fortunate subjects.

Favre's work is more complicated in its messages than Rhaïs's. Her social realism allowed her to criticize the society she had opted to live in. But her critique is essentially one of the metropolitan criticizing the provinces. It is also a class-based critique in a society where race and ethnicity formed the rungs of the social hierarchy rather than birth or education. While this suggests Favre's advocacy of more equality of opportunity for the Muslims, the author nonetheless reinforces many of the colonial narratives of the cultural backwardness and intractability of the Muslim population. Favre's work constituted a response to the growing dissatisfaction among native Algerians with their situation, which saw the emergence of the first protonationalist movements in the 1920s. Favre prodded for an improvement of the situation, rather than a reversal. In this she was in line with metropole liberals, such as Maurice Viollette, who advocated a more equitable situation for the Muslims, but whose projects the settler lobby blocked.[60] The subliminal message was that if "true" French values were adopted, harmony would be easier to attain.

It is in Favre's use of the themes of gender and sexuality that the social complexities of colonial society really come to the fore and her conservatism becomes more apparent. The racial and patriarchal hierarchies that the settlers strove to maintain originated in social and political anxieties and uncertainties. Native Algerian society had been thoroughly dislocated through land seizure. Pauperization had resulted in many parts of the country, and the dispossessed had migrated either to France as immigrant workers or to the urban centers of Algeria. As passive resistance gave way to more voluble forms of dissent, maintenance of the status quo to the settlers' advantage became more imperative. Colonial society had no desire for either Muslim or female upstarts. The depiction of Muslim women as generally beyond the pale of French influence was in fact a reas-

Novels of Elissa Rhaïs and Lucienne Favre 123

suring message. In the tug-of-war between the male *évolué* and the "backward" females of his entourage, it was the latter who won out in the long run. The family remained the seat of traditional values. In a similar message about the settlers, Ascension's social mobility is not related to the concept of emancipation. As her economic situation improves, she strives to become more "French," not more liberated, and she achieves this through her male relationships. Reproduction and the maintenance (or restoration) of order in men's chaotic lives is the woman's ultimate role. The theme of sexuality used to highlight cultural differences, deemed to be irreconcilable, is another way of endorsing the status quo. Favre had no desire to upset the apple cart.

The colonial space provided both Rhaïs and Favre with the wherewithal to develop their literary personalities. In different ways, both women responded to the literary scene and social climate in the metropole while ostensibly portraying the situation in the colony. Rhaïs abandoned her Jewish Algerian identity to assume that of a colonial persona, the exotic oriental female. She embarked on her literary career as an *évoluée*, obscuring her origins and her literary activities in an aura of mystery. Her sartorial exoticism and "Arab" hospitality provided a singular attraction at her literary gatherings. She played the card of mystery and exoticism to win a respected place on the literary scene for her work, the quality of which did not equal its appeal. Similarly, the colonial space provided Favre with an ideal setting to develop her literary authenticity through social realism. Her exposés (one can hardly call them critiques) of the tensions and animosities of colonial society were the basis on which her artistic reputation and credibility was founded. But for all the sharpness of her commentary, she in no way wanted to rock the colonial boat. Her criticisms were akin to those of a Parisian in the provinces; they were not those of the truly oppressed. She was a liberal, not a radical, and the colonial space provided her with the opportunity to be the former while appearing to be the latter.

The response of the metropole to the two women corresponded to the political and social concerns that shaped the period. Rhaïs's work responded to the ambiguous atmosphere of postwar France seeking to flee from the anxieties engendered by the disasters of war either by a hedonistic escapism or a return to traditional values. On the one hand, therefore, a public enamored with the idea of its universalism snapped up her exoticism, an exoticism whose cultural manifestations included *La Revue Nègre*, with Josephine Baker dancing to packed audiences at the Théâtre des Champs Elysées. Rhaïs's bittersweet tales of love and intrigue in the "Orient" fit well into the postwar hedonism that championed the "primitive" and the "exotic." On the other hand, the subliminal messages of order restored and tradition maintained, so integral to her plots, proved comforting to a public repelled by the perceived dissolution of established values. Favre's work appeared on the literary scene at the end of the twenties, when the decade's early flights of fantasy began to give way to the sobriety that would characterize the thirties. Scandals, depression, and political tensions reshaped preoccupations and led to a shift in French letters toward an expression of social concerns and social criticism. Favre's "realism" coincided with this literary development. Her depiction of Algerian society reinforced the French ideals of universalism by emphasizing the superiority of metropolitan French values, with regards to racial tolerance and harmony, over those of the neo-French. Her social "criticism" was circumscribed and the focus of her criticism distant enough to avoid the *succès de scandale* that so often accompanied mordant social criticism. As was the case with Rhaïs, Favre's response to metropole concerns and needs as much as her portrayal of colonial Algeria catapulted her to fame. For all the perceived literary innovation in the works of these two women, which ran into multiple editions, they remained ultimately conservative and therefore reassuring.[61] Behind the aura of originality, the subliminal messages reinforced the colonial status quo as well as endorsing a traditional gender hierarchy. The writers' popularity both in Algeria and in France, where the specter of social upheaval hovered in the atmosphere, was a measure of the need to escape the social realities of their times.

Notes

1   See, for example, Julia Clancy-Smith, "Islam, Gender, and Identities in the Making of French Algeria, 1830–1962," in *Domesticating the Empire: Race, Gender, and Family Life in French and Dutch Colonialism*, ed. Clancy-Smith and Frances Gouda (Charlottesville: Uni-

versity of Virginia Press, 1998), 156; Clancy-Smith, "La Femme Arabe: Women and Sexuality in France's North African Empire," in *Women, the Family, and Divorce Laws in Islamic History*, ed. Amira El Azhary Sonbol (Syracuse: Syracuse University Press, 1996), 52–63.

2 For example, Jenny Sharpe, *Allegories of Empire: The Figure of Woman in the Colonial Text* (Minneapolis: University of Minneapolis Press, 1993).

3 For example, Magli-Bosnard, Odette Keun, Annette Godin, Henriette Waltz, Maximilienne Heller, Marguerite Deval, Maria Bugeja, Gabrielle Quillery, Jeanne Faure-Sardet, Marcelle Capy, Anna Colnat, Lucienne Jean-Darrouy, Germaine Lassara-Bouchacourt, Françoise Berthault, and Marcelle Marty.

   Jean Déjeux states that there were at least sixty novels written by women on Algeria during the period 1919–39. Déjeux, "Élissa Rhaïs: Conteuse algérienne (1876–1940)," in *Le Maghreb dans l'imaginaire français: La colonie, le désert, l'exil* (Aix-en-Provence: Edisud, 1985), 73. This article also appeared in the *Revue de l'Occident musulman et de la Méditerranée* 37 (1984): 47–78.

4 Ibid., 50.

5 P.-O. Graillet, "Rhaïs (Elissa) — Les Juifs ou la fille d'Eléazar," in *Revue bibliographique*, 21 May 1921, 278–79. See also Firmin Roz, "Une forme nouvelle d'exotisme: Mme Elissa Rhaïs," *Revue bleue*, June 1920, 342–44.

6 Lucien Maury, "L'Orient des orientaux," *Revue bleue*, 10 January 1920, 27; this and all unmarked translations are mine.

7 Fernand Desonay, "Favre (Lucienne) — La noce," *Revue bibliographique*, July 1929, 333.

8 Pierre Mac-Orlan, preface to *L'homme derrière le mur*, by Lucienne Favre (Paris: Crès, 1927), ii.

9 Marius-Ary Leblond was a collective pseudonym for the cousins Georges Athénas (Marius), 1877–1953, and Aimé Merlo (Ary), 1880–1958. See Marius-Ary Leblond, *Après l'exotisme de Loti: Le roman colonial* (Paris: Vald Rasmussen, 1926).

10 Peter Dunwoodie, *Writing French Algeria* (Oxford, Clarendon, 1999), 133.

11 Déjeux, "Elissa Rhaïs: Conteuse algérienne," 69–70.

12 On the significance of the Grand Prix Littéraire de l'Algérie, see Jeanne Adam, "Polémique autour du premier Grand Prix Littéraire de l'Algérie: La situation des lettres algériennes en 1921," in *La Maghreb dans l'imaginaire français: La colonie, le désert, l'exile* (Aix-en-Provence: Edisud, 1985), 15–30; and Jean Déjeux, "Le Grand Prix Littéraire de l'Algérie (1921–1961)," *Revue d'histoire littéraire de la France*, 1985, 60–71.

13 Paul Tabet, *Elissa Rhaïs* (Paris: B. Grasset, 1982). Tabet backs his contention by reprinting letters from the various parties involved in the nomination and its aftermath. No archival sources are provided. Tabet's biography of Rhaïs had its own *succès de scandale* when it appeared in 1982. Tabet claimed Rhaïs had been illiterate and had forced her nephew and lover, Robert-Raoul, to write her stories for her. This reversal of the Willie-Colette scenario created a stir in Parisian literary circles. Tabet, whose book was promoted by Bernard-Henri Levy, was interviewed by Bernard Pivot on *Apostrophes*. In the book, Tabet claimed Rhaïs's behavior resulted from the fact she had been locked up in a harem as a beautiful young woman by her much older husband—and then neglected. It was her embitterment and desire to avenge herself on men that led to the harsh treatment of her nephew. Tabet's book was originally entitled *Elissa Rhaïs: Un roman*, but the subtitle was declared an editorial error and dropped. For a full description of the events surrounding the publication of Tabet's book and the uproar it caused, see Déjeux, "Elissa Rhaïs: Conteuse algérienne," especially 65.

14 Tabet, *Elissa Rhaïs*, 175.

15 Emily Apter, "Ethnographic Travesties, Colonial Realism, French Feminism, and the Case of Elissa Rhaïs," in *After Colonialism: Imperial Histories and Postcolonial Displacements*, ed. Gyan Prakash (Princeton: Princeton University Press, 1995), 304.

16 Jean Déjeux, *Femmes d'Algérie: Légendes, traditions, histoire, littérature* (Paris: La Boite à Documents, 1987), 262. (Louis Bertrand was elected to the Académie Française in 1925.)

17 André Spire, "Un conteur judéo-arabe d'Afrique du Nord: Elissa Rhaïs," 1929, in *Souvenirs à Bâtons Rompus*, ed. Andre Spire (Paris: Albin Michel, 1962), 249.

18 See, for example André Billy, "Elissa Rhaïs" in *La muse aux besicles* (Paris: Renaissance du Livre, 1920), 234–38.

19 Déjeux, *Femmes d'Algérie*, 262. Elissa Rhaïs was the pseudonym for Rosine Boumendil. She married a rabbi, Moïse Amar, whom she divorced. She then remarried Mardochée Chemouil, a well-to-do merchant. If her Jewish identity was unknown when Plon issued the communiqué, it did not remain so, as Spire's article indicates ("Un conteur," 249).

20 Déjeux, "Elissa Rhaïs: Conteuse algérienne," 61; and Déjeux, *Femmes algériennes*, 260–61. (Dejeux has thoroughly researched Rhaïs's background.)

21 See Charles-Robert Ageron, *Histoire de l'Algérie contemporaine: 1871–1954* (Paris, Presses Universitaires de France, 1979), 425–28. Anti-Semitism among the Europeans was prevalent. Flare-ups occurred from the time of the Crémieux Decree to the Second World

War. See also John Ruedy, *Modern Algeria: The Origins and Development of a Nation* (Bloomington: Indiana University Press, 1992), 110, 140.

22 Sakina Messaadi, *Les romancières coloniales et la femme colonisée: Contribution à une étude de la littérature coloniale en Algérie dans la première moitié du XXe siècle* (Algiers: Entreprise nationale du livre, 1990), 49.

23 Mac-Orlan, preface, iii.

24 Messaadi, *Les romancières coloniales*, 50–51.

25 Desonay, "Favre (Lucienne) — La noce," 333.

26 Messaadi, *Les romancières coloniales*, 53.

27 Fernande Feron, quoted in Messaadi, *Les romancières coloniales*, 51. Due, apparently, to a printer's oversight, there is no footnote providing the source of this quote.

28 Roz, "Une forme nouvelle d'exotisme," 344.

29 Ibid., 342.

30 Ibid., 344. For more on Bertrand, see chapter 8 in Patricia M. E. Lorcin, *Imperial Identities: Stereotyping, Prejudice, and Race in Colonial Algeria* (New York: St. Martin's, 1995); and Lorcin, "Decadence and Renascence: Louis Bertrand and the Concept of *Rebarbarisation* in Fin-de-Siècle Algeria," in *New Perspectives on the Fin-de-Siècle in Nineteenth- and Twentieth-Century France*, ed. Kay Chadwick and Tim Unwin (London: Edwin Mellen, 2000). See also Louis Bertrand, *Le sang des races* (Paris: P. Ollendorff, 1899).

31 Desonay, "Favre (Lucienne) — La noce," 333.

32 Quoted in Dunwoodie, *Writing French Algeria*, 134. Marcel Berger, "Littérature coloniale: Hier et aujourd'hui," *Revue des deux mondes*, 1929, 416.

33 Mary Louise Roberts, *Civilization without Sexes: Reconstructing Gender in Postwar France, 1917–1927* (Chicago: University of Chicago Press, 1994), 213.

34 The 1930 Violette-Blum bill, for example, which would have given Muslims some of the rights (although not all) accorded to the settlers, was quashed by the colon lobby. For an account of this and for the development of the nationalist movements in Algeria, see Ruedy, *Modern Algeria*, 114–50.

35 Luigi Pirandello, *Les oeuvres libres* (Paris: Fayard, 1927); the other collected work is entitled *Blida* (C. Trumelet, ed. [Algiers: A. Jourdan, 1887]), with a preface by Louis Bertrand. This collection includes works by Gaston Ricci, Ferdinand Duchêne, and Robert Migot. Of these, Duchêne was the first to receive the Grand Prix Littéraire de l'Algérie when it was established in 1921.

36 Elissa Rhaïs, *La riffaine* (Paris: Flammarion, 1929), 43, 45. All subsequent references will be given parenthetically in the text.

37 Elissa Rhaïs, *Kerkeb*, in *Un siècle de nouvelles franco-maghrébines*, ed. Denise Brahimi (Paris: Minerve, 1992), 89–108.

38 Elissa Rhaïs, *La fille des pachas* (Paris: Plon, 1922), 96. See also 46–47.

39 Ibid., 262.

40 Elissa Rhaïs, *Le mariage de Hanifa* (Paris: Plon, 1926), 38; Sid Ali in *Le mariage de Hanifa*.

41 Sid Mustapha Pacha in *La lille des pachas*, 4; Sid El Hadj in *La riffaine*, 45–46.

42 Andre Billy, who thought Rhaïs overrated, points out the shortcomings of her literary style. Billy, "Elissa Rhaïs," 235.

43 Roz quotes Rhaïs as follows: "I never write unless I am haunted by something, unless my heart is tight with suffering, there is always something of me in my books," adding that in effect "all her books record only the most vivid sensations." Roz, "Une forme nouvelle d'exotisme," 344.

44 Maury, "L'Orient des orientaux," 26.

45 Ibid., 28

46 Jules Roy, "Le mythe d'une Algérie heureuse," *Le Monde*, 1982.

47 Lucienne Favre, *Mille et un jours: Mourad* (Paris: Denoel, 1944), was the only one of her novels translated into English: *The Temptations of Mourad, a Novel* (New York: William Morrow, 1948). Favre, *Orientale 1930* (Paris: Grasset, 1930).

48 Lucienne Favre, *Bab-el-Oued* (Paris: Crès, 1926); Favre, *La noce* (Paris: Grasset, 1929); Favre, *Mille et un jours: Les aventures de la belle Doudja* (Paris: Gallimard, 1946); and the play *Isabelle d'Afrique*.

49 See, for example, *Mille et un jours: Mourad*, 32, 174, 368; *Dans la Casbah* (Paris: Fayard, 1936), 36, 43; and *Orientale 1930*, 28, 70.

50 Fatima was the prophet Muhammad's daughter. In a similar fashion, the collective name for Muslim men was Mohamed. The connotations of religious subordination and marginalization are obvious.

51 *Orientale 1930*, 9, 12. All subsequent references will be given parenthetically in the text. A *marabout* is a holy man (living saint in Islam); a *marabouta* is a holy woman.

52 See, for example, Favre, *Mille et un jours: Mourad*, 305. All subsequent references will be given parenthetically in the text.

53 Favre, *Bab-el-Oued*, 111. All subsequent references will be given parenthetically in the text.

54 Favre, *Dans la Casbah*, 14. All subsequent references will be given parenthetically in the text.

55 *Bicot* is one of the derogative terms used to denote Arabs.

56 Little is known of Favre's private life. My attempts to locate family

and/or papers through the houses that published her work remained unfruitful.

57 Namely, the liaisons of Ascension in *Bab-el-Oued* or of Dominique in *La noce*.

58 The book opens with a description of this demimonde.

59 "Les filles de la Casbah ont un sens aigu des valeurs hiérarchiques et des différences raciales. Les Filles des Magasins méprisent les Filles des Maisons qui entre elle font la moue pour parler des Fille Indigènes."

60 See Ruedy, *Modern Algeria*, 140–41. Maurice Viollette tried to get a bill passed in 1936, known as the Viollette-Blum bill, which would have given Algerian Muslims French citizenship without having to renounce the personal statute (which for a Muslim equals apostasy).

61 For example, Rhaïs's *Saada, la Marocaine* ran to twenty-six editions; *La fille des pachas* to fifteen editions. Favre's *L'homme derrière le mur* ran to fourteen editions; *Dans la Casbah* to seven editions.

Dana S. Hale

French Images of Race on Product Trademarks

during the Third Republic

During the Third Republic (1871–1940), supporters of overseas expansion succeeded in making economic development and the "civilizing mission" key policies in controlling regions of Africa and Asia. Nineteenth-century racial theories and popular views about culture and nonwhite races helped propel numerous conquests abroad during a period of French military decline in Europe. French forces asserted control over much of North and West Africa, portions of equatorial Africa, the island of Madagascar, and the area in Southeast Asia the French named "Indochina" (Vietnam, Cambodia, and Laos).

Commercial trademark images were one important medium through which ideas about Africans and Asians in the French territories reached the public during this period. Trademark illustrations document an important aspect of cultural history because they represent images the French encountered in their daily home environment (such as on bottles of laundry bleach or tea canisters) — images that had the power to mold or reinforce ideas about race.[1] By incorporating imagery from eighteenth-century plantation scenes or contemporary depictions adapted from colonial propaganda and mass advertising, French entrepreneurs and their designers depicted Africans and Asians in ways that not only corresponded to how they perceived them visually, but also corresponded to the roles that they *wanted* them to fill in the empire. Essentially, business owners portrayed colonial subjects as agricultural laborers, craftsmen, household servants, and entertainers. Most trademarks perpetuated an exotic view of Africans and Asians already familiar to the French populace through images in the popular press, ethnographic spectacles, and government-sponsored colonial fairs.[2] As Vanessa Schwartz has pointed out, French culture at the end of the nineteenth century was increasingly becoming a culture of the spectator and of "visual entertainments."[3] Increased advertising and the growing variety of exotic commercial images may be seen as part of this transformation. The repeated use of racial stereotypes in trademarks from this period suggests that the public often accepted these fashioned images as appealing and believable.

An examination of registered trademarks provides us with additional evidence about consumer and popular culture during the modern phase of French imperialism. Research by Jacques Marseille has established the overall economic significance of colonial expansion and investment to the *métropole* throughout most of the Third Republic.[4] But how might the French consumer have experienced these changes? Studies on consumer culture in modern France underline the expanding number of consumer goods available and the increasing number of citizens able to purchase them. Analyses by Rosalind Williams and Whitney Walton give special attention to the impact of technological advances, mass production, and commercialism on bourgeois values and practices.[5] These studies, however, do not attempt to evaluate changes in the consumption of basic products — such as foodstuffs, beverages, hygiene soaps, and cleaning products — in workers' households. The increasing number of trademarks representing these products reflects a growing market and indicates that these items entered more homes during this period. Colonial goods such as tea, bananas, cotton cloth, cocoa, and items derived from palm oil and rubber were among the new products purchased for French households. An examination of trademark designs can illuminate how entrepreneurs presented their wares and what led consumers to buy them.

This essay focuses on trademark images that depict colonized peoples under French administration in Africa and Asia — as specified in labels (e.g., *l'Algérien* or *l'Indochinoise*) — and those that depict the generic black, Arab, or Asian. During the Third Republic, business owners adopted a common definition of race that separated humans into four categories based primarily on physical characteristics. The four races, according to a formulation greatly popularized by racial theorist Gustave Le Bon, were white, yellow, red, and black — in descending order of intelligence, beauty, culture, and moral qualities. This classification allowed for ranking within racial groups, so that the French defined Arabs as inferior Caucasians, usually referring to a separate Arab "race."[6] Entrepreneurs used labeling, clothing, facial expression, and decoration in their trademarks to accentuate the exotic qualities of the three *subject* races.

The history of French trademarks during the Third Republic

also demonstrates the growing importance of intellectual property rights. Prior to the nineteenth century, a myriad of trademark regulations existed for certain industries, such as soap making and cutlery. One problem with these regulations was that they stipulated different penalties for fraudulent use of registered trademarks depending on the product in question. It was not until the 1840s and 1850s, under the July Monarchy and the Second Empire — governments eager to encourage and protect commerce — that officials seriously discussed changes to industrial property regulations. In 1856, Emperor Napoléon III presented the chamber and senate with the outline of a law on trademarks, which clarified registration procedures, legal rights of the owner, and penalties for abuse and fraudulent use of trademarks. After modifications, the assembly adopted the June 1857 *loi sur les marques de fabrique et de commerce*. This law created a uniform policy for official registration and the legal protection of products manufactured in France, sold by French entrepreneurs living abroad, or sold in France by foreign-owned companies. Although the government did not require an entrepreneur to register product trademarks, without official registration a person had no legal recourse if their products were counterfeited. Those desiring this protection could register their trademark, in duplicate, with the clerk at their local *tribunal de commerce*. The law required foreign companies to register at the Seine (Paris) tribunal.[7]

By the terms of the law, industrial products and foodstuffs were divided alphabetically into seventy-four classes. At the time of registration, the clerk would attach a class designation to the trademark. Common product categories included coffee, chicory, and tea (class 10), cotton cloth (class 67), and soaps (class 64). Registration cost one franc per trademark, plus a fee for the official stamp. Established trademarks were valid for fifteen years and could be renewed. The government modified the terms of this legislation in 1890 and 1920.[8]

The trademarks examined for this study were registered from 1886 to 1940 in Paris and Marseille, France's two largest cities and active centers for colonial organizations and overseas trade.[9] In order to compare annual trademark statistics, we begin in 1886, the first full year following the conference in Berlin that inaugurated an important phase of colonial conquest in Africa. The survey concludes with the end of the Third Republic and the creation of the Vichy regime in 1940. Table 1 shows the number of trademarks

Table 1. Trademarks Registered in Paris and Marseille, 1886–1940

Regional/Racial Groups	Totals in Categories	Yearly Averages
North African (Arab)	810	14.72
Sub-Saharan African (Black)	656	11.92
Indochinese (Asian)	259	4.70
Survey totals	1725	31.34

registered in Paris and Marseille that incorporated depictions of individuals from the three main regional and racial groups within the French empire.[10] A discussion of each of the regional/racial groups and the most common trademark images follows.

North Africans: Mysterious Arabs and Orientals

North Africans appeared on French trademarks and product labels between 1886 and 1940 more than images of any other group. French trademark designers used oriental scenes that evoked images taken from *The 1001 Arabian Nights* as the backdrop for many product labels. Turbaned men seated in Moorish courtyards smoked from long Turkish pipes. Alluring women lounged in palace salons. Arabs on camelback led caravans across endless deserts. Images of the Orient and Arab North Africa meshed, making it impossible to pinpoint the specific location of each scene from the collection of trademarks in this category. The individuals, dwellings, and decor portrayed in these labels describe an exotic oriental world utterly unlike continental Europe. In addition to using these exotic images, merchants depicted North Africans as producers of a range of agricultural products common to their region. Finally, business owners also emphasized Islam to characterize those depicted on the product labels.

Entrepreneurs regularly used exotic scenes of the Orient and North Africa, apparently to draw the French consumer's attention to common products. Merchants marketed items as diverse as Camembert cheese, shoe polish, and silks with trademarks depicting snake charmers, camel caravans, palm trees, and desert oases. The exotic Arab woman or oriental "harem" woman also found her place in French trademarks. In 1907, a company from

Marseille registered a trademark for Chocolat de la Mauresque, which showed a coquette woman with dark hair and eyes holding a fan in one hand and a chocolate bar in the other. The 1938 trademark for Anis El Djenna anisette liqueur presented a woman dancing in a Moorish palace. A number of trademark illustrations for beauty products presented oriental or North African femininity hidden behind Islamic veils. In 1921 Antoine Foucassier named his line of makeup Eclat des Yeux, Sourme! His trademark pictured the head of a Muslim woman wearing a full veil decorated with a crescent and star. The most striking female image in this study appeared on Maurice Viret's 1930 trademark for Fatoüma, a cosmetic product. The label used a sensual photograph of a young North African woman. "Fatoüma" wore a hair scarf, a necklace, and a cape, but had her breasts exposed.

A common exotic portrayal of North African or Arab men incorporated the theme of belligerence or violence. Entrepreneurs pictured Muslim zealots and North African warriors on a variety of trademark labels. Zealot labels depicted pious Muslims or Islamic political leaders as proud men. Warrior trademark labels presented a military figure (identified in the name of the trademark), an individual brandishing a weapon, or both. Sheikhs, *Kroumirs,* and caliphs were among the Muslim warrior "types" shown in trademarks around the turn of the twentieth century. These figures served as popular images for Marseillais businessmen selling soaps, flours, and semolina. Joseph Rougier registered Le Kalife soap trademark in 1892. His label bore a caption in French and in Arabic, and it pictured a man with a sword dangling from his wrist. In 1903 and in 1910 André Allatini's soap company used Le Cheik as its trademark. The *cheik* stood next to his horse, wore a turban, vest, and harem pants, and held a gun. The *Kroumirs,* a Tunisian ethnic group reportedly known for raiding and pillaging, served as a trademark symbol for a number of products. Entrepreneurs used the *Kroumir* image on soap trademarks in 1896, 1909, 1924, and 1939, on a flour label in 1910, for bleach in 1908, and for coffee in 1911. Café le Targui (1930), with its silhouette of a turbaned man on camelback, typifies the warrior trademarks (fig. 1). Other images of North African fighters — albeit nonthreatening members of French colonial units known as *Zouaves* (infantry) or *Spahis* (cavalry) — adorned an array of product labels. *Zouaves* appeared on dozens of trademarks for cigarette papers, particularly those registered by the Braunstein Brothers, throughout the fifty-five years of this survey.

Figure 1. Café le Targui trademark (Marseille, 1930), P. Agostini and M. Cheminaud

Trademark labels featuring Muslim religious figures were easily identifiable from the name of the product — often a religious title or the name of a Muslim order. In the 1890s and early 1900s, the Islamic marabout (ascetic) graced several French trademarks, including F. Cordeil and Company's Les Deux Marabouts soaps (1904). A Marseillais business owned by Maurin and Bontoux selected Le Senoussi, a Muslim brotherhood, as its grains' trademark (1913). The Senoussi pictured on the trademark label wore a white, hooded robe and had a sad expression on his face.

Many French entrepreneurs who pictured North Africans or Arabs on their trademarks did so not necessarily because such representations had exotic appeal, but because the product they were marketing came from the region. The Mediterranean coast of North Africa flourished in the production of fruits and grains. Indeed, after soaps and cleaning products, the most common class of products that featured North Africans or Arabs on trademarks was grains, with about 10 percent of the total trademarks belonging to this regional/racial category. Companies from Marseille registered nearly all of the grain trademarks included in this survey — an indication of their major role in the flour and semolina market in France. These businesses often chose a drawing of a turbaned head, a *tête d'Arabe*, or of men with exotic Arabic names or historical significance. Marseillais businessman Coundouris named his grains after the twelfth-century Egyptian sultan Saladin. Merchants also named their flours and semolinas after North African women. Popular figures included *la Bédouine* and *la Tunisienne*. French entrepreneurs affixed drawings of North Africans on their trademarks for other regional products such as dates, oranges, and wine.

Sub-Saharan Africans and Blacks

The sub-Saharan African and the "black" (*le noir* or *le nègre*), who represented a generic model of people of African descent, appeared prominently on hundreds of registered trademark illustrations between 1886 and 1940. Certainly the most famous trademark of the period belongs to Banania, the nutritional breakfast drink that featured a West African soldier remarking "Y'a Bon!" The association of Banania with Africa during World War I and afterwards proved tremendously successful, and the product is still a popular beverage for children in France. Few are aware, however, that the banana-chocolate cereal beverage originated in Nicaragua. Pierre-François Lardet, founder of the Banania company in Courbevoie, France, tasted the drink when visiting an Indian village in 1909.[11] The Banania trademark and the numerous posters with the grinning *tirailleur sénégalais* illustrate two themes in trademarks of the 1920s and 1930s — blacks in the role of the child and as soldiers. French trademarks registered in this period also presented sub-Saharan Africans as entertainers and, especially, as laborers for whites. This last theme is evident in the earliest trademarks of the nineteenth century.

Commercial images of blacks and Africans in the late 1880s evoked the plantation slavery system, which had only been dismantled in the middle of the century. Drawings of black domestic servants and black agricultural workers on these early trademark labels were essentially familiar drawings of house slaves and field slaves from the Caribbean. Some of these scenes showed French planters in tailored, white, three-piece suits surveying their lands, while black workers in loincloths and shifts labored over crops.

Such drawings made master and servant roles clear, confirming the inferior position of the black to the consumer.

Even more prominent than the plantation scenes, which appeared infrequently after 1900, were the trademarks that featured blacks as domestic servants. Many of these trademarks were for dark-colored products such as coffee, cocoa, and chicory, and they emphasized blackness as a positive attribute. They also displayed two relationships between the black image and the product. First, the dark pigmentation of Africans and mulattoes represented the color of the beverages. Second, blacks played an important role in harvesting coffee and cocoa in plantations in America and Africa and, moreover, had the job of preparing and serving the beverages as servants in European households. Usually, black servants in these labels wore fancy butler uniforms. The Bamboula label (1926), however, depicted a man wearing only striped shorts, dancing and playing a tambourine in the center of a table decorated with cups of steaming coffee (fig. 2).

Although coffee and chocolate trademarks associated blackness with the strength or qualities of the products, trademark labels for soaps, bleaches, and household cleaning products defined blackness as a decidedly negative trait. Several companies humorously asserted that their product was powerful enough to bleach a black person white. A laundry bleach called La Négresse, registered in 1888, presented a "before and after" drawing to suggest that La Négresse whitened the best. Jeffh, Savon à la Pierre Ponce (1911), pictured the special soap cleaning black children. In trademark depictions like these, French products washed or bleached away blackness, and, moreover, black adults and children in the drawings actively cooperated with the process. The soap and bleach trademarks promoted the often-cited idea that black people were under the "curse of Ham," and that their dark skin color and inferior status constituted a punishment from God.[12]

Three unique images of blacks appear in trademarks between 1914 and 1940. With the advent of the Great War, entrepreneurs adopted images of West African colonial soldiers on their new product trademarks. Thousands of the African soldiers fought and died in the trenches or supported the war effort from military bases in southern France. The *tirailleur sénégalais* was portrayed as a friendly and harmless character. Except for his uniform, little in his appearance or disposition communicated strength or military preparedness. The *tirailleur* images on trademarks presented blacks as

Figure 2. Bamboula trademark (Marseille, 1926), Etablissements V. and M. Carretier

carefree and childlike, quite unlike depictions of proud, fierce African warriors that appeared in the popular press and in some trademarks in the 1880s and 1890s.

Between 1915 and 1925, ten businesses incorporated the *tirailleur sénégalais* image into their trademarks for products ranging from chocolate to water-purifying tablets. Half of these trademarks were registered in 1915, the year when the grinning Banania "Y'a bon!" soldier first appeared on advertising posters. The popularity of the Banania image sparked two imitations. Chocolat! Y a Bon! combined the soldier image with the traditionally black advertising scheme for the chocolate bar, and the Kir-re-gal, Y a bon! trademark marketed a line of canned foods. The Kir-re-gal soldier held up a can in one hand and, with wide eyes and a big smile, tried to persuade the viewer to purchase the delicacy. His expression, as in most of the *tirailleur sénégalais* labels, was jovial and carefree. The Kir-re-gal soldier reflected the stereotype of the *bon noir* or *bon nègre* — a harmless, infantile black figure, devoid of power despite his military role.

Another category of trademarks presented Africans and blacks as children and childish adults. Most of these portrayals characterized young blacks as mischievous, simpleminded, ignorant, and unruly. Often the drawings were unflattering or humorous caricatures. For example, in 1922, the Café des Gourmets label depicted a mischievous child naked except for his white socks. As the child drank

Race on Product Trademarks 139

from the spout of a coffeepot, most of the beverage spilled from the top of the pot onto the ground. Alexandre Rannou and Company of Marseille selected a drawing of a black man climbing a date palm tree for their Honey Brand and Nigger Brand date products (1922). The comic figure clung to the trunk of the palm, trying to munch on dates, as his long legs and big feet dangled in the air. Another Marseillais business adopted a hideous drawing of a black dunce for its Yoyo Soda trademark. The character contorted his face as he sipped from a straw placed in a dish of soda. This was one of the most demeaning images in the survey.

The last new type of image found on Parisian and Marseillais trademarks in the postwar period was that of the entertainer. In the 1920s, a series of trademarks pictured blacks as musicians and dancers. Undoubtedly, this new image reflected changes in postwar French society, including official praise of black soldiers and a growing interest in black American entertainers in Paris, such as Josephine Baker. Several of the trademark labels with black entertainers included unique designs. In 1923, the Cafés Négrita label showed a black showgirl seated on a crescent moon, holding out a cup of steaming coffee. Pierrot the clown was climbing a ladder, hoping to reach her. In 1927, French entrepreneurs Jeanne and Marie Le Blanc registered their new cookies with the name Biscuits Black-Bottom and used a black saxophone player to illustrate the label. As the large-lipped man played his saxophone, cookies escaped out the end of his instrument. In the same year, a Marseillais company pictured a black male dancer on its Charleston label for household and industrial soaps. The man was dressed in tight white shorts and struck a dance pose. In addition to the nightclub scenes, ten other entertainer labels pictured African drummers and percussionists.

In these newer trademark depictions of sub-Saharan Africans and blacks, entrepreneurs tempered black strengths with comic, infantile images. The black African soldier never had a serious expression on his face. Black men and children served as commercial buffoons. Images of nightclub entertainers portrayed blacks in a more realistic but still stereotypical role. Through their trademark labels, business owners showed French consumers that blacks were childlike beings, destined to amuse and entertain them.

Indochinese and the Asian "Race"

Trademarks registered in France between 1886 and 1940 presented an exotic view of Indochina as part of a generic Far Eastern culture. Generally, French entrepreneurs portrayed people from the Far East as members of a single "race" with Chinese or Japanese cultural traits. Some, however, distinguished among Vietnamese, Cambodians, and their Asian neighbors to the north. In the trademark images, merchants relied on a stereotype that accentuated the manual skills and mild disposition of Asians. This survey includes all trademark labels that represent a product specified as Indochinese and all those that depict Asian people, but have no clear link to any particular country.

The Indochinese labels displayed three distinguishing aspects. First, they used traditional Asian symbols to help define the exotic nature of the product. Second, they usually marketed a limited variety of regional products. Third, with some exceptions, the labels included stereotypical portrayals of diligent Asian workers and servants. These three elements combined to reinforce the representation of Indochinese as gentle people who made humble French subjects.

The commercial image of Asians and Indochinese near the beginning of the twentieth century was associated with special cultural symbols. Emanating from religious beliefs or artistic traditions, these symbols made up one dimension of the exotic portrayal of the race. Companies that registered trademarks with Asian themes generally used drawings with elements that evoked beauty and nature. Trees, flowers, plants, and gardens were the most common natural symbols used. They served as the centerpiece or background of the trademark label designs. Some labels included birds and domesticated animals — Chinese symbols of spiritual resurrection (birds) and a good or peaceful life — while others were decorated with wild animals and mythical creatures such as dragons and giant-winged birds. For Asian consumers, the dragon had cultural significance as the controller of life-giving rain.

The majority of the "exotic Asia" trademarks communicated beauty and serenity in common situations and natural settings. They presented people in a variety of poses — standing outdoors with hats and parasols, seated in homes and on terraces, drinking or serving tea, and meditating. In 1892, the Maumy Brothers of Paris, fabric merchants, registered a trademark with a woman standing on a porch, dressed in a kimono, and holding a fan. The scene was framed with bamboo (a symbol of longevity), and in the background were plants and birds. In 1909, a company in Marseille named its pepper condiment Le Saïgonnais and registered a trademark label with a mustached man wearing a wide-brimmed hat. Paris-based F. Marquis Chocolate company used an illustration of an Asian woman standing in a garden to sell its candies in 1921.

The most important regional products marketed with images of Asians or Indochinese were tea, rice, and natural fibers in the form of thread or cloth. The bamboo-framed illustration for Fleurs de Souchong d'Annam (1904) pictured a woman in a garden holding up a branch of tea leaves. Another tea label, Fleur de Thé Imperiale d'Annam (1912), contained panels with the Chinese dragon and a woman wearing a Japanese kimono and hairstyle. This trademark is an example of how the French mixed images and symbols from different Asian countries to create a product label for an "Annamite" (Vietnamese) tea. A tea trademark design belonging to the Société de Produits Coloniaux Français (1933) offered a contemporary rendition of an Indochinese woman (fig. 3).

French entrepreneurs often pictured Asians at work on their product trademarks. We can divide the trademarks that include worker scenes into two categories: group work scenes and individuals at specific tasks. When examining the labels, the primary image coincides with the general theme of Indochinese or Asians as mild-mannered and diligent people. Women were depicted as gracious and submissive; men as meticulous craftsmen or laboring "coolies." Drawings on several labels showed distinctions between upper-class Asians and workers. A few labels pictured Indochinese serving European clients.

The best examples of groups depicted at work are Thé Noir, Thé pour Déjeuner (1913), Les Lolos (1910, 1912), and Laque Dubois (1907, 1922). On the Thé Noir label, the illustration contained two parts: one section pictured Asian workers cultivating tea leaves, and the second part showed servants carrying an Asian dignitary in a palanquin. The Lolos labels used the image of male workers with braids weaving fabric at a loom.[13] On the Laque Dubois label, three women in kimonos were painting vases.

The majority of the trademarks with Indochinese or Asians, however, featured one person at work or demonstrating the product. In 1909, Marseillais businessman Paul Vian marketed Le Pousse Pousse brand of flours and semolina. The *pousse-pousse* (rickshaw)

Figure 3. Tea trademark of Indochinese woman (Paris, 1933), Société de Produits Coloniaux Français

driver in the label pulled along a white female passenger. The Etablissement Weeks used an Asian man in its 1927 trademark for varnishes and paints. Seated cross-legged on the ground and wearing a straw hat, the man held up a jar of Weeks paint and a paintbrush. Philippe Millot, a Paris businessman, chose an Asian motif for his Fagoda, Polish Oriental in 1923. In the foreground of his illustration, a man shook the product onto a sponge. In the background stood a pagoda, perhaps waiting to be polished. Millot seemed to have a gift for clever labels. Just a month and a half after registering the Fagoda Polish, he established two trademarks for Aladdan Shampoo, a laundry soap. The most interesting of the two showed a woman in a kimono pulling an oriental carpet with a box of the shampoo visible to the side. Millot's Aladdan Shampoo illustration is a unique and poignant example of the mixture of stereotypical images. The blend of *Arabian Nights* imagery and the Asian launderer stereotype must have caught the attention of consumers. Although there are a number of striking trademark images depicting Indochinese and Asians, they made up a small number of the total trademarks in this survey. On the average, only four to five companies registered these product trademarks annually — about half the number of the trademarks incorporating sub-Saharan Africans or blacks and one-third the number with North Africans and Arabs.

Through the images they incorporate, French commercial trademarks registered during the Third Republic demonstrate how entrepreneurs imagined race during a period of European economic and territorial expansion in Africa and Asia. Entrepreneurs associated racial categories with specific products, relying on symbolic linkages between physical traits, such as complexion, and the characteristics of their wares. They also featured drawings of people from colonial regions where their products originated. Quite often, however, these drawings were generalized portrayals according to familiar racial or cultural markers. For example, a woman in a Japanese kimono could appear on a label for "Vietnamese" tea or a woman wearing Caribbean attire could represent a product from Senegal. Except for the new images of Africans and blacks as soldiers, entertainers, and children from the 1910s on, portrayals of race and racial stereotypes remained constant over the fifty-five-year period of this survey. By the 1930s, French entrepreneurs relied on a limited repertoire of visual symbols to embellish their trademarks. The most common of these were the turbaned head of the Arab nomad, the infantile grin of the African, and the wide-brimmed straw hat of the Indochinese worker. As entrepreneurs placed these and other symbols on their trademark illustrations, they contributed to the French consumer's view of colonial peoples as exotics, laborers in the battlefield or rice field, and inferiors who stood to benefit from the government's "civilizing" efforts.

On a recent visit to France, I was reminded of the lingering nostalgia of the empire and the power of commercial images. During a trip to the supermarket, a box of Banania glared out at me from the breakfast drink aisle. The head of a grinning wide-eyed African soldier had replaced the image on the 1990s Banania box. One side of the box contained a brief history of the Banania trademark, complete with an insert of the original 1915 poster featuring a *tirailleur sénégalais* sampling the beverage. On the opposite side, the Bestfoods France company encouraged consumers to participate in "Opération Banania" by sending in proof-of-purchase labels and money to buy Banania memorabilia. Ironically, the recycled African soldier image on the new boxes was first used in 1959, a date that marked the end of the French empire in Sub-Saharan Africa. This recent Banania campaign is a poignant commercial illustration of how, decades into the postcolonial period, myth and racial stereotypes thrive in France.

Notes

1 In this article I use the term *race* in the French context of this period to mean categories of human difference based on phenotypical and cultural traits.

2 Studies on this topic include William H. Schneider's *An Empire for the Masses: The French Popular Image of Africa, 1870–1900* (Westport, Conn.: Greenwood, 1982); Catherine Hodeir and Michel Pierre, *L'exposition coloniale* (1931; Brussels: Complexe, 1991); Raymond Bacholet et al., *Négripub: L'image des noirs dans la publicité depuis un siècle* (Paris: Somogy, 1992); Nicolas Bancel, Pascal Blanchard, and Laurent Gervereau, eds., *Images et colonies: Iconographie et propagande coloniales sur l'Afrique française de 1880 à 1962* (Paris: ACHAC, 1993); David Prochaska, "L'Algérie imaginaire: Jalons pour une histoire de l'iconographie coloniale," *Gradhiva* 7 (1989): 29–38; and Christraud M. Geary and Virginia-Lee Webb, eds., *Delivering Views: Distant Cultures in Early Postcards* (Washington, D.C.: Smithsonian Institution Press, 1998).

3 Vanessa R. Schwartz, *Spectacular Realities: Early Mass Culture in Fin-de-Siècle Paris* (Berkeley: University of California Press, 1998).

4 Jacques Marseille, *Empire colonial et capitalisme français: Histoire d'un divorce* (Paris: Albin Michel, 1984).

5 Rosalind Williams, *Dream Worlds: Mass Consumption in Late Nineteenth-Century France* (Berkeley: University of California Press, 1982); Whitney Walton, *France at the Crystal Palace: Bourgeois Taste and Artisan Manufacture in the Nineteenth Century* (Berkeley: University of California Press, 1992).

6 These ideas are grounded in the thought of George-Louis Leclerc de Buffon, Ernest Renan, and Arthur de Gobineau. For a description of the evolution of French racial thought, see Tzvetan Todorov, *On Human Diversity: Nationalism, Racism, and Exoticism in French Thought*, trans. Catherine Porter (Cambridge, Mass.: Harvard University Press, 1993); and William B. Cohen, *The French Encounter with Africans: White Response to Blacks, 1530–1880* (Bloomington: Indiana University Press, 1980).

7 See the discussion on the background of the 1857 law in *Annales de la propriété industrielle, artistique et littéraire* 4, 1 (1858): 9–70.

8   In the 1920 revision of trademark regulations, the government created a new classification system that included eighty product classes, separated into nine groups respectively: agricultural products; untreated materials to be crafted; semiprocessed products; tools, equipment, machines, and transportation devices; construction; furniture, household goods, and housekeeping articles; threads, cloth, rugs, dyes, and clothing; novelty items; foodstuffs; education/teaching, sciences, fine arts, miscellaneous.

9   Portions of this research appeared in my doctoral dissertation entitled "Races on Display: French Representations of the Colonial Native, 1886–1931" (Brandeis University, 1998). I am grateful to Brigitte Lainé of the Archives de Paris for pointing out the trademark registers and their significance.

10 Annual statistics for this period, which are compiled by the French trademark and patent office (Institut National de Propriété Industrielle — INPI) and published in the *Bulletin officiel de la propriété industrielle*, give national totals of trademark registrations separated by class, rather than by departmental totals. The total number of trademarks registered in 1886 was 5520. Statistics for several years between 1910 and 1920 are unavailable, but it appears that registrations increased steadily until World War I. (They surpassed 20,000 in 1912.) The average annual number of registrations between 1920 and 1940 was 14,828. The 20,000 mark was not reached again until 1946.

11 For the complete history of Banania, see Jean Garrigues's *Banania: Historie d'une passion française* (Paris: Du May, 1991); and Daniel Cauzard et al., *Le livre des marques* (Paris: Du May, 1993), 28–29.

12 See Gen. 9:20–27 for the root of this myth. Noah, not God, pronounces the curse.

13 Most likely, the Lolos label refers to the Lolos ethnic group in Laos.

Leora Auslander and Thomas C. Holt

Sambo in Paris

Race and Racism in the Iconography

of the Everyday

This article on the meanings of race and perceptions of racialized representations in late-twentieth-century France was born of a summer afternoon's chance encounter in Paris almost a decade ago. Following lunch in the Place des Vosges, we were wandering through the arcades and curio shops that frame the square, making our way aimlessly toward the pleasing strains of a jazz band we had heard at a distance, slightly out of view amidst the afternoon crowd. As we approached, we noticed first that all the musicians were white, an observation that did not greatly surprise us in a European city enjoying a decades-old love affair with this particular art form. Our second discovery, however, was dumbfounding. Instead of using the conventional hat or music case to collect the offerings of the audience, the band had chosen a life-size statue of a black man (fig. 1). The statue — in its too-bright shirt and pants, open collar, loose tie, thick, exaggeratedly red lips, servile smile, and bulging eyes — fully embodied the traditional stigmata of racist imagery. The statue was not only racist, but was a thoroughly American racist representation, pulled directly from the nineteenth-century minstrel theatrical tradition. The use of such a relic of America's racist past by musicians who clearly had a deep respect for contemporary African American music was jarring. Indeed, the depth of our dismay was perhaps attributable in large part to the sense of betrayal — of having been emotionally conned — that this bizarre juxtaposition evoked.[1] This feeling was perhaps even stronger because we, as leftist Americans who spend a significant amount of time in France, absolutely did not expect to encounter American racist representations there.

The Place des Vosges incident might well have passed on to become just another amusing anecdote — fit for casual party conversa-

Figure 1. Life-size, minstrel-like figure used to collect contributions by a jazz band at Place des Vosges, Paris, August 1992. Photograph by Auslander and Holt.

tion rather than scholarly investigation — had it not been reinforced by similar encounters that summer. Having become sensitized to these kinds of images, we rapidly discovered their ubiquity in our neighborhood, the Marais (in the fourth arrondissement), as well as elsewhere in Paris. We found statues presenting menus at the entrances to restaurants, black figures used in shop window displays, and even a store in the rue Saint-Antoine offering for sale a whole bazaar of racialized figures, including miniaturized jazz orchestras and a life-size "pickaninny" seated on a couch. Some of these objects were *racist*, by which we mean representations that deform, exaggerate, or render grotesque the body or face, or that represent the figures as servile or stupid. Other objects were, by contrast, *racialized*, that is, figures having stereotyped faces or bodies without being deformed. More than an anomaly, therefore, the band's use of a "sambo" seemed one instance of a common practice. In addition to the omnipresence of these images, we also came to be struck by another phenomenon — differences in how people perceived those images.

A few days after that first encounter, seeking a place to have

Figure 2. Bellhop figure used as menu-holder at Place St. Catherine, Paris, August 1992. Photograph by Auslander and Holt.

lunch, Leora suggested a restaurant, about half a block away, that had caught her eye. Tom followed her gesture and quickly responded, "No, I don't think I want to eat there." This abrupt response puzzled Leora until she realized that this particular restaurant was using a statue of a life-size black man (this time wearing something like a bellhop's uniform) to offer its menu to the view of the passersby (fig. 2). This incident added a new concern to our puzzle. Why, particularly given that we had been talking about this issue for the past several days, had one of us seen, in the literal sense of the word, the figure before the other? Differences in experience of race could, in part, provide an explanation for why Tom, who is black, saw the image immediately, while Leora, who is white, did not. We do not want to suggest racial categorization as the only salient experience for perception, but in this case, it would appear to be the most important. In the course of our analysis, we have come to understand more profoundly how the senses, too, are socially constructed: what we see, what we hear, what we "sense," differs according to our collective as well as our personal experiences; that is, according to both the experiences we endure and our conscious reflection on them.[2]

Our different modes of seeing were echoed when we described our encounters to some good friends and colleagues. None of them—all native French, longtime residents of Paris, active leftists, and firm antiracists—had noticed the flourishing of these portrayals. In fact, we had to convince them that the imagery was indeed as ubiquitous a presence in the city as we claimed. They then argued that we were misinterpreting the statues, that we had to understand that their context in France differed from that in America. French racism did not target blacks, it targeted North Africans. Since France did not have a history of metropolitan slavery, twentieth-century France had not inherited the same relation to racial difference as existed in the United States. We were, partially, in agreement with this argument. It is surely true that colonial history in France and the history of slavery in the United States left different traces behind. We did not want to suggest that the racist statues meant exactly the same thing in the United States and France; but we were also not ready to accept that they had no racialized meaning at all in the French context, that they said nothing about the construction of racial difference in France.

Our friends then added another argument about the national differences between the United States and France. They suggested that the symbolic did not have the same meaning on the two sides of the Atlantic. One needed to understand that the statues, in France, belonged to the same category, to the same semiotic system, as the cakes called *tête de nègre*, or a bar called Au Petit Nègre, a system that also embraced ordinary cakes, like the *religieuses* (or nuns) or *jésuites*. Names, images, and race just did not mean the same thing in France as in the United States. Because of the differing place of the arts in French and American educational systems, Americans tended to be literal in their visual practice, while the French showed more sophistication. Once again, we both agreed and were not completely convinced. It is certainly probable that French people and Americans do not perceive in the same way—just as white and black Americans do not see the same things—but we were not persuaded that a *jésuite* and a *tête de nègre* are quite comparable, or did the same symbolic work, in a context in which racialized images (but not religious ones) abounded and in which racist incidents and debates over racism were almost daily events.

These encounters—with the objects themselves and with variations on the theme of their invisibility—left us with a set of questions, some simple, some more complicated. First of all, what were these objects doing in France in the late twentieth century? How did they get there and what political or cultural role did they play? Had their racial meanings completely changed or been lost? Were they tied to contemporary French racial, cultural, or national identity, and if so, how? A second order of query involved perception, politics, and everyday life. We started off wondering why people of very similar political position and vision of the world perceived these objects so differently (at least at first). This took us to a broader interrogation of the manner in which we perceive the objects that furnish our everyday lives. Here again, the word *perceive* is used in a dual sense, meaning both the act of literal, physical recognition and the attribution of meaning. This interest in perception led us back to the objects themselves, pressing us to inquire into how everyday iconography shapes contemporary life in general and race relations in particular. We sought to understand the degree to which goods produced in one commercial context, in moving across time and space, could both transport and lose their original meanings. In each case, the objects seemed to have a great fluidity, were susceptible to radically different uses, and could mean very different things in the present or the past, in the United States or in France. And yet, notwithstanding this plasticity, there exists a necessary intertextual relation between these contemporary objects and their original prototypes; they can never be completely detached from their birthplace, their original meanings, or their historicity.

We have come to see, therefore, that these images may well provide clues to two urgent intellectual and political questions of our age: the interrelationship of the global and the local and the current configurations of race, racialization, and racism. A detailed study of the objects' physical and historical character — as well as of the trajectory of their production, distribution, and consumption in France and America (with some preliminary explorations in Japan and Germany as well) — demonstrates concretely the oft-made theoretical observation that capitalist cultural forms are fantastically, magically, it seems, adaptable. The racialized objects in France, the United States, Germany, and Japan are *simultaneously* global and local. They would not exist without global media, cultural, and commodity flows, but they are differentiated and particularized in each local habitat. But we hope to contribute not only to the better understanding of the national's relation to the transnational; we also attempt to understand the making of race in that global/local world. We will argue that the complex interplay of desire and repulsion, adoration and vilification, mimesis and alterity that define the Parisian racialized objects and their use, characterize the construction of race generally in the late twentieth century. Thus the conceptual key to many global — and often abstract — issues, we believe, lies in the study of commonplace experience and the concrete objects of everyday life with which and from which ordinary people invest and draw extraordinary meanings.

Our research started, then, with a set of questions concerning race, racism, perception, and systems of representation. As we turned, or returned, to the literatures on these topics, we realized that although national traditions mark all three, national marking surfaces particularly in the case of the scholarship on race and racism. Given the centrality these issues have had in the United States since the nation's founding, a very long tradition of research on race exists. The French literature is of more recent date, and different in emphasis. In this research project, we have used both the American and French literatures, acknowledging diversities within each national intellectual production and borrowing from each conceptualizations that seemed most helpful to untangling our particular set of puzzles.[3] Because both the national practices of racialization and modes of thinking about race seemed most salient here (and complex enough on their own), we also chose to focus on those issues here, leaving the more elaborated discussion of perception and the everyday to another moment.[4]

The Physical and Historical Description of the Objects

Given this methodological commitment to the concrete phenomena of everyday life, it is important to begin with a more detailed description of the objects themselves and of their location in French space. The majority are statues, with a clearly American referent, depicting black men and women in various poses of work or leisure, ranging in size from the very small (suitable for a tabletop or display case) to the life-size (most likely for commercial display purposes). Also available on the market, although rarer, are statues of North Africans and of "moors."

The objects we encountered fall into four categories: Some are antiques — American, French, Austrian, English, or Japanese in origin. Some are contemporary French, Chinese, and American reproductions of those antiques, often accompanied when displayed for sale by certificates of authenticity. The third group comprises the

Figure 3.
Minstrel-like
figures on sale at
the Saint Ouen
flea market,
August 1994.
Photograph by
Elisa Camiscioli.

pseudoantiques, closely modeled after the genuinely old, but either slightly modified for reasons of copyright or modernized. The last category consists of objects of current French design, manufactured either in France or in China. Differentiating between exact reproductions of old objects and new objects inspired by those same old forms is important because the two have different relationships to history. The reproductions simply make a scarce commodity or object of collection available to a wider market. The new "old" forms necessitate the production of new kinds of representation.

The putatively old figures are sold by antique dealers, in curio shops, at the *marché aux puces* in Saint Ouen just outside Paris, and at annual antique fairs (fig. 3). The antiques of North American design or provenance, we discovered, come largely out of the American minstrel tradition and depict servile characters, such as bellhops, caddies, shoeshine boys, or liveried figures. The genuinely old American objects, therefore, tend to be unambiguously racist representations of blacks as dumb, servile, and comic. These we have designated collectively as sambo images. The figures of Japanese origin available on the antique and used goods markets also appear as statues largely of this American genre, but produced in Japan.

The genuinely old French and European objects are more varied. They include figurines of jazz musicians and entertainers from the 1920s, especially Josephine Baker, but others as well. (There is also a strong interest in the Paul Colin posters advertising Josephine Baker shows.) Like the American minstrel figures, these are stereotyped forms, complete with bug-eyes, thick lips, and bodily contortions.[5] Alongside these statuettes and images exist varied representations emergent from France's colonial history, including bellhops with vaguely semitic features and advertising materials, such as the notorious Banania *tirailleur* and the Kabyle water carriers. Finally, available through the antique market, are moorish and orientalist clay or bronze figures. These statues, depicting barely clothed sub-Saharan or North African men and women, sometimes freestanding, often bent under a heavy burden, frequently enslaved, were produced mostly by the Goldscheider company.[6] Lastly, there are also a very few statues and paintings dating from the eighteenth century which represent "moors."

Demand, in the 1990s, for these older renditions of American, moorish, and North African figures appears to have exceeded supply. We found a lively market in reproductions, which not only increased the quantity of goods, but also made them accessible to those on a smaller budget. A number of companies seem to have engaged in this production, including the Parisian firm Apparence, which bought the license to make reproductions of Goldscheider casts. Claims to authenticity appear important; the figures have a label marked "réédition" on the bottom, and they carry a tag stating: "Réédition Collection Goldscheider 1885, peint à la main, créé à l'ancienne" [Reproduction, Goldscheider 1885 Collection, hand painted, created in the traditional style]. Other companies also produced statues based on the Goldscheiders, but copyright concerns required them to make variations in their designs.

The design, production, and distribution history of the reproductions, modernized copies, and new figures is thus very complex. As best as we have been able to determine, six major producers of these figures based in or selling heavily in France existed in the 1990s: Apparence, Artedosa, Optimum, Statueo, Ros, and All That Jazz. In addition, there appear to have been some independent artisans producing for sale at the Saint Ouen flea market. The figures marketed by All That Jazz were made in China, but appear to have been designed in France.[7] Artedosa advertised the artisanal nature of its production and apparently manufactured figures in France. According to a salesclerk at a major retail outlet for Artedosa, Optimum, and Apparence, the same artist/designer may have worked freelance for several companies.[8] Finally, journalist accounts indicate that the company Etc. Collectibles in Bristol, Tennessee, which produced and distributed reproductions, also sold them in France.[9] By the mid-1980s, however, statues of French design, and often of French production, appear to have dominated the French market.[10]

Exact reproductions of the old and a liminal category between reproduction and new design—the pseudo-old, that is, designs that capture the spirit of the originals but with slight variations—coexist. Both American and orientalist figures serve as models for this kind of pseudoauthentic copying. The orientalist *terre cuite*, or bronze, representations of North Africans are ethnographic (the figures are all depicted engaged in "traditional" activities) and thereby profoundly othered, but their faces are not distorted, exaggerated, or otherwise grotesque. The American figures and the moorish category of European figures of this genre are, on the other hand, to our eyes systematically and stereotypically racist. These figures are shown with large gold rings through their ears (and often their noses), turbaned, often grimacing. They crouch, supporting tables on their backs, or most often, stand, holding lamps, or miniaturized into a rum set, carrying rum and glasses. The American statues are invariably servile or foolish, either footmen or pickaninnies. We think, as will be elaborated below, that it is not an accident that very few contemporary productions of frankly racist representations of North Africans exist and sell in France today.

But not all of the new statuettes claim an authentic referent. Tellingly, we have not been able to find any originary object for one of the most prevalent forms—representations of jazz musicians. Generally, these statues do not have exaggerated facial features, and their clothing and poses are not degrading (fig. 4). These figures appear genuinely new—French designers created them—produced either in France or in China, and distributed in France, Germany, and probably elsewhere in the world. Many of these are signed and copyrighted. For example, Apparence markets some of its figures with a label identifying them as designed by Jacky Samson for the Collection Apparence, and they thus have a certificate of authenticity that apparently refers to the contemporary creator rather than

Sambo in Paris 155

Figure 4. Life-size jazzman figure, Place des Vosges, Paris, August 1992. Photograph by Auslander and Holt.

an antique provenance. In addition, the label carries a notification of copyright. These figures highlight the complexity of these representations' meaning, especially as in the majority of cases (although certainly not all) they were sold side by side with indisputably racist statues.

African-produced parodies of colonial life further complicated this story of race and representation. These statues, depicting Africans in stereotypically European colonial dress, were also very visible on the French scene and drew quite high prices. Another example of a complicating image would be the figure holding the menu outside the restaurant La Soufrière in Paris (fig. 5). This is an Antillean restaurant, owned by black Martinicans, and the figure was produced in Martinique. When our research assistant Elisa Camiscioli interviewed a waiter in the restaurant, he found absurd her suggestion that the figure was racist. These figures were common in the Antilles, he claimed, known there affectionately as "Coco."

The range of racialized statues and statuettes available on the

Figure 5. "Coco" at La Soufrière, rue du Cardinal Lemoine, Paris, August 1994. Photograph by Elisa Camiscioli.

Parisian marketplace was thus very broad. We focus here, however, specifically on the figures of American provenance or reference. These figures are the most ubiquitous and, in some sense, the most surprising: since a long history of the representation of racialized others exists in France, why import American figures, or make new figures with an American referent? Discovering what figures were available for purchase covers only part of the story, however; it is equally crucial to determine where they sold, at what price, and to whom.

Our original impression that these figures were concentrated in the Marais and neighborhoods like it was both confirmed and contradicted over the course of our research. The Marais is one of the oldest neighborhoods in Paris, a prime tourist attraction, and the location of a lively gay male culture. It has joined the Latin Quarter as an expensive and chic place to live, without having become as stolidly bourgeois as the seventh, eighth, or sixteenth arrondissements. We have discovered that although various versions of these statues are to be found all over Paris, they seem to concentrate in more well-to-do neighborhoods there and elsewhere.[11] Prices for these objects also ranged widely, but they were generally relatively expensive (the cheapest were about 50FF, the most expensive about 5,000FF, with most costing several hundred).[12]

Both the scale of these objects and their cost, as well as simple curiosity, raise the question of who buys these figures. One clearly important market is commercial. These black figures are used to help sell things — from restaurant meals, to jewelry, to sweets — and to attract and entertain customers. An elegant jewelry store on the rue de Bellechasse in the fancy seventh arrondissement used a small statuette as part of its window display; the Pressing du Seine — a laundromat in the equally posh sixth arrondissement — had a life-size black caddy leaning nonchalantly on his customer's golf bag under a potted palm, and an expensive English shoe store on the rue des Archives in the fourth had a life-size mannequin equipped with leather apron and shoe-shining equipment. Restaurants all over Paris (and elsewhere in France) used the figures to hold their menus and as interior decoration.[13]

As we will show, these statues do not exist in isolation from other aspects of commercial culture in France, but are intimately related to the long history of the development of commercial culture and advertising. Racialized commercial objects (as opposed to both advertising and architectural and painterly depictions of blacks) date at least from the era of the First World War, and they reveal the clear historical linkages between such objects of common use and the ads shaping our everyday sentient space. Indeed, what often begins as an advertising logo soon becomes a freestanding commodity. In the 1920s, for example, the popularity of Josephine Baker was capitalized on by selling Josephine Baker dolls and other objects. Similarly, in the 1930s, the Senegalese *tirailleur* moved off the Banania box and posters and onto the daily breakfast table pitchers and mugs.[14]

The racialized statuary and advertising in Paris that has proliferated since the mid-1980s therefore forms both part of an older tradition and of something new; it is both linked to a global commodity network and is distinctively French. One aspect of those linkages, we will argue, is the complex relation between France and America in the twentieth century. We cannot begin to understand those relations, therefore, without understanding the original American historical context for the appearance and usage of the sambo images.

American Precedents and Analogies

It is neither accidental nor incidental that the most numerous and among the most objectionable of the figures found in Paris are faithful copies of poses, images, and characterizations popularized by the American minstrel theater in the early nineteenth century. The originals of these so-called mammies, Uncle Toms, dandies, and pickaninnies all served as stock characters in minstrel performances and were supposedly modeled on people found on southern slave plantations or in northern cities. But minstrel theater provides more than the physical, historical precedents for contemporary sambo figures; it also provides analogs for interpreting their meaning.

From their birth in the 1830s, minstrel caricatures had a continuing influence on American theater throughout the nineteenth and early twentieth centuries, including strong echoes in twentieth-century vaudeville and early radio and television. That influence proved pervasive and extensive across all strata of society, from theaters catering to the working class to performances before American presidents and the royal courts of Europe. The minstrel show was, moreover, an art form claiming authentic black provenance, though articulated by white artists in the service of assuaging white angst; one whose essence lay in the derogation and stereotyping of African Americans, yet one that provided practically the only access blacks had to professional theatrical careers from the late nineteenth to the mid-twentieth centuries. In all of this, minstrelsy resonates with the sense of contradiction, fragmentation, and ambivalence characteristic of the Parisian encounters described above and, indeed, characteristic of modern race relations more generally.

The first widespread appearances of racist curios and objects occurred contemporaneously with the flourishing of minstrelsy. Although some of these, like trading cards and hitching posts, had origins predating the minstrel craze, most appear to date from the 1850s and post–Civil War eras. Changes in the packaging of consumable goods as well as new networks of distribution and a greatly expanded national market all proved crucial factors in the provenance of racialized commercial objects, but the stock characters and themes pioneered by the minstrel shows defined much of their style and content. For example, the Aunt Jemima character, who, significantly, had its debut as the symbol on packaged pancake mix at the 1893 Chicago world's fair, copied the venerable mammy of the slave plantation. Her visage vouched not only for the authenticity of the product, but suggested the reassurance and nurturance of a family retainer—American-style. A like analysis could be made of the Cream of Wheat man and a plethora of similar products that emerged in that era.[15]

However, the emergence of these advertising images—contemporaneous with similar ones in France—was accompanied by the development of a parallel market in the simulacra of such symbols intended for household and other uses. Aunt Jemima soon graced not only the pancake box, but salt and pepper shakers, a to-do list holder, and countless other domestic tools and decorations. Although they often had their origins in the promotional schemes of commercial products or entertainments, their ubiquity suggests both independent sources and more complex motives for their buyers than merely responding to the propaganda of capitalist entrepreneurs.[16] Well into the mid-twentieth century, images of grinning, subservient black men, women, and children filled the yards and domestic spaces of white American homes.

The presence of racially thematized advertisements, minstrel-like entertainment (as found in the Amos 'n' Andy show and local amateur performances), and racist curios seems to have faded in the post–World War II era. Ironically, the primary site for their production shifted to Japan and other Far East cheap labor locations. By the 1960s and 1970s, America's racial climate—if not conscience—had been sensitized to the more blatant forms of degradation, making such displays a high-risk affair. Of course, it is possible that other soon-to-be-contested symbols, such as the Confederate flag, took over their place and function. Still, racist figurines were more likely to be found in the possession of collectors than ordinary consumers.[17]

In the early 1980s—roughly contemporaneous with their resurgence in France—racist objects found an entirely new American market. African Americans, in increasingly large numbers, eventually displaced whites as the predominant customers for what one commentator has dubbed "contemptible collectibles." Although their announced motives differ substantially from those of white buyers—most claimed an interest in preserving an aspect of black American history—their investments had the bizarre effect of revitalizing the market. Reports of prices quadrupling over periods as short as three or four years became common. Examples of even more astonishing profits over a longer time frame are not unusual. For example, an Aunt Jemima cookie jar purchased for 25 cents in the year Martin Luther King Jr. was assassinated (1968), could be sold for $175 twenty-five years later.[18] Not surprisingly, individual vendors now count sales in millions of dollars annually, and distribution and production networks stretch from Route 80 in Tennessee to the streets of Taiwan.[19] It is highly likely that some of the earliest versions of these objects — especially the so-called antiques — found their way to France via this emerging market network.

The Prism of Race, the Prison of Racism

What, then, does this bizarre history suggest about the meaning of these objects in contemporary race relations, and especially about their seemingly incongruous appearance in France? Certainly the simpler, straightforward accounts, wherein these images fit neatly into a conscious strategy of subordination and oppression, are grounded in a utilitarian — and ultimately functionalist — logic. They don't add up. It is much more likely that these objects occupy a role in contemporary race relations as complex as the original minstrels from which they are drawn did in the nineteenth century. Thus, just as the minstrel portrait of happy slaves and inept freedmen did not simply constitute a response to attacks on slavery or a transparent effort to induce false consciousness in the slaves' potential white worker allies, the childlike, naïve black of postemancipation iconography was not simply propaganda to discredit black competition in the labor market, or to justify lower wages.[20] Although these make for likely aspects of their ultimate effect, they don't really explain the imagery.

Recent work has made clear that minstrelsy cannot be dismissed as simply a gross collage of racist caricatures — though it was certainly that as well.[21] Its earliest innovators were mostly northern or foreign-born men of middle-class, urban backgrounds writing for audiences made up of urban, working-class, northern white men — often immigrants or natives recently migrated to the city. The content of minstrel shows, its music, and its social setting suggest that for these men, it served profound cultural-political functions: on stage, in the audiences, and on the streets, minstrel conventions provided the discourse and performative media for fashioning as well as expressing white male identity in an era of profound political and economic tensions.[22] Conflicts over slavery, westward expansion, and repressed conflicts over class and gender relations within the emerging wage labor economy could be played out on stage behind thinly disguised blackface conventions.

In this sense, then, minstrels enacted the well-known conventions of displacement, wherein fools, children, and comics can speak of political or emotionally dangerous matters. But there was a compensatory aspect, as well, wherein minstrelsy invoked the imagined community of the southern plantation, comfortingly placid, paternalistic, and innocent. Such images served as a balm for white — especially white male — anxieties at a moment of tremendous economic, social, and cultural transformation. Black stereotypes provided antebellum whites with the means for displacing anxieties and fashioning new identities: they could define who they were against — the negative referent of what they most feared within themselves — while imaginatively constructing a world that was the diametric (and forbidden) opposite of the one they actually inhabited.

As powerful and convincing as these arguments are, however, they do not fully account for the staying power of the minstrel tradition. Obviously, the social conditions that gave rise to minstrelsy's antebellum popularity changed with the Civil War, a maturing capitalistic political economy, and vast transformations in the American racial and cultural habitus. Of course, minstrelsy also changed, even as the fundamental racist conventions and stereotypes that it had given life to endured deep into the twentieth century. In the 1980s and early 1990s, one black man could actually hold the highest position in the American military services (Colin Powell) and another could creditably aspire to hold the nation's highest political office (Jesse Jackson); and yet the minstrel stereotypes — "they can all sing and dance," "they are all natural athletes," and the like — were almost as strong as ever, not only in America, but globally. The reality of black success in taking advantage of the opportunities in musical and athletic fields, and of these being America's primary cultural exports, offers only a partial answer to this phenomenon. Rather, a more complete answer lies in the complex roles race and racial stereotyping have come to play in the modern world. Minstrelsy was not only a founding moment in that play historically, but it also gave form and expression to a process that since its inception has unfolded globally, although with specific local variations.

Anthropologist Michael Taussig's exploration of mimesis and alterity and of how commodity fetishes work in modern life provides one clue as to what that process might be. Following and elaborating the thought of Walter Benjamin, Taussig suggests that the desire to copy or mimic the other also involves "connecting with" and appropriating aspects of that alterity into one's desired self.[23] Historian Eric Lott's apt phrase "love and theft" is helpful in applying Taussig's ideas specifically to explain the minstrel phenomena.[24] By theft Lott refers to minstrelsy's appropriation and distortion of an actual African American experience; love refers to the intense fascination with an imagined black life and character. Taussig's analysis suggests that when a mimetic process such as this takes the form of commodity fetishism, the copy swallows up "the real" object of desire.[25] In the case of minstrelsy, a displacement function clearly existed wherein desired but repressed, imagined but distorted aspects of black life and character were symbolically, indeed sometimes literally, put on—on stage, in street parades, and even enacted during riots.[26] In the process, the whole of black life and character was colonized, that is, blacks became *only* song, dance, and sexuality—in a word, "joy." At the same time, blacks took on those aspects whites feared—the flip side of what they desired—the dangerous, the lustful, the bestial. Like the two sides of a coin, the contrary images of the Janus-faced black were mutually constituting. Thus the ridiculed, denigrated whole could not be simply left behind—excluded and rejected. It needed to be held close, because without it what had been appropriated—"stolen"—would only atrophy and die. There could be no joy without the threat of succumbing to lust. Donning a blackface enabled one to safely take that risk.[27]

The very anomalies of racial stereotyping and denigration suggest something of the plausibility of this reading. Among those anomalies we find the pervasive claims the creators and performers of the stereotypes made for their authenticity. The claim of faithful representation of actual black life has been a central trope in the advertising of such performances, from the antebellum performer Jim Rice, who insisted that he had based his Jim Crow dance and characterizations on observations of street performers in New Orleans, to Charles Correll and Freeman Gosden, the twentieth-century creators of *Amos 'n' Andy*, who claimed to have studied the southern black migrants to Chicago's South Side.[28]

Such claims cohabited with another, parallel, seemingly divergent, minstrel pattern, however. In the late nineteenth century (what one historian has called the "baroque period" of minstrelsy),[29] performers began to advertise as "blackface performers" rather than "negro impersonators." Significantly, it was during this period that the evolution toward vaudeville began and the original plantation tradition framework became more a conceit on which romantic songs and narratives more clearly about white subjects were overlaid. Blackface male performers singing of their longing for blond maidens could not possibly have been accepted as "real" black men. More likely, the convention of a black mask gave license to express romantic love, even if — perhaps especially because — white romantic love was thought to contrast so vividly with black lust. And yet the romantic love drew its energy, its power, from that forbidden lust.

This latter development suggests that the force and staying power of the minstrel tropes lies not in the putative "grain of truth" of racial stereotypes, but in their appropriation of what is taken as the desired essence of the racial Other. The claim to authenticity (*mimesis*), then, lies in tension with the claim to actually constitute an improvement on the original (*alterity*, in the sense of having become otherwise) — either because one has reduced the original to its essence or because (in the case of lust) one has domesticated it. But the tension is a necessary one, as are the related tensions between denigration and fascination, rejection and attraction.

These oppositions are crucial to resolving the puzzles we encountered in Paris and the more general problematic of racism in the late twentieth century. They help explain, perhaps, why the racism historically embedded in contemporary objects of consumption does not actually appear as racism to many well-intentioned antiracists. And, on the other hand, it explains how it is in fact *not* racism in its traditional guises and meanings — or not quite.

Such oppositions may also suggest solutions to a parallel but quite different puzzle — the appearance of African American collectors simultaneous with these commodities' resurgence in Europe and Asia. Black consumers of racist iconography would appear to complicate any simplistic analysis of the more general phenomena. Black collecting was enabled by and reflects the recent growth of the American black middle class. Although many blacks have been actively collecting for decades, in the 1980s some moved from other forms of collecting — such as African art — to these racist objects.[30] Their class location is further underscored by journals who have recently touted collecting in general as a smart form of investment.[31]

But just as clearly, something more than economic capacity or interest motivated this dramatic development and its timing. The phenomenon may be related, as one journalist has argued, to the general African American interest in reclaiming black history, evidenced by the one hundred new museums in the 1980s and 1990s devoted to that project alone.[32] Pressing that argument further, one can imagine a black middle class — economically embattled during the Reagan-Bush era — turning to the nation's racist history, but in a way that clearly marks the collector as experientially distanced from those conditions, even as (or perhaps because) he or she embraces their relics. A not uncommon sentiment among black collectors is that they rather than whites should own such objects and that through their possession "black people rob them of their power."[33] This may also help explain the incongruity of an ostensibly anti-racist purpose and the fact that statuary figures not only dominated the market, but that the most derogatory of them commanded the highest prices.[34] Despite ostensibly benign motives, these African American consumers, in search of their history, unwittingly further its commodification; indeed, the black experience itself is literally commodified and fetishized. And much like the commodity fetishes Taussig found among the Cuna Indians, these, too, become available for the multiple, if ambiguous deployments that the buyer may choose.[35]

It is a Faustian paradox, however, although one that should not be reduced to a mere dichotomy in which one forces a choice between racist and benign effects. The sheer power and tenacity of the form — its ability to reproduce itself over a century of time and a world of space — may derive precisely from its capacity to encompass both. If our hypothesis of a displacement effect among the black middle-class collectors during the Reagan-Bush repression is correct, then it is a process of resolution of racial and class tensions not entirely dissimilar to that of the white working-class devotees of the minstrel show of the last century, who worked out their own issues of identity and anxiety through the ancestral progenitors of the contemporary objects. The point here is not to conflate these responses — their emotional sources, motives, and outcomes were surely very different. Rather the juxtaposition intends to suggest the power of such fetishes in everyday lives and consciousness, and especially their capacity to mediate states of being at the societal/national levels of experience and those at levels more personal and immediate.

Even more profound, perhaps, is their enabling capacity for the persons who possess, view, or deploy them — even if ultimately the fruits of that capacity prove illusory and false. In short, it is that illusory power that explains their fascination and the strength of their grip, even as they wreak devastation on the peoples caricatured. Thus Alice Walker is only half right when, referring to African Americans, she asserts: "These caricatures and stereotypes were really intended as prisons."[36] They were and remain spiritual prisons for white Americans as well.

French Exceptionalism? Race and Representation

But can the same be said of France in the decade of the 1990s? Do parallels exist there to the American effects of displacement and symbolic resolution of social tensions? Is it there also a case of "love and theft"? As in all comparative analyses, one must guard against making analogies too facilely and rapidly between nations with strikingly different racial histories and contexts.[37] The parallels and divergences in French and American histories of racialized imagery reflects — in some measure certainly — the parallels and divergences in their racial and national histories. There are two important sets of distinctions between the French and American cases: first, the history and use of these racialized objects in the two countries is different; and second, they have distinct respective histories of race and nation.

The objects being sold at auctions and fairs in the United States were antiques or reproductions of antiques, usually bought for collections. They entered public (as opposed to domestic) space only when they served as outdoor statuary in people's gardens, or in museum exhibitions. We found no evidence of widespread use of black statues in American restaurants or bars, and rarely did we encounter them even in domestic exterior spaces. It is also not at all clear that people used them to decorate the interiors of their homes. Many of the black collectors declared explicitly that the purpose of their collection was *not* decorative, but rather commemorative of a history that links them collectively to ancestors and offspring. One collector even kept her then very valuable ensemble in a closet, pulling them out only for display at explicitly pedagogic and political exhibits.[38]

Obviously, the American-derived objects for sale and use in France could not be consumed in the same way. The descendants of the people to whom they refer, either admiringly or viciously, do not live in France. These objects are not, in any direct way, part of France's present or past. The consumers are necessarily largely white, necessarily largely French. Thus the French experience offers a doubled displacement: people did not buy objects playing on either the past or present of French colonialism, but rather ones emerging out of white Americans' distorted visions of black Americans.

And yet, although their displacement in space and time cannot completely detach the American-derived objects from their original meanings, it is likely that these figures did indeed change their meaning in their French incarnation, partly because racialized images with other histories — ones embedded in an explicitly colonial history more than a history of slavery — flanked them. Understanding both the continuities and the changes, therefore, requires understanding France's particular history of race making, colonialism, nation making, and "Americanization" in three key periods — the 1880s and 1890s, the 1920s, and the 1980s and 1990s, all periods in which definitions of Frenchness were under challenge and racialized images proliferated.

Racialized advertising images have a long history in France, as they do elsewhere; in every instance their origins appear linked to the late-nineteenth-century congruence of maturing international markets for consumables and the strengthened European (including French) imperialism that brought greater exploitation of colonial labor and resources. In France, from the 1870s to the First World War, such images became highly visible in illustrated magazines, school books, and advertisements.[39] Unsurprisingly, given the link to colonialism, images of blacks were not used indiscriminately in advertising, but rather to sell products of either colonial origin or ones closely associated with ostensibly black preferences and tastes — in advertisements for cotton, coffee, cocoa, tropical fruit, rum, and rice in the first instance, and bicycles and chicken in the second. In contrast with the period before the 1870s, when most of the black images appearing on posters had been borrowed from American minstrelsy, those from the 1880s to the 1890s represented blacks mostly as "tamed" Africans. Thus the King of Dahomey — who led many revolts against the French — was depicted in an advertisement in 1894 touting the virtues of a French bicycle![40]

These images must be read in the context of a fin de siècle characterized by the expansion of the French empire and the encouragement of European immigration brought in to assuage the labor shortage. This was a period of cultural unification for France, when both a diverse French-born population and large numbers of white, Catholic (and a far fewer number of non-Catholic) immigrants were integrated into the nation, reaffirming the principle of citizenship dating from the French Revolution.[41] In theory at least, all who were born and many who lived on French territory could become juridically French if they so chose and were willing to embrace French culture — speak French, attend French schools, accept the ostensibly secular (though in fact Christian) calendar, eat French food, have French taste.[42] Representations of blacks were limited to colonial imagery — Goldscheider and other like statuettes, "mooresque" lamps derived from the period of slavery, the wild savage, or the domesticated colonial consumer.

In this period, essentially no blacks and few North Africans lived in the metropole. Blacks were represented as the exotic Other — sometimes tame and sometimes savage, but always safely distant; they were represented as available for service — carrying water, a table, or demonstrating the capacities of a cleaning powder. The theory of universal citizenship was adhered to in this period, perhaps because it went essentially unchallenged. The immigrants who came in this period were desired and defined as "assimilable" — despite occasional xenophobic outbreaks — and the colonial world was safely in its place.[43]

The First World War fundamentally shook this commitment to an expansive France. The French relied heavily on the military and labor help of their colonies to sustain the war effort. For the first time, significant numbers of Africans were living and working on French soil, and African soldiers were saving French lives. Perhaps because of this new proximity and dependence, the very derogatory advertising images of blacks prevalent at the turn of the century disappeared during this period. Their loss was, however, compensated by the creation of a new figure in 1914–15 — the Banania *tirailleur*.[44] Given French dependence on colonial soldiers and labor during the war, the caricature may crystallize a particular trope in the highly ambivalent relation between a racialized culture and subordinated blacks — admiration, fear, and dependence. The trademark figure, emblazoned on every box of an immensely popular breakfast food, simultaneously brought the heroic Senegalese soldier into almost every home, making him the familiar of all small French children, and ridiculed him.

The Banania *tirailleur* gained even greater presence in the 1920s and 1930s, as his face appeared on mugs, bowls, and pitchers as well as on the box itself. At first glance this profusion and banalization of a stereotyped racist image seems surprising because the 1920s would appear, in contradistinction to the turn of the century, as a highpoint in French race relations. Beginning in the 1920s and continuing through the 1950s, celebrated African American musicians, dancers, artists, and novelists—Josephine Baker, Sidney Bechet, Loïs Mailou Jones, Richard Wright, Chester Himes, James Baldwin, and others—found a welcome contrast to American racism in their reception in Paris.[45] In the same period, African art forms were incorporated into avant-garde sculpture and painting.

During the 1920s, the hypervalorization of African American cultural forms and of African art, as well as the policy of assiduously cultivating a tiny French-trained indigenous elite in France's African colonies, occurred at precisely the moment when the vast majority of the inhabitants of French colonies were excluded from the right to live on French territory as well as from French citizenship. There were stringent exclusionary measures to return African and North African workers, imported during the war years, to their "homes."[46] Thus France's generous vision of *la plus grande France*, which supposedly embraced all the colonized, proved, as analyzed in the writings of Senghor, Césaire, and others, far more problematic in practice.[47] It is no accident, then, that it was in this period that the notion of a "white" French identity began seriously to challenge the traditional universalist vision of French citizenship.[48]

Finally, France in the 1920s lived uncomfortably with the memory of having required not only the help of its colonial subjects during the war, but also that of America. Not only had the United States played a critical role in World War I, but in the 1920s its political and economic dominance became clearer and clearer. As the historian Richard Kuisel has suggested, France in this period defined itself, at least to a certain extent, through opposition to the United States. French support of African American artists and musicians who had been badly treated at home may have served as a means of marking a difference with the United States and establishing a French identity.[49]

In this context of global politics, both the choice of African American artists to go to Paris and their reception there takes on new meanings. It would appear that these men and women embraced the lesser of two evils. Josephine Baker was barred from the stage at moments in the United States, while in France she was lionized—as long as her show was adequately "wild" and "African," reproducing established stereotypes of blacks on the Parisian stage.[50] Those stereotypes were also plastered all over Paris on the posters advertising the *Revue Nègre*, and it was not just the Banania infantryman and the traditional moorish figures who appeared in Parisian homes in the 1920s, but also grotesquely stereotyped figures of jazz musicians — produced both in the United States and in France.

French toleration, even lionization, of a very few African American performing artists and writers cannot be read as evidence of France's absence of racism. Rather than proof of less racist treatment, it more nearly suggests a *different* kind of racism. While elements of "primitive" cultural forms were celebrated on the stage, placed in museums, and incorporated into cubism, and jazz themes were melded into classical musical composition, these borrowings rather meant to reinvigorate "European" traditions than create new, collaborative, syncretic forms and practices. The limits of 1920s cultural hybridization reveal themselves starkly when compared with forms of the 1980s and 1990s.[51]

The world in which France of the 1980s and the 1990s finds itself repeats some of the tropes of the 1920s, but with crucial differences. Cultural and literary critic Kristin Ross has made the persuasive argument that it is impossible to understand French history in the 1950s and 1960s without grasping France's position as simultaneously dominated (by American capital and culture) and dominating (of its colonies).[52] This narrative is extended by Richard Kuisel into the 1970s, during which, he argues, the French no longer perceived Americanization as the dominant threat and the country's practice, common in the late 1940s and 1950s, of identifying itself in contrast to the United States became obsolete. There was a turn, instead, toward looking to the French past to find a basis for a French identity.[53] The Second World War and the Algerian War, however, greatly complicated this turn toward a French past because it thus required forgetting as much as remembering.[54]

Indeed, one can clearly see the dream of assimilation and its paradoxes in the relations between France and Algeria.[55] (And, as well perhaps, in the *beurs'* relation to France.) In a country in which race is not supposed to matter, an explosion of discourse linking issues of race with the survival of the French nation has occurred. Thus France's decision to support Algeria's secular government against the Islamic opposition may have been in part motivated by a fear of the "Islamicization" of France's large population of Algerian immigrants, their children, and grandchildren.[56] The integration/ assimilation of people of Algerian origin since Algeria's independence in 1962 proved both a success and a failure. Adolescents and young adults of Algerian parentage found themselves fully French in that they spoke French, were distant from Algeria, and often did not practice the daily rituals of Islam. In sum, they had expectations for their lives very similar to their "white" friends. These same young adults, however, found themselves on the margins of society. They often grew up in crowded housing projects on urban peripheries; their unemployment rate was higher than that in the population at large; their success at school was lower; and they encountered both explicit and subtle racism in many moments of their everyday lives.[57]

This exclusion and experience of racism may be part of the reason why many French youth adopted and transformed contemporary urban African American art forms, especially hip hop, graffiti art, film, and street fashion.[58] Far more extensively than in the 1920s, French musicians are producing music modeled on African American sounds.[59] Rather than adding sounds and rhythms into existing musical forms, this syncretic music is actually based on North American hip hop, also incorporating North African, West African, Caribbean, and French musical elements.[60] Many of these musicians were themselves the product of decolonization — often of West African or North African descent. For many *beurs* and blacks, the immersion in this transcultural "black" music signified that, for them, the assimilationist dream was over. This music did not, however, gain popularity only among the children and grandchildren of decolonization, but was played by "white" youth as well and has become a mainstream commercial success. The music's aggressive refusal to be "French" in a recognizable form, including the acknowledged influence of North American sounds, has caused it to be perceived as a general threat to Frenchness — from both Americanization and immigration.

In contrast to French youth responses — which reflect a hybridization of cultures — the thrust of successive French governments and the larger French public have been largely toward a defense of the traditional model of Frenchness and a renewed commitment to the principles of assimilation. In the early 1980s, for the first and a very brief time only (with the exception of Vichy), the French government itself challenged the assimilationist model.[61] Following the 1981 elections, the newly founded socialist government endorsed a pluralist cultural policy, providing financial and administrative assistance to groups organized on the basis of regional ethnic/linguistic origin.[62] The speed with which the government retreated from this position and even repudiated it gives an indication of three challenges it faced. Initially conceived to allow Bretons, Basques, and Alsatians to maintain regional cultural forms, such attitudes, even within the socialist party, changed when it became a question of enabling Algerians, West Africans, and Vietnamese to maintain their linguistic, religious, and other practices. Secondly, those who remained convinced of the necessity for a universal French people challenged the policy, as did, finally, the meteoric rise of the Far Right, which changed the field of political discourse. In 1983, just as the new pluralist vision of the nation was being implemented, the National Front party achieved astounding electoral successes, rising well above its traditional 1 percent of the vote.[63] The socialists rapidly retreated from their programs, by 1989 going so far as to declare that the "limit of tolerance" for immigration had been reached in France and making the decision to reduce support for France's ex-colonies in Africa. Meanwhile, the centrist right parties moved closer to the frankly xenophobic and racist discourses of the National Front.

After this brief, failed experiment in pluralism, French politicians and intellectuals of all political colors returned with renewed conviction to the assimilation project, arguing that the only way France could survive as a nation was for all to be alike. The language of such alikeness — among the "respectable" political parties at least — became cultural rather than racial. It was echoed in the suspicions expressed later (again across the political spectrum) concerning identity politics and demands for the right to difference.[64] Thus even those who made arguments for generous immigration policies based them on justice — not on the idea that those who come from other places and other cultures might have something valuable to contribute to the collective life of France.

Unlike the youth's syncretic approach, this vision of assimilation remains very distant from one of collage or hybridization. It is one of transformation — that newcomers will become like the inhabitants of longer standing and not the other way around. Black is to become white. Both the view's power and its ambivalence can be seen in a rather painful way in a poster advertising a "Nuit Métis: Musiques, Cultures, et Vidéos" in Marseille in the summer of 1995 (fig. 6). The upper right of the poster is occupied by a distinctively

Figure 6. Advertisement for "Nuit Métis," Marseilles, August 1995. Photograph by Auslander and Holt.

African looking man, standing in profile, turned toward the middle of the poster. The bottom left corner is occupied by a very blond woman, also in profile, also turned in toward the center of the poster. In the middle of the poster, in the diagonal between the black African man and the white French woman is NOTHING. The space connecting them, the space between them, remains blank, empty. It is revealing of the power of the assimilationist ethos of France that even in this poster publicizing a clearly antiracist event, whose goal was clearly to promote cultural and social hybridization, the place of mixture, of *métissage* appears beyond the imagination.

Within this general deployment of racialized icons in France, the American-derived figures occupied a particular location. Both very positive and very negative images of American blacks — themselves a dominated group within a dominating polity and society — had a particular grasp on the imagination in late-twentieth-century France. Within the widespread resentment concerning the hegemony of American culture and commodities (the most visible forms of capital), African American art forms retained a very complicated kind of legitimacy. They exemplified the production of those also exploited by the powerful. Could the analog of white reactions to American minstrelsy prove suggestive here? Could it be that because of both their power and their distance, American blacks could become both the object of desire and the object of derision, of love and of fear? Just as anxious working-class northern men in the United States neither mocked nor appropriated intimately known (and very threatening) cultures, but rather were attracted to supposedly authentic (yet clearly inauthentic) representations of black life in antebellum plantations and cities, so people in France of the 1990s, anxious about the future of their country, their economy, their culture, appropriated — in order to admire and mock — supposedly authentic but often inauthentic representations of a far distant (but also close) culture. A culture they could not avoid, but could not fully embrace either. In both cases, there was a kind of appropriation, consumption, even devouring of the least threatening of one of the invader's gifts. We argue that it is the *American* images (not the North African or the moorish) that were invested with this particular power. America embodied what was loved and feared, desired and hated, and thus black American images — representing the innocence and joie de vivre of the dominated — could become the perfect fetish.

Toward a Transatlantic Politics of the Everyday? From *Tête de Nègre* to *Meringue au Chocolat*

Our encounters with sambo in Paris, then, elucidate some important aspects of the relation between globalization and the politics of the everyday. It suggests, first, that the most effective way of avoiding the scylla of assumptions that everything is now everywhere the same and the charybdis of a stubborn attachment to belief in local autonomy comes through the analysis of specific manifestations of globalism in the everyday. The apparition of sambo in Paris simultaneously tells us something about the history of race and racism in America and in France, the circulation of African American culture throughout and out from the United States and the Americas from the mid-nineteenth century to the 1990s, and the ways in which France, the United States, Europe, and Japan were commercially and semiotically linked. The racialized images were and were not the same objects when they turned up in France and the United

States, however. Their distinct histories and their various presents necessarily made them different. But the interpenetration of American and European culture in the last two hundred years also made them like.

The story we have told here is obviously not yet over. In the beginning, our French friends suggested that French modes of sight might differ from American ones as a result of pedagogical practices. That may be true, but clearly those national visual and political cultures are also subject to transformation by processes of globalization as well as by internal changes.[65] When we saw those first sambo images, it was with "American" eyes that saw stereotypes and racist contempt; such images seemed to us eruptions from a hidden canker at the heart of French society. Our friends argued that people—whether white or black—raised in France and educated in a French visual culture, would see something radically different in these images. They thought it possible that the musicians who chose to use a sambo figure as their collection box saw in this an intertextual joke—one that actually signified on the sambo figure.[66] Thus the "sambo" statues could refer to the *jouissance* of a Josephine Baker or a Richard Wright, and not to the realities of French race relations. Or, people eating a *tête de nègre* could imagine themselves in the same field of benign references that named the *réligieuse*, and the *jésuite*, and *not* Antillean slavery, Senegalese forced labor, or—most certainly *not*—the Algerian War.

And yet perhaps just as jazz, hip hop, and sambo have crossed the Atlantic, so, too, have modes of seeing, of political mobilization, and—of resistance. Certainly our own thinking has changed since those initial encounters in the summer of 1992. So has that of our friends. They, too, now see the everyday with different eyes. With those "new" eyes, they spotted a newspaper article that suggested even broader changes in French perceptions of the sambo phenomenon underway, changes that resonate with the *beurs* and other French youth who have responded to cultural transformations so differently than their elders. In April 1995, a woman in Nancy engaged in a gesture of protest much like those that the French press, reporting on the United States, have vilified as emblematic of the foolishness and dangers of American identity politics and political correctness. Esther, a young woman who had moved to France from the Ivory Coast fifteen years before, decided to contest in court the nomenclature of the cakes called *tête de nègre* on the grounds of its racist insult and defamation. Her argument: "I am expecting a child, and I don't want him or her to be able to eat or suck on *têtes de nègre* or for anyone to call him or her a nigger [*nègre*]. . . . it's unbearable and my African friends have reacted like me." Her lawyer defended the seriousness of the case arguing, "It's not a question of outlawing sweets, but to open a debate on the problem of ordinary racism."[67] It is striking both that Esther (the paper did not give her last name) seems to have not "seen" the cakes and their name for fifteen years (or at least not to have been bothered by them) and that she apparently was moved to action by her associations of the present existence of the *têtes de nègre* and future abusive treatment of her not-yet-born child. She seemed hopeful, and her lawyer's position reinforces the position, that taking these cakes off the market, or renaming them, is part of the process of social change that will protect her future child from being called "nigger." It is still too early to tell the long-term legal import of Esther's suit, but the mere fact of the complaint having been lodged appears to have won a small victory. In the summer of 1995, we returned to the bakery where we originally photographed the *têtes de nègre*. We found that they now bore a new name—*meringues au chocolat*.

Notes

We would like to thank Elisa Camiscioli and Nayan Shah for their crucial assistance researching this essay. Nayan traced much of the American and European primary and secondary source material; Elisa did field work in Paris, including interviews and photography. We are also grateful to Jim Miller for researching some of the general background literature for the French case. We would like to thank Françoise Basch, Alice Conklin, Fred Cooper, Jacqueline Feldman, Susan Gal, Lisa Moses, Michel-Rolph Trouillot, and Alison Wylie as well as participants in the workshop on contemporary European culture at the University of Chicago for their perceptive and helpful comments. Special acknowledgment is owed to Rosine Fefferman, Jean-Claude Zancarini, and Michelle Zancarini-Fournel who labored to put this text into French and find it a French public.

1   Another example of Parisians' complex mixture of admiration for African American culture and distrust of African Americans can be seen in the following article in the *Los Angeles Times*: " 'I'm [an African American living in Paris] walking down the street one day with a white colleague after a business meeting when this white policeman jumps out and asks me for my papers,' he says, sitting in a

Parisian cafe where James Brown's song, 'I Feel Good' is playing in the background. 'We're both in suits. He [asked] me what's in my bag and then starts going through it.'" Tammerlin Drummond, "Adieu Utopia," *Los Angeles Times*, 22 March 1993. Our thanks to our colleague Julie Saville for calling this article to our attention.

2   For discussions of the status of lived experience in shaping perception, see Denise Riley, *"Am I That Name?" Feminism and the Category of "Women" in History* (Minneapolis: University of Minnesota Press, 1988); Joan W. Scott, "The Evidence of Experience," and a response by Thomas C. Holt, "Experience and the Politics of Intellectual Inquiry," in *Questions of Evidence: Proof, Practice, and Persuasion across the Disciplines*, ed. James Chandler, Arnold I. Davidson, and Harry Harootunian (Chicago: University of Chicago Press, 1994), 363–96; Laura Lee Downs, "If 'Woman' Is Just an Empty Category, Then Why Am I Afraid to Walk Alone at Night? Identity Politics Meets the Postmodern Subject," *Comparative Studies in Society and History*, 35, 2 (1993): 414–51. See also Joan W. Scott's reply in the same issue. The literatures in psychology and anthropology on the question of perception are too large to engage here.

3   We cannot, obviously, provide overviews of these two vast literatures here. For Tom Holt's reading of the U.S. literature please see his, "Explaining Racism in American History," in *Imagined Histories: American Historians Interpret the Past*, ed. Anthony Molho and Gordon S. Wood (Princeton, N.J.: Princeton University Press, 1998), 107–19. Among the French work we have found most useful for this particular conundrum, we would include Balibar's contributions to Etienne Balibar and Immanuel Wallerstein, *Race, Nation, and Class: Ambiguous Identities* (New York: Verso, 1991); Collette Guillaumin, *Racism, Sexism, Power, and Ideology* (New York: Routledge, 1994); Michel Wieviorka, *L'espace du racisme* (Paris: Editions du Seuil, 1991); and Pierre-André Taguieff, "The New Cultural Racism in France," *Telos* 83 (1990): 109–22.

4   We have each written on this topic elsewhere, and Leora Auslander continues to pursue the problematic of objects, perception, and the everyday. The texts that have most influenced our reflection on the everyday (in our disagreements with them as well as in our agreements) are: Henri Lefebvre, *Critique de la vie quotidienne* (Paris: L'Arche, 1958–1981); Michel de Certeau, *The Practice of Everyday Life*, trans. Steven F. Rendall (Berkeley: University of California Press, 1984); Allan Pred, *Lost Words and Lost Worlds: Modernity and the Language of Everyday Life in Late Nineteenth-Century Stockholm* (Cambridge: Cambridge University Press, 1990); Roland Barthes, *Mythologies* (Paris: Le Seuil, 1970); and Pierre Bourdieu, *Outline of a Theory of Practice*, trans. Richard Nice (Cambridge:

Cambridge University Press, 1977). Our own work has most clearly addressed these issues in Thomas C. Holt, "Marking: Race, Race-Making, and the Writing of History," *American Historical Review* 100 (1995): 1–20; Thomas C. Holt, *The Problem of Race in the Twenty-First Century* (Cambridge, Mass.: Harvard University Press, 2000); Leora Auslander, *Taste and Power: Furnishing Modern France* (Berkeley: University of California Press, 1996), particularly the introduction and conclusion; Leora Auslander, " 'Jewish Taste'? Jews and the Aesthetics of Everyday Life in Paris and Berlin, 1933–1942," in *Histories of Leisure*, ed. Rudy Koshar (Oxford: Berg, 2002), 299–318; and Leora Auslander, "Bavarian Crucifixes and French Headscarves: Religious Practices and the Postmodern European State," *Cultural Dynamics* 12, 3(2000): 183–209.

5 See, for example, the French art deco figure of a banjo player, produced by Robj in Paris around 1920. Illustrated in P. J. Gibbs, *Black Collectibles Sold in America* (Paducah, Ky.: Collector Books, 1987). Illustrations of the Paul Colin posters advertising the *Revue Nègre* (1925) may be found in Max Gallo, *The Poster in History*, trans. Alfred Mayor and Bruni Mayor (New York: American Heritage Publishing, 1974).

6 Stéphane Richemond, "Terres cuites orientalistes des XIXe et XXe siècles," *L'objet d'art* 290 (1995): 54–65. The market for orientalist antiques boomed in the early 1980s, followed by a fall in prices in 1986–87. The theme remains popular, however, and as Richemond notes, "Orientalism continues to be an appreciated theme, and, given equal quality, a kabyle musician will always sell better than a sower from Picardy" (64). All unmarked translations are mine.

7 All That Jazz also appears to have production and distribution sites in southern Illinois, but its connection to the French company is unclear.

8 Salesperson at Coste, interview by Elisa Camiscioli, July 1995, 11 rue de Rivoli, Paris.

9 George E. Curry, "Color of Money Keys Return of Racist Curios," *Chicago Tribune*, 11 December 1992.

10 Two of the major producers for whom we have detailed information — Optimum and Apparence — were founded in 1986. Optimum produces, imports, and exports statuettes of a variety of kinds, but specializes in images of children. In 1995, they were headquartered in Paris, had a workshop in Saint Clement, and a retail outlet in Montpellier. It was a relatively small firm, with three employees and 150,000FF in capital. They exported approximately 600,000FF worth of plaster statues to Belgium, Germany, Portugal, Switzerland, Austria, Turkey, and Guadeloupe, and imported about 70,000FF worth of goods from Portugal. By contrast, Apparence, located in a

suburb of Paris, with 50,000FF of capital, employed between eleven and eighteen people, engaged in only a very small export business, and had no retail store of its own.

11 We, Elisa Camiscioli, and various friends have found them in locations ranging from the City Lights Restaurant-Bar at Saint-Paul in the Marais, to a gift and lamp store, Regali, in the sixteenth arrondissement, to the gift shop/newspaper stand at the Gare de Lyon, to furniture stores in the Faubourg Saint-Antoine, to a discount shop at the metro Saint-Fargeau in the twentieth, to a toy store in the first. Finally, while our comparative labors have been far from exhaustive, we have also discovered a similar range of statues in well-to-do sections of Honfleur, on the Normandy coast, in Nyons in the south of France, in Strasbourg, on the German border, in the American Place restaurant in the Marriott hotel in Hamburg, in a curio shop in that city (both for sale and used as decoration), and in San Francisco's waterfront district.

12 For example, among the cheapest was about 50FF for a six-to-eight-inch-tall jazz man (with a discount price of 348FF if one bought a whole band of eight) at Regali, 45, avenue Victor-Hugo. The middle range was between 200 and 400FF for the small figures and around 1700FF for a larger model (about a foot and a half tall). These were found, among other places, at the City Lights Restaurant-Bar, 20 rue Saint Paul. Also available was a 105-centimeter boy in baseball clothes (or others) for 4,180FF (Coste, 11 rue de Rivoli).

13 Examples include: Les Jardins d'Elisa, 101 rue de Charonne; and Italian Restaurant, place du Marché Sainte Catherine. In addition, a *salon de thé* in Besançon was decorated with a Banania motif, and we noted the use of moorish lampholders in a very elegant clothing store in Hamburg.

14 Raymond Bachollet et al., *Négripub: L'image des noirs dans la publicité* (Paris: Somogy, 1992), 79; and Phyllis Rose, *Jazz Cleopatra: Josephine Baker in Her Time* (New York: Doubleday, 1989).

15 Regarding the history of the Aunt Jemima figurine, see Jackie Young, *Black Collectables: Mammy and Her Friends* (West Chester, Pa.: Schiffer, 1988).

16 For example, self-rising pancake mix was invented by Chris L. Rutt of St. Louis in 1889; he reputedly named it after a cakewalk song performed by a vaudeville team, Baker and Farrell. The company was purchased by R. T. Davis Milling Co., who launched a national advertising campaign at the 1893 Columbian exposition in Chicago. The recipe was sold to Quaker Oats in 1925. Part of the myth promoted by the company was that the recipe had been purchased from "a smiling mammy cook who was a slave on Colonel Higbee's plantation in the State of Louisiana" and supposedly fa-

mous for her secret pancake recipe. This story was used to promote the product until the 1960s. "The Aunt Jemima Story," in Young, *Black Collectables*.

17 Historian Kenneth W. Goings attributes mid-twentieth-century changes to the fight against Nazis and fascists in the 1930s, which undermined racist views and resulted in the appearance of black collectibles reflecting the change. "Items, particularly housewares, became more functional and decorative. The skin tones on the collectibles were brighter, and some of the images of black women were slimmed down." During the civil rights movement of the 1960s, these images disappeared altogether, giving way to the subtler stereotypes of the 1970s. Goings, "Memorabilia That Have Perpetuated Stereotypes about African Americans," *Chronicle of Higher Education*, 14 February 1990; Curry, "Color of Money"; regarding Japan's prominent role, see Young, *Black Collectables*.

18 "Cookie Jars of Oppression," *Newsweek*, 16 May 1988, 75.

19 Stan Pantovic, "Black Antiques Reveal History of Stereotypes," *Sepia*, 23 July 1974, 44–48; "Cookie Jars of Oppression," 75; and Marcia Davis, "Black History in Bric-a-Brac," *Washington Post*, 15 October 1992. For examples of prices: "In Washington, D.C., in 1989, a ceramic toothpick holder with a Black face sold for $75. In Kansas in 1991, a 15-inch vase that featured a Black girl and a banjo sold for $600. In Pennsylvania in 1989, a wood carving of a Black man that once stood in front of an inn sold for $12,800," Joy Duckett Cain, "Heritage Collectibles," *Essence* 24 (February, 1994). Also see Gibbs, *Black Collectibles Sold in America*.

20 For examples of such interpretations, see *Ethnic Notions: Black Images in the White Mind*, on an exhibition of African American stereotype and caricature from the collection of Janette Faulkner, held at the Berkeley Art Center, 12 September–4 November 1982 (Berkeley: Berkeley Art Center, 1982), 12, 19.

21 For a somewhat more extended discussion than is possible here of the recent American literature and its implications for analyzing racial phenomena, see Holt, "Marking."

22 For an analysis of street parades and urban riots where these phenomena were literally acted out, see David R. Roediger, *The Wages of Whiteness: Race and the Making of the American Working Class* (London: Verso, 1993), 115–19; and Eric Lott, *Love and Theft: Blackface Minstrelsy and the American Working Class* (New York: Oxford University Press, 1993).

23 See Michael Taussig, *Mimesis and Alterity: A Particular History of the Senses* (New York: Routledge, 1993), xviii–xix, 21–22, 67.

24 Lott, *Love and Theft*, 45–46, 225.

25 Taussig, *Mimesis and Alterity*, 20–21.

26 See discussions of the Astor Place riot in Roediger and Lott.

27 In the context, one can begin to understand the apparently insatiable appetite for and fierce loyalties to performances within the genre. The first is attested to by the extensive network devoted to putting on amateur minstrel performances; the second by the fact that for a decade America stood still — stopping all familial and official activities — to listen to the *Amos 'n' Andy* radio show. See Melvin Patrick Ely, *The Adventures of Amos 'n' Andy: A Social History of an American Phenomenon* (New York: Free Press, 1991), 23–46.

28 Lott, *Love and Theft*; and Ely, *Amos 'n' Andy.*

29 Kenneth W. Goings, *Mammy and Uncle Mose: Black Collectibles and American Stereotyping* (Bloomington: Indiana University Press, 1994).

30 For example, a Los Angeles dental hygienist, who has purchased 1,400 items (which she describes as "symbols of racism in its concretest form"), began by collecting African art and hails from a family of collectors. Paula Parker, "Contemptible Collectibles," *Perspectives: The Civil Rights Quarterly* 12 (1980): 19–23.

31 Julianne Malveaux, "Investing by Collecting," *Essence*, December 1986, 113–14.

32 Carol Hernandez, "Black Memorabilia Find Big Demand," *Wall Street Journal* (August 10, 1992): B1.

33 "Cookie Jars of Oppression," 75.

34 Ibid. Here, however, it might prove useful to compare the recent generation of collectors with one of their elders: "I'm old enough to have grown up [seeing] these [negative] things," he said. "Now that we've gotten away from it, I certainly wouldn't go out and pay money to bring something like that into my house." Davis, "Black History in Bric-a-Brac."

35 Taussig, *Mimesis and Alterity*, 176–77, 191–92.

36 Quoted in *Ethnic Notions*, 11–12.

37 For an analogous effort to determine the meaning of a racialized form in Europe, see John Blair, "Blackface Minstrels in Cross-cultural Perspective," *American Studies International* 28, 2 (1990): 55–65.

38 Parker, "Contemptible Collectibles," 23.

39 On mass media, see William H. Schneider, *An Empire for the Masses: The French Popular Image of Africa, 1870–1900* (Westport, Conn.: Greenwood, 1982); and Thomas August, *The Selling of the Empire* (Westport, Conn.: Greenwood, 1985).

40 Marie-Christine Peyriere with Jean-Barthelemi Debost, "L'image mediatique: Sous le regard de Grace Jones," in *Autres images, autres langues*, 113.

41 The classic on this issue remains Eugen Weber, *Peasants into Frenchmen: The Modernization of Rural France, 1870–1914* (Stanford, Calif.: Stanford University Press, 1976).

42 The classic work on this subject is Gérard Noiriel, *The French Melting Pot: Immigration, Citizenship, and National Identity*, trans. Geoffroy de Laforcade (Minneapolis: University of Minnesota Press, 1996). For a different approach to the nation-building project, see Auslander, *Taste and Power*, chap. 10.

43 On the 1889 consolidation of jus soli and the attribution of citizenship to second-generation immigrants, see Rogers Brubaker, *Citizenship and Nationhood in France and Germany* (Cambridge, Mass.: Harvard University Press, 1992), 85–86, 107–10.

44 For the dating of this advertising practice, see Bachollet et al., *Négripub*, 22, 78.

45 See Tyler Stovall, *Paris Noir: African Americans in the City of Light* (New York, Houghton Mifflin, 1996); and Michel Fabre, *From Harlem to Paris: Black American Writers in France, 1840–1980* (Urbana: University of Illinois Press, 1991).

46 Tyler Stovall, "Colour-Blind France? Colonial Workers during the First World War," *Race and Class* 35 (1993): 41–55. The "tolerant" 1920s and 1930s also saw the marked increase in already tangible anti-Semitism in France.

47 Gary Wilder, "Greater France between the Wars: Negritude, Colonial Humanism, and the Imperial State" (Ph.D. diss., University of Chicago, 1999).

48 Herve Le Bras, *Le sol et le sang* (Paris: Editions de l'Aube, 1994), 85, 91, 102.

49 Richard F. Kuisel, *Seducing the French: The Dilemma of Americanization* (Berkeley: University of California Press, 1993).

50 Rose, *Jazz Cleopatra*, 6, 21, 98.

51 On this issue in the plastic arts, see Marianna Togovnick, *Gone Primitive: Savage Intellects, Modern Lives* (Chicago: University of Chicago Press, 1990); Sally Price, *Primitive Art in Civilized Places* (Chicago: University of Chicago Press, 1989); Charles Harrison, Francis Frascina, and Gill Perry, *Primitivism, Cubism, Abstraction: The Early Twentieth Century* (New Haven, Conn.: Yale University Press, 1993); and especially Hal Foster's analysis in "The 'Primitive' Unconsciousness of Modern Art, or, White Skin Black Mask," in his *Recodings: Art, Spectacle, Cultural Politics* (Port Townsend, Wash.: Bay, 1985), 181–210. For music, see William A. Shack, *Harlem in Montmartre: A Paris Jazz Story between the Great Wars* (Berkeley: University of California Press, 2001); and Ludovic Tournès, *New Orleans sur Seine: Histoire du jazz en France* (Paris: Fayard, 1999).

52 Kristin Ross, *Fast Cars, Clean Bodies: Decolonization and the Reordering of French Culture* (Cambridge, Mass.: MIT Press, 1995), 7.

53 Kuisel, *Seducing the French*, 6.

54 See Henry Rousso, *Le syndrome de Vichy, 1944–198-*, (Paris: Seuil, 1987); and Benjamin Stora, *La gangrène et l'oubli: La mémoire de la guerre d'Algerie* (Paris: Editions La Découverte, 1991).

55 For a discussion of this phenomenon within the context of the so-called headscarf affair, see Françoise Gaspard and Farhad Khosrokhavar, *Le foulard et la république* (Paris: La Découverte, 1995); David Beriss, "Scarves, Schools, and Segregation: The *Foulard* Affair," *French Politics and Society* 8, 1 (1990): 1–13; and Auslander, "Bavarian Crucifixes and French Headscarves."

56 See Peggy A. Phillips, *Republican France: Divided Loyalties* (Westport, Conn.: Greenwood, 1993).

57 Paul A. Silverstein, "Sporting Faith: Islam, Soccer, and the French Nation-State," *Social Text* 65 (2000): 25–54; Adil Jazouli, *Les années banlieues* (Paris: Editions du Seuil, 1992); and Alex G. Hargreaves and Mark McKinney, eds., *Post-colonial Cultures in France* (New York: Routledge, 1997).

58 See, for example, the three important films from the period: *La haine, Rai*, and *L'état des lieux*, all of which focus on life in the housing projects.

59 John G. Russell, "Narratives of Denial: Racial Chauvinism and the Black Other in Japan," *Japan Quarterly* 38, 4 (1991): 416–25; Russell, "Race and Reflexivity: The Black Other in Contemporary Japanese Mass Culture," *Cultural Anthropology* 6, 1 (1991): 3–25; and Nina Cornyetz, "Fetishized Blackness: Hip-Hop and Racial Desire in Contemporary Japan," *Social Text* 12 (1994).

60 Hugues Bazin, *La culture hip-hop* (Paris: Desce de Brouwer, 1995); Francesca Candade Sautman, "Hip-Hop/scotch: 'Sounding Francophone' in French and United States Cultures," *Yale French Studies* 100 (2002): 119–145. Marie Caffari and Agnès Villette, "Le rap français: Evaluation de textes contemporaines," in *Black, Blanc, Beur: Youth Language and Identity in France*, ed. Farid Aitsiselmi (Bradford: Department of Modern Languages, University of Bradford, 2000), 95–112. For hip-hop film see Dominique Bluher, "Hip-Hop Cinema in France," *Camera Obscura* 16, 1 (2001): 77–96.

61 Vichy refused to assimilate the foreign completely.

62 Judith E. Vichniac, "French Socialists and Droit à la Différence: A Changing Dynamic," *French Politics and Society* 9, 1 (1991): 40–56; and Miriam Feldblum, *Reconstructing Citizenship: The Politics of Nationality Reform and Immigration in Contemporary France* (Albany: State University of New York Press, 1999).

63 For a helpful, succinct account of the National Front's rise, see Martin A. Schain, "The National Front in France and the Constitution of Political Legitimacy," *West European Politics* 10, 2 (1987): 229–52.

64 See Taguieff, "The New Cultural Racism in France."
65 On the issue of transatlantic movements of political form, see David Pinto, "The Atlantic Influence and the Mellowing of French Identity," *Contemporary France* 2 (1988): 117–33, esp. 128–29.
66 For discussion of the visual in French education, see Auslander, *Taste and Power*, chap. 9.
67 Our translation of Robert Trinca, "Des 'têtes de nègre' male digerées,'" *Libération*, 1–2 April 1995. Our thanks to Michelle Zancarini-Fournel for bringing this to our attention.

3

Colonial and Global Perspectives

Michael G. Vann

The Good, the Bad, and the Ugly

Variation and Difference in French Racism

in Colonial *Indochine*

The experience of race in the colonies has traditionally been re-garded as a question of dualism: colonizer versus colonized, op-pressor versus oppressed, or black versus white. In the francophone world, the work of prominent intellectual critics of empire, such as Frantz Fanon, Albert Memmi, and Jean-Paul Sartre, utilized this dualism in support of the nationalist and anticolonialist cause.[1] Often, historians have adopted this reductionist sketch of colonial life and reproduced a colonial bipolar disorder in their own work. This essay, which discusses the different ways in which people of color were classified in *Indochine Française*, takes issue with the classic texts of colonial theory. I argue that the model of colonial versus *indigène* constitutes an oversimplification of the racial expe-rience in *Indochine*. Based on my archival research, it is clear that the experience of race in the colonial world was not a Manichaean dichotomy, but something closer to a hierarchical scale with the white "race," of course, at the zenith; a situation closer to Gobineau than to Fanon.[2]

Colonial racism did not operate by homogenizing the nonwhites into a single entity. Instead, several distinct categories existed into which the various nonwhites fit. While these variations and dif-ferences in the construction of "race" reflected an understanding of real and important ethnic distinctions, they also expressed rac-ist prejudices in the dominant *mentalité* of the *Indochine* French. These prejudices stemmed from two sources: racial thinking in France brought to the colonies and racial assumptions based on the experience of the colonial encounter. An example of racial thinking exported to the colonies would be the commonly held views of Africans as hypersexualized or of Jews as miserly, attitudes one could characterize as a sort of racial general knowledge.[3] Conversely, the notion that Vietnamese were industrious but naïve was a racial stereotype that arose out of the colonial context, the lived experience of life in the imperial contact zone, indicating a more advanced or specialized racial knowledge.[4] As France emerged from the colonial scramble of the late nineteenth century, the general and the specialized forms of racial knowledge formed a nexus of racial (and, assuredly, racist) understanding of the other. In the colony, these imported and indigenous racial views fused into a generalized understanding of racial difference that transcended both the official and popular minds of imperial France. These patterns of French racism present an insight into the construction of white identity.[5] This identity, born out of the French colonial conquest, occupation, and rule of lands in Africa, Asia, and Oceania, returned to France first during *la grande guerre* and the interwar years, and later, in force, with decolonization and the creation of a postcolonial but multicultural France.[6]

In broad strokes, the French gaze placed nonwhites into several categories. Due to the thorny issues of citizenship in the colony, the colonial state accorded much weight on distinguishing between *indigènes* and *asiatiques étrangers*. The first group included *Annamites*, *Laotiens*, *Cambodgiens*, and *Moïs* (a catchall term for a variety of "hill people" and "savages").[7] In the second group we find Chinese and Japanese. Throughout the colonial era, the two categories of a third group, the *Chetty* of French India and the métis or mix-bloods, posed serious obstacles for clear and coherent administrative classification.[8] Racial thinking was not limited to legal concerns; economics and culture also shaped French perceptions of others. This paper explores the clusters of stereotypes surrounding each of the main racial groupings with the intention of illustrating the various ways that racial oppression operated in colonial *Indochine*. For the sake of brevity, the discussion focuses on the French views of *Annamites*, Chinese, Japanese, and *Chetty*.

Vietnamese

In the colonial lexicon, an *Annamite* was a Vietnamese. The French use of the term, drawn from the derogatory Chinese term for "pacified south," was designed to counter nationalist resistance and grated on the nerves of many Vietnamese. Following a classic divide-and-rule strategy, the French banned the term *Vietnam* and divided the nation into three colonies. *Annamites* were labeled *Co-chinchinois*, *Annamites*, and *Tonkinois*, following the south to north administrative divisions of Vietnam. These officially sanctioned terms influenced the way in which colonials thought about the colonized. Rather than dealing with some 20 million members of a nation with an autonomous history, the French belittled the *indigène* as a mere regional native, not part of a larger entity. The very act of defining and naming was bound up with the French strategy of domination by creating differences.[9] In their quotidian experiences, the French encountered the Vietnamese not as individuals but as representatives of certain types. The most common were the mandarin, the boy, the *congaï*, and the *nha-que*. During the conquest and pacification of Tonkin, the pirate was an inescapable image, but this faded after the turn of the century. These stereotypes nested in both the official mind and the popular sphere of French colonialism.

The figure of the mandarin entered the French colonial collective consciousness early in the history of the French penetration of Southeast Asia. Explorers and conquerors were the first to interact with these much maligned and poorly understood local officials. Adventurers who returned to France and published their stories, such as Jean Dupuis, presented the mandarin as an Asiatic despot only concerned with his own interests.[10] Few of these heroic narratives observed that the white interlopers muscled in on the mandarins' legal domain. The martyrdom of missionaries and the massacres of converts added to the unfavorable image of the mandarin by invoking deep cultural memories of the crusades.[11] Despite being a fairly rational act undertaken by indigenous leaders concerned with the obviously disruptive impact of Catholicism, this form of resistance cast the Vietnamese leaders as wicked and cruel villains engaged in a fight against Western values and beliefs. In addition to their violent barbarism, an unnatural vanity was projected onto these men. Their fondness of ritual and costume indicated moral flaws and a childish desire for self-glorification — a curious critique from the land of Louis XIV and Napoléon. Finally, they were condemned as decadent for their corruption and opium use (vices not unknown to the French). Republican France's overthrow of the anachronistic mandarins constituted a central component of the mythic *mission civilisatrice*. Colonists, who saw themselves as representatives of a universal and rational modernism, never felt at ease with these medieval holdouts. French reliance on the mandarins after the pacification and the willingness of many mandarins to cooperate with the new rulers resulted in an interesting paradox. While the popular anticolonial movements of the interwar years, be they nationalist or communist, fought against the mandarin class as an aspect of the colonial order, the French still viewed their closest collaborators with racist contempt.[12]

The most common contact between whites and nonwhites occurred in the employment of domestic help.[13] While the institution slowly died in France after the Great War, throughout the colonial era, it was unusual for a colonist to remain without servants. Even the lowest-level official in the state bureaucracy was expected to budget a portion of his income for the employment of a boy and a *bếp* (cook).[14] Widespread domestic employment revived atavistic social patterns which resonated with contemporary racism.[15] Boys were often seen as dishonest or of limited intelligence, supposedly due to their *déraciné* background.[16] Cartoons from the period lampooned the boy as the source of petty thefts. According to general consensus (and the daily papers), boys were likely to go through an employer's pockets, steal watches while one slept, or make off with other household items.[17] The rare and extreme cases where boys were suspected of murdering their patrons fed the paranoid French community's collective neuroses.[18] Nonetheless, employment of Vietnamese in the home constituted a necessary risk of colonial life.[19] Few colonials stopped to consider the temptations that would naturally arise from the dramatically different levels of wealth between master and servant. Rather, the view of the boy as criminal reinforced existing white suspicions of the *indigène*'s moral character.[20] White commentators deemed the Vietnamese too mysterious and hypocritical for them to understand. To the French, the native's mind was impenetrable and *malin*. At best, one might get used to the natives, but a real connection remained impossible.[21]

The lack of tact among *Annamite* boys made for another widespread stereotype. Numerous jokes circulated in which the naïve boy let slip some indiscreet detail about madame or monsieur's private life. On other occasions, the boy was far too literal and failed to understand the nuances of French culture.[22] The similarity between this form of humor and anecdotes about children is inescapable. Hence the French drew as a conclusion from these popular vignettes that the Vietnamese mind was childlike and immature. On the positive side, white colonials noted that Vietnamese boys were very eager to please. Despite their suspect *déraciné* identity,[23] many white observers praised their skills at imitation, suggesting Homi Bhabha's concept of the "mimic men."[24]

After the boy, the next most frequently encountered type was the *congaï*. Thanks to the romanticization of colonial sexual relations and to the changing nature of the institution, an exact definition of *congaï* is difficult.[25] Suffice it to say that the *congaï* was a young Vietnamese female somewhere between a prostitute and a mistress. While the experience could range from a cash-for-sex exchange to a long-term relationship with real emotional bonds, the common image suggested that of a professional live-in girlfriend, a sort of domestic employee for sexual service. However, following World War I, the French community evolved, as a wave of interwar immigration shrunk the colonial gender gap.[26] With more white women about, it became less common and less acceptable for French men to be openly *encongaïé*.[27] Both demographics and social attitudes were responsible for this sociosexual shift and the corresponding increase in social distance between white men and native women. Nonetheless, throughout the colonial era, the Vietnamese woman was associated with complacent sexuality and a lack of agency. She was willing but distant, taking no enjoyment in the act. Frequently, literary sources linked the Vietnamese woman with the other sensual yet alienating pleasure of *Indochine Française* — opium. One need look no further than Jean Lartéguy's or Graham Greene's portraits of the waning days of French rule in Asia to find this stereotype.[28]

As for the figure of the *nha-que*, or Vietnamese peasant, there is much less to say, since very little contact took place between the colonial rulers and the vast majority of their subjects. The French stayed in their urban strongholds and rarely ventured into the countryside.[29] If they did leave the safety and order of the French quarters of Hanoi or Saigon, it was often at the greatest speed possible and toward another white enclave, such as the beach resorts of Cap Saint Jacques and Do Son or the hill stations of Dalat, Tam Dao, and Sapa. Because the contact with the peasantry remained so limited, the racial stereotypes were even stronger. With little or no personal experience on which to base their ideas, literary sources frequently provided the images for French understanding of the *nha-que*.[30] Exoticist novels such as Jean Marquet's prizewinning *De la rizière à la montagne* and *Du village à la cité* gave a racial stereotype of the Vietnamese peasant as honest but superstitious.[31] Naively pure, the peasants paradoxically possessed a sage wisdom and inner peace. Simple creatures, they were prone to the corrupting influences of the outside world.[32] The trip to the city was destined to lead to ruin, and those who sought to cheat and exploit the *nha-que* found fertile soil in the small villages.[33] These images were closely related to the long-held French myth of the noble savage. Another stereotype concerned the *Annamite* peasant's impassivity in the face of fate. Even death itself produced a nonchalance unfathomable to the Westerner. In the French mind, the symbol of the peasant child atop a water buffalo summarized the eternal calm and monotony of the *Annamite*'s rural experience. France's self-proclaimed civilizing mission involved kick-starting the inertia-bound rural natives. Only through colonial modernization and motivation would these peasants be able to achieve their full productive potential.

There were also more generalized racist stereotypes about the Vietnamese, such as the commonly held belief that they had a terrible business sense. Related to their notion of the boys' naïveté, the French saw the Vietnamese as mere babes in the woods when it came to commerce. The *indigènes'* supposed lack of entrepreneurial drive and commercial sense constituted a central justification of France's civilizing mission in Southeast Asia.[34] *Indochine* had to be developed in spite of the Vietnamese. That the French had to protect the *indigènes* from the more active, shrewd, and unscrupulous Chinese made for a corollary to this thesis. As one observer remarked: "Que les chinois sont malins et que les annamites sont ignorants!"[35] This racist attitude toward the Vietnamese illustrates an important cultural manifestation of the colonial economic order. To justify imperial rule, the dominator debased and ridiculed the colonized, presenting colonial tutelage as the only solution. The colonizer is thus not only absolved of his sins, but also anointed with the sacred crusade of modernization. This two-way process denigrated the Asian as it exalted the European.

Related to their lack of business sense, the Vietnamese were depicted as compulsive gamblers. Observers noted the mania and lack of control that overtook the Vietnamese when involved in a game.[36] Conveniently forgetting their own fascination with games of chance as well as the fact that gambling was a state-run industry in *Indochine*, the French belabored the spread of this vice.[37] Of particular concern was the so-called *Jeu de Trente-Six Bêtes*. While it is true that the game wrecked many individuals' lives, the French were more concerned with their failure to control the syndicate running the game than with the game as a social ill. That a Chinese secret society controlled the game proved even more worrisome.[38]

Finally, the various superstitions the Vietnamese followed often amused the French. Few Westerners, typically orientalists, attempted to understand the local population's traditional and popular beliefs. Rather, the French mocked indigenous rituals and practices as typical of an immature and backward people. Conveniently forgetting the irrational traditions of provincial folk culture described by Eugen Weber,[39] white colonials used Vietnamese superstitions as a sign of French cultural, moral, and intellectual superiority. In patterns similar to Parisian contempt for rural France, colonials often mocked Vietnamese beliefs and expressed frustration with their alien worldview. Again, the contempt for superstitions reinforced the popular image of the Vietnamese as a childish and irrational people. Such paternalist racism rationalized French rule. It was France's mission, her white man's burden, to bring these people out of the darkness and into the light. Thus we find that cultural constructions, in this case racism, worked in synchronicity with economic and political forms of domination.

Chinese

The case of the overseas Chinese best demonstrates the colonial world's racial complexity and its lack of a clear racial bipolarism. Due to the centuries-old process of the Chinese diaspora and the chaos of nineteenth- and twentieth-century China, *Indochine*, as all of Southeast Asia, had a substantial Chinese population. Concentrated in the cities, this community's importance in the financial life of the region far outweighed its demographic size. The very success members of this community enjoyed in the commercial realm caused unease in the minds of the French.[40] Chinese transnational identity and their seemingly secretive social order increased the colonial overlords' anxiety, one articulated as racialized discourses on political and health issues.

The most common racial stereotype of the Chinese was economic. They were characterized as extraordinarily venal and motivated solely by the desire to amass wealth. Admittedly, crucial sectors of *Indochine*'s economy, especially trade, were dominated, if not controlled, by Chinese. Both the Vietnamese and the French resented their prosperity, be it as shopkeepers, landowners, or usurers. One observer doubted if the French were masters of *Indochine*, suggesting that the real power lay with the Chinese.[41] Interestingly,

The Good, the Bad, and the Ugly 193

the colonizers brought with them a prefabricated racial discourse for such a successful minority. Numerous reactionary elements fleeing the disgraceful and decadent Third Republic imported anti-Semitism, in full bloom in France throughout the period of high colonialism, to *Indochine*.[42] Hostile French colonials deployed their homegrown hatred of Jews and their supposed financial prowess against the Chinese. The racist cliché of "the Jew of Asia" was an oft-repeated slur of the era. As one local poet wrote:

> The celestial counts the sum
> which he stole and, smiling,
> seems hardly angry that he is called
> the Jew of the Far East.[43]

The constant scheming for money characterized Chinese women as well. A cartoon entitled "Chinese Diplomacy" showed a white woman asking one of her servants why the baby was crying. The Chinese nanny replied that the child was upset because the nanny was only paid fifteen piastres a month.[44]

As previously mentioned, the French regularly belabored the inability of either the white or Vietnamese community to replace the Chinese economic role. Since the white community was demographically weak, the French did what they could to encourage the Vietnamese to build up their financial skills.[45] This increased tensions between the Chinese and Vietnamese, which boiled over on several occasions. The anti-Chinese riots that began in Haiphong and soon spread to Hanoi in August of 1927 proved particularly frightening for the administration. The speed with which the violence erupted, the intensity of the anger, and the inability of the French to quickly restore order indicated the weakness of French control in *Indochine* and the dangers of a divide-and-rule policy.[46]

The system of regional connections offers one explanation for Chinese prosperity. Merchants could rely on extended family or other relationships that blended the personal and the professional to raise capital, secure commodities, or find outlets for their products. On one level, the existence of these networks frustrated French officials, who saw them as an unfair advantage. On a deeper level, the secret and closed nature of the networks caused a great deal of anxiety and suspicion.[47] It was suspected, and often the case, that smuggling rings were closely tied to legitimate Chinese trade. As a result, the administration became increasingly concerned with these networks and the existence of Chinese secret societies.[48] The threatening image of the mysterious Chinese underworld became a common nightmare in the official and popular minds. Unable to understand, let alone control, Chinese organized crime, the colonial rulers looked on all Chinese as likely criminals. In short, the imperial gaze racialized organized crime and branded all Chinese as potential criminals.

The political ferment and disorder in China added to the prejudice against the Chinese. The organization of political parties in response to the perceived threat to China from the West constituted an ominous development in the eyes of the French. First Sun Yat-sen's nationalist Kuomintang (KMT) and later the Chinese Communist Party posed the possibility of organized attacks on the existing social-political order in Asia. The French Sûreté closely watched cadre from both organizations.[49] Due to official paranoia and the clandestine work of the revolutionary groups, surveillance was extended to the general Chinese population as well.[50] The community was suspected of importing revolutionary ideas and fomenting revolt amongst the Vietnamese. With the revolution of 1911 and the ensuing chaos of civil war and warlordism, French administrators deemed China and the Chinese sources of disruption. After the outbreak of hostilities between Japan and China, the administration intensified efforts to monitor the Chinese community.[51]

The discourse of health and disease frequently expressed anti-Chinese sentiment. French medical thinking singled out China as the origin of numerous epidemics and the Chinese as vectors in the spread of illness. Colonial physicians regularly mentioned the bubonic plague and tuberculosis as two diseases that the Chinese brought to *Indochine*.[52] Sinophobia reached such heights that even Chinese food was deemed too risky for European consumption. A health manual for military personnel stationed in Saigon in the mid-1930s warned soldiers to avoid Chinese restaurants and cautioned married officers not to leave their children alone with servants lest they feed them sweets from Chinese merchants, a sure source of dysentery.[53] Chinese resistance to outside interference regularly frustrated the administration, and health officials were often suspicious and fearful of Chinese who resisted French attempts at social hygiene.[54] Municipal health authorities declared streets and buildings inhabited exclusively by Chinese as breeding grounds for disease and a danger to public health.[55]

In the colonial mind, the Chinese represented a pathogenic peril to the health of *Indochine Française*. The construction of this ethnic group as a biological danger was condensed with the alleged economic, criminal, and political threats into a generalized sinophobia. The porous border with China and the ambiguous legal status of Chinese immigrants strengthened the notion of that community as an uncontrollable element. The inability of the French to understand Chinese culture or to effectively penetrate the secret societies further added to the ominous air of mystery and distrust surrounding the Chinese. French racial attitudes thus centered around the idea that the Chinese posed a chaotic threat to their social order.

Japanese

The Japanese were another group of *asiatiques étrangers* that caused much concern. Despite their demographic insignificance in the colony, the Japanese were extremely important to the history of French racism in Asia. French views of the Japanese were complex and make a simple dichotomy of European versus Asian impossible. While obvious derogatory racial stereotyping existed, the French also admired many things about the Japanese. As Japan's regional ambitions grew and tensions between the two nations intensified, with Japan actually displacing French rule in World War II, French views of the Japanese became even more contradictory and ambiguous.

In the popular mind, the most common image of the Japanese was that of the geisha. This was due to two factors. First, many Europeans arrived in Asia with preconceived notions about Japanese refinement and sensuality. The fact that most, if not all, the Japanese women in the colony were *filles publiques* reinforced these ideas.[56] Brought to *Indochine* for the sex industry, Japanese women were a fetishized commodity. As it did the rare *valaque*, or white prostitute, the disproportionately male colonial community worshiped Japanese women. Thought to possess erotic knowledge and expertise not known to Vietnamese or Chinese women, the females advertised by the red lanterns of Japanese brothels held a special significance for the colonial male libido.[57] The white man's fantasy of the geisha was generalized into a hypersensual stereotype of the Japanese as a whole.

One of the most fascinating aspects of the Japanese case is the begrudging way in which their official status changed as Japan was transformed in the post-Meji era. The European nations were more than pleased with Japan's westernizing revolution. Praising the country for accepting science and modernizing its political structure, the European states signed treaties with Japan and welcomed the Japanese into the international community of nations. In stark contrast to the treatment of colonized peoples, the Japanese, despite being people of color, were to be treated as Europeans.[58]

However, the official view often conflicted with the popular racism of daily life. In May of 1912, a Monsieur Hessebe arrived in Saigon. As he disembarked, he was guided to a long line of other Asians and not to the short line for Europeans. Thereafter he was subjected to a medical examination along with numerous Chinese coolies. Since his protests to this "humiliating" treatment went unheeded by the local officials, the imperial consulate of Japan filed a formal protest on Hessebe's behalf. If this surprised local health inspectors, they were stunned when their superiors in the *gouvernement général d'Indochine* informed them that by the treaties of 4 August 1896 and 10 June 1907, Japanese citizens were to be treated as assimilated Europeans.[59] Another example proves even more telling. A visitor to *Indochine* in the early 1930s recounts the story of a "petit homme jaune" patiently waiting in line at the post office. As his turn came and he approached the window, he was rudely seized by the shoulders and thrown back from the window by a young European. As he began to conduct his business, the white man stated: "Je suis pressé!" The incident, evidently normal French behavior toward *indigènes*, turned few heads in the *bureau de poste*. However, to the surprise of the witnesses, the "little yellow man" handed the European a calling card and demanded an apology. The card read: "Matsuoko, Captain of the Imperial Guard, Tokyo, Japan." In the ensuing affair of honor, the friends of the Frenchman explained that he was very sorry but that he had taken Matsuoko for an *Annamite*.[60] Evidently the white man was new to the colony and did not have the sophisticated colonial gaze necessary to organize Asians according to the hierarchy of races in *Indochine*. This anecdote illustrates that privilege and status were not constructed in the simple black-and-white model, but were subject to the complicated racial calculus of life in the colonies.

Chetty

Because of their unique financial role and their glaring cultural differences, the *Chetty* constituted a much despised community. Hailing from the port cities of India, they were members of the *Civaïte* sect. Their numbers were small in both Saigon and Hanoi, but they were rather visible due to their overrepresentation in the usury trade, which often fed on the difficult economic plight of the rural Vietnamese population.[61] Referred to as a *fléau* and considered a worse threat than the Chinese, the *Chetty*'s financial dealings, which admittedly often involved steep interest rates, provoked hatred from both the French and the Vietnamese. Their exploitation of desperate Vietnamese villagers provoked bitterness from peasants who found that their business dealings were not a solution to their personal fiscal crises and from French authorities who feared that they were only increasing rural poverty. The local press vilified them as "morally and physically repugnant" and mocked their white robes.[62] Their ornate and wealthy temples provoked curiosity, and their religious processions caught many an eye but could not overcome the popular contempt for them. Michael Herr tells us that as late as 1968 they continued to be involved in Saigon's legal and extralegal economy.[63]

A report to the Popular Front's Commission Guernut (a special committee investigating colonial abuses) referred to them as "Shylocks" who would soon cause a *jacquerie* amongst the Vietnamese peasantry if their ways were not curtailed.[64] Again, we see French anti-Semitism deployed to explain racial difference and express racial hatred in Asia. We should note that the journalist who filed the report, Albert Celmenti, was a man of the left with a long history of political agitation for Vietnamese rights. That Clementi, who flirted with more radical strains of socialism, would condemn usury is not surprising, as this constituted a common criticism of high colonialism's economic violence. If one were to forget the intensity with which racial stereotyping saturated the colonial world, it might seem odd that a progressive would resort to such racist terminology. However, colonial racial and racist thinking frequently transcended political identity amongst the white community and was able to split left-wing organizations. Even the French Socialist Party (SFIO) succumbed to the racist logic of the colonies. On 22 April 1937, an organizational meeting was held to establish a local branch of the French Socialist Party. Under orders from Paris, the SFIO gathering and the Tonkinese branch of the party were to include both French and Vietnamese members. Despite their progressive ideology, the colonial whites resented being forced to create a multiracial organization. Forty-four whites and thirty-two nonwhites made it to the meeting. Unable to challenge the party hierarchy directly, the French members used their numbers to vote for measures that would ensure that the native party members held no power.[65]

Despite French and Vietnamese contempt, the administration tolerated the *Chetty*. The colonial community patronized these *Chetty* loan sharks, indicating that they did fill a niche in the local economy. Their legal status complicated the issue. Most of them came from ancien régime territories in India, such as Pondicherry. This gave the *Chetty* the special status of French subjects, allowing them to move about the French colonial empire with an ease not enjoyed by Vietnamese and other people who came under French domination in the late nineteenth century. This special status also meant that the administration had little power to enact the punitive measures called for by the group's local enemies. Furthermore, in the context of the institutionalized exploitation of the empire, French calls for the protection of the Vietnamese from the *Chetty* must be taken with a grain of salt, perhaps indicating jealousy rather than benevolent concern. As seen with the case of the Japanese, legal status could run counter to popular racial hatred, indicating some of the contradictions and complexities of French colonial racism.

The examples I have discussed show the complexity of white racism in *Indochine Française*. Rather than a clear case of colonizer and colonized, the ways in which people of color were treated in the colony depended on how the colonial gaze sorted and classified them. The various racial definitions resulted from prejudices brought to the colonies combined with the daily experiences of the colonial encounter itself. An understanding of this process provides a window into the functioning of official and popular racial oppression. Furthermore, the study of white racism provides insight into how the colonial context constructed white identity. While it is well known that the colonials defined themselves in opposition to the other, it is important to recognize that this other did not constitute a single entity, but rather a heterogeneous collection of ethnicities. Both the act of colonial autodefinition and the system of racial ordering reveal the workings of the colonial mind. The patterns of colonial racism and its influence on white identity played a central role in shaping France as it transformed into a postcolonial and multicultural society in the last third of the twentieth century. We should not overlook the fact that much of France's understanding of racial difference stemmed from the day-to-day realities of the empire.

Notes

This article was originally presented at the annual meeting of the Western Society for French History in September 1997, and it won the Edward Gargan Prize for best paper by a graduate student. An earlier version of this work appeared in *The Proceedings of the Western Society for French History* (1998). Research for this paper was conducted in France and Vietnam with support from a J. William Fulbright grant and several research grants from the History Board, University of California, Santa Cruz. I will use the following abbreviations in my notes: GGI for gouvernement général d'Indochine; IDEO for Imprimerie d'Extrême-Orient; CAOM for Centre des Archives Outre-Mer; AF for Ancien Fonds; HNA for Hanoi National Archives; MH for Marie de Hanoï; SLOTFOM for Service de Liaison avec les Originaires des Territoires Françaises d'Outre-Mer; and RST for résident superieur du Tonkin.

1   Frantz Fanon, *Peau noire, masques blancs* (Paris: Edition du Seuil, 1952); Fanon, *The Wretched of the Earth*, trans. Constance Farrington (New York: Grove, 1968); Fanon, trans. Haakon Chevalier, *A Dying Colonialism* (New York: Grove, 1967); and Albert Memmi, *The Colonizer and the Colonized*, trans. Howard Greenfeld (Boston: Beacon, 1967).

2   Arthur de Gobineau, *The Inequality of Human Races*, trans. Adrian Collins (New York: Fertig, 1967); and Tzvetan Todorov, *On Human Diversity: Nationalism, Racism, and Exoticism in French Thought*, trans. Catherine Porter (Cambridge, Mass.: Harvard University Press, 1993), 129–40.

3   See William B. Cohen, *The French Encounter with Africans: White Response to Blacks, 1530–1880* (Bloomington: Indiana University Press, 1980), for a study of European views of the African other. Also, T. Denean Sharpley-Whiting, *Black Venus: Sexualized Savages, Primal Fears, and Primitive Narratives in French* (Durham, N.C.: Duke University Press, 1999); and Victor Kiernan's revised classic, *The Lords of Human Kind: European Attitudes to Other Cultures in the Imperial Age* (London: Serif, 1995).

4 For the concept of the *contact zone*, see Mary Louise Pratt, *Imperial Eyes: Travel Writing and Transculturation* (New York: Routledge, 1992), 6–7.

5 For the theory of whiteness in American history, see David R. Roediger, *The Wages of Whiteness: Race and the Making of the American Working Class* (London: Verso, 1991); Eric Lott, *Love and Theft: Blackface Minstrelsy and the American Working Class* (New York: Oxford University Press, 1993); and Noel Ignatiev, *How the Irish Became White* (New York: Routledge, 1995). See also Theodore W. Allen, *The Invention of the White Race*, vol. 1, *Racial Oppression and Social Control* (London: Verso, 1994); Allen, *The Invention of the White Race*, vol. 2, *The Origins of Racial Oppression in Anglo-America* (London: Verso, 1997); Toni Morrison, *Playing in the Dark: Whiteness and the Literary Imagination* (New York: Vintage, 1993); Mike Hill, ed., *Whiteness: A Critical Reader* (New York: New York University Press, 1997); Ruth Frankenberg, ed., *Displacing Whiteness: Essays in Social and Cultural Criticism* (Durham, N.C.: Duke University Press, 1997); and Grace Elizabeth Hale, *Making Whiteness: The Culture of Segregation in the South, 1890–1940* (New York: Pantheon, 1998). For reviews of the growing field, see Liz McMillen, "Lifting the Veil from Whiteness: Growing Body of Scholarship Challenges a Racial 'Norm,'" *Chronicle of Higher Education*, 8 September 1995, A23; Shelly Fisher Fishken, "Interrogating 'Whiteness,' Complicating 'Blackness': Remapping American Culture," *American Quarterly* (1995): 428–66; and David W. Stowe, "Uncolored People," *Lingua Franca*, September 1996, 68–77.

6 Tyler Stovall, "Colonial Workers in France during the Great War" in *European Imperialism, 1830-1930*, ed. Alice L. Conklin and Ian Christopher Fletcher (New York: Houghton Mifflin, 1999), 165-77; Elizabeth Ezra, *The Colonial Unconscious: Race and Culture in Interwar France* (Ithaca, N.Y.: Cornell University Press, 2000); Herman Lebovics, *True France: The Wars over Cultural Identity, 1900-1945* (Ithaca, N.Y.: Cornell University Press, 1992); and Kristin Ross, *Fast Cars, Clean Bodies: Decolonization and the Reordering of French Culture* (Cambridge, Mass: MIT Press, 1995). For France's problematic history of extending democratic rights to people of color in the postcolonial era, see Maxim Silverman, *Deconstructing the Nation: Immigration, Racism, and Citizenship in Modern France* (New York: Routledge, 1992); Rogers Brubaker, *Citizenship and Nationhood in France and Germany* (Cambridge, Mass.: Harvard University Press, 1992); Emmanuel Todd, *La nouvelle France* (Paris: Editions du Seuil, 1988); and Todd, *Le destin des immigrés: Assimilation et ségrégation dans les démocraties occidentales* (Paris: Editions du Seuil, 1994).

7   GGI, *Annuaire statistique de l'Indochine: 1913–1923*   (Hanoi: IDEO, 1924), 23–26.

8   Ann Stoler, "Making Empire Respectable: The Politics of Race and Sexual Morality in Twentieth-Century Colonial Cultures," in *Imperial Monkey Business: Racial Supremacy in Social Darwinist Theory and Colonial Practice*, ed. Jan Breman (Amsterdam: VU University Press, 1990); and Stoler "Sexual Affronts and Racial Frontiers: European Identities and the Cultural Politics of Exclusion in Colonial Southeast Asia," *Comparative Studies in Society and History* (1992).

9   Christopher E. Goscha, *Vietnam or Indochina?* (Copenhagen: NIAS, 1995).

10 Jean Dupuis and Jules Gros, *La conquête du Tong-Kin par vingt-sept Français commandés par Jean Dupuis* (Paris: Maurice Dreyfous, 1885); Colonel E. Diguet de l'Infanterie Coloniale, *Annam et Indo-Chine Française* (Paris: Augustin Challamel, 1908); Jean Dupuis, *Le Tonkin de 1872 à 1886: Histoire et politque* (Paris: Augustin Challamel, 1910); Colonel Duboc des Troupes Colonailes, *L'Indochine contemporaine* (Paris: Charles-Lavauzelle et Cie, 1932); Jean Marquet and Jean Norel, *L'occupation du Tonkin par la France (1873–1874) d'après des documents inédits* (Saigon: n.p., 1936).

11 Charles Fourniau, *Annam-Tonkin, 1885–1896: Lettrés et paysans vietnamiens face à la conquête coloniale* (Paris: Editions L'Harmattan, 1989).

12 Herein lies the original inspiration for this article. I would suggest a comparison with British attitudes toward the Kikuyu as opposed to the Masai in Kenya or the Punjabis who staffed the Indian civil service and the troublesome groups of the northwest frontier under the raj. In both cases, the ethnic groups who made imperial rule possible were despised as contemptible toadies, while those who presented a thorn in the side of the conquerors were considered legitimate men of virtue, true to their culture.

13 Eugène Pujarniscle, *Philoxène, ou De la littérature coloniale* (Paris: Librarie de Paris, 1931), 90; and Alfred Meynard, "La vie européenne au Tonkin," *Bulletin de la Société de Géographie et d'Etudes Coloniales de Marseille* 32 (1908): 69.

14 Joleaud Barrol, *La colonisation française au Tonkin et en Annam* (Paris: Plon, 1899), 59–60.

15 Joseph A. Schumpeter, "Imperialism as a Social Atavism," in *The "New Imperialism": Analysis of Late-Nineteenth-Century Expansion*, ed. Harrison M. Wright, 2d ed. (Lexington, Mass: Heath, 1976), 69–88.

16 Pujarniscle, *Philoxène*, 96; see also the comments pertaining to this subject in "Rapport sur la situation politique et économique de

l'Indochine. GGI," 17 February 1905, box 9, file 51, CAOM, AF, Aix-en-Provence.

17 See the daily section, "Echos du Tonkin" of *L'Indo-Chine Française*, especially 26–27 January 1896 and 9–10 February 1896; "Nos Boys," *La Vie Indochinoise*, 28 November 1896; and Eugène Jung, *L'initiation coloniale: Guide à l'usage de tous les futurs coloniaux (fonctionnaires et colons)* (Paris: Jung, 1931), 18–19.

18 "Rapport sur la situation politque et économique de l'Indochine. GGI," 17 February 1905, box 9, file 51, CAOM, AF; and "Justice, affaires divers: Assassinat de Madame Vve Beljionne," 19 November 1906, CAOM, GGI 4664.

19 "Boys et indigènes," *L'Indo-Chine Française*, 16 June 1896.

20 M. le Dr. Roux, "Intelligence et moralité de l'Annamite Tonkinois," *Bulletin de la Société de Géographie et d'Etudes Coloniales de Marseille* (1906): 190–91.

21 Pujarniscle, *Philoxène*, 81; and Pujarniscle, "De la mentalité et de la criminalité ches les annamites," *La revue indochinoise*, 7 October 1901, 897–900.

22 "Boyerie," *La Vie Indochinoise*, 23 January 1897; "Oh! Ces boys!" *La Vie Indochinoise*, 15 May 1897; and "Nos chers boys," *La Vie Indochinoise*, 25 December 1897.

23 Pujarniscle, *Philoxène*, 96.

24 Homi K. Bhabha, "Of Mimicery and Man: The Ambivalence of Colonial Discourse," in *Tensions of Empire: Colonial Cultures in a Bourgeois World*, ed. Frederick Cooper and Ann Laura Stoler (Berkeley: University of California Press, 1997).

25 See Gail Hershatter's recent work for an excellent history of the transformation of the sexual economy in another Asian colonial city, *Dangerous Pleasures: Prostitution and Modernity in Twentieth-Century Shanghai* (Berkeley: University of California Press, 1997).

26 Gilles de Gantès, "La population française au Tonkin entre 1931 et 1938" (master's thesis, Université de Provence, Centre d'Aix, 1981); and Ronald Hyam, *Empire and Sexuality: The British Experience* (Manchester: Manchester University Press, 1990).

27 Louis Roubaud, *Viet-Nam: La tragédie indochinoise* (Paris: Librarie Valois, 1931), 243.

28 Jean Lartéguy, *La ville étranglée* (Paris: René Julliard, 1955); and Graham Greene, *The Quiet American* (London: Heinemann, 1955).

29 Michael G. Vann, "All the World's a Stage, Especially in the Colonies: The Hanoi Exposition of 1902" (paper presented at "Empire and Propaganda: French Popular Imperialism" conference, Institut Français, London, 19 September 1997).

30 Pierre Jourda, *L'histoire de la littérature exotique française depuis*

Chateaubriand (Paris: Boivin, 1956); Patrick Laude, *Exoticisme indochinois et poésie: Etude sur l'oeuvre poétique d'Alfred Droin, Jeanne Leuba et Albert de Pouvourville* (Paris: Sudestasie, 1990); Ronald Lebel, *L'histoire de la littérature coloniale en France* (Paris: Larose, 1931); and Louis Malleret, *L'exoticisme indochinois dans la littérature française depuis 1860* (Paris: Larose, 1934).

31 Jean Marquet, *De la rizière à la montagne* (Paris: Delalain, 1920); and Marquet, *Du village à la cité* (Paris: Delalain, 1921).

32 Pujarniscle, *Philoxène*, 96.

33 "Rapport sur la situation politque et économique de l'Indochine. GGI," 17 February 1905, box 9, file 51, CAOM, AF; and "Affaire Riviére," 1912, CAOM, GGI 4770.

34 "Rapport sur la situation de la ville de Hanoi et de la zone suburbaine du 1er Juillet 1911 au 30 Juin 1912," file 39, HNA, MH.

35 "A. S. de la répression des jeux á Hanoï, 1909," CAOM, GGI 4713.

36 Pierre Nicolas, *Notes sur la vie française en Cochinchine* (Paris: Flammarion, 1900), 192–98.

37 Georges Garros, *Forceries humaines: L'Indochine lititqieuse esquisse d'une entente franco-annamite* (Paris: André Delpeuch, 1926), 117.

38 "A. S. de la répression des jeux á Hanoï, 1909," CAOM, GGI 4713.

39 Eugen Weber, *Peasants into Frenchmen: The Modernization of Rural France, 1870–1914* (Stanford, Calif.: Stanford University Press, 1976).

40 French immigration to counter the Chinese demographic threat was encouraged in P. B., *Le rôle et la situation de la famille française dans nos colonies* (Paris: Journal des Colonaiux et L'Armée Coloniale Réunis, 1927), 3.

41 Brieux, *Voyage aux Indes et en Indo-Chine: Simples notes d'un touriste* (Paris: Librarie Ch. Delagrave, 1910), 154–56.

42 Michael Burns, *Dreyfus: A Family Affair, 1789-1945* (London: Chatto and Windus, 1991); and Eric Cahm, *The Dreyfus Affair in French Society and Politics* (New York: Longman, 1996).

43 "Les Chinois: Commerçant chinois," *La Vie Indochinoise*, 15 January 1898. This translation is my own, as are all unmarked translations in this essay.

44 Andre Joyeux, *La vie large des colonies* (Paris: Maurice Bauche, n.d.).

45 "Tonkin, RST à GGI, rapport politique," 1919, CAOM, GGI 64190.

46 "Incidents d'Haïphong entre Chinois et Annamites," 1927, subfile 11, CAOM, SLOTFOM III/39.

47 Jean Chesneaux, ed., *Popular Movements and Secret Societies in China, 1840–1950* (Stanford, Calif.: Stanford University Press, 1972).

48 "Renseignements sur les sociétés secrétes chinoises," 1903, CAOM,

RST 34573; "Service de la Sûreté du Tonkin: Rapport annuel (1 jul. 1922–30 jun. 1923)," CAOM, RST 1549.

49 "Copie d'une lettre du procureur général a. s. des agissements des Chinois," 1904, CAOM, RST 34561; "Tonkin: Rapport politique," 1905, CAOM, GGI 64176; and "Designation des Chinois sur les actes judiciares en Indochine," 1912, CAOM, GGI 19165.

50 "Service de la Sûreté du Tonkin: Rapport annuel (1 jul. 1922–30 jun. 1923)," CAOM, RST 1549; and "Projet d'attentat sur le premier président de la cour," 10 June 1932, CAOM, RST 6775.

51 "Agitation anti-Japonaise, (1931–1932)," CAOM, RST 6782.

52 Gaide and Dorolle, La tuberculose et sa prophlylaxie en Indochine Française (Hanoi: IDEO, 1930), 7; and Gaide and Bodet, La peste en Indochine (Hanoi: IDEO, 1930), 5, 27–28.

53 Marine en Indochine, Direction Service de Santé, Les maladies évitables à Saigon (Saigon: Imp. J. Nguyen-Van-Viet, 1936), 2, 11.

54 Maurice Rondet-Saint, Choses de l'Indochine contemporaine (Paris: Plon, 1916), 288.

55 "Procès verbal de la séance ordinaire du 22 Novembre 1897 du conseil municipale de Hanoi," CAOM, GGI 6366.

56 "Renseignements sur les Japonais établis à Hanoï," 1905, CAOM, RST 34509.

57 "Prêtresses d'amour," La Vie Indochinoise, 28 November 1896; "Comment elles se donnent," La Vie Indochinoise, 19 December 1896; "Moeurs Japonaises," La Vie Indochinoise, 13 February 1897; "Nippon Jorôya! Japonaiserie," La Vie Indochinoise, 29 January 1899; and see the numerous untitled cartoons in La Vie Indochinois.

58 Alexandre de Siebold, L'accession du Japon au droit des gens européen (Paris: Librarie Cotillon, 1900).

59 "Consulat Imperial du Japon à GGI," 25 May 1912, CAOM, GGI 19167; and "GGI á Inspection Générale des Services Sanitaires et Médicaux, circulaire No15-8, Hanoi," 13 June 1912.

60 Roubaud, Viet-Nam, 250–51.

61 M. C. Rodriguez, Les enjeux de la vie municipale, à travers l'exemple de Saïgon, Cholon, Hanoï, Phnom Penh et Vientiane (Fin XIXème–1930) (Université de Provence, Aix-Marseille I, 1993), 142.

62 Raymond Veyhel, "Les chetty," L'avenir du Tonkin, 9 October and 14 October 1903.

63 Michael Herr, Dispatches (New York: Vintage, 1977).

64 "Voeux de M. A. Clementi, directeur-fondateur de L'Argus Indochinois," La Commission Guernut, box 23, file BC, CAOM.

65 "Tonkin," 1937, file 64201, CAOM, GGI.

Richard Fogarty and Michael A. Osborne

Constructions and Functions of Race in French

Military Medicine, 1830–1920

This essay examines perceptions of the status of French and African peoples in relation to the health and staffing concerns pressing on French colonial and military administrators from the beginning of the French conquest of Algeria in 1830 to the cataclysm of the First World War. We argue that even during the mature Third Republic the view that human races were inalterable or fixed had failed to define the field. While not denying a growing concern with physical anthropology, we find that on balance, French racial theories as expressed in the military and colonial literature remained pluralistic and highly fluid. While emerging concepts of scientific racism, which stressed inherent biological distinctions between members of different races, were important in the French medical community and in the military, many doctors continued to stress the fundamental unity of the human family, and cultural understandings of difference also remained significant in definitions of race. In fact, French racial attitudes in general were and remain based on a mixture of biological and cultural factors. It is the persistent and continuing role of culture that distinguishes French racial attitudes from thinking about race in many other national traditions. Our examination of assumptions about race in the French military medical community during the nineteenth and early twentieth centuries highlights this persistence and problematizes the notion of a so-called triumph of scientific racism in France during the nineteenth century.

Biological Determinism or Anthropological Pluralism?

According to William B. Cohen, biological views of race and the notion of black Africans as innately inferior to Europeans had triumphed by 1850.[1] But this claim hinges largely on the appearance of Arthur de Gobineau's *Essai sur l'inégalité des races humaines* (1853–55), a study which Cohen notes was rarely read in France, but one which he interprets as synthesizing French thoughts on race.[2] More recently, Joe Lunn has extended and elaborated on the biological argument in his studies of the West African troops who fought for France in World War I. For Lunn, "the tenets of biological determinism (including its racist implications) were widely accepted," and he believes that, "far from providing an exception to the rule, French attitudes were consistent with the mainstream of western European thought."[3] The problem with these views is that the French scientific community, and the French construction of scientific racism, differed quite markedly from those found in other European countries. In many particulars, the idea of "hard" or "fixed" anatomical or behavioral characters runs counter to the history of French biology. Unlike Germany and Great Britain, France rejected Darwinism; French naturalists clung to variants of Lamarckian transformist ideas which privileged the biology of individuals, environmental agency, notions of plasticity, and the ultimate unity of biological types, including the races of humankind.[4] Additionally, the very concept of what constitutes a biological ("hard" or "separate") race, and what was needed to keep that race firm or "fixed," requires contextualization. Darwin had only rudimentary ideas of particulate inheritance, and certainly nothing as sophisticated as Mendelism. In the five editions of *On the Origin of Species* subsequent to the original of 1859, Darwin grew ever more favorable to the agency of acquired characters and so-called Lamarckian factors as influences on the life of the organism. The belated acceptance of Mendelian genetics in France is telling, for Mendelism, prior to its recognition as a source of variation, might have provided a scientific logic for firming racial boundaries. But French scientists were as insistent in their rejection of Mendelian genetics as they had been of Darwinian ideas. This circumstance distinguishes France from the sort of thinking typified by American physicians like Paul Freer, who saw Filipinos as having a hereditary immunity to cholera and other afflictions of the tropics.[5] Not until the 1930s did some French bacteriologists embrace Mendelian approaches.[6] Given these circumstances, what we might call *plasticity*, as opposed to *firmness*, typified racial categories, which in some measure remained permeable to the influences of both culture and environment. Based on the scientific knowledge of the era, even biological races had some but probably not limitless ability to acquire and pass on through inheritance many of the elements of European culture such as the skills of singing, creating poetry, making fine wine, and operating a rifle. They merely needed to be exposed to these elements of culture.

Positing the mid-century as a triumphal dividing line between older ethnological views of race and the newer physical anthropology championed by Paul Broca and many members of the Société d'Anthropologique de Paris, which Broca founded in 1859, risks overinterpreting earlier racial theories as "softer" or perhaps more ethnological and literary. Broca's writings reveal him as a master of literary performance. But we must not read too much into Broca's posturing or his programmatic distinctions between the old and the new, nor must we imagine that his representations of the state of French anthropology remained unbiased. Above all, Broca was institution building, and he sought to define his activities and research as the new wave of the investigation of man. In fact, the discursive and methodological levels manifest a good deal of continuity in racial thought and anthropological techniques throughout the nineteenth century. For example, in the late eighteenth century, the Dutch anatomist Peter Camper, soon followed by the French comparative anatomist Georges Cuvier and a host of phrenologists, promoted the study of facial angles, an emblematic technique of anthropometry. Thus there was much overlap and continuity in the concerns of the Société Ethnologique de Paris, founded by the physician William Edwards in 1839, and Broca's group of 1859.[7] Edwards promoted an idea of racial types influenced by intermixture which does not map well onto later ideas of race. But his vision of a research program for the Société Ethnologique de Paris was eminently pluralistic and included the study of physical anthropology alongside the investigation of languages, moral character, and historical traditions.[8]

Even if one clings to the claim that physical anthropological methods and ideas ascended after 1850, there still remain as many problems with singling out physical anthropology as the main taproot of ideas on race as there do with the notion that biologically fixed concepts of race need to be read as impervious to culture. Diverse currents of biomedical thought, including medical geography, qualitative demography, and even mental medicine, melded into the synthetic discipline which became French anthropology. Beyond Broca, French anthropology remained quite ecumenical. Thus when in 1856 the zoologist and physician Armand Quatrefages de Bréau — perhaps second only to Broca in terms of celebrity, and second to none in terms of his volume of publications on anthropology and natural history — assumed the chair of anthropology at the Paris Museum of Natural History, he too, like Edwards, envisioned an inclusive anthropological science which would subsume traditions as diverse as ethnography, ethnology, anthropography, and the sociology and psychology of peoples.[9] Quatrefages de Bréau, while recognizing a small degree of ethnological immunity, felt that most diseases were common to all races, and that men shared a "nature fondamentale."[10]

In Napoleonic France, in North Africa in the 1830s, and even in the early twentieth century, French expeditionary and military physicians recorded physical attributes of race, but often assessed them in relationship to place and a long list of neo-Hippocratic and hygienic factors including climate, diet, appropriate clothing, and exercise.[11] Additionally, not all French army physicians thought physical characteristics alone determined a race's place in the hierarchies they reveled in constructing. As Patricia Lorcin has noted, French military physicians who studied the Arab and Berber peoples of North Africa in the years 1830 to 1870 elaborated their ideas "prior to a time when the superiority of French medicine could be delineated in technological terms and was thus measured according to philosophical, sociological or moral indexes."[12] After 1850, the methods used in the scientific and medical investigation of the peoples of humanity continued in a pluralistic mode. Ethnological methods, travel literature, and impressionistic accounts of the habits and languages of non-French peoples continued as a part of anthropology well into the Third Republic.

French Naval Medicine: Genres of Expression and Racial Immunity

Until the founding of the Service de Santé des Colonies et Pays de Protectorat in 1890, the navy trained the vast majority of colonial physicians. Concerned in general with preventive medicine and racial immunity, but more specifically with the diseases of Europeans in the tropics, the majority of these men published little and tended to be practitioners both first and last. Yet naval physicians were required to compose reports of voyages, and most colonial physicians wrote yearly reports on the health of their station. Many physicians who published something in addition to their medical theses often framed their work as a medical topography. This genre of expression, paradigmatic for naval physicians and common in tropical medicine, frequently eschewed the details of physical anthropology and promoted a place-based geographical view of disease and health. What these doctors tended to write about was more linked to the strategies of disease avoidance and the needs of hygiene than to therapeutic medicine.[13] As such, naval medicine, while it, too, rested on a foundation of surgery and pathological anatomy, was rather different in terms of methods and intellectual products from the more clinical approach to medicine promoted by the Paris Faculty of Medicine.[14]

Typical of French medical topography's narrative arc was a formulaic presentation with much attention to local details. Race often appears here, but a vast forest of details spanning geography, ethnography, demography, and comparative pathology most frequently subsume the concept.[15] For example, the naval physician Richaud, engaged in early French activities in Southeast Asia in the 1860s, wrote a medical topography of the region in which he evaluated the country's health dangers and its peoples. Earlier French medical literature had tended to characterize Cochin China as the country of cholera and ulcer, the latter of which affected many of the region's inhabitants. Richaud qualified the notion that only Asians contracted the ulcer and argued that while the disease was most severe among Asian peoples, it also affected Europeans and Africans. Thus his approach was to break down the idea that Europeans and Asians had radically different immunities or predispositions to disease. Noting that a comparative pathology of Europeans and *indigènes* remained to be written, he related that while the Annamite peoples appeared pale and rather sickly, they had many attributes of value to the French, including an aptitude for heavy and sustained labor. Given a better diet, they would rapidly gain even more strength. In their abilities as soldiers, they might even surpass Europeans, as "wounds, in general, are endured by the Annamites with a remarkable courage and perfect resignation. Is this lack of sensibility or is it Stoicism? At any rate . . . the Annamite dies with a resoluteness and calm rarely found among Europeans."[16] Neither scientific racism nor physical anthropology primarily drove the concerns of Richaud and others who adopted this genre of medical commentary.

Richaud's study of the etiology of ulcers was one of many to argue against absolute notions of firm racial immunity and, by extension, for the permeability of racial boundaries as regards morbidity. Others, too, noted that colonizer and colonized suffered from the same diseases, though perhaps in somewhat different proportions. Doctor J. Chapuis, first physician in chief of the colony of Cayenne in 1864, argued that the ulcers described by Richaud were identical with those that struck all races on the French prison colony of Guyana and the rainbow of ethnic groups in New Caledonia, Mozambique, Senegal, and the other corners of the French empire. Hinting that malaria constituted a universal phenomenon which also struck without much regard for race, he wrote of the ulcers that "no race is exempt, but the rapidity of progression, its extent, and its depth of some disorders are, for different races, in direct relation to . . . the distressing hygienic conditions that their social state induces."[17] Indicative of the trend of military medicine during the Third Republic, naval medical school professors began to question the firmness of other racialized categories of disease, such as the *mal d'estomac des nègres*.[18] In India, too, members of the Indian Medical Service began to see immunity in terms of a mixture of cultural factors, including sanitation, rather than in terms of race.[19]

In addition to the adoption of medical topography as a genre of expression and a medical focus on the etiology of disease, the heritage of placing the study of man within the purview of natural history mitigated against the notion of races as a narrow concept and one impervious to climatic and cultural agency. By the 1860s, the influence of Georges Cuvier had waned considerably.[20] French naval physicians were required to take classes in medical natural history and human anatomy as part of their professional training. These pedagogical traditions were themselves set within a larger program of botanical, general zoological, and climatological study. An oft-reprinted pamphlet solicited by the minister of the navy for its officers and crafted by professors at the Paris Museum of Natural History enunciated many aspects of this program. The text and recommended collection methods of the *Instructions pour voyageurs* of 1818, republished with only slight modifications in 1824, 1827, 1829, 1845, and 1860, called for reconnaissance and close enumeration of the three kingdoms of nature with an eye toward the exploitation of useful plants.[21] This pluralistic and utilitarian approach to exotic nature and its peoples continued within the French navy, as did the naval physicians' interest in how climate and culture intersected with physical anthropological ideas of race.

The French presence in West Africa grew markedly during the Second Empire. The naval physician Barthélemy Benoit, on the occasion of his departure for Senegal in 1859, requested that the new Société d'Anthropologie de Paris draft instructions for anthropological research on the region's peoples. Authored by three early members of the group, including the zoologist and critic of Georges Cuvier, Isidore Geoffroy Saint-Hilaire, and Broca, the instructions appeared in 1864 in the official voice of naval medicine, the *Archives de médecine navale*. The authors asserted the primacy of West Africa for anthropological investigation and noted how "no region of the globe offers the anthropologist a field of observations more fertile than our colony of Senegal."[22] The methodology suggested to guide investigations in Senegal combined cultural and ethnological approaches with physical anthropology.

French anthropologists recognized three great races in the region: Yoloffs, Mandingues, and an invading race, the Foulahs. The latter were described as having a reddish brown complexion and smooth hair and being largely of the Islamic faith. In terms of physical anthropology, the scientists hoped to gather crania and skeletons, or failing these, a cast of a cranium or at least craniometric and dentitional information.[23] Yet even here the brief proved pluralistic in intent, for in addition to skeletal characteristics, the anthropologists also asked whether African newborns were born white and then changed color, and for information on the languages and religions of the regions, and on the native inhabitants' use of domesticated animals.

In placing the peoples of West Africa within a racial hierarchy, it is well again to frame this exercise in terms of practical applications or specific aptitudes, rather than reducing all to a narrow focus on the physical features of race. Realizing that naval physicians would likely be caught up mainly in medical duties and that physical anthropological research would need to come second, if at all, the anthropologists saw the major task of the naval physician as one of constructing a comparative pathology of the races. People living in or nearly at the "savage state" were thought to be mostly free of cancers, aneurysms, and mental diseases common among Europeans. Even childbirth seemed easier for some colonized peoples than for Europeans.[24] As regards susceptibility to disease, Broca asked "if these more or less complete immunities depend on race, or a savage mode of life, or on diet, or climate." He continued, "The influences of the races appear to be demonstrated at least for some cases, and naval physicians will be able to furnish important information on this point. The question of acclimatization, so important from all points of view, is equally among the questions still awaiting solution."[25] The medical study of human acclimatization, and more broadly the ability of Europeans to adapt to life in the tropics — whether through regimes of public and personal hygiene or through individual physiological adaptation to new disease ecologies — was linked with anthropological concerns and also with neo-Lamarckian biology.[26] As one historian of anthropology put it, "The utilitarian objectives of colonialism made acclimatization the fundamental scientific question it raised."[27] With such a list of responsibilities, and given the multitude of colonial physicians' tasks, race clearly could only emerge as one factor of study among many others.

Among the naval physicians who found time to write on West African anthropology and racial immunity, none wrote more than Jean-Baptiste Laurent Bérenger-Féraud. Bérenger-Féraud first went to West Africa in 1855 at the age of twenty. Over the course of a career that lasted some four decades, he spent nearly half his time on ship or posted in the colonies at stations including Senegal, the Caribbean, Tunisia, and Pondichéry. As Cohen notes, the polygenist Bérenger-Féraud wrote against racial intermixture,[28] but his views did not define the field, and other anthropologists such as Paul Topinard thought that racial intermixture might actually strengthen resistance to disease.[29] Bérenger-Féraud, after serving with distinction at the army's Val-de-Grâce hospital during the siege of Paris, gained a promotion and a posting to the West African outpost of Gorée. Shortly thereafter, he obtained the directorship of the health service of Senegal, a function in which he served during 1872 and 1873.[30] A two-volume book on the illnesses of Europeans in Senegal published soon after his tour of duty reveals him as a stern critic of the idea that Europeans could ever adapt to life in West Africa.[31] But Bérenger-Féraud's methodology was only that of physical anthropology. Author of some fifteen books and one hundred articles, his anthropological writings included ethnographical studies of African and French provincial stories, songs, migrations, and habits.[32] Yet even hard-line racialists like Bérenger-Féraud could adopt a more pluralistic approach in their medical writings, and toward the end of his life his stance on the absoluteness of racial immunity softened.

Although originally a surgeon, Bérenger-Féraud studied fevers for much of his career. Publishing an informed historical study of yellow fever in Senegal in 1874,[33] a colony visited by epidemics of the disease in 1830, 1837, 1859, 1866, and 1867, he returned to the topic in 1891. Impressed with the new science of parasitology and Louis Pasteur's germ theory, he was open to the idea that an as yet unknown microorganism might cause the disease.[34] Espousing a medical pluralism, he saw race as only part of the etiological riddle. Reviewing both racial and environmental factors on a global scale in the white, black, and intermediary — or creolized — races, he concluded that the white race was most susceptible to the disease. All the same, immunity was only relative, and while prior contracting of the illness seemed to confer some immunity, it was never, for any race, an absolute immunity. The "question of the immunity of races and individuals as regards yellow fever," he wrote, "is variable and too often contingent."[35] Hence, though inclining toward biological and fixist notions of race, even Bérenger-Féraud, in his investigations of ethnicity and disease, left considerable place for extra-racial factors. Other naval physicians went even further, including a future professor of tropical medicine at the new naval medical school at Bordeaux, who in his medical school thesis of 1886 argued that "the immunity of negroes is not an immunity of race; it is acquired by a visit to countries conquered by yellow fever, and the white race is subject to the same laws."[36] Thus, many years prior to the 1928 International Congress of Tropical Medicine and Hygiene, when W. H. Hoffmann of Cuba's Instituto Finlay declared that racial immunity to yellow fever did not exist, the research of naval physicians like Bérenger-Féraud had destabilized biological notions of race in matters of health.[37] This, of course, constitutes precisely the *opposite* of received versions of the evolution of biological racism in France.

By the first decade of the twentieth century, some sectors of colonial medicine had become civilianized, and Bordeaux, Marseille, and Paris boasted institutes of tropical medicine. While it was not quite true, as a backer of the Institute for Colonial Medicine at Paris claimed, that "in looking at our books on pathology, we can see that there is no mention of the illnesses specially attacking the black race," a number of physicians now enamored by the germ theory of disease were discounting the thesis of a firm and absolute racial immunity.[38] On medical grounds, at least, commonalities rather than differences typified the races of humanity. Having reviewed some of the elements of French naval medicine that informed a pluralistic approach to racial theory, we now turn to the deployment of medicalized ideas of race in the French army during World War I.

Race and Health in a New Century

If the most important military observers of race during the nineteenth century were in the navy, the more active voices came from within the army by the beginning of the twentieth century. This shift occurred for two main reasons. First, in 1900, the navy lost direct administrative control over military matters in the colonies. The Ministry of the Navy had first surrendered some of its exclusive control over the colonies in 1893, with the creation of the Ministry of the Colonies. Still, throughout the nineteenth century, the navy and its marine troops were primarily responsible for colonial security, though the army took part in major campaigns.[39] Many army officers took temporary transfers into the marines in order to escape dreary and uneventful garrison life in France, as colonial service was a way to see real action and gain more rapid promotion than available in the metropolitan army. But in 1900, the legislature created a separate *armée coloniale* under the authority of the Ministry of War, transferring most marine troops, including *troupes indigènes* (as nonwhite colonial soldiers were known), away from naval command.[40]

A second event that increased the relative importance of the army in racial matters was the outbreak of the First World War in 1914. The navy's primary role in the conflict was to patrol the Mediterranean and protect troop movements between North Africa and France, while the British kept the German fleet bottled up in the North Sea. The main theaters of the war were on land, and for the French, specifically on the Western Front. Not only was the army's primary role here obvious, but hundreds of thousands of troops from the colonies came to the metropole to help drive out the German invaders. Among these were nearly 500,000 *troupes indigènes*, and the presence of so many nonwhite soldiers in the army and in France provoked a great deal of commentary about race. Although North Africans made up the bulk of *troupes indigènes* in France, and thousands of Madagascans, Indochinese, and Antilleans also served, the most prominent soldiers in the army's and the public's eyes were men from West Africa. Their fame as "shock troops" and ferocious warriors had more to do with stereotypes about black

Race in French Military Medicine 215

Africans than with reality, but their notoriety and the fact that the army often assigned them to combat duty at the front guaranteed that much of the discourse about race in the ranks would center on West Africans.[41]

Even before the war, West African soldiers (known collectively, despite their provenance from many different areas of France's huge West African territory, as *tirailleurs sénégalais*) had gained fame, primarily through the publicity surrounding Colonel (later General) Charles Mangin's efforts to persuade the army to raise large numbers of troops from the area. Mangin pitched his ideas as the only adequate response to an increasingly populous and powerful Germany, which threatened the national security of a France plagued by a declining metropolitan birthrate. His arguments about the soldierly qualities of West Africans demonstrated the same mix of biological and cultural factors that would characterize racial thinking throughout the Great War.[42]

Mangin maintained that the "much less developed" nervous systems of black Africans rendered them more stable under fire, especially heavy artillery fire, than white soldiers. In fact, the "extreme nervousness of civilized peoples" was one of the main dangers of modern war, he claimed, and the use of West African troops would address this problem.[43] Yet this inherent characteristic was not the only quality that made West Africans ideal soldiers. Mangin explicitly rejected the biological deterministic argument that Africans could not live in cold climates, a position that would render these troops useless in a European war, or even in conflicts in many parts of North Africa. With minimal precautions, he argued, *tirailleurs sénégalais* could be deployed in colder weather, and their ability to adapt to extreme climates was one of the most compelling reasons for recruiting them. Mangin even cited the example of black Americans living in the northern parts of the United States as proof of his assertions.[44] Moreover, he claimed that Africans did not have any special illnesses that would affect either their performance or the health of whites with whom they came in contact.[45]

Finally, it was not only different biological characteristics, but different histories that rendered the warlike instincts of black Africans superior to those of Europeans. Mangin remarked that throughout its history, Africa had been "a vast battlefield,"[46] and he spent a large part of his 1911 treatise on the subject of raising an army in West Africa, *La force noire*, reviewing the brilliant history of black troops from the days of the ancient Egyptians to the Franco-

Prussian War. He concluded that this warlike past had prepared Africans for service in the French army and that the continuing hardships of life in West Africa had hardened its inhabitants, resulting in the legendary endurance of the *tirailleurs sénégalais* during colonial campaigns.[47]

Mangin's ideas had a great influence on the views of others toward West African soldiers and race, and a similar mixture of biological and cultural racism characterized thinking in the army throughout the First World War. During this period, the medical staff assigned to serve with *troupes indigènes*, especially those serving with the West African soldiers, emerged as a critical group of observers. With their expertise in medical and health issues, army doctors were likely to address issues of biology and race in their observations about illnesses among the *tirailleurs*, but they, too, stressed cultural factors in explaining racial difference.

Race and the Contingencies of War

After the war began in Europe, many doctors in training at military medical schools or on other duties found themselves suddenly called to service at the front.[48] A number of these men were attached to units of the colonial army or to camps in the south of France, where the army stationed many *troupes indigènes* during the cold winter months. As active duty interrupted the studies of some of these medical personnel, several completed abbreviated theses in order to complete their medical degrees at the University of Bordeaux. A few chose as the subject of their *thèses de guerre*, as one of them called his work, *pathologie exotique*, a subject they had ample occasion to observe while treating colonial subjects.[49] A particular concern within this field was the incidence of pneumonia among West African soldiers.[50] Though these men spent the cold, damp European winters away from the front in the relative warmth of southern France or North Africa, they demonstrated a marked susceptibility to respiratory illnesses, in particular bronchitis and pneumonia. The discussions of the etiology, symptoms, and treatment of this affliction in the wartime Bordeaux theses devoted to illness among the *tirailleurs sénégalais* make clear the mixture of cultural and biological factors that underlay racial thinking among military physicians, and these works are representative of the broader current of thought within the army on issues of health, medicine, and race.

Pierre Jandeau, a medical officer in the *armée coloniale*, published his doctoral thesis in 1916.[51] He reported that on arriving at a camp for West African soldiers at Arcachon (near Bordeaux), the proportion of pneumonia cases among the pulmonary infections he examined immediately struck him. Fifty-seven percent were pneumonia, a much higher rate, he claimed, than found among white troops. From this he concluded that "the pneumococcus so widespread, in a normal state, in the nasopharynx, finds in the *tirailleur sénégalais* a terrain very favorable to its development."[52] In some ways, he noted, the course of the disease among Africans was similar to that observed among alcoholics, as both often suffered from heart complications and even death due to cardiac arrest during treatment. Yet Jandeau warned against too facile a comparison of the two groups, as the weak heart and high blood pressure of West Africans had a very precise cause: the habitual consumption of kola nuts. In fact, Jandeau characterized the daily consumption of large numbers of these nuts as an "abuse" leading to a perpetual state of hypertension. He supported this claim by comparing the pulse and blood pressure of several men who ate kola nuts regularly with that of the one soldier in the battalion who did not eat the nuts.[53] Still, despite the very real danger of complications arising from this hypertension while suffering from pneumonia, West African patients responded well to treatment that addressed this special condition.

It was not merely the weakened state of the *tirailleurs'* hearts that rendered them particularly vulnerable to serious cases of pneumonia. Jandeau noted that recent recruits were qualitatively different from the career soldiers who had helped the French during their conquest of West Africa and who had made up the first contingents sent to France early in the war. The soldiers that began to arrive in increasing numbers in 1916 were not such *soldats de métier*, hardened by long years of service and campaigning and used to diverse climates. The new troops were not only younger, but they were "drawn from villages where their natural indolence and the ease of life had kept them in nearly complete idleness." In fact, it was the "pacific administration" of the French that had made life so easy, erasing the warlike character of the West Africans. In an argument that echoed certain strains of the then-current discourse about "degeneration" among Europeans corrupted by modern modes of existence, Jandeau maintained that as a result of France's destruction of the reign of the sultans, slavery, and cannibalism, inhabitants of the rich and fertile countries of West Africa no longer had any reason "to exercise their muscles, to tire their bodies," and merely "savored the benefits of pacification."[54] Added to this was the hasty recruitment into the French army, the abrupt introduction of a harsh regimen of training, fatiguing travel to a strange land, and a sudden change of climate. Even though the south of France experienced fairly mild weather during the spring, heavy rains, hot days, and cool nights all combined to lower the Africans' resistance to disease.

Certain habits among the *tirailleurs* only made the situation worse. Jandeau argued that West Africans were incapable of defending themselves from the cold, as they did not like to wear warm clothes and were ignorant of the most basic rules of hygiene. Even strict surveillance by their officers did not always improve the situation. The *tirailleurs* went to bed only very late at night, "risking their pay and their health in interminable nocturnal parties" at which they indulged their love of gambling. They slept "nearly nude," often without covers, drank enormous amounts of cold water after exercise, failed to remove wet clothing after long marches, exposed themselves to the cold naïvely, and bathed in cold water while still sweating after strenuous work.[55] All of these factors — poor hygiene, poor physical condition, the long voyage, abrupt climate change, and consumption of kola nuts — combined to provide a *terrain de choix* for the pneumococcus.[56] To these factors Jandeau added the possibility of a biological proclivity of Africans to pneumonia. Emile Marchoux had claimed that he had succeeded in restoring the virulence of attenuated pneumoncocci in a solution by adding blood taken from a black person. If this was true, Jandeau remarked, then it was no wonder that West African troops were suffering inordinately from pneumonia while in France.[57]

Ultimately, Jandeau concluded that despite some differences in the response of the *tirailleurs* to their illness, and corresponding differences in treatment, the course of pneumonia among Africans was similar to that observed in whites. The "fatalistic" attitude of the *tirailleurs* rendered *médication morale* ineffective, as they lacked the "will to heal" that whites possessed. The only treatment that might help in this regard was the application of cupping glasses, in which West Africans placed great faith. Preventative treatment was also unlikely to be very effective, as the West African soldier would "always be a big child, resistant to the elementary rules of hygiene," and also because the sudden change of circumstances and climate was the most decisive factor in bringing on illness.[58]

Henry Templier, in his 1917 Bordeaux thesis, expanded Jandeau's earlier observations. Both men characterized the onset of pneumonia as a "hatching" (*l'éclosion*) of the disease within the *tirailleurs*.[59] The term strongly implied a biological proclivity toward pneumonia among West Africans, but cultural, environmental, and other factors seemed equally, and often more, important. Templier's study was based on his service in the hospital at the Courneau camp, just south of Bordeaux, where he treated numerous cases of pneumonia among the *tirailleurs sénégalais*. At the outset, he remarked that the low incidence of pneumonia among the white staff at the camp's hospital, while the *tirailleurs* suffered at a high rate, led him to affirm that West Africans were particularly sensitive to the pneumococcus bacteria. Emile Marchoux's work with the blood of Africans had verified this "dogma of colonial pathology."[60] But added to this inherent weakness was the West Africans' general laziness and indolence, which, following Jandeau, Templier attributed to the benefits of peaceful French rule; the poor health of new, young recruits; the rapid change of location and climate; and the failure of *tirailleurs* to observe elementary rules of hygiene.[61] Templier also repeated Jandeau's observations about the deleterious effect of kola nut consumption on the cardiac health of the soldiers.[62]

If Templier's study merely confirmed most of Jandeau's earlier observations and conclusions, the later work was more thorough, noted a higher incidence of death from pneumonia, and insisted more forcefully on the role of an inherent proclivity toward the disease. Yet Templier failed to mention a crucial factor in the virulence of the outbreak of pneumonia at Courneau, one that helps explain the higher rate of fatalities there when compared to Jandeau's earlier experience. The sanitary state of Courneau was nothing short of disastrous, and the influx of increasing numbers of recruits from Africa put growing strain on the camp's limited resources. On 9 December 1916, Blaise Diagne, the black African legislator who represented the Four Communes of Senegal in the French Chamber of Deputies, told that body that Courneau's sanitary state was such that he felt compelled to demand its immediate evacuation.[63] From the institution of the camp in March onward, there had been serious problems, but the Service de Santé declared the problems ameliorated and claimed that conditions at Courneau were no worse than at other camps.[64] As late as November, the commandant of the camp argued that the problems were minor and conditions were steadily improving.[65]

In fact, the epidemic of pneumonia during that summer and autumn was not restricted to Courneau, as many West Africans suffering from the disease were also admitted to hospitals at Menton and Fréjus. In all areas, the *tirailleurs* experienced a high mortality rate.[66] Yet a thorough inspection of Courneau in December 1916 provided a clear picture of the horrendous conditions. The camp was near a swamp, and rain, humidity, and lack of drainage made for an unhealthy climate. Moreover, facilities proved inadequate: the barracks had leaky roofs, so the *tirailleurs* often had to sleep under their beds; the floors were of sand and therefore impossible to clean and disinfect, especially as the soldiers spit on them, creating an ideal situation for the spread of pneumonia bacteria; conditions were overcrowded, with barracks holding twice their capacity; shower facilities were inadequate; heat was insufficient; and rations were meager. The statistics spoke for themselves: soldiers admitted to the hospital at Courneau suffered a mortality rate of 8.92 percent, while hospitals elsewhere recorded fewer overall hospitalizations and a mortality rate of 2.23 percent. Part of this situation doubtlessly resulted from the fact that the chief medical officer at Courneau, rather than being a doctor with experience in the colonies, was an obstetrician from Paris.[67]

In such conditions, it was hardly surprising that the *tirailleurs* suffered inordinately from pneumonia at Courneau. The army administration made further efforts to improve the camp, but conditions remained poor through Templier's stay in the spring of 1917. The West Africans finally left the camp for good that summer to make room for a mutinous contingent of Russian soldiers fighting on the Western Front. The camp remained unsanitary, even after the Russians left and American troops moved in.[68] Clearly, the camp at Courneau constituted a particularly unhealthy environment for the *tirailleurs*. Although Templier did not mention them explicitly, these conditions no doubt contributed to the pneumonia epidemic. Had he taken these conditions into account, he likely would have placed an even greater emphasis on soldiers' hygiene, as opposed to their inherent biological characteristics, than he did. As it was, the bias he shared with other French military personnel caused him to regard the hygienic problems as arising out of the *tirailleurs'* natural uncleanliness.

Another doctor stationed at Courneau, Lucien Viéron, showed a greater recognition of the decisive role of external factors such as hygiene and sanitation in determining the *tirailleurs'* propensity to contract pneumonia. His thesis, published in 1917, acknowledged the natural vulnerability of West Africans to pneumonia, readily apparent even in the colonies, but he focused on the circumstances that exacerbated this inherent condition. Given that soldiers had suffered from pneumonia during recruitment in West Africa — the disease taking a significant toll in training camps there during 1915–16 — it was unlikely that the cold weather of France worked as the decisive factor. In fact, Viéron argued, "displacement" constituted the most important variable.

Two specific incidents had helped to convince him of this. First, the worst outbreak of pneumonia occurred in August 1916, immediately after the arrival of new recruits from West Africa and during the hottest days of the summer.[69] The outbreak began to ease by September, and the percentage of men afflicted with the disease was eight times lower by February, one of the coldest months of the winter. The second incident was the aftermath of the battalion's move from Courneau to a camp at nearby Bayonne (though Viéron does not mention this, the movement resulted from the army's recognition of the overcrowding and poor conditions at Courneau). Immediately following this move, which involved only a minor displacement, the number of cases of pneumonia increased for a short period, before settling down again in February. Clearly, according to Viéron, the movement from one place to another, with the attendant change in climate, fatigue, alterations in eating habits, emotional and mental strain, and "always defective installations in the hubbub of an arrival, where everything is planned, but nothing is ready," reduced the resistance of *tirailleurs* to "that continual host of the respiratory pathways that is the pneumococcus."[70]

For this author, the external factors, rather than race, proved crucial in bringing on pneumonia epidemics among West Africans. Although a biological proclivity to the disease marked the starting point for his analysis, he cited the usual cultural factors in determining Africans' vulnerability to the pneumococcus, such as poor hygienic habits, apathy, and general ignorance. As such, his work lends itself as a good example of the pluralistic approach to race and disease that characterized thinking in the military medical community. This same approach was evident in attitudes toward *tirailleurs sénégalais* and their health among other military personnel as well. A mixture of biological and cultural factors were important, though the emphasis was usually placed on behavioral aspects that arose from the West Africans' racial identity. A December 1916 report by the headquarters of the Armée de l'Afrique du Nord proved particularly revealing in this regard. The document described the condition of two companies of *tirailleurs* during their winter stay in Algeria and offered suggestions concerning policy toward West African troops in areas ranging from clothing and food to health and hygiene.[71]

The report went into the greatest detail concerning the clothing of the *tirailleurs*: the main problem was that they did "not 'know' how to dress," and thus soon ended up in varying states of undress as time went on. Viéron had pointed out that buttons were "mysteries" to the Africans,[72] and the report echoed this assertion, claiming that the *tirailleurs* failed to understand how to use them and thus were unable to protect themselves from the cold. The report suggested it would be best to do away with them altogether on their uniforms, and to replace them with laces. As for boots, the author of the report considered these an unnecessary luxury, claiming that the *tirailleurs* preferred to be without them anyway. Footwear only slowed down "these big, agile monkeys." With unintentional irony, the report noted that it was important not to force the Africans to wear boots out of a "bias or preconceived idea" that soldiers should have them.[73]

Lacking any sense of the utility of warm clothing when the weather was warm (and this testified to the Africans' supposed inability to plan ahead), the *tirailleurs* discarded garments they would later need. Since he preferred to sleep outdoors, and "the sleep of the black is heavy," white officers had constantly to be on their guard that the soldier did not catch a chill and "contract all the pulmonary ailments to which he is sensitive." The same concern lay behind the report's questioning of the wisdom of forcing West Africans to carry regulation army knapsacks. In Africa, the *tirailleurs* customarily carried their belongings in goatskin sacks, most often on their heads. The European-style sack was for them "an instrument of torture," and the straps caused them to sweat in the area around their chests. When they removed the sacks and the air cooled this area, respiratory infections often ensued. Although the report did not go so far as to suggest that West Africans carry their sacks on their heads in the trenches, it did recommend that the soldiers be allowed to modify their sacks as they saw fit or to use musette bags if goatskins were not available.[74] In fact, the overall thrust of the report was to advocate modifying the circumstances of West African soldiers in ways that would better conform with their habits, habits of a primitive people unaccustomed to European ways. Templier had noted precisely the same kind of problems in his thesis, remarking that among the elements that contributed to the *tirailleurs'* vulnerability to pneumonia was the "irritation caused by clothing to which they are not accustomed and which they hasten to leave behind when they can," and "a thoracic trauma caused by carrying the knapsack, for which the tirailleur manifests a certain repugnance."[75] For both the doctors who treated West African soldiers and for the staff of the Armée de l'Afrique du Nord, the clash of the African troops' primitive cultures and customs with the constraints of military service provided one of the keys to their physical health.[76]

Such attitudes characterized the observations of many French military officials. In the early years of the conflict, military authorities eagerly used the African soldiers in the Dardanelles operation (spring 1915) and the southern European front (in Greece and Macedonia, to which France and Britain sent troops in late 1915) because of their supposed immunity to malaria.[77] The *tirailleurs* were also supposed to be ideal for duty in Turkey because they would resist the hot climate better than would Europeans.[78] This assertion of course failed to take into account the cold, wet winters of the region, which proved disastrous for the health of the West Africans. Yet added to this biological determinism was the widespread belief that these men could adapt to European climates. After the war ended in 1918, the French used West African troops to occupy conquered areas of the German Rhineland, and the question of their resistance to cold weather gained new importance. The desire to use them for occupation duty during the winter clashed with their demonstrated lack of resistance to cold weather. However, many argued that not only could the army takes steps to keep the troops warm, but that cold weather duty would rapidly acclimatize the *tirailleurs*, making them acquire the constitutions and habits necessary for survival during the winter months.[79] Clearly, when it came to health issues and the *tirailleurs sénégalais* during the First World War, relatively fixed notions of scientific racism and biological determinism coexisted alongside more fluid ideas associated with environment and culture.

There is no doubt that scientific ideas about race were important during the period between 1830 and the end of the First World War. Concepts associated with evolution combined with physical anthropological views of racial difference to reinforce a racial hierarchy with white Europeans firmly at the top. Yet cultural and environmental factors never receded, at least in France, to the extent that one can speak of a triumph of scientific racism in the late nineteenth and early twentieth centuries. The two strands of French racial thinking — cultural and biological — coexisted throughout the period. Although after the First World War hard, scientific perspectives on racial difference gained greater currency in the French medical and scientific community, strict biological racism never fully defined the field. Up to the 1920s, the ideas of famous French theorists of scientific racism, such as Arthur de Gobineau and Georges Vacher de Lapouge, proved much more influential outside France than within the country. French eugenicists, as William Schneider has shown, remained marginal until the interwar period and the Vichy years provided an opportunity for them to influence state policy more directly with their ideas about biology and race.[80] Similarly, Alice Conklin has demonstrated that it was during the 1920s that French policy in West Africa began to display a heightened consciousness of race and of the irreducible difference between white Europeans and black Africans.[81] Yet Stephen Wooten has identified what he terms a resurgence of cultural understandings of difference in the work of French ethnographers working in West Africa between 1900 and 1940. Although he argues that these ideas modified the polygenist, scientific racism prevalent in the late eighteenth century, he does identify a continuing "strain of relativism" in French racial attitudes.[82] In fact, these attitudes demonstrated a marked continuity throughout this period, with both scientific and cultural assumptions clearly in evidence.

These competing strands of thought manifested themselves in debates over colonial policies of "assimilation" and "association." In his pioneering study of these ideas, Raymond Betts identifies the growing importance of scientific notions of race as contributing to the shift from assimilation (which was an attempt "to absorb the native societies administratively and culturally into the French nation") to association (which "would emphasize retention of local institutions and which would make the native an associate in the colonial enterprise") between 1890 and 1914.[83] Theories of inherent biological difference helped to discredit the idea of assimilating allegedly inferior "natives" to superior white culture, and many French observers thus deemed association a more realistic approach. Yet, as Betts points out, assimilationist ideas never really died out completely, and the two approaches tended to overlap even after association became official policy after 1918.[84] Similarly, cultural understandings of difference continued to be important in French racial thinking even as voices advocating heredity and biology as the bases of racial differences became more influential.

The stress on the acceptance of French culture as a largely sufficient prerequisite for citizenship and belonging to the French nation, for erasing the distinction between French and non-French, has proven one of the salient characteristics of thinking about national identity, ethnicity, and race in France.[85] To be sure, this openness to assimilation often becomes problematic, especially for nonwhites, immigrants, and former colonial subjects. Scientific notions of race have never disappeared entirely, but the racist policies of the Vichy regime in France, the Nazis in Germany, and segregationists in the United States have discredited such thinking among large segments of the French population. Though there are benefits to examining racism as a European phenomenon, as George Mosse has done with the goal of explaining the intellectual precursors of the violent apotheosis of biological racism in the Holocaust during the Second World War, it is important to keep in mind national differences.[86] Each nation in Europe has possessed its own current of thought on race — based on history, tradition, culture — while drawing from and contributing to the larger European intellectual environment. In this context, it is critical to take into account the particularities of racism in France.

This imperative has led some scholars to stress culture as the decisive factor in determining French racial attitudes. David Beriss has pointed out the importance of identifying the specificities of racial thinking in France, arguing that the dominant tendency is to discriminate and exclude foreigners on the basis of culture, although cultures "constrain people in ways that resemble race."[87] This cultural understanding of French identity often results in a sort of cultural chauvinism similar to racial discrimination but different from the more biologically driven racism prevalent in American society. Although Beriss and others are quick to admit the important role that "harder" notions of race play in current debates over national identity and immigration, notably in the prominence and electoral success of the xenophobic and overtly racist Front National, "softer," more ambiguous cultural understandings of difference remain predominant.[88]

This contemporary stress on culture is much easier to understand and explain if we problematize the notion of a triumph of biological racism in the late nineteenth century, identifying instead a greater continuity in French racial attitudes.[89] Although scientific racism constituted an important aspect of racist thought in France during the late nineteenth and early twentieth centuries, many in France continued to consider cultural and environmental factors of great importance in explaining racial difference. Pierre-André Taguieff has identified these two discourses on race as "hetero-racialization" and "auto-racialization," the former type being universalizing and assimilationist, while the latter is particularist and more exclusionary.[90] Michel Wieviorka has further explored these discourses, arguing that they constitute two "logics" of racism which often coexist in racist attitudes and practices.[91] This coexistence was evident in the approach of the French military to racial difference during the nineteenth and early twentieth centuries. Both biology and culture proved important in informing French racial attitudes throughout this period, and it is the complex relationship between these two ways of viewing race, rather than the predominance of one or the other, that should be the focus of historical inquiry.

Notes

The authors, who are solely responsible for the views expressed in this essay, thank Stephen R. Wooten for bibliographic assistance and Paul Spickard for constructive criticism. Additional thanks for critical discussions on this topic go to Matthew Aberman, Eric Boyle, Sandra Dawson, David Schuster, Greg Whitesides, and Vicki Vantoch of the Second Author's 2001 History of Medicine Seminar at the University of California, Santa Barbara.

1   William B. Cohen, *The French Encounter with Africans: White Response to Blacks, 1530–1880* (Bloomington: Indiana University Press, 1980), 210–62. Cohen later noted the persistence of cultural and albeit anemic ethnographical ideas of race in "French Racism and Its African Impact," in *Double Impact: France and Africa in the Age of Imperialism*, ed. G. Wesley Johnson (Westport, Conn.: Greenwood, 1985), 305–17.

2　Cohen, *French Encounter with Africans*, 210.

3　Joe Lunn, " 'Les Races Guerrières': Racial Preconceptions in the French Military about West African Soldiers during the First World War," *Journal of Contemporary History* 34 (1999): 517–36, quote on 517 n. 2. See also his *Memoirs of the Maelstrom: A Senegalese Oral History of the First World War* (Portsmouth, N.H.: Heinemann, 1999), as well as his dissertation of the same title, completed in 1993 at the University of Wisconsin, Madison.

4　See Pietro Corsi and Paul J. Weindling, "Darwinism in Germany, France, and Italy," in *The Darwinian Heritage*, ed. David Kohn (Princeton, N.J.: Princeton University Press, 1985), 683–729.

5　Warwick Anderson, "Immunities of Empire: Race, Disease, and the New Tropical Medicine, 1900–1920," *Bulletin of the History of Medicine* 70 (1996): 94–118.

6　Richard M. Burian, Jean Gayon, and Doris Zallen, "The Singular Fate of Genetics in the History of French Biology," *Journal for the History of Biology* 21 (1988): 357–402.

7　Martin S. Staum, "Paris Ethnology and the Perfectibility of 'Races,' " *Canadian Journal of History/Annales canadiennes d'histoire* 35 (2000): 222–38.

8　Ibid., which quotes William Edwards, *Mémoirs de la Société Ethnologique de Paris* 1 (1841): i, iii, iv.

9　Jacques Léonard, *La médecine entre les savoirs et les pouvoirs: Histoire intellectuelle et politique de la médecine française au XIXe siècle* (Paris: Editions Aubier Montaigne, 1981), 168–69.

10　See Anderson, "Immunities of Empire," 100 n. 23. Quote from Armand de Quatrefages de Bréau, *L'espèce humaine* (Paris: Librairie Germer Baillière et Cie, 1877), 310; emphasis original.

11　Michael A. Osborne, "Resurrecting Hippocrates: Hygienic Science and the French Expeditions to Egypt, Morea, and Algeria," in *Warm Climates and Western Medicine: The Emergence of Tropical Medicine, 1500–1900*, ed. David Arnold (Amsterdam: Rodopi, 1996), 80–98.

12　Patricia M. E. Lorcin, "Imperialism, Colonial Identity, and Race in Algeria, 1830–1870: The Role of the French Medical Corps," *Isis* 90 (1999): 653–79, summarizes the contributions of several military physicians to racial ideas. Quote on 655.

13　Michael A. Osborne, "The Geographical Imperative in Nineteenth Century French Medicine," *Medical History*, supplement 20 (2000): 31–50.

14　The editors examine changing ideas of the Paris Clinical School in "Paris Medicine: Perspectives Past and Present," in *Constructing Paris Medicine*, ed. Ann La Berge and Caroline Hannaway (Amsterdam: Rodopi, 1998), 1–69.

15 Osborne, "The Geographical Imperative," 41.

16 Richaud, "Essai de topographie médicale de la Cochinchine française," *Archives de médecine navale* 1 (1864): 198–225, 341–62. See especially 211–21, 357. Quote on 358. This translation and all unmarked translations are mine.

17 J. Chapuis, "De l'identité de l'ulcère observé à la Guyanne française avec celui décrit sous les noms de Gué-Ham, ulcère de cochinchine, de Saigon, ulcère Annamite," *Archives de médecine navale* 1 (1864): 375–81. Malaria comment on 377; quotation on 381 n. 1.

18 Fonssagrives et Le Roy de Méricourt, "Du mal-coeur ou mal d'estomac des nègres," *Archives de médecine navale* 1 (1864): 362–75.

19 Anderson, "Immunities of Empire," 100, 113, provides a case in point in the person of Colonel Kenneth MacLeod.

20 Goulven Laurent, *Paléontologie et évolution en France de 1800 à 1860: Une histoire des idées de Cuvier et Lamarck à Darwin* (Paris: Editions du C.T.H.S., 1987), especially 467–96.

21 Lorelai Kury, "Les instructions de voyage dans les expéditions scientifiques françaises (1750–1830)," *Revue d'histoire des sciences* 51, 1 (1998): 65–91.

22 Isid [ore] Geoffroy Saint-Hilaire, de Castelnau, and P [aul] Broca, "Instructions anthropologiques pour le Sénégal," *Archives de médecine navale* 1 (1864): 255–65.

23 Ibid., 256–58.

24 "L'école de médecine de Pondichery," *Annales d'hygiène et de médecine coloniales* 5 (1902): 507–10.

25 Saint-Hilaire, de Castelnau, and Broca, "Instructions anthropologiques," 264–65.

26 Michael A. Osborne, *Nature, the Exotic, and the Science of French Colonialism* (Bloomington: Indiana University Press, 1994).

27 Henrika Kuklick, "Islands in the Pacific: Darwinian Biogeography and British Anthropology," *American Ethnologist* 23, 3 (1996): 611–38, quote on 628.

28 Cohen, *French Encounter with Africans*, 235.

29 Anderson, "Immunities of Empire," 102.

30 "Bérenger-Féraud, Jean-Baptiste Laurent," individual file, série 2e moderne, box B 20, Service Historique de la Marine, Vincennes, France.

31 L.-J. B. Bérenger-Féraud, *Traité clinique des maladies des Europeéns au Sénégal*, 2 vols. (Paris: Adrien de la Haye, 1875–1878). See especially "Hygiène des Européens au Sénégal," 2:325–531.

32 [L.-J. B. Béranger-Féraud], *Notice sur les services et les travaux scientifiques de M. L.-Bérenger-Féraud, directeur du service de santé de la marine* (Toulon: Imprimerie du Var, 1887). Anthropological titles include *La race provençale au point de vue de ses origines* (Paris:

Octave Doin, 1883) and *Les peuplades de la Sénégambie: Histoire, ethnographie, moeurs, coutumes* (Paris: Ernest Leroux, 1879).

33 The *Traité clinique des maladies des Europeéns au Sénégal* had more than eighty tables, but only a few of them list disease frequencies by race.

34 L.-J. B. Bérenger-Féraud, *Traité théorique et clinique de la fièvre jaune* (Paris: Octave Doin, 1891), 745.

35 Ibid., especially 461–82. Quote on 482.

36 A. Le Dantec, *Recherches sur la fièvre jaune, critique des théories microbiennes émise en Amérique au sujet de cette maladie* (Paris: Imprimerie des Ecoles, Henri Jové, 1886), 49.

37 See Sheldon Watts, *Disease, Power, and Imperialism* (New Haven, Conn.: Yale University Press, 1997), 216.

38 [F.] Le Dantec, "La médecine coloniale," *Le caducée: Journal de chirurgie et de médecine d'armée, guerre-marine-colonies* 3 (1903): 29–32, quote on 32.

39 All statements about colonial administration are subject to qualification, given the great variety of approaches in different areas of the French empire. The navy was largely responsible for colonial security, though it was the army that conquered and administered Algeria between 1830 and 1870.

40 For accounts of the marines, the colonial army, and the 1900 legislation, see Kim J. Munholland, "The Emergence of the Colonial Military in France 1880–1905" (Ph.D. diss., Princeton University, 1964); Jean-Charles Jauffret, *Parlement, gouvernement, commandement: L'armée de métier sous la 3e République, 1871–1914*, vol. 2 (Vincennes: Service Historique de l'Armée de Terre, 1987); Jauffret, "Genèse de la loi du 5 juillet 1900 portant organisation des troupes coloniales," *Revue Historique des armées* 218 (2000): 10–18; Douglas Porch, *The March to the Marne: The French Army, 1871–1914* (Cambridge: Cambridge University Press, 1981); and *Les troupes de marine, 1622–1984* (Paris: Charles-Lavauzelle, 1986).

41 For West African troops, see Lunn, *Memoirs*; Charles John Balesi, *From Adversaries to Comrades in Arms: West Africa and the French Military, 1885–1918* (Waltham, Mass.: Crossroads, 1979); Marc Michel, *L'appel à l'Afrique: Contributions et réactions à l'effort de guerre en AOF (1914–1919)* (Paris: Publications de la Sorbonne, 1982); and Myron Echenberg, *Colonial Conscripts: The Tirailleurs Sénégalais in French West Africa, 1857–1960* (Portsmouth, N.H.: Heinemann, 1991). Richard S. Fogarty, "Race and War in France: Colonial Subjects in the French Army, 1914–1918" (Ph.D. diss., University of California, Santa Barbara, 2002), examines French ideas about race and the army's use of soldiers from North and West Africa, Madagascar, and Indochina.

42 Lunn also notes this mixture, although he stresses the biological roots of Mangin's thinking, and the biological determinism of French racism generally in this era: "He based these premises on a series of racist arguments consistent with the widely held belief in biological determinism of the age, but, where appropriate, Mangin also invoked cultural relativism to buttress his case." Lunn, "'Les races guerrières,'" 519–20. Echenberg also notes the mixture of "cultural" and "racial" explanations for Africans' martial prowess in Mangin's thought; see his *Colonial Conscripts*, 29. In addition to these works, see the following for discussions of Mangin's campaign for the use of West African troops: Balesi, *From Adversaries to Comrades in Arms*, 57–78; Michel, *L'appel à l'Afrique*, 7–12; Lunn, "Memoirs" (Ph.D. diss.), 76–99.

43 Charles Mangin, "L'utilisation des troupes noires," *Bulletins et mémoirs de la Société d'Anthropologie de Paris* 2 (1911): 90–1. See also his *La force noire* (Paris: Hachette, 1911), 252.

44 Mangin, *La force noire*, 248–52; Mangin, "L'utilisation," 93.

45 Mangin, "L'utilisation," 93 ff.

46 Ibid., 89. This argument was itself actually at once biologically deterministic — as the best warriors would have been selected over time in a Darwinistic, evolutionary process — and cultural — as the constant state of war would have conditioned each generation of Africans for fighting.

47 Mangin, *La force noire*, 247–48, 252–54. Though not precisely relevant to this essay, Mangin and others also made distinctions among the various "races" that made up the West African population and ranked them according to their soldierly qualities and warlike propensities (medical officers do not seem to have made much of these kinds of racial distinctions in their work). See Lunn, "'Les races guerrières.'" For an explicit discussion of the various "races" and their qualities, see Service Historique de l'Armée de Terre (hereafter SHAT) 16N198: *Notice sur les sénégalais et leur emploi au combat* (Paris: Grand Quartier Général, 1918).

48 Even doctors and medical students technically attached to the navy received postings to the army, as the need was much greater in the latter service. This was an ironic reversal of the nineteenth-century trend of army officers seeking marine appointments in order to gain combat experience and promotion in the colonies.

49 Lucien Viéron, *Quelques réflexions sur la pneumonie des troupes noires et son traitement* (Bordeaux: Imprimerie de l'Université, 1917), 15.

50 West African soldiers' problems with pneumonia became legendary among the officers who commanded them, leading officers to expect outbreaks of the illness as a matter of course. General Blondlat,

Commander of the second corps of the colonial army, wrote in a report that the then-current health problems in the 80th Senegalese Battalion would no doubt soon be complicated by "the most common affliction among the Senegalese: pneumonia." Blondlat to Commandant of the 10th Army, "Au sujet du 80e Bataillon Sénégalais," 14 September 1916, SHAT 16N196 (Vincennes, France).

51 Pierre Jandeau, *Contribution à l'étude de pneumonie chez le tirailleur sénégalais traitement* (Bordeaux: Imprimerie de l'Université, 1916).

52 Ibid., 16.

53 Ibid., 16, 19, 26–27.

54 Ibid., 18. The classic formulation of the concept of degeneration is the Paris-based Hungarian journalist Max Nordau's *Entartung* [Degeneration], first published in 1892. The work was widely translated and enormously influential in discussions of degeneration and the emerging movement of eugenics. Historical treatments of the concept of degeneration include, Daniel Pick, *Faces of Degeneration: A European Disorder, c.1848–c.1918* (Cambridge: Cambridge University Press, 1989); Jacques Hochmann, "La théorie de la dégénérescence de B.-A. Morel, ses origines et son évolution," in *Darwinisme et société*, ed. Patrick Tort (Paris: Presses Universitaires de France, 1992), 401–12; and Robert A. Nye, *Crime, Madness, and Politics in Modern France: The Medical Concept of National Decline* (Princeton, N.J.: Princeton University Press, 1984).

55 Captain DeLettre, of the 2d Senegalese Battalion, also noted that his men often contracted pulmonary illnesses, even in the summer, because sweat induced them impulsively to submerge themselves in washtubs full of cold water. "Renseignements fournis par le Capitaine DeLettre, du 2e btn de tirailleurs sénégalais d'algérie," n.d., SHAT 7N2121. The report likely dates from late 1914 or early 1915.

56 Jandeau, *Contribution*, 18–19.

57 In reality, Africans would have had less immunity to common European ailments like pneumonia, while they had more resistance to diseases, like malaria, which were widespread in West Africa.

58 Jandeau, *Contribution*, 22, 39.

59 Ibid., 47; Henry Templier, *Observations etiologiques, cliniques, pronostiques et thérapeutiques sur la pneumonie des noirs de l'Afrique Occidentale Française au Camp du Courneau* (Bordeaux: Imprimerie de l'Université, 1917), 16ff.

60 Templier, *Observations*, 15.

61 Ibid., 16–17, 42.

62 Ibid., 22, 29, 41.

63 See the *Journal officiel de la République Française, débats-chambre*, 10 December 1916. Diagne represented the *quatre communes de*

plein exercise, comprised of the urban centers of Gorée, Saint-Louis, Rufisque, and Dakar, the citizens of which had become French citizens and obtained electoral rights in return for their republican loyalty during the 1848 revolution. For discussions of conditions at Courneau and other camps, see Balesi, *From Adversaries to Comrades in Arms*, 103–4; Michel, *L'appel*, 363–75; and Lunn, *Memoirs*, 106.

64 Direction des Troupes Coloniales, "Note pour le Cabinet du Ministre: Situation sanitaire du Camp du Courneau," 12 December 1916, SHAT 7N440.

65 Colonel Fonssagrives to Directeur des Troupes Coloniales, 1 November 1916, SHAT 7N440. Even earlier, in August, the Inspecteur de Contingents Indigènes, General Simonin, had visited Courneau and declared that the sanitary state and facilities of the camp were "very satisfactory," despite problems with the weather. "Rapport d'inspection du Général Simonin, Inspecteur de Contingents Indigènes," 12 August 1916, SHAT 16N196.

66 For example, out of seventy-seven cases treated at the hospital at Menton during July, twenty-four were fatal. Service de Santé, "Note pour l'Etat-Major de l'Armée (3ème Bureau)," 26 August 1916, SHAT 7N440.

67 "Rapport de M. le Controleur général Chapelle," December 1916, SHAT 6N97. For further information and statistics on Courneau and other camps that housed *tirailleurs sénégalais* in France, see the documents in SHAT 7N1990.

68 On the Russian expeditionary force, see Jamie H. Cockfield, *With Snow on Their Boots: The Tragic Odyssey of the Russian Expeditionary Force in France during World War I* (New York: St. Martin's, 1998). American expeditionary force commander General John J. Pershing called the camp "the most unsanitary place I have ever seen"; quoted in Cockfield, *With Snow on Their Boots*, 207.

69 A report by the Service de Santé also noted the seeming irrelevance of cold weather to the problems with pneumonia, citing figures that showed numerous cases, many of them lethal, of the illness throughout the summer months of 1916 in diverse regions of France. Service de Santé, "Note pour l'Etat-Major de l'Armée (3ème Bureau)," 16 August 1916, SHAT 7N440.

70 Viéron, *Quelques réflexions*, 17–19, quotes on 18.

71 Armée de l'Afrique du Nord, État-Major (3ème Bureau), "Note sur les modifications à apporter au régime des Sénégalais," December 1916, SHAT 6N97.

72 Viéron, *Quelques réflexions*, 22.

73 Armée de l'Afrique du Nord, État-Major, "Note sur les modifications."

74 Ibid.

75 Templier, *Observations*, 17.

76 Médecin Major Verdier noted that same kind of culture clash, mixed with West African soldiers' allegedly natural tendency toward certain physical ailments. In a 17 November 1914 report, he noted that the soldiers' habit of shedding their shoes while on duty in France exacerbated "the well-known predisposition of this race to lymphatic problems and edemas." "Rapport du Médecin Major Verdier," 17 November 1914, SHAT 16N194.

77 Michel, *L'appel*, 294, 312, 334. Authorities often included Vietnamese troops in the same category with regard to resistance to disease. Discussing the stationing of West African soldiers with the Army of the Orient in Greece, the high command asserted, "Indigènes being more resistant to malaria than Europeans, their deployment in the Orient will economize on [the use of] French soldiers." Grand Quartier Général, "Avis de la Section des TOE sur l'utilisation des bataillons indigènes en 1917," 24 November 1916, SHAT 16N196. On the role of malaria and the use of indigenous troops in the French conquest of empire during the nineteenth century, see William Cohen, "Malaria and French Imperialism," *Journal of African History* 24 (1983): 23–36; and Philip D. Curtin, "Disease and Empire," in *Death by Migration: Europe's Encounter with the Tropical World in the Nineteenth Century* (Cambridge: Cambridge University Press, 1989), 133 n. 6, and 135 n. 10; here, Curtin challenges some aspects of Cohen's argument.

78 Typical of this thinking was the officer who argued that West African companies would have even more solidity in Turkey than would white units, "whose men, fatigued by the great heat of the summer, would offer less resistance than the Senegalese." "Rapport du Chef de Bataillon Malafosse sur l'emploi des Sénégalais," 23 August 1916, SHAT 16N196.

79 For example, see "Extrait d'un rapport de M. le Professeur Borrel relatif à l'utilisation des tirailleurs Sénégalais en territoire occupé," n.d., SHAT 16N199. The date was probably early 1919. This report argued that although there would be "inevitable" outbreaks among the troops during the first year, even as they were maintained in West Africa for training, and during the second year at camps in the south of France, by the third year the soldiers would have overcome their problems with *déplacement* and climate change and would be available for duty in Germany. As it was, West Africans served in the Rhineland without the benefit of such a long process of acclimatization.

80 The fall of the Vichy regime marked the end of this brief period of ascendancy. William H. Schneider, *Quality and Quantity: The Quest*

for Biological Regeneration in Twentieth-Century France (Cambridge: Cambridge University Press, 1990); and Schneider, "Towards the Improvement of the Human Race: The History of Eugenics in France," *Journal of Modern History* 54 (1982): 268–91. See also Pierre-André Taguieff, "Eugénisme ou décadence? L'exception française," *Ethnologie française* 24 (1994): 81–103.

81 Alice L. Conklin, *A Mission to Civilize: The Republican Idea of Empire in France and West Africa, 1895–1930* (Stanford, Calif.: Stanford University Press, 1997).

82 Stephen R. Wooten, "Colonial Administration and the Ethnography of the Family in the French Soudan," *Cahiers d'études africaines* 131, 33-3 (1993): 419–46, quote on 426.

83 Raymond F. Betts, *Assimilation and Association in French Colonial Theory, 1890–1914* (New York: Columbia University Press, 1961), quotes on vii.

84 Ibid., 165 ff.

85 Rogers Brubaker, in his *Citizenship and Nationhood in France and Germany* (Cambridge, Mass.: Harvard University Press, 1992), notes the distinctive strength of "assimilationist nationalism" in France. This is a long-standing heritage, deriving from the French Revolution, and influenced legislation on citizenship throughout France's republican history. Even here, though, biological, racist notions have complicated this essentially cultural approach to national identity. Brubaker himself notes the parallel existence of a competing "exclusionist" tendency in debates over citizenship, and this corresponds to Michel Winock's "open" and "closed" forms of French nationalism: Michel Winock, "Open Nationalism and Closed Nationalism," in *Nationalism, Anti-Semitism, and Fascism in France*, trans. Jane Marie Todd (Stanford, Calif.: Stanford University Press, 1998), 5–26. Gérard Noiriel, in *The French Melting Pot: Immigration, Citizenship, and National Identity*, trans. Geoffroy de Laforcade (Minneapolis: The University of Minnesota Press, 1996), 54–56, has pointed out the concessions to "advocates of 'race' and 'heredity,'" such as the denial of immediate full civic rights to naturalized French citizens, contained in the otherwise quite liberal 1889 citizenship law. Also, legislation during the 1990s has significantly restricted the right to automatic citizenship of children born in France to immigrant parents. The fact that this latter measure strikes hardest at immigrants of color, along with the rhetoric surrounding the legislation and immigration in general, gives ample evidence of both biologically and culturally racist attitudes on the part of many people in France.

86 George L. Mosse, *Toward the Final Solution: A History of European Racism* (1978; Madison: University of Wisconsin Press, 1985).

Mosse makes very little effort to delineate specific national histories of racism in this work, though of course Germany's experience is central to the narrative. This pan-European focus is in some senses justified, as the community of writers, scholars, scientists, and politicians was international, but the approach ultimately blurs distinctions between nations.

87 David Beriss, "Culture-as-Race or Culture-as-Culture: Caribbean Ethnicity and the Ambiguity of Cultural Identity in French Society," *French Politics, Culture, and Society* 18, 3 (2000): 40.

88 The power of this cultural understanding of difference has led French demographer Emmanuel Todd to assert the continuing power of assimilationist attitudes in informing contemporary reactions to immigrants. As a result, he downplays the existence of racism in France, attributing the success of the Front National and other manifestations of xenophobia to "a perversion of French egalitarian and universalist principles," rather than to "a manifestation of racism in the narrow sense of the word." For him, the French attitude stands in stark contrast to British and American "differentialism" and biological racism. "Le paradoxe français," *L'histoire* 193 (1995): 36. See also his *Le destin des immigrés: Assimilation et ségrégation dans les démocraties occidentales* (Paris: Editions du Seuil, 1994).

89 Cohen, *French Encounter*, 210–63, is the best example of this notion. William H. Schneider, *An Empire for the Masses: The French Popular Image of Africa, 1870–1900* (Westport, Conn.: Greenwood, 1982), also identifies a rising predominance of scientific racism, though his later work, *Quality and Quantity*, reveals the marginal nature of much of this kind of thinking in France until the 1930s and 1940s.

90 Pierre-André Taguieff, *La force du préjugé: Essais sur le racisme et ses doubles* (Paris: Editions La Découverte, 1988).

91 Michel Wieviorka, Introduction to *Racisme et modernité*, ed. Wieviorka (Paris: Editions La Découverte, 1993), 7–20.

Gary Wilder

Panafricanism and

the Republican Political

Sphere

In the context of our current round of globalization, scholars across the disciplines have begun to question the adequacy of the nation-state as an analytic category. Paul Gilroy has claimed that "the structures and presuppositions of the nation-state" are "outmoded."[1] Arjun Appadurai claims that "we are in the process of moving to a global order in which the nation-state has become obsolete" and counsels us "to think ourselves beyond the nation."[2] In contrast, Partha Chatterjee exhorts scholars to "think within the nation-state" in order to address the internal tensions that have contributed to current transnational phenomena.[3]

But rather than focus on this movement from the national to the transnational, we may also historicize the nation-state itself as a political form characterized by an open-ended relationship between territory, state, and people. In my work, for example, I have tried to approach France as an imperial nation-state in which a parliamentary republic is articulated with its administrative empire to compose a single, albeit fractured, political formation that has exceeded supposedly national boundaries since its inception. From this perspective, processes that we now identify as *trans*national can be located within the nation-state itself. Such an optic would allow us to better understand the seeming tension between national and transnational commitments that marked anticolonial politics in twentieth-century French history. In this essay, I would like to discuss the relationship between Panafrican projects pursued by racialized colonial subjects and the national, republican space in which they were located.

Postcolonial Panafricanism

I was challenged to think about the relationship between Panafrican organizing and republican political culture when in 1994 I attended several meetings of the Institute for Historical Truth and Identity at a progressive community center in Belleville, a largely immigrant neighborhood in Paris. The institute provided classes taught by volunteers in Creole and Swahili language, African history, and small-business skills to subscription-paying members: young African students and slightly older petit bourgeois Caribbeans, both men and women.

The institute's founder hailed from the Caribbean himself, seemed to be in his late forties, and went by an African-inflected name that he himself chose. Sekou Manga was a community organizer who also hosted a talk radio show focused on issues of concern to the Antillean (Caribbean) community in France. The show became a forum for his francophone Afrocentrism, which he also elaborated in weekly lectures at the institute. These discourses blended a post-*négritude* celebration of primordial Africanness shared by diaspora blacks with a Garveyist/Nation of Islam message of black separatism and capitalist self-help.

Sekou was remarkably preoccupied by Jews, about whom he spoke with a mixture of suspicion and envy. He explained that Jews "arrived" (the points of departure and destination remained unclear) with nothing, but they stuck together, insulated themselves from the larger society, and shared resources amongst themselves. This, for him, was the source of Jews' legendary racial cohesion and social power. He presented their putative dense social network, financial wealth, and political influence as a cultural model for the French black community, which he criticized as fragmented, self-interested, and passive. Sekou also spoke admiringly of the community solidarity and public profile that black identity politics in the United States and Britain had been able to achieve. At one meeting, he proposed a plan that would have institute members circulating through Paris selling canonical nationalist texts to francophone blacks, including those by Frantz Fanon, Cheikh Anta Diop, and Malcolm X. Although the immediate objective would have been to raise money for the institute, this enterprise was also supposed to promote consciousness raising, community building, and black entrepreneurship.

Sekou was a cultural separatist, but he also called on Parisian blacks to claim their rightful place *within* French social and public life. The institute was precisely the kind of voluntary association supposed to characterize democratic civil society, and broadcast radio the kind of medium constituting a republican public sphere. But Sekou was careful to insist that his was not a political project; by his account, the institute concerned itself only with promoting cultural discovery and social improvement.

This tone shifted abruptly one Friday when he announced that his radio show, located on the frequency guaranteed by the state to the Antillean community in France, was cancelled. He emphasized that a white woman had made this decision based on the program's supposedly inappropriate content. Sekou suggested that French society tolerated Antilleans as long as they focused on *zouk* music and dance, but not when they began addressing their real sociopolitical problems and interests. At his invitation, members made plans to protest this injustice. There would be public demonstrations that would include speeches, music, and mass support—just like the ones they had in the United States, according to Sekou. The goal would be to win the sympathy of French left liberals and the Socialist Party in the midst of a presidential election campaign. Here the institute's cultural separatism was oriented toward public opinion and electoral politics, elements of the republican public sphere. The group seemed animated and politicized.

But two weeks later, the Friday meeting took an unexpected turn. It began with a member standing to denounce Sekou and his wife as Jehovah's Witnesses and con artists stealing members' money and manipulating the group. The meeting devolved into tense shouting matches between the leader's supporters and detractors until Sekou and his wife left angry and indignant. Temporarily, at least, the Institute for Historical Truth and Identity had imploded. My account is anecdotal, not ethnographic. I was in France as a historian, not an anthropologist. I neither researched the organization, nor interviewed its members, or learned whether the institute was ever reconstituted. But my archival research soon helped me recognize that historical precedents existed for precisely this cycle of organization, mobilization, and collapse in the field of black cultural politics in Paris.

Paris had hosted the international Pan-African congresses in 1919 and 1921.[4] But during the interwar period, a number of lower-profile Panafrican initiatives were pursued in France by various groups who found it difficult to sustain transnational racial solidarity within the imperial metropole, including black communists, radical separatists, and moderate cultural nationalists.[5] The French Communist Party's decision to create a Committee for Colonial Studies in 1921, followed by the multiracial Intercolonial Union, facilitated this activity.[6] Communist support later enabled Lamine Senghor, a former colonial soldier and prominent labor organizer from Senegal, to found the Committee for the Defense of the Black Race (CDRN) and its affiliated newspaper, *La Voix des Nègres*, in 1926.[7]

The committee was committed to internationalism; it advocated "permanent collaboration with organizations that truly struggle for the liberation of oppressed peoples and for the world revolution."[8] It also professed a Panafricanist commitment to work for the "social evolution of the black race."[9] Senghor declared, "Blacks do not belong to any European nationality."[10] The organization exhorted blacks to overcome racializing distinctions between *hommes de couleur* (educated blacks), *noirs* (newly assimilated blacks), and *nègres* (the poorest and most "indigenous" colonized blacks). An editorial in the paper called for a reappropriation of this last category, declaring "The youth of the Committee for the Defense of the Black Race have lifted this name out of the mud . . . in order to make a symbol out of it. . . . We feel honor and glory to call ourselves *Nègres*."[11]

By 1927, ideological conflicts led to a split within the group between a reformist faction, led by Maurice Satineau (from Guadeloupe), and a communist faction, led by Senghor (from Senegal) and another African, Tiemoko Garan Kouyaté (from the French Sudan). The latter two seceded to create the more explicitly revolutionary League for the Defense of the Black Race (LDRN) whose newspaper *La Race Nègre* was also partly funded by the French Communist Party.[12] The paper was distributed within France and French West Africa; metropolitan and colonial governments monitored its publication, sought to disrupt its distribution network, and harassed its subscribers.[13] Internal tensions also challenged *La Race Nègre*. By the end of the year, Kouyaté accused Senghor of being a brigand and having expropriated funds from the league set aside for printing costs.[14] When Senghor resigned as president of the league because of illness, Kouyaté denounced this activity as a ruse to evade investigation for his financial irresponsibility.[15] Senghor died soon thereafter, and Kouyaté assumed responsibility for the group and its newspaper.[16]

Under Kouyaté, the league developed a nationalist agenda and promoted Panafrican solidarity. In 1928, it distributed posters addressed to the black community in Paris, calling on them to cease their internal struggles and begin the reconciliation necessary for group unity.[17] *La Race Nègre* declared that "the end of racial prejudice will arrive when a great black state will be constituted on a modern foundation: African Zionism."[18] Yet the league also demanded democratic rights for the republic's colonial subjects: freedoms of the press, speech, association, movement, and religious belief, as well as local governing assemblies and a fair judiciary.[19] This position perhaps contituted a response to the organization's constant police surveillance and censorship of *La Race Nègre*. The group also formulated a number of social demands, including the right to work, the end of monopoly trade concessions for metropolitan firms, and military exemptions for colonized natives.[20] But its political scope was not restricted to France or the empire; the League of Nations, for example, asked the league to send it a report on the question of forced labor.[21]

Under Kouyaté's leadership, the group also pursued a black internationalism that placed it in a close but precarious relationship to the Communist Party. In 1929, he traveled to the Soviet Union to raise funds for his movement; in return for financial support, Moscow requested that ten black students be sent to the USSR for their education.[22] Several months later, Kouyaté angered the militant French Confédération Générale du Travail Unitaire (CGTU) when he created a black trade union independent of the Communist Party in Bordeaux and Marseille.[23] The league sent delegates to the international Black Workers Congress in Hamburg in 1930. While there, they received promises of "moral and material support" from sympathetic organizations and were asked to create a multiracial "League against Imperialism and for National Independence" in Paris.[24]

More important, Kouyaté returned to face a smear campaign against him from within the league. Despite his courting the Comintern, he had undermined the group's relationship with its local sponsor, the French Communist Party, by refusing to grant it over-sight of articles to be published in *La Race Nègre*.[25] Kouyaté was a communist who nevertheless insisted on ideological and institu-tional independence for his nationalist movement. This meant that by 1930, the league faced a financial crisis; the journal was kept afloat by Emile Faure, a black nationalist more concerned with racial purity than revolutionary communism.[26] What began as an ideological conflict between Kouyaté and Faure escalated into a fully blown power struggle within the league, again over financial impropriety. When Faure was unable to pay the printer to publish *La Race Nègre*, he accused Kouyaté of misusing funds the latter had used to subsidize a sailors' union in Marseille.[27] This conflict even-tually led the league to split into two factions in 1931, each of which published its own version of *La Race Nègre*.[28]

Kouyaté finally abandoned this struggle and created the Union of Black Workers (UTN) in 1932, with support from the colonial com-mittee of the CGTU, as a vehicle for Panafrican political organiz-ing.[29] Already in 1930 several members of the league had sought to create an "Institut Nègre de Paris," in which Panafrican connec-tions would help to improve living conditions for black students *within* French society by providing "natives of color, without dis-tinction of nationality" with a library, meeting rooms, lodging, and a restaurant.[30] This group was led by Leo Sajous, a Haitian national influenced by Marcus Garvey (whom he had once met in the United States), and included Kouyaté, Faure, Paulette Nardal, and Hélène Jaffard.[31] Although independent of the French Communist Party, the organization was monitored as radical by the colonial admin-istration and attacked by the anticommunist far right press.[32] The institute never materialized; perhaps the conflict between Kouyaté and Faure over control of the league undermined its creation.

Through the new Union of Black Workers, Kouyaté pursued this vision of transnational and cross-class alliances that included Afri-cans and Antilleans, labor militants and moderate students. In 1933, he had the union invite the leaders of black organizations in Paris to a number of meetings in the basement of the Café la Samari-taine.[33] The goal was to establish a common list of grievances and provide moral as well as material support to black students in France. Like Sajous, Kouyaté proposed creating a "Maison des Nègres," which would include lodging and a library. The group would also address the problem of repatriation for impoverished students. Kouyaté avoided revolutionary rhetoric and calls for po-

litical independence and simply proposed unifying, and thus em-
powering, the weak and fragmented black community in Paris. To
literally demonstrate solidarity, they agreed to invite other groups
to march with them to the grave at Père Lachaise of Victor Schoel-
cher, who abolished slavery in the French empire in 1848.[34]

Despite Kouyaté's moderation, the representatives of colonial student organizations, including Léonard Sainville and Léopold Senghor, were anxious about protecting their members' scholarships.[35]
They proposed explicit political discussions to be prohibited in the
new federation, and they objected to Kouyaté's plan to extend the
union's organizing work to colonial West Africa. Union members
argued with them about the need to engage in direct political action;
no agreement could be reached. Student support wavered as Senghor, who at the first meeting had promised to recruit twelve more
Senegalese students for the group, declined to serve on the group's
study commission and refused to formally affiliate the West African
Student Association without its approval.[36] Despite these tensions,
the project collapsed of its own accord later that year when Kouyaté
was expelled from the Communist Party for having tried to maintain the union's independence and then found himself forced out of
the union as well for collaborating on Panafrican projects with
moderates such as Satineau, Faure, and René Maran.[37]

Eventually the union itself—whose members composed perhaps
the most successful and enduring radical Panafrican alliance of
the interwar period—was threatened with dissolution by its own
sponsors. In October 1935, the colonial section of the Communist
Party sought to divide the Union of Black Workers into separate
African and Caribbean sections, each with its own newspaper.[38]
Members protested this authoritarian and fragmenting directive.
One Antillean placed Panafrican solidarity over party loyalty and
exclaimed, "we are all nègres here, and we are united to pursue a
common project . . . it is disastrous to divide les nègres."[39] After
months of institutional conflict, during which the colonial activists
found themselves accused of not being genuine communists, this
same man complained, "The Communist Party that leads us treats
blacks like children."[40] Ultimately the French representative from
the party's political bureau expressed his exasperation through a
racial outburst: "I work with Arabs and Indochinese, but I cannot
manage work with nègres."[41] He then withdrew from the project
and requested that sanctions be imposed on the recalcitrant union
comrades.

Communist Party anticolonialism in the thirties clearly had its institutional contradictions. But there were also internal tensions within the union, again expressed by Martinican and Guadeloupean student representatives who had participated in these meetings. One student, Jules Monnerot, protested the party's attempt to divide the union, arguing that "there is no distinction between black Africans and Antilleans." But another, Sainville, acknowledged: "We must be realistic. It is a fact: there is some difficulty between Africans and Antilleans. There are also problems between black workers and students. We need two organizations and even three journals: for workers, intellectuals, and Africans."[42]

The Cultural Panafricanism of Colonial Elites

Sainville, Monnerot, and Senghor belonged to a cohort of colonial students who also worked to create Panafrican community in Paris. But they were more influenced by a current of anticolonial politics practiced by educated elites, affiliated with publications like *La Dépeche Africaine* and *La Revue du Monde Noir*, than they were by the radical tradition of the Committee for the Defense of the Black Race, The League for the Defense of the Black Race, and the Union of Black Workers.[43] They were neither affiliated with the Communist Party, nor were they labor organizers. These colonial moderates were never as organized or activist as their radical counterparts, but they were perhaps more successful at maintaining Panafrican cultural alliances without imploding from external and internal pressures.

Contributors to *La Dépeche Africaine* included black colonial lawyers, journalists, administrators, students, and writers, primarily from Guadeloupe and Martinique, and it was edited by Maurice Satineau, an original member of the earlier Committee for the Defense of the Black Race, who would later be elected to the French national assembly. The journal stated an explicitly Panafricanist goal: "To serve as a link between nègres of Africa, Madagascar, the Antilles, and America, in order to establish a universal correspondence between men of color."[44] The paper contained notices on black arts and cultural events in Paris, and an English page devoted to ideas derived from Garveyism and the New Negro movement in the United States. Its writers sought "to examine in common the most favorable means for the evolution of their backward brothers to permit the elite of the Negro race to bring its spiritual contribution to the common patrimony of humanity."[45]

Yet the editors also declared: "This is not a nationalist project."[46] Rather, they explained, "[Our conceptions] will be republican, that is to say based on the immortal principles of the glorious French Revolution, which proclaim . . . that 'all men are born free and equal under the law,' that 'the rights of man are sacred and must be defended without distinction of race or color.' "[47] In short, their antiracist program did not lead them to reject the French nation. On the contrary, they endeavored "to point out and combat the injustices and errors which are still too often committed in the colonies so that the true face of France can shine forth, maternal and just."[48]

The *Dépeche* published articles that focused on colonial abuses in French Africa and demanded that the metropolitan state extend republican politics to its overseas territories, including citizenship for all colonial subjects, the protection of human rights, social welfare legislation, a fair judiciary based on rational law, and a separation of governmental powers. In short, this was an organization simultaneously Panafrican and republican, anticolonial and patriotic, in which Antillean writers expressed racial solidarity with their African brothers by invoking "the great principles of equality, public liberty, and social justice, which serve as the foundation of all modern democracies."[49] Like the more radical organizations, *La Dépeche Africaine* was under close police surveillance, provided by paid informants from their own ranks; the paper was regularly confiscated before arriving at its colonial destinations, and those involved in the production and distribution of the paper suffered monitoring and harassment.[50]

In 1931 and 1932, established Antilleans in France published a parallel bilingual cultural journal influenced by the American Harlem Renaissance. The paper, *La Revue du Monde Noir*, declared itself the "official organ" for "the intelligentsia of the black race" whose aim was "to study and to popularize . . . all that concerns BLACK CIVILIZATION . . . to create among the Negroes of the entire world, regardless of nationality, an intellectual and moral tie, which will permit them to know each other better, to love one another, to defend their collective interests more effectively, and to glorify their race."[51] This educated vanguard undertook to "awaken race consciousness" through articles on black arts, folklore, ethnography, poetry, and history, as well as stories on Haiti, Cuba, Liberia, Ethiopia, and black America.[52]

Yet this Panafricanist project was also articulated with French national concerns. Paulette Nardal, a cofounder of the review, affirmed: "We are fully conscious of our debts to Latin culture, and we have no intention of discarding it."[53] She expressed the group's racial transnationalism in a universalist idiom: "The two hundred million individuals who constitute the Negro race, even though scattered among the various nations, will form over and above the latter a great Brotherhood, the forerunner of universal Democracy."[54] In fact, *La Revue du Monde Noir* addressed a Panafrican community concerned with life *in France*, not in some imagined black republic. The journal reviewed and announced cultural events related to the black colonial community in the metropole. A series of articles devoted to the question of how blacks in Europe should dress in order to minimize ridicule indicates the group's concern with this community's ability to integrate into French society.[55]

Although the review didn't last long, it made a lasting impression on those who not only read the paper but who participated in the Nardal cultural salon, legendary Sunday teas at which the black diasporic community in Paris converged. Students, writers, politicians, and professionals from Africa, the Antilles, and the United States came together to recite poetry, sing the blues, and, as one participant recalls, discuss "Paris or world news . . . colonial and interracial problems, the growing place of men and women of color in French life . . . [and] every manifestation of racism."[56] Here republican civil society allowed displaced colonial subjects to make transnational connections and cultivate a Panafrican consciousness, which then addressed how this racialized community could participate in French society.

Attending this salon were the younger Africans and Antilleans who would develop the cultural project of negritude. This cohort never created a formal organization; the group was founded on interlocking friendships and common concerns, which included creating a black poetry, exploring their African heritage, and analyzing their location in French imperial society. The project to claim a common transhistorical black identity led these colonial students to create an intentional Panafrican social network transcending the distinct African, Guadeloupean, Martinican, and Guyanese student communities. The founding group included Léopold Senghor and Aimé Césaire, presidents, respectively, of the West African and Martinique Student Associations, as well as Léon Damas (from Guyane), Soulèye Diagne, and Birago Diop (both from Senegal).

Senghor worked to encourage African and Antillean students to overcome mutual suspicion and share meals at the Cité Universitaire. They would also meet in Diop's residence hotel, where a series of discussions led to the creation of *L'étudiant noir* in 1935, the first negritude publication.[57]

Although these students did not create a formal organization, their journal sought to address as well as create a diasporic student community in France. The title's general racial designation marked a deliberate attempt to transcend national particularities. Damas described *L'étudiant noir* as "a corporate journal of struggle," whose objective was "the end of tribalization, of the clannish system that rules in the Latin Quarter." He hoped that the journal would help colonial subjects of different nationalities merge into "one single and same black student/*étudiant noir*," declaring, "life in isolation is over."[58]

In its first and only surviving issue, essays by Gilbert Gratient, Léonard Sainville, Léopold Senghor, and Aimé Césaire interrogated racial identity and explored the ground on which a Panafrican community might be constructed.[59] The writers grappled with their own problematic cultural status as educated colonial elites enmeshed within a European social order. There were brief pieces on issues that touched colonial students' everyday lives in the imperial metropole, such as their inadequate scholarships, the student organizations' leadership failures, and French national politics. Student readers were warned specifically of "the imminent dangers posed to their life and liberties by the rise of fascism."[60]

L'étudiant noir thus intersected with the broader field of interwar national politics. Numerous black organizations participated in the mid-1930s Popular Front mobilization in defense of the national republic. Nancy Cunard, the avant-garde socialite and Negrophile, described the 1935 Popular Front Bastille Day parade led by the anthropologist Paul Rivet, in which she identified not only radical organizations like the Union of Black Workers, but also this group around *L'étudiant noir*. Like the other demonstrators, colonial groups rallied for the republic. But Cunard reports that they were also chanting slogans such as "Africa for the Africans" and carrying banners that said "Equal Rights and Equal Status for North African and Colonial Workers," or "Fight Mussolini's Aggression on Ethiopia."[61]

Interwar blacks thus directed their Panafrican networks to republican national ends even as they took advantage of the republican public space to pursue Panafricanist politics. By bringing diverse colonial organizations together with a common objective, Popular Front coalition politics opened the possibility for various transnational projects. The Panafricanist enterprise at this time was galvanized by the Italian invasion of Ethiopia. Léopold Senghor, for example, wrote a long poem in response to this imperial war, titled "At the Call of the Race of Sheba," which stages Panafricanism as a worldwide epic struggle. The poem's speaker presents a vision of global black community mobilized around and symbolized by the Ethiopian homeland: "I become equal with the sons of prisoners, and am friends of Moors and Tauregs, congenital enemies / Because the mountainous cry of Ras Desta has cut across Africa, like a long sure sword."[62]

The invasion of Ethiopia led to the creation of a number of anti-imperialist organizations which included members from across the empire, such as the Federation of Colonized Peoples. Created in 1935, this group was composed of students, journalists, lawyers, politicians, and militant socialists from France, Indochina, North Africa, West Africa, and the Antilles. Its goal was to "make known colonial grievances in the metropole and work for their rectification" by informing public opinion about colonial injustices. Yet this federation also wanted "to reconcile colonial peoples' attachment to their respective homelands with the deep love we have for the revolutionary ideal of the France of 1789."[63] Here again, political practices in the republican public space mediated a Panafrican and internationalist vision on the one hand, and a commitment to the French national tradition and its political culture on the other.

When *L'étudiant noir* appeared in 1935, it was thus implicated in the larger milieu of Panafrican, anticolonial, and antifascist politics in France. Like other journals of this time, *L'étudiant noir* was subject to police surveillance.[64] Yet in contrast to the examples I have cited, the end of this journal only marked the beginning of the negritude movement. Even without an institutional locus, negritude's moderate Panafricanism lasted for a generation and shaped the terrain of cultural nationalism for the next. In part, this relative success may have been due to the group's formation at a moment of national republican crisis. In an era of defensive Popular Front alliance, negritude's cultural nationalism within a republican framework must have been less threatening to the French state than the earlier forms of black political nationalism within the revolutionary framework that I discussed.

Several observations emerge from this schematic inventory of interwar Panafricanism. First, the cycle of organization and implosion endemic to Panafrican politics suggests that the combination of internal and external pressures made anticolonial alliance politics around racial identity very difficult to maintain at this time. The French Communist Party seemed unwilling to recognize black nationalism as an autonomous radical movement, radical black nationalists were unable to support the pragmatics of collaborating with moderate but race-conscious reformers, and colonial elites, especially students, were reluctant to commit to the struggles of colonial workers. Chronic financial crisis and constant harassment by the Paris police and colonial government added to this organizational stress. These may be reasons why the informal and cultural Panafricanism formulated by the negritude students proved to be more stable and enduring—if politically moderate—than the more organized and revolutionary Panafricanism of their politicized elders.

Second, despite the entropic and internecine character of interwar organizing, the Panafrican vision continued to animate anticolonial politics during this period, but in a historically specific way. Notably, its advocates were influenced by political and cultural ferment among black Americans. But these interwar activists were not only concerned with African independence and a common diaspora culture. They also used transnational forms of racial identification in order to secure a place *within* French *national* society, even as they were identifying with a diasporic community that contained its own political possibilities.

These brief examples indicate that republican political culture enabled Panafrican solidarity, which then became a standpoint for engaging in republican politics and demanding democratic rights. Moreover, it appears that this was neither a matter of tension nor complementarity *between* national and transnational black politics in France. I want to emphasize that in an imperial nation-state—containing a multinational population spread across disjunctive territories and subject to diverse regimes of governance—nation-centered politics may themselves be transnational. And transnational forms of identification become a modality through which to participate in the national politics of an imperial power. Within this system, Panafricanism and republicanism often entailed one another.

Finally, as my opening vignette suggests, it seems important to establish the genealogical relationship between Panafrican politics in the imperial nation-state of the 1930s and Afrocentric politics in the postcolonial nation-state of the 1990s and beyond. Within France there has been a history of engagement between transnational identity politics and republican political culture which requires more sustained historical attention.

Postcolonial Cultural Politics

In several respects the cultural field in which Sekou Manga's Institute for Historical Truth and Identity emerged and collapsed was as charged as the interwar one was. This grassroots Panafrican organization was not only undermined by internal and interpersonal tensions. French political culture in the mid-1990s proved hostile to precisely the kind of identity politics that the institute's members promoted. The Balladur government began applying the 1993 Pasqua Laws which, among other provisions, made family reunification for legal immigrants more difficult and initiated a war against *les clandestins*. Mass deportations of illegal African immigrants on chartered planes began. As sudden and public document checks became routinized, all French residents of color became coded as "immigrant," regardless of their citizenship status.[65] Prompted by a series of exploding bombs in central Paris metro stations and street markets, the French public was able to watch a television broadcast of gendarmes tracking and executing Kelkal Khaled, a suspected terrorist in the hills outside Lyon.[66] This organized state violence, both mediated and direct, against immigrants converged with the National Front's renewed program of terror against "foreigners" at this same time.[67]

Such official and renegade anti-immigrant sentiment as well as the conservative preoccupation with French national identity and border security intensified at a moment when the Algerian civil war, France's loss of legitimacy in central Africa following the Rwanda genocide, and riots in French Polynesia in response to Chirac's resumption of nuclear tests there threatened French neocolonial authority.[68] At the same time, a liberal-left consensus developed against American-style multicultural identity politics and so-called political correctness, which, it was feared, would spread to France and infect the social body.

Sekou Manga's Institute for Historical Truth and Identity thus emerged at a moment when state policy, neofascist violence, and liberal fear worked to criminalize immigrants, racialize foreigners, and marginalize identity politics. Given this context, we can appreciate why he insisted on the institute's cultural, rather than political, character. We can also recognize the potential subversiveness of his gesture of looking across the Atlantic to African American cultural nationalists as cultural examples.

Sekou Manga's institute and the Panafrican projects of the interwar years were both enabled by respective rounds of capitalist and cultural globalization. French historians have recently shifted their attention to processes such as immigration and imperialism, which disrupt conventional histories of the nation. But much of this work remains nevertheless *within* a national history paradigm — concerned especially with the impact of these processes on national *identity*. There results a risk, especially with the new colonial history, of reproducing national narratives on a wider scale, rather than rethinking them in a more fundamental way.

To paraphrase Wallerstein, we need to *unthink* national history. When studying French imperialism, there is no reason to assume the nation as the most fruitful grid of intelligibility; it should not be invested a priori with privileged explanatory power. Studying imperialism on its own terms, through other nonnational optics, means historicizing the French nation as a *feature*, not a *container* of imperialism. The project then would be not only to expand the field of French history to include the empire, but to reorder the field itself from an imperial perspective. Recent research on French colonialism has demonstrated that French national history cannot be grasped apart from the imperial context through which it was forged. We now need to write history from a properly imperial perspective.

Such work requires categories adequate to the multiple and overlapping spatial and temporal coordinates of empire. It would thus be fruitful for historians to engage recent work on the history and geography of globalization, transnationalism, and diaspora. In turn, by historicizing, rather than presuming, the nation, European historians can make a signal contribution to these discussions about the changing forms of our political modernity. Colonial historians especially can help link the current round of globalization to the earlier global configuration of high imperialism and thus correct certain ahistorical scholarly tendencies.

Notes

1 Paul Gilroy, *The Black Atlantic: Modernity and Double Consciousness* (Cambridge, Mass.: Harvard University Press, 1993), 2–29. Gilroy recognizes that postemancipation Panafrican politics have synthesized national and transnational approaches. But he ultimately submerges the national within the transnational by focusing his analysis on diasporic cultural politics.

2 Arjun Appadurai, *Modernity at Large: Cultural Dimensions of Globalization* (Minneapolis: University of Minnesota Press, 1996), 69, 158, 167.

3 Partha Chatterjee, "Beyond the Nation? Or Within?" *Social Text* 56 (1998): 57–69.

4 For general accounts of Panafricanism, see Colin Legum, *Pan-Africanism: A Short Political Guide* (New York: Praeger, 1962); J. Ayodele Langley, *Pan-Africanism and Nationalism in West Africa, 1900–1945: A Study in Ideology and Social Classes* (Oxford: Clarendon, 1973); P. Olisanwuche Esedebe, *Pan-Africanism: The Idea and Movement, 1776–1991*, 2d ed. (Washington, D.C.: Howard University Press, 1994); and the essays collected in Sidney J. Lemelle and Robin D. G. Kelley, eds., *Imagining Home: Class, Culture, and Nationalism in the African Diaspora* (London: Verso, 1994). Following Lemelle and Kelley, I am working with a broad definition of Panafricanism in this essay, which is not restricted to political movements seeking African independence. Lemelle and Kelly, "Imagining Home: Pan-Africanism Revisited," in *Imagining Home*. I signify this difference by not using the standard orthography, that is, *Pan-African*, which would refer to the more deliberate and formal international political movement.

5 For general accounts of this field of activity, see Philippe Dewitte, *Les mouvements nègres en France, 1919–1939* (Paris: Editions L'Harmattan, 1985); and James Spiegler, "Aspects of Nationalist Thought among French Speaking West Africans, 1921–1939" (Ph.D. diss., Oxford University, 1968).

6 Dewitte, *Les mouvements nègres*, 95–102.

7 Ibid., 130. For the CDRN's troubled affiliation with the PCF see 137.

8   Lamine Senghor, "Ce qu'est notre Comité de Défense de la Race
    Nègre," *La Voix des Nègres*, January 1927, 1. Copies of this journal
    may be found in ANSOM/SLOTFOM V in Aix-en-Provence. This and
    all unmarked translations are mine.

9   Ibid.

10 Ibid.

11 Le Comité, "Le mot 'nègre,' " *La Voix des Nègres*, January 1927, 1.

12 Dewitte, *Les mouvements nègres*, 150–54; "Rapport de 'Desiré,' "
    12 January 1929 and "Rapport de 'Paul,' " 25 October 1929, AN-
    SOM/SLOTFOM V/3. It appeared in Paris, Aix-en-Provence, Mar-
    seille, Bordeaux, and the Midi, as well as in Senegal, Ivory Coast,
    Guinea, and Dahomey. "Rapport de 'Desiré,' " 31 August 1927,
    10 September 1927, 13 October 1927, 22 October 1927, 28 Novem-
    ber 1927, 28 February 1928, and 12 January 1929; "Rapport de
    'Coco,' " 10 August 1929, ANSOM/SLOTFOM V/3.

13 For example, the governor-general of Afrique Occidentale Française
    (AOF) distributed a circular throughout the federation instructing
    administrators to interdict the newspaper. Reported in "La généro-
    sité française sous la IIIème république," *La Race Nègre*, September
    1927, 1. Copies of this journal may be found in ANSOM/SLOTFOM
    V. The police infiltration of the LDRN and *La Race Nègre* is docu-
    mented in the detailed police reports in ANSOM/SLOTFOM V/3. The
    newspaper appeared in Paris, Aix-en-Provence, Marseille, Bordeaux,
    and the Midi, as well as in Senegal, Ivory Coast, Guinea, and Da-
    homey. "Rapport de 'Desiré,' " 31 August 1927, 10 September 1927,
    13 October 1927, 22 October 1927, 28 November 1927, 28 Febru-
    ary 1928, and 12 January 1929; "Rapport de 'Coco,' " 10 August
    1929, ANSOM/SLOTFOM V/3.

14 "Rapport," 5 November 1927, ANSOM/SLOTFOM V/3.

15 "Rapport," 19 November 1927, ANSOM/SLOTFOM V/3.

16 La Race Nègre, "La ligue est en deuil: Son très dévoué président
    Senghor Lamine est mort," *La Race Nègre*, May 1928, 1. "Rapport
    de 'Joe,' " 2 November 1929, ANSOM/SLOTFOM V/3.

17 Quoted from one of the posters in a letter from the prefect of police,
    Paris, to the minister of colonies, 28 February 1928, ANSOM/SLOT-
    FOM V/3.

18 "Vers l'élaboration d'un programme," *La Race Nègre*, March 1929,
    1. In 1929, the group resolved to block the arrival of blacks imported
    from the colonies for the coming international colonial exposition.
    "Rapport de 'Joe,' " 2 November 1929, ANSOM/SLOTFOM V/3.

19 Dorarlie, "Expliquons-nous," *La Race Nègre*, September 1927, 1.

20 "Ordre du jour," *La Race Nègre*, September 1927, 1.

21 "Rapport de 'Paul,' " 28 June 1930, ANSOM/SLOTFOM V/3.

22 "Rapport de 'Paul,' " 11 October 1929, ANSOM/SLOTFOM V/3.

23 "Rapport de 'Paul,'" 16 January 1930, 28 June 1930, ANSOM/
    SLOTFOM V/3. Only lack of funds kept him from also organizing
    black unions in Le Havre and Dunkurque. "Rapport de 'Paul,'"
    17 April 1930, ANSOM/SLOTFOM V/3.
24 "Rapport de 'Paul,'" 28 June 1930, 12 November 1930, ANSOM/
    SLOTFOM V/3.
25 "Rapport de 'Paul,'" 25 October 1929, ANSOM/SLOTFOM V/3.
26 "Rapport de 'Paul,'" 16 January 1930, 17 April 1930, ANSOM/
    SLOTFOM V/3.
27 "Rapport de 'Desiré,'" 17 September 1930, "Rapport de 'Paul,'" 12
    November 1930, ANSOM/SLOTFOM V/3.
28 "Rapport de 'Paul,'" 25 November 1930, 11 December 1930; "Rap-
    port de 'Joe,'" 15 March 1931; "Rapport de 'Claude,'" 15 June
    1931, ANSOM/SLOTFOM V/3; "A tous nos abonnés, membres, et
    lecteurs," La Race Nègre, Kouyaté edition, April 1931, 1; La Rédac-
    tion, "Avis," La Race Nègre, Faure edition, April 1931, 1.
29 Koyaté created the UTN in May 1932 with promises of financial sup-
    port from the colonial commission of the PCF. But the UTN neither
    immediately submitted to party authority nor subscribed to positions
    determined by the international, so the colonial commission came to
    distrust the group. Dewitte, Les mouvements nègres, 284–304.
30 Letter from minister of colonies to the governor-generals of AOF,
    (AEF), and Madagascar, 2 March 1930, ANSOM/SLOTFOM III/112.
31 "Rapport de 'Desiré,'" 6 December 1927; "Rapport de 'Joe,'" 2 No-
    vember 1929, 22 December 1929, 14 July 1930, 15 May 1930, and
    27 December 1931, ANSOM/SLOTFOM V/3; "Rapport de 'Desiré,'"
    15 March 1930, ANSOM/SLOTFOM III/112.
32 "Rapport de 'Desiré,'" 15 March 1930, ANSOM/SLOTFOM III/112.
    See also "Contre le communisme: Un institut revolutionnaire nègre
    en plein Paris," L'Ami du Peuple, 26 May 1930, also in ANSOM/
    SLOTFOM III/112. Sajous, perhaps because of his affiliation with the
    moderate Revue du monde noir, presented himself to the préfet de
    police and protested the inclusion of his name on the list of members
    of the LDRN, insisting that he no longer belonged to the group. "Rap-
    port de 'Joe,'" 5 May 1931, ANSOM/SLOTFOM V/3.
33 Participants at the first meeting included African, Antillean, and
    Malagasy communists from the UTN who had formed the radical
    faction of the LDRN, including Kossoul, Ramanajato and his wife
    Ebele, and Julians. Also present were a number of students: Léonard
    Sainville from the Guadeloupe Student Association, Megrone from
    the Martinique Student Association, and Léopold Sédar Senghor
    from the African Student Association as well as two other unaffili-
    ated students, Jalton and Danglemont. At least two police infor-
    mants attended the meeting. "Note sur la propagande révolution-

naire interessant les pays d'outre-mer," ANSOM/SLOTFOM III/61; "Rapport de 'Joe,' " 23 June 1933; and "Rapport de 'Paul,' " 23 June 1933, ANSOM/SLOTFOM III/73.

34 Kouyaté hoped this would lead to a multiracial conference in Paris that would include all the peoples colonized by France. "Note sur la propagande révolutionnaire interessant les pays d'outre-mer," AN-SOM/SLOTFOM III/61; "Note sur la propagande révolutionnaire interessant les pays d'outre-mer," 31 July 1933, ANSOM/SLOTFOM III/61. During this period, Kouyaté also pursued his multiracial anti-colonial organizing. In early May 1934, he organized a meeting along with Faure and Beton, which included blacks, Indochinese, and North Africans. The goal was to create a "Comité Intercolonial" that would include representatives from all French colonies in order to "defend the moral, material, cultural, and political interests of populations oppressed by French imperialism and that would work for the national liberation and social emancipation of French colonies." "Note sur la propagande révolutionnaire interessant les pays d'outre-mer," 31 May 1934, ANSOM/SLOTFOM III/61.

35 The UTN participants had composed the radical faction of the LDRN and included Kossoul, Ramanajato and his wife Ebele, and Julians. Two other "nonaffiliated" students were present, Jalton and Dangle-mont. "Note sur la propagande révolutionnaire interessant les pays d'outre-mer," ANSOM/SLOTFOM III/61; "Rapport de 'Joe,' " 23 June 1933, ANSOM/SLOTFOM III/73; "Rapport de 'Paul,' " 23 June 1933, ANSOM/SLOTFOM III/73.

36 "Rapport de 'Joe,' " 23 June 1933; and "Rapport de 'Paul,' " 23 June 1933, ANSOM/SLOTFOM III/73; "Note sur la propagande révolutionnaire interessant les pays d'outre-mer," 31 July 1933, ANSOM/SLOTFOM III/61. Senghor's name is not even listed in the police account of that 31 July discussion, which means he was either silent or did not even show up.

37 "Note sur la propagande révolutionnaire interessant les pays d'outre-mer," 31 October 1933, ANSOM/SLOTFOM III/61; "Note sur la propagande révolutionnaire interessant les pays d'outre-mer," 3 November 1933, ANSOM/SLOTFOM III/61. On 31 October 1933, the communist *Humanité* published a notice announcing Kouyaté's expulsion, accusing him of misusing party funds and maintaining relations with party enemies. "Note sur la propagande révolutionnaire interessant les pays d'outre-mer," 31 October 1933, ANSOM/SLOTFOM III/61. In February 1934, after finally being forced out of the UTN, *Le Cri des Nègres* — the newspaper published by those who comprised the radical communist faction of the *La Race Nègre* — also published a notice denouncing Kouyaté for collaborating with politically unacceptable figures. "Note sur la propagande révolutionnaire

interessant les pays d'outre-mer," 28 February 1934, ANSOM/SLOT-FOM III/61.

38 Letter from Bureau Politique du Parti Communiste, Section Coloniale, 3 September 1935; "Note: Réunion de la Section Coloniale du Parti Communiste," 10 October 1935, ANSOM/SLOTFOM III/73.

39 "Note: Réunion de la Section Coloniale du Parti Communiste," 10 October 1935, ANSOM/SLOTFOM III/73; "Réunion de la Section Coloniale du Parti Communiste," 11 October 1935, ANSOM/SLOT-FOM III/73. Despite this challenge to party discipline, both Kossoul and Rosso were members of the PCF's colonial commission. Claude Liauzu, *Aux origines des tiers-mondismes: Colonisés et anticolonialistes en France (1919–1939)* (Paris: Editions L'Harmattan, 1982), 230. Although Kouyaté had been expelled from the party, and despite Kouyaté's bitter political, organizational, and legal conflict with Faure, it was believed that Kouyaté and Faure would both show integral involvement in this new African organization. "Note from L.S.," 12 November 1935, and "Note from L.S.," 23 November 1935, ANSOM/SLOTFOM III/73.

40 "Réunion de la sous-section nègre du Parti Communiste," 18 December 1935, ANSOM/SLOTFOM III/73.

41 Ibid.

42 "Réunion de la sous-section nègre du Parti Communiste," 11 October 1935, ANSOM/SLOTFOM III/73.

43 For a fuller discussion of the anticolonialism practiced by *La Dépêche Africaine* and *La Revue du Monde Noir*, from which the following is partially extracted, see Gary Wilder, "Practicing Citizenship in Imperial Paris," in *Civil Society and the Political Imagination in Africa: Critical Perspectives*, ed. John L. Comaroff and Jean Comaroff (Chicago: University of Chicago Press, 1999).

44 "Notre but, notre programme," *La Dépeche Africaine*, February 1928, 1. (Available in ANSOM/SLOTFOM V/2.)

45 Ibid.

46 Ibid.

47 Ibid.

48 Ibid.

49 Ibid.

50 See the dossiers in ANSOM/SLOTFOM V/2.

51 "Our Aim," *La Revue du Monde Noir*, 1931, 2.

52 Paulette Nardal, "Eveil de la conscience de race," *La Revue du Monde Noir*, 1932, 31.

53 Ibid.

54 Ibid.

55 "Nos enquêtes," *La Revue du Monde Noir*, no. 2, 60, and, no. 4, 51–52.

56 Louis Achille, preface to *La Revue du Monde Noir/Review of the Black World* (Paris: Jean-Michel Place, 1931), xv.

57 For histories of these social connections, see M. a M. Ngal (Mbwil a Mpaang), *Aimé Césaire: Un homme à la recherche d'une patrie* (Paris: Présence Africaine, 1994); Janet G. Vaillant, *Black, French, and African: A Life of Léopold Sédar Senghor* (Cambridge, Mass.: Harvard University Press, 1990); Daniel Racine, *Léon-Gontran Damas: L'homme et l'oeuvre* (Paris: Présence Africaine, 1983); *Hommage posthume à Léon-Gontran Damas (1912–1978)* (Paris: Présence Africaine, 1979); Birago Diop, *La plume raboutée: Mémoires* (Paris: Présence Africaine, 1978); *Hommage à Léopold Sédar Senghor: Homme de culture* (Paris: Présence Africaine, 1976).

58 Damas quoted in Racine, *Léon-Gontran Damas*, 29–30.

59 Aimé Césaire, "Nègreries: Jeunesse noire et l'assimilation," *L'Etudiant Noir*, March 1935, 3; Léopold Sédar Senghor, "L'humanisme et nous: René Maran," *L'étudiant noir*, March 1935, 4; Henry Eboué, "Langage et musique chez les nègres du Congo," *L'étudiant noir*, March 1935; Paulette Nardal, "Guignol Oulouf," *L'étudiant noir*, March 1935, 4–5; Léonard Sainville, "Un livre sur la Martinique," *L'étudiant noir*, March 1935, 5; Gilbert Gratient, "Mulatres . . . pour le bien et le mal," *L'étudiant noir*, March 1935, 5–7.

60 Léonard Sainville, "Simples questions à Je Suis Partout," *L'étudiant noir*, March 1935, 8.

61 Nancy Cunard, "Tricolor with International," 14 July 1935, AN-SOM/SLOTFOM III/73.

62 Léopold Sédar Senghor "À l'appel de la race de Saba," *Poèmes*, new ed. (Paris: Editions du Seuil, 1984), 59–60. Senghor's invocation of Panafrican solidarity exceeds the Ethiopian conflict as the poem quickly moves to a vision of general anticolonial revolt and African liberation entailing "the final assault against the bureaucracies that govern the governors of colonies." But the poem's last verse elaborates a vision of working-class internationalism to supplement the racial transnationalism. The speaker announces "we are all reunited here . . . different costumes custom language; but . . . the same chant of suffering"; this group includes not only colonial Africans and Asians, but also "all the white workers in fraternal struggle" and Jewish victims of German persecution. Here Panafrican politics seems to enable worldwide working-class politics; it does not just mirror them.

63 "D'un agent: La Féderation des Peuples Colonisés et Nguyen The Truyen," 11 March 1935, 12 March 1935, and 13 March 1935; "Lettre de la Federation des Peuples Colonisés"; "Note d'un agent," 21 March 1935; all in ANSOM/SLOTFOM III/119.

64 "Rapport de L.S.," 3 May 1935, ANSOM/SLOTFOM III/73.

65   Bernard Philippe and Nathaniel Herzberg, "Les entraves administratives se multiplient envers les étrangers," *Le Monde*, 19 April 1995.

66   Eric Collier, "L'homme a tiré, les gendarmes ont riposté et l'ont abbatu," *Le Monde*, 2 October 1995.

67   Luc Leroux, "Une sale histoire marseillaise," *Le Monde*, 6 March 1995, Bernard Phillip and Erich Inciyan, "Un morocain a été tué pendant la manifestation du Front National," *Le Monde*, 3 May 1995. See Edward G. DeClair, *Politics on the Fringe: The People, Policies, and Organization of the French National Front* (Durham, N.C.: Duke University Press, 1999).

68   See Benjamin Stora, *L'Algérie en 1995: La guerre, l'histoire, la politique* (Paris: Michalon, 1995); Philip Gourevitch, *We Wish to Inform You That Tomorrow We Will Be Killed with Our Families: Stories from Rwanda* (New York: Farrar, Strauss, and Giroux, 1998): "Emeutes en Polynesie française: nombreuses manifestations dans le monde," Agence France Presse notice, 7 September 1995.

Dennis McEnnerney

Frantz Fanon, the Resistance,

and the Emergence of Identity Politics

The Third World liberationist Frantz Fanon (1925–61) has long appeared fundamentally anti-French. Not only did Fanon oppose the colonialist policies of the French state when his writings first gained widespread attention during the Algerian War, but he also challenged France's claims to legitimacy. Fanon insisted, for example, that racial discrimination and colonial domination were deeply woven into the French Republic and that the purported philosophical foundation of modern French republicanism, the principle of equal citizenship, was a sham. This Fanon seemed absolutely *not French*, and at least since that time most French intellectuals have agreed with this assessment. Perhaps partly as a result, Fanon's books have sold poorly in France, and as a recent biographer notes, "When he is read" in France, "the readings are negative."[1]

Yet only a decade before Fanon published his searing critique of French and European colonialism, *Les damnés de la terre* (1961), he had forthrightly rejected black nationalism in *Peau noire, masque blanc* (1952) and insisted on his French identity, asking,

> What is all this talk of a black people, of a Negro nationality? I am a Frenchman. I am interested in French culture, French civilization, the French people. We refuse to be considered "outsiders" [comme "à-côté"], we have full part in the French drama. When men who were not basically bad, only deluded, invaded France in order to subjugate her, my position as a Frenchman made it plain to me that my place was not outside but in the very heart of the problem. I am personally interested in the future of France, in French values, in the French nation. What do I have to do with a black empire?[2]

Perhaps, as some biographers have suggested, an "early," non-racial Fanon, interested in France and French culture, changed into a radically different, "late" Third World Fanon, hostile to all things French.[3] However, while atrocities during the Algerian War certainly did alienate Fanon from France, it is worth bearing in mind that rejecting the Fourth and Fifth Republics and renouncing French citizenship are not equivalent to becoming utterly non-French.

To be sure, Fanon was both original and radical in many respects. Yet he was also deeply shaped by his experiences as a black colonial Frenchman, both in the native Martinique of his childhood and in the metropolitan France of his young adulthood.[4] His originality and radicalism grew partly out of that black colonial French youth, marked by both aspirations for racial equality and disappointment with French racism. His critical engagement, as a young adult, with the problems of French identity — black colonial and white metropolitan — also marked his thinking. Drawing on repudiations of French republicanism within the white metropolitan French resistance, Fanon found concepts and categories that helped him to analyze black colonial identity and, eventually, to develop the liberationist theory that made him seem so un-French.

Disappointed Dissidence

Frantz Fanon's French colonial youth coincided with the Second World War. Martinicans like Fanon responded to the invasion and partitioning of France in quite different ways than did white metropolitans. Most of the latter, having lost faith in the Third Republic, quickly accepted the authority of Marshal Pétain's Vichy regime.[5] In contrast, the reactions of black and mixed-race Martinicans, such as the Fanons, were more varied. In 1940, substantial numbers of nonwhite Martinicans remained committed to some form of republicanism, long associated on the island with movements against slavery and for racial equality. When Pétain's signing of the armistice agreement with Germany in June 1940 prompted Charles de Gaulle to demand continued resistance, the island's mayors and *conseillers généraux* — most of whom were mixed-race or black — responded within days, pledging to assume "the ultimate sacrifices in order to achieve the final victory by continuing the struggle alongside the Allies and the French Overseas Empire."[6] But by then, Martinique had fallen under the authority of the senior white naval officer in the Caribbean, Admiral Georges Robert, high commissioner for the French West Indies and commander in chief of the West Atlantic fleet. Overruling the locals, Robert aligned Martinique with Vichy and set about installing an authoritarian regime that drew strongly on the island's small white Creole population, much of which sympathized with Vichy. Although some mixed-race and black Martinicans initially supported Robert's effort, the regime quickly lost any hope of broad support as nonwhite islanders began to see that the new order favored whites. In particular, Robert's replacement of elected mayors, most of whom were of mixed-race background, with appointees drawn from the white minority undermined the popularity of his cause.[7]

Not long afterward, black Martinicans, including the Fanon family, began inconspicuously listening to General de Gaulle's regular BBC broadcasts, transmitted from the neighboring British islands of Dominica and Saint Lucia.[8] As the naval authorities worked to establish a local version of Vichy, many if not most common black Martinicans came to reaffirm, as essential to their struggle against racial oppression, the republican principles and institutions defended by de Gaulle and attacked by Vichy.[9] Rejecting republicanism or France were options the majority never seriously entertained. Just as earlier generations of black Martinicans had embraced French republicanism in the course of rejecting Caribbean slavery, their descendents adopted de Gaulle as the leader in what they saw as a struggle against collaborationist *and* racist rule. The seventeen-year-old Fanon, following most of his elders, is said to have rejected the suggestion of a disaffected teacher who had argued that war among white Europeans could benefit blacks, calling him a "bastard." Instead, Fanon embraced the more common argument of another teacher, who had remarked, "When you hear people speaking ill of the Jews, . . . they're talking about you [too]." Building on such arguments, Fanon reportedly told his brother that "freedom is indivisible" and insisted that France's struggle was their struggle.[10] In these respects, the young Fanon was a typical black Martinican, though perhaps one more outspoken and determined than most.

However, as in mainland France, it took time for overt organized opposition to develop in Martinique, given the overwhelming strength of the naval authorities, who had force of arms as well as support within the island's small but relatively wealthy white minority. While portraits of Pétain, pasted on the walls of Fort-de-France in an effort to consolidate the new regime's authority, were regularly slashed as early as 1941, little else was done.[11] Only in the middle of 1942 did more overt signs of rebellion emerge in the form of acts recalling traditions of slave resistance: sugarcane fields were set on fire, and black Martinicans began fleeing by boat or raft to the neighboring British islands. Those remaining behind started refusing to bare their heads when the Marseillaise was played.[12] By early 1943, a pro-Gaullist *Comité de Libération*, dominated by mixed-race and black leaders but headquartered at the home of a prominent white Creole, organized to press for a change of administration. These varied opposition efforts came to be known as dissidence, which one of Fanon's biographers characterizes as "the Martinican equivalent to résistance."[13]

Eventually, hundreds of nonwhite Martinicans, along with some white sailors and soldiers, started to flee to Saint Lucia and Dominica, where they could enlist in de Gaulle's Free French army.[14] Fanon joined them in the spring of 1943, sailing to Dominica, where he underwent some basic military training. Then, in late June, the Vichy authorities in Martinique lost power to the Free French when a small contingent of army troops, including some nonwhite soldiers, joined the *comité de libération* in calling on the majority black population to revolt against the naval leadership.[15] On 29 June 1943, Martinican blacks demonstrated in large numbers, forcing Admiral Robert to begin negotiating a transition of power the next day. On Bastille Day, 14 July 1943, Free French authorities arrived on a battleship, claiming to have "brought back" or "restored" France and the republic to Martinique.[16] Shortly afterward, Fanon, who turned eighteen only on 20 July and may have been considered too young to enlist, was himself brought back to Martinique to finish secondary school. Fanon completed his coursework the following spring and, still eighteen, again volunteered for the Free French. This time they accepted him.[17]

Fanon may have been a precocious French republican, but he was also a black West Indian. Consequently, despite republican discourse about equal, universal French citizenship — long associated in Martinique with struggles for racial equality — Fanon soon encountered the racial underside of Gaullist Free France. The French army he joined was "structured around an ethnic hierarchy, with white Europeans at the top . . . North Africans at the bottom . . . Black colonial troops . . . superior to Arabs, and the position of West Indians . . . ambiguous in the extreme."[18] Fanon was placed in an almost exclusively black West Indian unit, which was first sent to North Africa and then, in September 1944, to the south of France, near Toulon.[19] Soon after, he and three friends from Martinique were incorporated into a black African unit from Senegal. The unit soon began moving north, where some hoped to take part in the invasion of Germany itself. But their hopes were disappointed in late October, when the French high command, acting on little more than racial and cultural stereotypes, decided that black Africans, unlike white Europeans, could not be expected to fight effectively in cold climates. Before engaging the Germans in the north, the high command ordered that the division undergo "whitening" (*blanchiment*): the black Senegalese soldiers were removed and the unit proclaimed officially "European." However, Fanon and the other West Indians were not removed, perhaps because, having come from what the French called their "old" or longstanding colonies, they were assumed to be more assimilated to French culture and thereby culturally "whiter" and more "European."[20] Whatever the reason, Fanon and his three Martinican friends were left in the uncomfortable position of being black-skinned French colonials in an officially whitened European division.[21]

Fanon was wounded seriously on 25 November 1944 by shrapnel from an incoming German mortar round while servicing a French mortar. Decorated for "distinguished conduct" and awarded the Croix de Guerre with a bronze star, he was evacuated to convalesce near Lyon, where he remained until, after a brief first visit to Paris, he returned to his unit in January 1945. By that time, the unit was conducting night patrols on the still insecure Rhine.[22]

At the end of the war, Fanon and all the surviving West Indians were reassembled in Toulon, where, despite their valorous service, they found themselves effectively segregated from the white city. While other troops were feted as heroic fighters, the Martinicans were shunned because, in that context, their racial and colonial backgrounds contrasted negatively with those of the dominant force in Toulon, white American troops. The white Americans made for attractive heroes, especially in the eyes of Toulon's women; by contrast, the West Indians, regardless of their purported assimilation into French and European culture, appeared to the white Toulonese women as scary black sexual predators.[23] From Toulon, Fanon's contingent was moved to Rouen in August 1945 for embarkment to Martinique, which took place the following October.

During his term of service, Fanon had only limited direct contact with white France, and those contacts were often marked by racism. When he left Martinique to join the Free French, Fanon had been convinced that "freedom is indivisible,"[24] that threats to other French people, especially racist attacks on Jews, endangered the freedom of all people, and that France's troubles were his own. By the end of the war, Fanon's outlook had changed. As he later explained in *Peau noire, masques blancs*, racial stereotyping and discrimination were common, not only in the army, but also throughout the French territories. Even French Arabs and Africans were prejudiced and acted on racial stereotypes.[25] Reflecting bitterly on his experiences, he wrote to his parents on 12 April 1945 that he had enlisted "to defend an obsolete ideal." He told them in so many words that French republicanism, which supposedly treated all citizens equally, was not the good cause: "This false ideology that shields the secularists and the idiot politicians must not delude us any longer. *I was wrong!* Nothing here, nothing justifies my sudden decision to defend the interests of farmers who don't give a damn."[26]

Fanon had started the war with acts of dissidence that he believed allied him with all other French republicans and that arguably showed him to be more loyal to France than most white French people had been. By the end of the war, however, he found that his dissidence left him an outsider, a black other, within a white-dominated French empire.

Marginal Résistance

Fanon's wartime experiences drove home how problematic French identity was for black Martinicans, and it set Fanon on a road that would ultimately lead to his militant rejection of the French Republic and French citizenship. Yet in the 1940s and early 1950s, troubles with French identity were not limited to people of colonial and non-European origin. Fanon shared the experience of questioning with important subcultures of white metropolitan France during and after the Second World War, although the very different trajectories of their respective wartime experiences and the very different characters of their respective troubles with French identity obscured this commonality.[27]

Mainland *résistants* began the war as outsiders in a society where virtually all groups not only accepted the Vichy regime in 1940, but also remained relatively supportive of it until the war began turning against the Axis powers in late 1943. By contrast, black *dissidents* entered the war on the side of the Allies relatively early on, well aware that most nonwhite Martinicans shared their hostility both to the white naval officers who took control of the island in 1940 and, more generally, to Vichy collaborationism. The experience of mainland résistants differed in other ways too. For example, they initially found themselves much more isolated than their West Indian cousins: listening to the BBC proved far more difficult on the mainland than in Martinique; and escaping to Allied territory in order to join the Free French was almost impossible in occupied France and quite hazardous in the Vichy zone during the early years of the war, whereas fleeing Martinique in the years before authority on the island passed to the Free French, though risky, was not extremely dangerous.

The actions taken by dissidents and résistants during the war also differed markedly. After the Robert government disavowed the initial Martinican declarations of support for the Free French and actions were taken to control public life on the island, dissidence seems to have taken the form of following news about de Gaulle and the Allies in private while discreetly discussing the progress of the war with trusted friends and family members. For example, Fanon notes in passing that as a fourteen-year-old schoolboy, he listened to the BBC with his family and that as early as February 1941, he was cheering the British rout of Italian forces at Benghazi, Libya.[28] Such actions became increasingly open and assertive as dissatisfaction with Robert mounted in 1942. Ultimately, for young men like Fanon, dissidence took the form of escape from the island and enlistment in the Free French. When they accepted Fanon in 1944, he, along with the other Martinican volunteers, found that dissidence had led to a role familiar to generations of men, that of the lowly foot soldier.[29]

By contrast, the life of a résistant was more irregular and self-directed. The resistance was not one formal organization, but many loosely connected groupings of often highly individualistic people. As was the case in Martinique, public conformity and worries about surveillance marked the first months following the armistice on the mainland. However, given the metropole's overwhelming support for Vichy, it took much longer for opponents of the regime there to emerge, recognize one another, and begin organizing. Whereas nonwhite Martinicans could assume most other nonwhite Martinicans were unsympathetic to their white metropolitan naval rulers — given their common history of racial grievances — mainland French people could not count on any group of people for understanding, let alone support. Even when resistance members began to form networks, those networks couldn't offer the social support, direction, and solidarity typical of more normal social and political organizations. Under the conditions of the occupation and Vichy, authority had to be dispersed, and members were typically more isolated and self-directed than common soldiers were.[30] The actual opposition that résistants presented to the German and Vichy authorities was consequently highly restricted, even after organized groups emerged, since the internal resisters, with few exceptions, had limited access to weapons. Whereas Fanon and his Martinican compatriots came to be armed and eventually fought on open battlefields, résistants lacked the means to affect much around them. Indeed, until fairly late in the war, they were reduced largely to announcing their résistance, often in anonymous flyers and at underground meetings. Even the occasional assassination, like the more frequent act of vandalism, was tied to the logic of making résistance known. Such actions had little effect on the outcome of the war, but they at least made metropolitans aware of *some* risk of punishment, admonishing them to think twice before collaborating.

Though their actions remained limited and negative, resisters in metropolitan France nevertheless did accomplish three important things in announcing (albeit anonymously or pseudonymously) their résistance. First, they uncovered an internal capacity for holding out. In the extraordinary circumstances of the occupation and Vichy, isolated partisans made manifest a capacity for résistance simply by speaking out in favor of it. Resisters thus demonstrated that the otherwise powerful Vichy and occupation authorities could be challenged and limited, even if only in the constricted arena of consciousness and self-consciousness. Second, they opened up what in essence was a cultural and psychological battlefield in which that capacity was tested. To announce one's résistance in wartime France was to challenge German and Vichy regimes that would brook neither opposition nor independence; one's announcement demanded a response, and it was generally received. But the resulting struggle took place in an arena over which even the impressive German army and Nazi propaganda machine could have only limited sway: "within" the French resisters, in their hearts and minds, in the ways they perceived, understood, and presented themselves and their experiences. Furthermore, because the partisans generally offered their verbal résistance in a surreptitious, anonymous manner, it was often impossible for the authorities to locate their opponents, let alone defeat them. The battle was engaged, but the struggle amounted to a kind of cultural guerilla war, one in which the authorities found themselves significantly disadvantaged. Third, by speaking out intelligibly, resisters also drew on a common French culture, using elements of that culture to establish a new kind of social solidarity and to begin building a counterculture or subculture of résistance.

Speech, writing, and consciousness thus became more central to the mainland movement eventually known as La Résistance than they did to the Martinican movement later known as La Dissidence. Here word choices prove revealing. Nonwhite Martinicans manifested dissidence in the face of the white Vichy authorities: that is, together they ceased to obey the established authorities, together they separated themselves as a group from the larger community to which they had been attached. When they joined de Gaulle's army, black and mixed-race Martinicans became part of *la France combattante* or *la France libre*. In short, their community removed itself from a "bad" authority and attached itself to a "good" one.[31] Mainland resisters, in contrast, sought to hold out against invasion and collaboration, to contest authority they considered illegitimate, and to act morally in a context in which all authorities had come into question. They offered résistance in the form of what, at first, were largely moral and often individual acts. Whereas *dissidence* has a relatively narrow and negative political meaning ("the act or state of withdrawing obedience or association," or "the group that withdraws such obedience or association"), *résistance* has a broad set of related senses combining physical, military, political, and moral meanings.[32] The internal Résistance movement wanted to oppose or respond to the physical pressure of invasion and coercion; it wanted to respond militarily to attacks; and it wanted to refuse political obedience to the German and Vichy authorities. But in practice, actual résistance could take none of those forms with regularity in occupied and Vichy France until late in the war. Instead, opponents of the occupation and Vichy took moral action.

Unlike the English term *resistance*, the French concept of *résistance* has since early modern times also had an explicitly moral meaning in addition to the physical, military, and political ones. *Résistance* has to do with the morally better part of oneself, the part that refuses seduction, a connection notably absent in English dictionary entries for *resistance*.[33] For a résistant, holding fast or standing against the occupation and Vichy in the first years of the war thus meant striking a moral stance largely on one's own. It amounted to coming to moral consciousness in relative isolation, while also making that consciousness manifest to others.[34] During the Second World War, French patriots invoked *résistance* in this sense with some regularity, and as a result the semantic range of the term expanded.[35] By 1943, the word *résistance* had become integral to a set of transformative speech acts, actions taken by relatively isolated and powerless persons who, in declaring their résistance (generally pseudonymously), discovered themselves to be obstacles, albeit small ones, to the occupation and Vichy. For resisters, in other words, imprudently speaking out for résistance in clandestine publications and secret meetings crystallized their respective senses of self: they committed themselves morally, and in doing so they began to see themselves and their world in a new light. The moral self-discovery and self-identification of résistants came to constitute a form of political action, a way of founding countercultures within occupied and Vichy France.

The struggles of the internal resistance movement gained literary expression and broad resonance in Albert Camus's underground *Combat* editorials, as well as in his wartime "Letters to a German Friend." In those pieces, Camus charted the actions of individuals who, on imagining the implications of fascism, discover within themselves a force that refuses to accept those implications. As Camus would put it later in *The Rebel*, "What was at first the man's obstinate résistance now becomes the whole man, who is identified with and summed up in this résistance." The result is rebellion, and "with rebellion, awareness is born": a new moral and political consciousness that demanded holding out against the seduction of collaboration then emerged from acts of stubbornness performed without calculation.[36] As Camus made clear in his *Combat* editorials, such acts stemmed neither from traditional patriotism nor from high moral principle, but from what he took as an internal moral capacity, "the delicacy of the heart that feels repugnance . . ., the capacity to say no."[37]

Résistance was therefore neither like the dissidence of Martinique — in the course of which whole nonwhite communities consciously withdrew their political allegiance from an authority they saw as illegitimate and transferred it to another — nor was it like that alternate authority itself, de Gaulle's Free French. Although de Gaulle's movement was sometimes also referred to as résistance, it was a movement based on a traditional patriotism and on the assertion that de Gaulle maintained the continuing authority of the republic in exile. (Hence the Free French could claim that they had "returned" the authority of France and the republic to Martinique.) By contrast, the internal résistance, drawing on elements of French moral and linguistic traditions, fashioned its own, new political authority through unplanned acts of moral self-discovery and self-recognition.

Just as the origins and actions of résistance and dissidence differed, so, too, did the initial results: whereas the Martinicans could enroll in de Gaulle's army and become players in the massive Allied offensives that destroyed Vichy and the occupation, internal résistants were largely limited to effecting symbolic changes and beginning the process of developing an alternative subculture. That alternative subculture, the internal French resistance, however, did not have wide support in the early years of the war. Even at the end of the war, it lacked the power to topple the occupation and Vichy, and it was never likely to gain that power — only the Allied armies, including the Free French forces in which Fanon served, had that potential capacity. The resistance's primary forces were those of culture and consciousness, not those of arms. Within the restricted environment of Vichy and the occupation, the internal resistance showed that presenting difference in the form of assertions of moral résistance made political action possible. Those assertions resonated with others; they opened discussions in which new moral standards against which to judge the actions of individuals and authorities began to take shape; and they thus started the process of forming an oppositional French subculture.

The movements of résistance and dissidence did share one commonality, however: both involved questioning French identity. For black Martinicans, as for many colonial French people, Vichy, with its implicitly racist paternalism, did not represent France. At the beginning of the war, to be French meant, in the eyes of nonwhite Martinicans, commitment to equal, universal, and therefore nonracial citizenship. By the end of the war, the realities of endemic racial discrimination and stereotyping within Free France, the restored republic, and the reworked colonial union raised questions about French identity, at least for sensitive Martinicans like Fanon. Similarly, for resistance leaders and sympathizers in metropolitan France, Vichy was not France, for a whole variety of different reasons. The internal resistance itself constituted France, a France in the process of rebirth and renovation.[38] To opponents of Vichy and the occupation in the metropole, being French, after 1940, meant embracing résistance and creating a new kind of politics, one based on the discovery, assertion, and development of identities in the course of continuing moral conflict and debate.

But after the Allies swept the Germans and collaborationists from power, the internal resistance failed to shape the postwar French state, in part because the political leaders who emerged in 1944, particularly Charles de Gaulle, had positive reasons to discourage attempts to institutionalize a politics of résistance.[39] For de Gaulle, the restoration of order and the imposition of normal lines of authority presented first priorities. In pursuit of these ends, de Gaulle insisted on the continuity of the French state during the war years, which meant that from his perspective, the legitimacy of the internal resistance stemmed from its acceptance of his purportedly "continuing" authority as legitimate leader of the French Republic. His provisional government, as well as its elected successors in the Fourth and Fifth Republics, thus sought to downplay significantly the rebelliousness of the internal resistance (as well as the initial popularity and legal standing of the Vichy regime), partially in order to undercut the legitimacy of continued political opposition in the postwar period.[40]

Following de Gaulle's lead, it became the conventional wisdom of the postwar era that the legacy of the internal resistance was solely moral, not political.[41] What the resistance demonstrated, it has been said, was the possibility of virtuous acts even when an illegitimate government perverts the laws.[42] At the same time, however, commentators have suggested that the sort of self-sacrifice involved in risking life and limb in a struggle against a lawless state is the stuff of heroes, not the sort of action expected of citizens and politicians living in "normal" states. Hence the failure of resistance leaders as postwar politicians: in a modern constitutional republic, heroes need not apply.[43] Recognizing the resistance in this manner was thus convenient both for the majority of the French and for state elites. Average citizens and political leaders could regard the resistance as a great moral example, though one without much consequence in the postwar world. Collaborators also found the arrangement advantageous since it allowed them to claim to have resisted deep in their "delicate hearts," which remained necessarily and conveniently unseen.[44]

The leaders of the republic, by removing debates over résistance from the political sphere, effectively minimized problematic moral disputes over national and subnational identities. Reviving the claim that citizenship in France was abstract and universal, state elites pronounced all of France one again in the republican spirit. Even Martinique was officially assimilated into France, thereby becoming in principle indistinguishable from the rest of the nation. As a result, mainland résistants and Martinican dissidents found themselves in similar positions not long after the war: their differences from the mainstreams of French political life had been effaced within official discourse and by state policies, while in practice they were pushed to the margins of the French polity, a polity that refused to see the difference between résistants and colonial blacks. Just as Fanon found it hard to identify with that polity, sensitive résistants found it difficult to accept the restored republic as their own, even while France celebrated them as its moral beacons.

The résistants of metropolitan France traveled a road quite different from that of the Martinican dissidents, but both groups reached a similar end: marginality. Résistants went from being obscure, unrealistic, isolated opponents of Vichy to becoming the official heroes of the restored French Republic who, in short order, found themselves to be minority outsiders in a France that refused to acknowledge or confront their continuing rebelliousness, a France that they increasingly had trouble recognizing and accepting as their own national order. Meanwhile, dissidents started the war as members of one of the few subcommunities of the French empire that remained loyal to the republic, and they ended it as subaltern players in the restored order, smarting from lack of recognition and respect within the republic and union.

Understanding at the Margins

When Fanon left Rouen for Fort-de-France in October 1945, having already come to see republican universalism as a "false ideology," he appears to have questioned what it meant for a black Martinican to be French. It is unclear what he knew about the internal resistance at the end of the war, but he probably learned little before leaving France that would have made him more comfortable with French identity. What he likely heard were stories that stressed French universalism, such as the popular saga of France united under de Gaulle in a struggle against the Germans, or the competing communist narrative of working-class France united against the Germans and a few bourgeois traitors. While in Normandy, Fanon did have at least one direct contact with someone active in the internal resistance, Marcel Lemonnier. Lemonnier, a prosperous and generous businessman, was one of the few white French people who took an interest in the Martinican soldiers. When Lemonnier heard, in early September 1945, that the West Indians were garrisoned in the area while awaiting return to the islands, he contacted the unit's commander to invite fifteen of the men to dinner with his family. Fanon, along with two of his friends, attended what seems to have been a successful evening. All the soldiers signed the family's visitors' book. An entry written by one of Fanon's friends, a Martinican who also served in the "whitened" unit, suggests that some version of French universalism colored the evening's discussion. Identifying the black Martinicans as "spiritual sons of the immortal France," the friend pledged that they "would continue to love our motherland and her children, who were so hospitable." Fanon, who had earlier demonstrated skepticism about French unity, wrote more simply, "With thanks for the generous hospitality and homely quality of the evenings spent with the Lemonnier family."[45]

Meanwhile, some activists in the internal resistance also questioned the apparent republican harmony that had emerged in France after the heady days of liberation in August 1944. Most résistants had hoped for a different kind of society, one more in line with the proclamation on the masthead of Camus's underground newspaper, *Combat*, "From Résistance to Revolution." While many former activists did accept de Gaulle as their leader, others deeply resented how Gaullists had swept the rebelliousness of the internal resistance under the rug of patriotic concord in the months following the German retreat. For instance, one historian of the liberation reports the following episode of extreme disillusionment on the part of a policeman formerly active in the resistance. In the midst of excited celebrations about a year after the liberation, just one month after Fanon had denounced republicanism to his parents, the policeman is reported to have taken the following actions:

> On 18 June 1945, as the trumpets and fanfares of a Gaullist march sounded through the streets of Paris, the *gardien de la paix*, Charles Chambon, of undoubted Resistance credentials, asked a colleague whether they should not join the march, but immediately answered his own question with the bitter words "what's the point, we count for nothing now." At 12:30 that day he lifted a gun to his chest and pulled the trigger.[46]

While Chambon's reaction was certainly extreme, it indicates the existence of an undercurrent of intense résistant dissatisfaction with the republic that de Gaulle had brought back to metropolitan France.

Fanon became familiar with this kind of discontent when he returned to France in late 1946 to complete his university education. By the time he finished medical school and clinical training in psychiatry in 1951, he had come to know intellectual versions of resistance discontentment, such as those contained in the writings of Jean-Paul Sartre and in the regular contributions to *Esprit*, a leftist Catholic journal regarded as "one of the great expressions of the spirit of the wartime Resistance."[47] However, when Fanon published *Peau noire, masque blanc* in *Esprit*'s book series in 1952, he seems to have doubted that colonial blacks were ready or able to embrace a politics of résistance.

What Fanon saw is that French colonial blacks lacked two prerequisites for effective résistance. First, résistance required enough experience acting on one's own to have developed a sense of self that one cannot abandon, that one will stubbornly assert in the manner described by Camus. Second, it required that one's résistance resonate, both with those against whom it is offered and, eventually, with others who come to identify with it.

Fanon doubted that French blacks had had enough experience acting on their own to be able to assert themselves. He complained that French blacks had been the passive recipients of republican rights, including the most basic freedoms. Parodying French history, Fanon explained slave emancipation in this manner: "One day a good white master who had influence said to his friends, 'Let's be nice to *les nègres*.' The other masters argued, . . . but then decided to promote the machine-animal-men to the supreme rank of *men*." So it was announced, "*Slavery shall no longer exist on French soil*." But Fanon noted, "The upheaval reached the Black from without."[48] Unlike their American counterparts, French colonial blacks, he complained, didn't have to fight for their rights. As a result, their potential moral character remained undeveloped, leaving them dependent on white France for their identities. Earlier in the book, Fanon recounted Anna Freud's discussion of ego-withdrawal in an effort to explain this problem in another way. Normal young people, Freud noted, sometimes withdraw from the pain and pressures of social life as they develop. "When the ego is young and plastic,"

Fanon quoted Freud, "its withdrawal from one field of activity is sometimes compensated for by excellence in another, upon which it concentrates." In a similar manner, the wartime résistants may be seen as having withdrawn from normal social life, where the pain of collaborationism was too great, and as having instead focused on developing the heightened moral sense and political will that made confronting the occupation and Vichy possible. By contrast, Freud argued, when an ego becomes "rigid or has already developed an intolerance of 'pain' and is so obsessionally fixated to a method of flight, such withdrawal is punished by impaired development. By abandoning one position after another it becomes one-sided, loses too many interests and can show but a meagre achievement." French colonial blacks were in this position, Fanon argued, because white French culture made them feel insignificant, inadequate, and insular. In their situation, he argued, "there is only one way out, and it leads to the white world." Fanon knew this well when he returned to metropolitan France for education. "Ego-withdrawal as a successful defense mechanism is impossible for the Negro" because, Fanon concluded, the colonial black "needs white approval," which effectively ruled out a politics of résistance.[49]

A greater obstacle to its further development, however, was the lack of resonance that greeted the rare instances of black résistance. Whites would simply refuse to recognize it: either they didn't see black résistance as something in itself or they transformed what they saw into predictable stereotypes of black behavior. Fanon complained, "The black man has no ontological résistance in the eyes of the white man."[50] Every act of a black gets dissolved, either into acts of "man" or acts of a "race," both of which are categories of an essentially white world, categories created in the process of colonization. Nothing new, nothing unique was recognized as coming from the colonized black. Other blacks, meanwhile, given their identification with white authorities, would flee from black résistants. Summarizing his frustrations, Fanon said that "with all my strength I refuse to accept" racial prejudice, but then, as "I wanted to stand up, . . . eviscerating silence flowed over me, paralyzing my legs [ses ailes paralysées]."[51]

Fanon concluded *Peau noire* by arguing that the only way for the French black to move forward was "to engage himself ceaselessly in disclosing résistance, opposition, challenge" [*sans cesse il va se préoccuper de déceler*], meaning that blacks had to press white France to reveal the prejudices it concealed within, to expose the rifts between white and black French people.[52] Only by this means would it be possible for French blacks to find themselves, to develop their potential as independent moral beings, and to force white French people to recognize them as different — and French.

Black in and out of France

Fanon's early proclamation of French identity, quoted in the introduction, then, is more consistent with his later Third World liberationist politics than may appear at first. Fanon embraced white France in 1952, not in order to assimilate to it, but in order to challenge it, to root out the differences that had to be worked through if blacks were to achieve freedom and if whites were to overcome their narcissism. Although Fanon believed he was equal to other French citizens, he learned unhappily during the Second World War that he was French *and* an "inferior" other. Working through the experience of the internal resistance after the war, he then learned how to understand the difficulty of resisting the fantastic republican universalism that obscured French racism.

When he later renounced French citizenship and embraced Third World revolution, Fanon didn't abandon these French beginnings. Insisting on the equality of colonized nonwhite peoples, he encouraged Algerians to show the world how to force Europeans to recognize independent subaltern existences, beginning in small ways, such as by insisting on the traditional veiling of Islamic women, which he argued amounted to a highly visible "strategy of résistance" that inflicted "a spectacular setback" on modernizing French authorities.[53] He also encouraged the clandestine radio broadcasts of the *Voice of Fighting Algeria*, explaining that their stories of résistance would resonate among oppressed colonials and oppressive colonizers. Recalling how "listening to the voice of *Free France*" had kept alive "the spirit of résistance" and had amounted to "a form of combat" during the Second World War, Fanon argued that listening to the *Voice of Fighting Algeria* similarly brought Algerians to recognize one another in a common combat.[54] More important, the broadcasts also broke the "old monologue of the colonial situation," and as a result, "the occupier's voice was stripped of its authority."[55]

What Fanon found in Algeria was the resonance that he lacked as a black colonial in France. This he called "a common life, common experiences and memories, common aims," which he argued showed him that he "was a stranger in France." He asserted, "I was not French," and "I had never been French. Language, culture — these are not enough to make you belong to a people."[56] Yet ironically, it was his French colonial determination to overcome inequality and his French resistance conceptual language that led him to see how a politics of résistance could flourish in Algeria and that eventually made French authorities recognize him, albeit by rejecting him. In theorizing Third World liberation, Fanon contributed to the development of movements across the globe which built on subaltern and subcultural resistances. That is, by connecting racial and colonial status to strategies of résistance, Fanon laid the theoretical groundwork for what has since become known as identity politics or multiculturalism, which some French intellectuals, in another irony, now attack for being as un- or anti-French as Fanon supposedly was.[57]

Notes

1 David Macey, *Frantz Fanon: A Life* (London: Granta, 2000), 21. The first edition of Fanon's most influential book, *Les damnés de la terre*, sold only 3,300 copies in France. In contrast, Macey reports that the 1965 publication of an American translation turned the book into a best-seller "that was reprinted twice before it reached the bookstores and [that] went through five paperback reprints within the space of a year." The book was also translated into eighteen other languages. Macey, *Fanon*, 17.

2 Frantz Fanon, *Black Skin, White Masks*, trans. Charles Lam Markmann (New York: Grove, 1967), 203. The French original appears in Frantz Fanon, *Peau noire, masques blancs* (Paris: Editions du Seuil, 1952), 164. Because I have altered some of the English translations of this text, I cite both the English and French versions of the book in the following notes.

3 David Caute, for instance, distinguishes between a "young" Fanon, who was a reformist psychiatrist more interested in the individual, and a "mature" Fanon, who became a revolutionary activist more interested in sociological and institutional forces. Implicitly, the young Fanon may be described as "French," while the mature Fanon may be described as "anti-French." David Caute, *Frantz Fanon* (New York: Viking, 1970), 38–39.

4 It is worth noting that while Fanon himself was dark-skinned, the family was said to be partly Alsatian. Macey, *Fanon*, 48.

5   See Robert O. Paxton, *Vichy France: Old Guard and New Order,*
    1940–1944 (New York: Knopf, 1972); H. R. Kedward, *Occupied*
    France: Collaboration and Resistance (Oxford: Blackwell, 1985);
    and Henry Rousso, *The Vichy Syndrome: History and Memory in*
    France since 1944, trans. Arthur Goldhammer (Cambridge, Mass.:
    Harvard University Press, 1991).

6   Camille Chauvet, "La Martinique au temps de l'Amiral Robert
    (1939–1940)," in *Historial antillais,* vol. 5 (Fort-de-France: Société
    Dajani, 1985), 423–24, quoted in Macey, *Fanon,* 79–80. See also
    Richard D. E. Burton, " 'Nos Journées de Juin': The Historical Sig-
    nificance of the Liberation of Martinique (June 1943)," in *The Liber-*
    ation of France: Image and Event, ed. H. R. Kedward and Nancy
    Wood (Oxford: Berg, 1995), 227.

7   Macey, *Fanon,* 81–82, 84. Burton stresses, however, that the Robert
    regime did receive support in 1940 and 1941 from "sections of the
    local coloured and, to a lesser extent, black populations," though
    such support "was visibly dwindling" by late 1942. Burton, " 'Nos
    Journées,' " 228.

8   Macey, *Fanon,* 84, 86. Among the many biographies and studies of
    Fanon, Macey's biography contains the most detailed historical ac-
    count of Fanon's life available, and I rely on it heavily in the follow-
    ing. Also useful, though sketchier, is Irene L. Gendzier, *Frantz Fanon:*
    A Critical Study (New York: Pantheon, 1973).

9   Macey, *Fanon,* 84.

10 Macey, *Fanon,* 88. Fanon quotes his teacher in *Black Skin, White*
    Masks, 122; *Peau noire,* 98.

11 Macey, *Fanon,* 84; Burton, " 'Nos Journées,' " 229.

12 Macey, *Fanon,* 86; Burton, " 'Nos Journées,' " 229. See also Frantz
    Fanon, "West Indians and Africans," in *Toward the African Revolu-*
    tion: Political Essays, trans. Haakon Chevalier (New York: Monthly
    Review, 1967), 23.

13 Macey, *Fanon,* 87.

14 Burton reports that there were as many as 5,000 new recruits from
    Martinique and Guadeloupe in West Indian transit camps, preparing
    to ship out with the Free French by April 1943. Burton, " 'Nos Jour-
    nées,' " 229.

15 The exact racial composition of the troops is uncertain, but they
    certainly included some Africans from Senegal, as well as black or
    mixed-race Martinicans. See Burton, " 'Nos Journées,' " 231.

16 A representative of the Free French, Henri Hoppenot, announced
    to a crowd in Fort-de-France on 14 July 1943, "I return France and
    the Republic to you" [Je vous ramène la France et la République].
    Quoted in Burton, " 'Nos Journées,' " 232. See also Macey, *Fanon,*
    90.

17 Macey, *Fanon*, 89–91.

18 Macey, *Fanon*, 93. It should be noted that the French were not alone in creating armies organized along segregated lines.

19 Macey, *Fanon*, 91–98. The officers and NCOs were white or of mixed race.

20 Fanon himself discusses the notion of black Caribbeans being seen as "more European" than Senegalese troops in *Black Skin*, 25–27; *Peau noire*, 20–21.

21 Macey, *Fanon*, 100–101.

22 Macey, *Fanon*, 102–3.

23 Reflecting on such experiences, Fanon later argued such white women typically imagined that blacks desired to subject them to "all kinds of . . . cruelties," "sexual abuses," and other "immoral and shameful things." Fanon cites his experience in Toulon as one of the first in which he realized how widespread what he called "Negrophobia" was among white Europeans. Fanon, *Black Skin*, 156; *Peau noire*, 127.

24 Quoted in Macey, *Fanon*, 88. Macey's source for this quotation seems to be interviews with Fanon's brother, Joby, though the citation is unclear.

25 Fanon, *Black Skin*, 102–3; *Peau noire*, 83–84.

26 Quoted in Macey, *Fanon*, 103–4.

27 For studies of the resistance, see Kedward, *Occupied France*; John F. Sweets, *The Politics of Resistance in France, 1940–1944: A History of the Mouvements Unis de la Résistance* (DeKalb: Northern Illinois University Press, 1976); and James D. Wilkinson, *The Intellectual Resistance in Europe* (Cambridge, Mass.: Harvard University Press, 1981).

28 Fanon, *Black Skin*, 194–95; *Peau noire*, 157. See also Macey, *Fanon*, 86. (Macey seems to list the date of Benghazi incorrectly as 7 February 1940.)

29 Given that the U.S. armed forces were officially segregated during the Second World War, it would be reasonable to say that virtually all of Fanon's wartime experiences, including the discrimination he encountered, were fairly typical for the time.

30 Historian J. C. Simmonds, for example, reports that members of the communist Carmagnole-Liberté group, who were responsible for taking direct action against Germans and collaborationists in Lyon, were told "to live as solitary a life as they could manage. They were not allowed to write to their families, socialize with other members of the group or contact anyone except their 'chef.' " Later Simmonds notes, "Such a life took a terrible psychological toll on men and women, who were young and constantly in fear. Their lack of social contacts and conversations, even within their group or the wider

MOI and FTP [resistance organizations], meant an isolation which was profound." J. C. Simmonds, "Immigrant Fighters for the Liberation of France: A Local Profile of Carmagnole-Liberté in Lyon," in Kedward and Wood, *Liberation*, 35, 36.

31 Richard Burton notes that "by 1943, Robert, his associates and the creole whites who supported them had coagulated into a single, overwhelming negative image: they were *mauvais blancs*, pure and simple. In June 1943, coloured and black Martinicans joined forces with a group of *'bons Français'* to overthrow a negative white father-figure, Robert, only to replace him with a new, and still more potent, paternal image, a white superego of quite prodigious charismatic force — Charles de Gaulle." Burton, " 'Nos Journées,' " 235.

32 The noun *dissidence* is given two general meanings in most French dictionaries: the action, by an individual or group, of ceasing to obey an established authority or of breaking with a community; and the group of people who cease to obey or break with a community. For example, see *Dictionnaire usuel illustré Flammarion*, s.v. "dissidence." *Larousse* adds a third meaning, an ideological divergence that leads persons or groups to separate from the community, country, or party to which they had previously belonged. *Grand dictionnaire encylopédique Larousse*, s.v. "dissidence." On *résistance*, see the following notes.

33 For example, the *Grand Larousse* lists fifteen meanings for *résistance*, the *Grand Robert* ten; and among those meanings, both dictionaries cite ones specifically having to do with the action of opposing morally questionable pressures, with the internal force that allows one to oppose such pressures, and with the action of opposing seduction, particularly sexual seduction. *The Oxford English Dictionary* cites six general meanings for *resistance*, none of which has to do with moral actions or forces specifically. *Grand Larousse de la langue française*, s.v. "résistance"; *Grand Robert de la langue française: Dictionnaire alphabétique et analogique de la langue française*, 2d ed., s.v. "résistance"; and *The Oxford English Dictionary*, 2d ed., s.v. "resistance."

34 For a detailed discussion of these conceptual innovations and their relation to the thought of Sartre and Camus, see Dennis John McEnnerney, "The Concepts of *Résistance* and *Libération* and the Politics of Consciousness in Twentieth-Century French Thought" (Ph.D. diss., University of California at Berkeley, 1995).

35 Both *Larousse* and *Robert* list new meanings associated with the war, including ones having to do with moral character. In order to help the reader bear in mind the French term's distinctive meanings, I use the French word throughout, even when making or citing English translations.

Fanon, Resistance, and Identity Politics 279

36 Albert Camus, *The Rebel: An Essay on Man in Revolt*, trans. Anthony Bower (New York: Vintage, 1956), 14–15. The passage from
which this quotation comes, first appeared in an essay Camus wrote
in March 1944 about the rebel "functionary" who refused to collaborate. Later, Camus reworked the piece, turning the functionary into
a slave. See Albert Camus, "Remarque sur la révolte," in *Essais*, ed.
R. Quillot and L. Faucon (Paris: Gallimard, 1965), 1682–97. The
essay originally appeared in *L'existence* in October 1944.

37 Albert Camus, *Between Hell and Reason: Essays from the Resistance
Newspaper Combat, 1944–1947*, trans. Alexandre de Gramont
(Hanover, N.H.: University Press of New England, 1991), 75. As I
suggest below, Fanon embraced exactly this notion of résistance in
the struggle against the French occupation of Algeria, while Camus
first argued for compromise in Algeria within the context of the
French Republic and then fell into silence when the FLN pushed for
national liberation.

38 Other possible Frances were not considered much. Metropolitan resisters largely ignored the loyalty and patriotism of France's colonies,
and de Gaulle seemed distant and uninspiring to many internal résistants in the first years of Vichy and the occupation.

39 Simmonds's account also suggests another reason: the clandestine
character of some kinds of resistance activities left activists with
relatively few direct contacts and little skill at building formal organizations in open environments. Simmonds, "Immigrant Fighters,"
36.

40 For a popular discussion of the various strategies of normalization,
see Herbert R. Lottman, *The People's Anger: Justice and Revenge in
Post-Liberation France* (London: Hutchinson, 1986).

41 For instance, see Gordon Wright, *France in Modern Times: From the
Enlightenment to the Present*, 4th ed. (New York: Norton, 1987),
401–2.

42 For a recent restatement of this point of view, see the opening paragraph of Wilkinson, *Intellectual Resistance*, 1.

43 This argument was first made by an intellectual résistant, Maurice
Merleau-Ponty, who rejected Sartre's call to continue the wartime
struggle because the end of the war had been followed by a return to
institutional politics and impersonal forces. See Wilkinson, *Intellectual Resistance*, 88–89.

44 Since subjective experiences, by definition, are hidden from view, and
since the resistance as a movement could generally appear only in
disguised forms, it became quite possible after the war for some to
assert that they had resisted, when in fact they had done nothing, and
for many to claim that résistance was always in their hearts, waiting
to be flushed out, even if they had failed to act or had done so only

late in the war. Who could prove otherwise, particularly in the latter cases? Indeed, I suspect some may have convinced themselves, retrospectively, that from the start of the war their hearts had really been delicate too.

45 Quoted in Macey, *Fanon*, 108.

46 Simon Kitson, "The Police in the Liberation of Paris," in Kedward and Wood, *Liberation*, 52–53.

47 Macey, *Fanon*, 154.

48 Fanon, *Black Skin*, 220; *Peau noire*, 178.

49 Fanon, *Black Skin*, 50–51; *Peau noire*, 41. Fanon quoted the French translation of Anna Freud, *The Ego and the Mechanisms of Defense* (New York: International Universities Press, 1946), 111.

50 Fanon, *Black Skin*, 110; *Peau noire*, 89.

51 Fanon, *Black Skin*, 140; *Peau noire*, 114.

52 Fanon, *Black Skin*, 222; *Peau noire*, 180.

53 Frantz Fanon, "Algeria Unveiled," in *A Dying Colonialism*, trans. Haakon Chevalier (New York: Grove, 1965), 49, 47.

54 Frantz Fanon, "This Is the Voice of Algeria," in *Dying Colonialism*, 93–94.

55 Fanon, "Voice of Algeria," 95.

56 Frantz Fanon, "Algeria's European Minority," in *Dying Colonialism*, 175.

57 For a thoughtful criticism of dogmatic French universalistic republicanism and dogmatic versions of American multiculturalism, see Jean-Philippe Mathy, *French Resistance: The French-American Culture Wars* (Minneapolis: University of Minnesota Press, 2000), especially chaps. 4–6.

4

Race and the Postcolonial City

Lynn E. Palermo

Identity under Construction

Representing the Colonies at the Paris

Exposition Universelle of 1889

A true marvel . . .
On the left, the colonies and the protectorate countries in a delicious glow of color, in an exquisitely disordered confusion of silhouettes. . . . This whole corner of the Esplanade is still charming; gathered here are exotic types of construction, corners of colonial villages (Pahouin, Alfourou, Malgache), an Annamite theater, the Saldé tower from Senegal; here there is a suite of enchanting, animated sketches of African and Asian life.

The diverse colonial exhibitions laid out on the Esplanade des Invalides are, after the Eiffel Tower and the Gallery of Machines, the main attraction of the 1889 Exposition Universelle. The fidelity of their architecture, their picturesque qualities, their tone, and above all the liveliness with which they are infused by the presence of colorfully dressed guests from all the colonies represented on the Esplanade, have attracted crowds from the very first day.

Therefore, let us give you some advice:
For your visit to the colonial section of the exposition,
choose a hot, sunny day.[1]

These quotations taken from the *Guide bleu du Figaro et du Petit Journal* illustrate the enthusiasm that greeted the colonial section of the *exposition universelle* of Paris in 1889. From 5 May until 6 November 1889, the extensive fairgrounds covered more than 228 acres in the heart of Paris, filling the Champ de Mars military parade grounds, spilling across the Seine to the Trocadéro Palace, then stretching along the riverbank and onto the Esplanade in front of the Hôtel des Invalides military hospital. During its six-month existence, the exposition attracted more than 32,350,000 visitors; it was one of the few such events to earn its way, netting a profit of about $600,000.[2] From financial, aesthetic, and popular perspectives, the exposition was judged an enormous success.

By 1889, France's colonial possessions encompassed an area ten times the size of the *métropole*, making the French empire second only to that of England. The colonial section at the exposition signaled France's military strength to her rivals, as well as providing grounds for optimism and pride for citizens of the French Third Republic, a regime still haunted by a recent political crisis.[3] At the same time, expansionist policy proved controversial for economic, political, and moral reasons. Therefore, the contradictions inherent in showcasing both France's imperial conquests and its republican tradition in a single exhibition posed inevitable problems of representation. What message did the *exposition universelle* send to the public concerning colonization? What role did the architecture, layout, and displays play in communicating and reinforcing that message? Were imperialist values successfully reconciled with the cherished "Rights of Man and Citizen"?

Architecture: A Gauge of Progress and Exoticism

A key to the enormous success of the 1889 *exposition universelle* was architecture, an area in which the French claimed to have made remarkable advances thanks to a blending of art and science through the cooperative efforts of architects and engineers. The immense buildings on the Champs de Mars pushed the architectural and technical possibilities of iron to the limit and amazed visitors with their extraordinary dimensions and harmonious proportions. The Eiffel Tower, the tallest building in the world, soared to a record-breaking height of three hundred meters.[4] The Galerie des Machines enclosed an unprecedented fifteen-acre space unimpeded by supporting columns.[5] As the *Gazette des beaux-arts* phrased it, "All is clear, expressive, in scale, [so that] even the immensity of the Eiffel Tower does not seem to clash with its surroundings, thanks to its harmonious design and fine proportions."[6]

On the nearby Esplanade des Invalides, the colonial pavilions served as a counterpoint to these superhuman feats of architecture and engineering. Modest in size, they instead appealed to the senses through exotic design, profuse color, elaborate ornament, and organic building materials. The largest among them was the Palais

Figure 1. The Palais des Machines as shown in *L'Exposition Universelle de Paris (1889)*, 25 May 1889, supplemental plate between
pages 100 and 101. Reproduced with the permission of Rare Books
and Manuscripts, Special Collections Library, The Pennsylvania
State University Libraries.

Central des Colonies. Designed by Sauvestre, also the architect of
the Eiffel Tower, the palais was a wooden, polychrome structure.
The *Guide bleu* states that it was an unremarkable seventy-three
meters long; its central dome attained the "reasonable height of
50 meters."[7] The most interesting feature of the palais was its design
and ornament, not its structure. This held true in assessments of the
other colonial pavilions as well.[8]

The *L'Exposition Universelle de Paris (1889)* newspaper praised
Sauvestre for having "blended the styles of diverse colonies, without
allowing any of them to dominate,"[9] although it would be more
accurate to say that the Palais Central blended *French* architectural
styles found in the colonies. In any case, Sauvestre exhibited the
architect's tendency to conceive of each colonial pavilion as a con-
glomeration — or "synthesis" — of the various styles found in a particular territory. For example, portions of the Algerian pavilion
were inspired by the mosques of three different Algerian cities. The
Tunisian pavilion seamlessly joined elements of two mosques and a
monumental tomb.[10] Cambodian architecture was "summarized"

Identity under Construction 287

Figure 2. The colonial section on the Esplanade, with the Hôtel des Invalides in the background. Reproduced in *1889: La Tour Eiffel et l'exposition universelle: Exposition présentée au Musée d'Orsay, 16 mai–15 août 1989* (Paris: Editions de la Réunion des musées nationaux, 1989) from an original photograph at the Bibliothèque de la Ville de Paris.

in a reproduction of a tower from the temple of Angkor Wat.[11] This approach, lauded in the press and official publications as giving a condensed yet stylistically authentic vision of a colony's architecture, effectively created a distinct image for each colony. Ultimately, French architects (since all the architects of the colonial pavilions *were* French) constructed a specific identity for each colony, making it easier for exposition visitors to identify and distinguish them from one another. Synthesizing a colony's architectural styles and motifs into a series of harmonious wholes also made ethnic cultures appear to correspond—whether naturally or rationally—to the colonial borders recently imposed by European powers.

Paradoxically, architects of the pavilions, while praised for their faithful reproduction and authenticity of indigenous styles, were equally applauded for their individual creative powers—even in cases where fantasy outweighed fidelity to existing styles. With regard to the Palais Central, for example, the *Guide bleu* said, "Monsieur Sauvestre wanted to realize his creative dreams, and not [simply] copy such-and-such a colonial style. . . . His Palais Central had to be original, above all."[12] This emphasis on the architect's creativity can be explained partly by the architectural eclecticism of the second half of the nineteenth century, which allowed the relatively free borrowing and adaptation of historical styles. During this period, the primary criterion on which an architect was judged was not how "correctly" he used a particular style, but rather his skill in manipulating a variety of design elements inventively.[13] Thus representing each colony through its pavilion became a personal challenge for the designing architect. To some extent, this aspect of the project displaced attention from the colonial territory in question to the individual French architect, for whom the colony served as a vehicle for demonstrating his creative virtuosity.

Not only were the colonial pavilions designed by French architects, but French carpenters and stonemasons completed the structural work, while architectural details and ornament were left to indigenous artisans.[14] Although this practice was presented as genuine collaboration, a hierarchy of labor clearly operated here — one that echoed the unequal relationship between metropolitan France and its colonies. Structure (a product of applied science), showcased in French architecture on the Champs de Mars, was more highly esteemed than decoration. In fact, when the actual structure of a pavilion proved uninteresting to architects, as in the small villages scattered behind the larger pavilions, native artisans imported from the colonies were simply handed materials and told to build their own huts under French supervision. Thus emerged a further hierarchy based on the presence or absence of "worthwhile," or monumental, architecture. These hierarchies of culture, architecture, and labor converge in an observation made by an amused French journalist: "[The native colonial artisans] are sober, docile, and polite; when they meet one of the [French] engineers overseeing their work, they stop and, lifting hand to turban, salute him in military style."[15]

In many cases, the design of the colonial pavilions was based on existing indigenous religious structures, such as mosques or temples. But when "recreated" on the Esplanade des Invalides, they were emptied of any sacred significance, leaving shells then assigned the function of museum. Filled with exhibits boasting their colony's rich natural resources and growth in productivity, these buildings were reinvested, in the manner of a Barthesian myth, with the materialistic and positivist values of bourgeois, nonsectarian, Republican France. The wealth of samples displayed and of statistics quoted reveals a desire to employ science, the "modern religion," in the service of advancing France's "civilizing mission," part of which involved demonstrating an exhaustive, encyclopedic knowledge of each colony to justify France's intervention.[16] That this type of knowledge was considered primary to the destiny of the colonies is underlined by the fact that the only expression of cultural identity left to the colonized peoples themselves was the "packaging" of the exhibits—that is, a veneer of colorful wooden decoration applied to pavilions conceived, built, and filled for them by the French, according to French priorities.

One element of a colonial pavilion that did retain its original function was the minaret of the Algerian pavilion, from which Muslims were called to prayer on the Esplanade. However, manifestations of Islamic spirituality were exploited for profane purposes: the spectacle of the Muslims at prayer constituted one of the tableaux vivants, or ethnographic exhibits, that first became an integral part of the colonial section in 1889.

From Architecture to Inhabitants: Tableaux Vivants, Exoticism, and Cultural Hierarchy

From their inception in 1851, world's fairs were used as educational tools.[17] In fact, in *Ephemeral Vistas*, Paul Greenhalgh calls education the "fetish" of exposition planners. In the early years, organizers directed their efforts toward the affluent (educated) classes.[18] But as early as 1867, and increasingly until the end of the nineteenth century, emphasis shifted to targeting the working and artisan classes.[19] In the process, the goal of governmental planners became two-fold: to inform the people on whom the vitality of the republic depended for stability; and to exercise influence on public opinion in a young age of universal suffrage.[20] By 1878, however, public enthusiasm for purely didactic, encyclopedic displays had waned, resulting in substantial financial loss for that year's universal exposition. Consequently, fundraising for the 1889 exposition underwent change to reduce the state's role: over half of the financial burden fell to two banks and the city of Paris. Feeling increased pressure to generate profit—and to compete with unauthorized vendors and entertainers who set up booths just beyond the official festival grounds—organizers consciously expanded the amusement factor of the exposition exhibits to bolster attendance.

In 1889, the Esplanade had become a fully developed exhibition site, considered by the press to be well worth a full day's visit. For the first time at a world's fair, the construction of villages, including indigenous people going about "normal" daily activities, constituted a central component of the exposition.[21] In addition to watching Muslims kneel in prayer at the foot of the minaret of the Algerian pavilion, visitors could enter a Kabyle home to observe women weaving at their looms; watch a family of New Caledonian Canaques prepare dinner over an open fire; or poke their head into the tent of a nomadic desert family. According to most accounts in *L'Exposition Universelle de Paris (1889)*, the indigenous people imported from the colonies to live their life on the Esplanade seemed "unaffected" by the presence of European observers. One exceptional article, however, reported conversations with indigenous *figurants*, or "extras," which revealed their discomfort at being placed in such a situation. "We are very humiliated," commented Samba Lawbé Thiam, master jeweler from Senegal, in very good French, "to be exhibited this way, in huts like savages; these straw and mud huts do not give an idea of Senegal. In Senegal . . . we have large buildings, railroad stations, railroads; we light them with electricity. The Bureau of Hygiene does not tolerate the construction of this type of hovel. Those [existing ones] that fall into disrepair are not replaced." Colonial natives also found the French to be "decidedly lacking in courtesy," and complained of cruel remarks made by visitors who wrongly assumed that those on display spoke no French. Exclamations such as, "What an ape! A monster! My heavens, he's ugly!" had, according to the journalist, "plunged some of the colonials into an inconsolable melancholy," and left more than one in tears. "We forget," he commented, "that these are people and not exotic animals that we are watching behind the fences."[22] An anthropologist who lamented the lack of scientific rigor in the 1889 exposition anthropological displays also expressed concern about whether the tableaux vivants compromised the dignity of the people exhibited. However, realizing that the public would probably poorly receive any criticism, he decided to remain quiet and focus instead on the worthy scientific research spawned by the ethnographic exhibitions.[23]

Colonial people lent the weight of authenticity to the displays and architectural framework of the Esplanade; moreover, their presence implied that they were playing a cooperative role in France's so-called civilizing mission, with its fundamental notions of cultural

Figure 3. A tableau vivant, part of the Algerian exhibit in the colonial section, as shown in *L'Exposition Universelle de Paris (1889)*, 6 July 1889, 149. Reproduced with the permission of Rare Books and Manuscripts, Special Collections Library, The Pennsylvania State University Libraries.

hierarchy. Effectively, the indigenous colonized people became a natural extension of the exhibits housed in the pavilions — to use Hinsley's words, "another colonial raw material."[24] Indeed, in the first proposal for such "ethnographic" displays at a universal exposition, two anthropologists drew little distinction between people and goods: "It would be most desirable for native populations to accompany the products of the land which they inhabit to the Exposition Universelle."[25]

The visitors' penetration into the colonized people's intimate space, where they performed domestic tasks and worked at traditional trades (referred to as "colonial industries"), also objectified the colonial natives. The practice of displaying imported human beings in a supposedly "authentic" setting created an unequal relationship between European (observer) and non-European (observed), illustrating what Edward Said has termed the "whole complex series of knowledgeable manipulations by which the Orient [meaning the non-Western world] was identified by the West. . . . Knowledge of the Orient, because generated out of strength, in a sense *creates* the Orient, the Oriental, and his world."[26] The juxtaposition of ethnographic exhibits with didactic exhibits that claimed scientific objectivity through the accumulation of artifacts and statistics implied that the more theatrical — not to say, fanciful — tableaux vivants should also be considered scientific. The press underscored this assumption: "All these natives will live the life of their country there [on the Esplanade des Invalides] and, in a few hours, one will be able to become completely informed about their customs and their favorite activities."[27]

The tableaux vivants, which added a crucial element of animation to the more traditional didactic exhibits, in fact became the greater attraction, attracting crowds from the first days of the exposition. However, at nightfall the Esplanade stood deserted, as visitors flocked to the Champ de Mars to view the illuminated Eiffel Tower and Fountain of Progress. In response to pressure from the entrepreneurs and exhibitors on the Esplanade, exposition officials permitted the establishment of Tuesday evening festivities designed to keep crowds in the colonial section after dark.[28] Each week, events began with a parade down the *allée centrale*, with all the indigenous people in full traditional dress and many of them playing music. Traditional dances by Canaques and theater performances by the Annamese followed, after which visitors could visit the Javanese kampong (village) or take refreshment in the Moorish and Creole cafés. Thus while the pavilions still displayed samples, artifacts, and statistics in a mission to educate the public, that goal was being eroded in the name of entertainment conceived to attract an audience of consumers. Henceforth world's fairs (in general, not just in France) would become increasingly amusing, not simply through an increased number of restaurants, cafés, and spectacles, but also more subtly, by tilting previously "serious" exhibits toward entertainment.[29] Even the displays of colonial objects were increasingly left to speak for themselves "without the need for long passages of accompanying text."[30] The result blurred fact and fiction, as the colonial section evolved into a "theater of the most engaging fantasies,"[31] enhanced through the exploitation of exoticism. As Pascal Ory puts it, "The whole logic behind the local color is in the slippage from discovery to voyeurism."[32]

The exotic atmosphere of the colonial section was induced, in part, by the concentration of several architectural styles in a single building, and then accentuated by placing in close proximity styles normally separated by miles, if not oceans. The effect was then heightened by the presence of diverse indigenous peoples in their brightly colored, traditional dress. Add a variety of languages, sounds of drums and music, lush vegetation, dancers, and a confusion of odors emanating from the exotic restaurants and noisy street markets, and it is easy to understand how nineteenth-century visitors could indeed have felt transported to another world. The press, as well as officially authorized publications, enthusiastically evoked the ambiance, although occasional incidents of exaggeration did surface. A journalist covering the New Caledonian village noted, for example, that compared to the engraving accompanying his article, the costumes actually worn by the Canaques on the Esplanade were "less picturesque and less . . . primitive."[33] As the level of exoticism increased, so did the feeling of cultural distance between the colonial native and the European visitor, in whose own section on the Champ de Mars thrills derived more from rational than sensual sources: the immense strength and scale of modern machinery, which, along with a wealth of statistics, testified to the human mastery of nature.[34]

From the many colorful descriptions in guidebooks (such as the one quoted at the beginning of this article) and the press, it becomes evident that exoticism constituted a highly valorized quality of the colonies. Still, a certain ambivalence about the extent to which the colonies could or should be Europeanized underlay the fantastic descriptions. For example, an article in the *Guide bleu*, which extols the material progress of Algeria under French tutelage, concludes with the comment, "If an excessively Europeanized Algeria disturbs your nostalgia for the exotic, be sure not to leave [the pavilion] without seeing the desert [exhibit]."[35] Expressed here is regret that progress, as defined by nineteenth-century positivism, might very well destroy what was perhaps most appealing about the colonies, their human scale and village life — qualities that may also have aroused a parallel nostalgia for the rural France fading into the industrial, urban republic.

Spatial Organization and Hierarchy on the Esplanade

The same sort of hierarchy implied in the tableaux vivants and by the architecture of the pavilions also operated in general in the spatial arrangement of pavilions on the Esplanade des Invalides. The location of the colonial section directly across from the ministry of war classically opposed European and other — with Europe, and specifically France, holding the position of strength and dominance.

In addition, within the colonial section itself, a further hierarchy among the various colonies emerged. Those pavilions characterized by a type of monumental architecture, and which lined the *allée centrale*, represented only the North African and Asian colonies. Scattered about them — very possibly not even visible from the main boulevard — were the ethnographic villages, representing sub-Saharan black Africans, New Caledonian Canaques (considered a hybrid black-Asian racial group), and the Tonkinese. Thus the use of monumental architecture as a gauge of "civilization" did not cut neatly along the lines of the three main races recognized at the time as "white," "yellow" (or Mongol), and "black." However, Asian and North African superiority over blacks was implied in that the last group's representation remained completely limited to ethnographic villages.[36] Anthropological circles at the time passionately debated the issues of race, racial hierarchy, and racial origin.[37] But one point that seemed to receive consistent support was that, either permanently or temporarily, the black race occupied the lowest position in the racial and cultural hierarchy. Not credited with any large-scale edifices at the 1889 exposition, this racial group was accordingly relegated to the back row of the exhibit grounds.[38] Curiously, in all the coverage of France's empire by the eighty-issue *L'Exposition Universelle de Paris (1889)*, the islands of Saint-Pierre and Miquelon (off the coast of Newfoundland) with their fishing villages go unmentioned — even though they had been French possessions since 1763. The fact that the inhabitants were mostly of French descent (albeit largely Basque and Breton) could have caused awkwardness had they been represented by an ethnographic village alongside non-European colonial "natives," or described in the press with the same level of exoticism.[39]

On the Esplanade des Invalides, assumptions about the level of cultural complexity can be read through the presence or absence of urban or monumental architecture. In this way, a stroll from the war ministry pavilion, across the *allée centrale*, and through the side streets leading back to the ethnographic villages could be experienced as a walk backwards through the development of "civilization": evolutionary distance increased with growing spatial separation from the sphere of French influence. The partial regularization of the colonial pavilions, and the highlighting of monumental architecture, represented the French empire as a work in progress and signaled France's intent to "create" the colonies in its image. Through the same strategies used to develop and unify the diverse peoples of the "Hexagon," the colonies would become an extension of the modern, highly civilized industrial nation represented on the Champ de Mars.

France the Republic, France the Imperial Power

"The superior races have a right because they have a duty. They have the duty to civilize the inferior races," declared Jules Ferry, the prime minister of France under whom colonization gained momentum.[40] Believing in the universality of the values of rational republicanism, the Third Republic set out to organize its far-flung colonies by applying the same model for unification used in its own territory. Colonial administration resembled metropolitan administration; "pacification" was followed by the establishment of schools and human services. Visitors found this strategy echoed in the colonial pavilions, where education and public health displays took their place among exhibits detailing the economic benefits of colonization.

The republic's plan for colonial development paralleled the plan for national development already under way; progress and its benefits for the French working class were demonstrated in the pavilions of public assistance, hygiene, and housing in the social economy exhibit across from the colonial section. Thus visitors could come to view colonization as a natural extension of the social work accomplished within France. While fostering economic development, the Third Republic was also creating a single identity for the ethnically diverse people within each colony, and, eventually, a common "French" identity for all colonies, based on the same values that had operated to forge the diverse peoples of metropolitan France into a single nation. The use of real French workers in parts of the social economy exhibit indicates that the criteria for civilization transcended, at least partially, simple categorization by race.[41] With that much established, all that remained was to complete the process of assimilation.

And yet, the colonized peoples were undeniably *not* French (except the inhabitants of Saint-Pierre and Miquelon) — nor could they ever *become* French in the fullest sense, given the immutable cultural and racial hierarchy communicated through the exposition, which overlaid the criteria for civilization. Therefore colonization could never lead to total assimilation (and indeed, the policy would gradually be abandoned), despite official policy that argued for it and shaped colonial action accordingly.[42] More gravely, admitting the impossibility of assimilation might lay bare the oxymoron of republican imperialism. In the face of these overriding contradictions in principle, policy, and reality, as well as the inconsistencies in efforts to characterize, classify, and — by extension — hierarchize cultural and racial groups, the project of promoting assimilationist colonialism seemed to become even more dependent on exploiting exoticism in the quest for public approbation. The gap separating the Western peoples on the Champs de Mars and the non-Western peoples on the Esplanade des Invalides denoted the most obvious cultural hierarchy, for none of France's colonial possessions could boast the machinery or industrial power necessary to produce an Eiffel Tower. But because racial and cultural categories did not always correspond, their representation on the Esplanade also required the use of poetic license to help gloss over inconsistencies. The silence surrounding Saint-Pierre and Miquelon points to some recognition of the problem of justifying republican imperialism once the veneer of "civilizing mission" is removed. The theatrical setting of the colonial exhibitions, reinforced by a seductive, exotic atmosphere, emphasized entertainment, at the expense of education,[43] while the pavilions and exhibits were praised for their fidelity and authenticity. Ultimately, the universal exposition as educational tool had the power to lull people into passive acceptance, rather than stimulate critical thinking, as the cumulative effects of exoticism encouraged visitors to suspend judgment about what was real, logical, natural, or morally right — and to just enjoy the sensual pleasures of the spectacle before them.

Notes

An earlier version of this paper was presented at the 1994 conference of the Western Society for French History. My thanks to Willa Z. Silverman and Vera Mark for their comments as this paper evolved.

1   *Exposition de 1889: Guide bleu du Figaro et du Petit Journal* (Paris: Imprimerie Chaix, 1889), 25, 246; boldface original. All translations in this essay are my own.

2 John E. Findling and Kimberly D. Pelle, eds., *Historical Dictionary of World's Fairs and Expositions, 1851–1988* (New York: Greenwood, 1990), 108.

3 I am referring to the period of instability after the fall of Jules Ferry from the post of prime minister in 1885, which culminated in the Boulangist crisis.

4 The Eiffel Tower attained a height of 986 feet (300.51 meters). The *Guide bleu* devotes thirty pages to the Eiffel Tower alone, detailing its history, dimensions, construction, elevators, staircases, and degree of oscillation experienced at the top on a windy day. The guidebook also includes a scale drawing of the Eiffel Tower, comparing it to the other "tallest monuments" in the world. Amongst the statistics, the guide carefully points out that before the tower's construction, the world's tallest edifice had been the Washington Monument, measuring 169.25 meters — just over half the height of the Eiffel Tower. During the course of the exposition, nearly 2 million people paid supplemental admission to ascend the Eiffel Tower (Findling and Pelle, *Historical Dictionary of World's Fairs and Expositions*, 112).

5 The Galerie des Machines, situated at the opposite end of the Champ de Mars from the Eiffel Tower, measured 1,452 feet by 380 feet wide. The roof span of 377 feet without a central support was without precedent. An electrically operated platform with a capacity of two hundred people provided a panoramic view of the machinery on display, as it rolled along a track that ran the length of the pavilion above the two-story galleries (ibid.).

6 Louis Gonse, "L'architecture," *Gazette des beaux-arts*, 465.

7 *Guide bleu*, 257.

8 At least in the *Guide bleu*, and the official publications and press sources quoted in this essay.

9 "L'Esplanade des Invalides," *L'Exposition Universelle de 1889 de Paris: Publiée avec la collaboration d'écrivains spéciaux*, 15 June 1889, 123. Edition enrichie de vues, de scènes, de dessins et gravures par les mêmes artistes. This newspaper was published by Librairie Illustrée in eighty weekly issues, from 15 October 1888 to 19 February 1890.

10 See Zeynep Çelik, *Displaying the Orient: Architecture of Islam at Nineteenth-Century World's Fairs* (Berkeley: University of California Press, 1992), for a study of the representation of Islamic cultures through the prism of the architecture of the pavilions during the colonial era.

11 The temple of Angkor Wat, located in Cambodia (the French colony of Annam in 1889) and built in the first half of the twelfth century, was one of the main centers of Khmer Buddhism in that country. A

reproduction of the entire temple at one-quarter its size would be the centerpiece of the Exposition Colonial Internationale de Paris in 1931.

12 *Guide bleu*, 257.

13 Norma Evenson, *Paris: A Century of Change, 1878–1978* (New Haven, Conn.: Yale University Press, 1979), 125.

14 G. Lenotre, "Les coloniaux à l'Exposition Universelle," *L'Exposition Universelle de Paris (1889)*, 6 July 1889, 151.

15 Frantz Jourdain, "Les travaux de l'Exposition Universelle," *L'Exposition Universelle de Paris (1889)*, 4 May 1889, 80.

16 Paul Greenhalgh discusses the relationship between encyclopedic knowledge and the plotting of various peoples on an "evolutionary scale" in *Ephemeral Vistas: The Expositions Universelles, Great Exhibitions, and World's Fairs, 1851–1939* (Manchester: Manchester University Press, 1988), 87–90.

17 The first exhibition of world's fair proportions was the Crystal Palace Exhibition (1851) in England. The first French universal exposition took place in Paris in 1855 and was followed by others in 1867, 1878, 1889, and 1900. In the twentieth century, French expositions became more specialized: The International Exposition of Modern Decorative and Industrial Arts (1925); The International Colonial Exposition (1931); and The International Exposition of Arts and Techniques (1937), which emphasized rural life and regionalism. These nationalistic displays ended in France with the advent of World War II.

18 At least in France, by focusing on the educated classes, the government also hoped to attract greater private investment in the colonies.

19 Greenhalgh, *Ephemeral Vistas*, 21.

20 Ibid., 29.

21 However, this type of display did have a precedent in ethnographic exhibitions at the Jardin d'Acclimatation in Paris. For a discussion of the evolution of ethnographic exhibitions in Paris, see William H. Schneider, *An Empire for the Masses: The French Popular Image of Africa, 1870–1900* (Westport, Conn.: Greenwood, 1982).

22 All the quotes in this paragraph come from Hugues Le Roux, "Psychologie exotique," *L'Exposition Universelle de Paris (1889)*, 27 July 1889, 170–71. It must be said, however, that the author tended to minimize the complaints of the indigenous people, rather than defend them.

23 Emile Cartailhac, "Un projet d'exposition anthropologique dressé en 1867 et en partie réalisé en 1889," *Anthropologie* 1 (1890).

24 Curtis M. Hinsley, "The World as Marketplace: Commodification of the Exotic at the World's Columbian Exposition, Chicago, 1893," in *Exhibiting Cultures: The Poetics and Politics of Museum Display*,

ed. Ivan Karp and Steven D. Lavine (Washington, D.C.: Smithsonian Institution Press, 1991), 345.

25 Quoted in Cartailhac, "Un projet d'exposition anthropologique dressé en 1867," 633.

26 Edward W. Said, *Orientalism* (New York: Pantheon, 1979), 40.

27 "L'Esplanade des Invalides," 123.

28 See Philippe Augier, "Fête coloniale à l'Esplanade," *L'Exposition Universelle de 1889 de Paris*, 5 October 1889, 8; and Augier, "Fête de nuit à l'Esplanade des Invalides," *L'Exposition Universelle de 1889 de Paris*, 12 October 1889, 18. Note that these weekly events did not make their debut until over four months into the exposition.

29 Greenhalgh, *Ephemeral Vistas*, 42.

30 Madeleine Ribérioux, "Au tournant des expositions: 1889," *Le mouvement social* 149 (1989): 10. (A special issue entitled "La mise en scène et vulgarisation: L'Exposition Universelle de 1889.")

31 Gonse, "L'architecture," 474.

32 Pascal Ory, *Les expositions universelles de Paris: Panorama raisonné avec des aperçus nouveaux et des illustrations par les meilleurs auteurs* (Paris: Editions Ramsay, 1982), 114.

33 "Le campement canaque," *L'Exposition Universelle de Paris (1889)*, 12 October 1889, 22.

34 For more on the French notion of *civilization* as defined in terms of human mastery of nature, see Alice L. Conklin, *A Mission to Civilize: The Republican Idea of Empire in France and West Africa, 1895–1930* (Stanford, Calif.: Stanford University Press, 1997).

35 *Guide bleu*, 250.

36 That is to say, the public was left to believe that the black race had never constructed large-scale edifices.

37 For discussions on these debates, see Linda L. Clark, *Social Darwinism in France* (Huntsville: University of Alabama Press, 1984); Jean-Marc Bernardini, *Le darwinisme social en France (1859–1918): Fascination et rejet d'une idéologie* (Paris: CNRS Editions, 1997); Elizabeth A. Williams, "The Science of Man: Anthropological Thought and Institutions in Nineteenth-Century France" (Ph.D. diss., Indiana University, 1983).

38 This same judgment was echoed in Charles Garnier's *History of Human Habitation*, a positivist exhibit situated at the base of the Eiffel Tower on the Champ de Mars, which traced the evolution of human lodging around the world from prehistory to the Renaissance (at which point Garnier had exhausted available funds). Habitations of the black race, however, were completely omitted, except for one example that served as part of a postscript displaying "primitive" housing still in existence in the modern world.

39 The two islands were only represented in the Palais Central des Colonies.

40 Quoted from a speech delivered before the French chamber of deputies on 28 July 1885 in Raoul Girardet, ed., *Le nationalisme français* (Paris: Editions du Seuil, 1983), 97.

41 For more on the social economy exhibit and its links with the colonial section, see Janet R. Horne, "In Pursuit of Greater France: Visions of Empire among Musée Social Reformers, 1894–1931," in *Domesticating the Empire: Race, Gender, and Family Life in French and Dutch Colonialism*, ed. Julia Clancy-Smith and Frances Gouda (Charlottesville: University Press of Virginia, 1998), 21–42.

42 For more on the inherent conflicts between the theory of assimilation and the contemporary belief in immutable ethnic differences (with the added layer of gender), see Alice L. Conklin, "Redefining 'Frenchness': Citizenship, Race, Regeneration, and Imperial Motherhood in France and West Africa, 1914–40," in Clancy-Smith and Gouda, *Domesticating the Empire*. By 1910, colonial policy had largely shifted from one of assimilation to one of association. For a discussion of assimilation versus association, see Raymond F. Betts, *Assimilation and Association in French Colonial Theory, 1890–1914* (New York: Columbia University Press, 1961); Charles-Robert Ageron, *France coloniale ou parti colonial?* (Paris: Presses Universitaires de France, 1978); Raoul Girardet, *L'idée coloniale en France de 1871–1962* (Paris: La Table Ronde, 1972).

43 For more on the theatrical dimension of colonial representation at universal expositions, see Sylviane Leprun, *Le théâtre des colonies: Scénographie, acteurs et discours de l'imaginaire dans les expositions 1855–1937* (Paris: Editions L'Harmattan, 1986).

Alice L. Conklin

Who Speaks for Africa?

The René Maran–Blaise Diagne

Trial in 1920s Paris

In 1924, Blaise Diagne, the first African deputy to be elected to the French parliament, sued the celebrated Caribbean novelist and former colonial administrator in Africa, René Maran, for libel in the *cour d'assises*, the second highest tribunal in France. Diagne was incensed by an unsigned article that had recently appeared in a new and struggling *pan-noir* journal critical of French colonial administration, *Les Continents*, of which Maran was vice president.[1] The article described Diagne as an agent of French colonialism and accused him of having accepted a bribe for each *tirailleur* he had recruited during World War I to fight in, and for, France. The accusation was the more sensational coming from the pages of a journal to which René Maran regularly contributed.[2] Like Diagne, Maran had breached the color barrier that defined French-colonial relations in the early twentieth century, albeit in a different context. In 1921, Maran became the first black man to win the prestigious Prix Goncourt. It was awarded for his novel *Batouala, véritable roman nègre*, which combined a crude ethnography of the people of Ubangi-Shari with a vicious indictment of French rule in their Equatorial African colony, although it did not call for independence.[3]

Two French black luminaries, then, confronted each other in the waning November days of 1924 over the fate of France's African subjects and the direction of its rule on that continent. The two-day trial was widely reported, allegedly catching the attention of *le tout Paris*. Much of the Parisian press supported Diagne.[4] As the ex–high commissioner of African troops, Diagne still had powerful political friends in Paris in the early 1920s. Maran's principal support, on the other hand, came from the tiny *mouvement noir* just now making its mark on the Paris literary and political scene. Made up of a few West African ex-soldiers who had stayed in France, a larger following of militant dock workers, and several Caribbean intellectuals such as Maran — all of whom had been radicalized by their wartime and immediate postwar experiences on French soil — this community shared a greater willingness to condemn the abuses of French colonialism and its methods than Diagne.[5]

Une querelle de famille — a relatively straightforward competition between two visions of how best to reform the empire — one might well conclude. And to the extent that historians have discussed the trial, this has been the dominant interpretation: Diagne and Maran were both committed critics of the French, but differed on how fast to go in the struggle for human dignity and freedom.[6] This interpretation is correct, but only to a point. Its principal weakness derives from its assumption that because both men were black, the only real difference between them had to be political. Underneath the men's political differences, however, lay a subtler and equally important one: a different conception of what it meant to be "*noir*," "African," and "French" in an imperial nation-state that did not draw distinctions only on the basis of skin color. To reduce the quarrel to one over the best means to reform the empire is to miss, if you will allow me an anachronism, the "identity politics" at stake in the Diagne-Maran confrontation at a highly charged moment in the history of French race relations.

Issues of identity — racial, national, and cultural/continental — were politicized in at least two different and related ways in the 1924 trial. First, Maran and Diagne's mutual recriminations must be understood in the context of international postwar Pan-Africanism, of which Diagne was initially a leader, then a critic. Pan-Africanism held that blacks everywhere were obligated to make common cause as "negroes" against their oppressors, regardless of their countries of origin. If they did not, they could only be stooges of the white establishment. As a black Frenchman from the Antilles serving in the colonial administration in Africa, Maran had encountered and witnessed sufficient racism from white Frenchmen and -women to see *le monde noir* in 1924 in these essentialist terms. From Maran's vantage point, Diagne appeared to place loyalty to white France over devotion to his fellow Africans. What Maran failed to see was that as an educated deputy from the Four Communes of Senegal, Diagne was as Senegalese as he was French. In short, both of these men moved in multiple worlds, with considerably more complex identities than simply black or white, French or *noir* than the sharp dichotomies of Pan-Africanism might suggest — complexities that echoed the permeable and unstable boundaries of the French color line overseas and at home.

Second, conflicting visions of Africa in an era of heightened nationalism also proved central to the politics of Frenchness and blackness that characterized the Diagne-Maran confrontation. One by-product of the awakening *mouvement noir* in France in this period, and indeed worldwide, was that Europeans lost their monopoly on speaking for the entity they called "Africa." Imperialism had always justified itself on the grounds that the white man alone knew what was best for the African and thus could fully represent him. Now men like Diagne and Maran were beginning to argue publicly, and in flawless French, that as educated men of color, they constituted the more legitimate and natural spokesmen for Africa. Yet in "daring" to speak for their *frères de race*, Diagne and Maran had very different understandings of what they were doing. Maran did not question the existence of a traditional Africa, and he spent more and more of his time in the 1920s seeking to know it. Diagne, in contrast, did not think in continental terms, but in nascent national ones. These constituted two alternate and ultimately incommensurate Africanisms — two modes of imagining and interacting with the peoples of that continent — at a time when an older idea of Africa in the West was coming unmoored.

The Trial

Imagine, first, a packed courtroom, "the room . . . bursting at the seams."[7] The audience was a mixed one, more white than black, but definitely integrated.[8] People had come here, into the second highest court of the land, because Blaise Diagne was pressing charges against an upstart newspaper. Libel cases usually came before a lower court, the *tribunal correctionnel*, but Diagne had exercised the prerogatives of his parliamentary office to claim a higher judicial review — and ensure, presumably, maximum publicity. In the *cour d'assises*, the burden of proof lay with the defendant; more important, trial was by jury, with no appeal: "the people's" verdict was final. In this particular case, those responsible for *Les Continents* must prove to the jury the veracity of a specific passage that appeared in the 15 October issue of their newspaper, in an article entitled "Le bon apôtre," which Diagne claimed to be defamatory. It described a conversation that allegedly took place in early 1918 between then–prime minister Clemenceau and Blaise Diagne, deputy from Senegal, when the former decided to ask the latter to lead one final recruiting drive in West Africa:

> M. Clemenceau, cunning as usual, was eager to let M. Diagne know by telephone that he would be accorded a certain commission per soldier recruited. The deputy from Senegal promptly rushed to the Presidency of the Council. He accepted [the offer]. M. Mandel will not gainsay our allegations. This was what M. Diagne calls fighting for France and for one's race.[9]

As Diagne himself put it, there was only one issue at hand for the court: "Whether, as I'm accused, I received a commission per soldier recruited."[10]

Eloquently and persuasively, Diagne then used his opening statement to recount what exactly had transpired six years earlier. He had accepted the mission to recruit soldiers out of a double sense of duty: first, "a duty of gratitude to France";[11] and second, a "duty of interest for the indigenous inhabitants of the colonies, for it did not escape them that in the case of defeat, the colonies would be the ransom demanded by Germany."[12] He carried out this mission, he continued, in a completely disinterested fashion. Up until 1917, recruitment had been highly coercive, and thus counterproductive: "Villages were targeted and prisoners taken." France, which in 1917 needed still more men, was ill-served by such inefficient methods: "It was then, in early 1918, that I gave into M. Clemenceau's pleas and left for Africa, where I substituted for forcible recruitment a system providing blacks with the opportunity to participate in a crusade of sorts against the enemy of France, their protector; thus an image of the motherland took shape in their minds."[13] In one month, and without a military escort, Diagne traveled 3,500 kilometers. In return for volunteers, he promised a medical school, a midwifery school, an agricultural school, and a veterinary school.[14] His efforts paid off. Hoping for 45,000 men, 77,800 signed up, without a single shot being fired. Diagne closed his peroration with what would remain his formal explanation for why he felt compelled to bring suit in France's high criminal court against a struggling newspaper few Parisians had heard of. The newspaper in question, *Les Continents*, circulated in Africa.[15] He did not want to leave his compatriots in Africa, whom France might again need, under the impression that they had sacrificed their lives for his personal enrichment.[16]

The calling up of witnesses for cross-examination occupied much of the remainder of the trial. Diagne had hired as his attorney another deputy of color, Alcide Delmont, from Martinique.[17] Delmont made his line of attack perfectly clear by suggesting right off the mark that the accusations against Diagne and his role in the recruitment formed part of a bolshevik conspiracy.[18] Diagne's lineup of witnesses, in contrast, was all white, and impressive by any count. It included many of the Third Republic's most visible and active politicians and civil servants, all of whom had been involved in the 1918 recruitment either as decision-makers or men on the spot. Diagne had called Georges Clemenceau and many of his wartime cabinet, including Georges Mandel, Paul Painlevé, André Maginot, Henri-Simon, and Pierre Masse. Colonial and military officials were also well represented: Gabriel Angoulvant, interim governor-general of Afrique Equatoriale Française (AEF) and Afrique Occidentale Française (AOF) in 1918, Auguste Brunet, former governor of the Sudan, and General Gouraud.[19] The reason for their selection — and for their willingness to serve — would have been obvious to contemporaries. In accusing Blaise Diagne, *Les Continents* had sought to reopen an old brief: the inhumanity of rounding up Africans to serve as cannon fodder for the French in *la grande guerre*, the ultimate symbol of French colonial abuses generally.[20] This charge could not be allowed to stand. France might again need its African army, and it was an article of faith among government officials that these men would serve the French as loyally in the future as they had in the past. Their loyalty, and especially the blood tax these subjects willingly paid for being ruled by a colorblind and generous France, was the ultimate proof of *la grande nation*'s success at colonizing.[21]

This, in short, was very much the line taken by the prosecution. Their witnesses revisited in lengthy detail the recruitment of African soldiers, Diagne's privileged role in guaranteeing its success, and the vital necessity of these troops to France. Clemenceau, Mandel, and Gouraud — much to the chagrin of many in the audience — did not actually appear, but sent letters testifying to the absolute integrity of Diagne and the heroism of the black troops. Clemenceau reminded the court that when offered the Legion of Honor for services rendered to the nation, Diagne had declined, stating that he was simply doing his duty and therefore deserved no special recompense. The other deputies and ex-ministers frankly agreed that "Diagne's gentle and human approach succeeded beyond all expectations where brutality had failed and provoked revolts."[22]

Given the unanimity and authority with which these witnesses spoke on Diagne's behalf, the defense did not even attempt to dispute the evidence presented. Instead, it entered a plea of guilty and then tried to justify publication of the libel. The defense's choice of witnesses and the plaintiff's attempt to discredit them generated the only fiery exchanges during the course of the trial. Technically, the defendant in the case was not René Maran, director of *Les Continents*, but Jean Fangeat, the twenty-three-year-old editor in chief and proprietor of the journal. It was, however, commonly assumed that Maran had written the article in question and that he was the *inspirateur* behind the whole *Les Continents* enterprise. He was, moreover, the defense's star witness, fueling the perception that the entire trial was "a duel between MM. Diagne and Maran."[23] In the end, Fangeat's principal role was to call attention to the fact that *Les Continents* was simply repeating a story that several other more established newspapers owned by whites had already printed.[24] Skirting for the moment the issue at stake — Diagne's venality or lack of it — Fangeat pleaded that a paper such as theirs, dedicated to the defense of the "negro race," received "hundreds of documents" raising charges against colonial administrators, as well as against Diagne. Although they attempted always to verify their accuracy, they did not always succeed. "The note concerning M. Diagne seemed to me to agree with similar notes already published in other newspapers."[25] At most, their correspondent might have exaggerated the claim.[26] Finally, alluding to Delmont's charge of communist machinations, Fangeat insisted that he at no point was himself or his journal accused of antipatriotism.

Fangeat's witnesses were, not surprisingly given his newspaper's marginalization, considerably more eclectic in outlook than Diagne's. He was defended by Maître Ernest-Charles, assisted by Maître Yvonne Netter. In addition to Maran, the defense called up two lesser-known generals: General Sarrail, who had commanded black troops in Salonika and had heard them complain about their "forced" recruitment; and General Verraux, who announced that he had never heard of Diagne, even though it was now being claimed that he had single-handedly "saved France"; two communist deputies, Ernest Lafont and André Berthon, who reported that they had personally witnessed Diagne's dramatic opposition to recruitment in the chamber before 1918 — thus making his "change of heart" all the more suspect; and Félicien Challaye, lycée professor and prominent member of the Ligue des Droits de l'Homme, called on to attest to the philanthropic vocation of *Les Continents*. Several personal friends of Maran and Fangeat also spoke to their morality and to the justice of *Les Continents'* cause as the first organ devoted to defending blacks in the colonies. These friends included Henri Béraud, another Goncourt laureate; Gouttenoire de Toury, also on the editorial board of *Les Continents* and a longtime defender of the rights of the peoples of Madagascar; J.-M. Renaitour, a young writer; and Colonel Finet. The final witness was the decorated ex-*tirailleur* Lamine Senghor, making his political debut by recounting the extreme disgruntlement of soldiers who had been forcibly recruited. These latter particularly resented the fact that soldiers from the Four Communes of Senegal received better pay than those from the rest of the federation.[27] Collectively, their testimony proved the rumors before the trial right. Their brief was not so much to prove Diagne's venality: "Does M. Diagne have sticky fingers? I'm perfectly indifferent on this score. I can't say yes, and I can't say no," Maran reportedly said.[28] It was rather to protest against the specious distinction being made between Diagne's good recruiting efforts and the "bad" ones that they replaced. This obscured the more fundamental issue of Mangin-le-Boucher's murderous, not to say illegal, use of black troops in France in the first place,[29] as well as the infamy of France being the first "to send innocents to their death . . . without anything in return."[30] Last but not least, they were protesting against "the force and assaults exercised upon the natives, and against the discretionary powers of the governors, then and now."[31]

Yet if the defendants hoped to use the excesses of the war years to focus attention on a continuing need for colonial reform in the present, they had underestimated their opponent's skill. In what became the centerpiece of the trial, Diagne let Maran raise the issue he felt most passionately about — colonial violence, particularly during the war years — in order to make a stunning revelation to those assembled. When Maran was still working for the colonial administration, Diagne asked, had he not been fined fifty francs on 26 June 1919 by a *tribunal correctionnel* for excessive use of violence against a native?[32] Had not this native later died from his blows? "M. Maran," Diagne continued, "even though negro himself, strikes me as poorly qualified to take on the defense of blacks."[33]

Maran immediately denied that he had inflicted the blows in question, insisting that he had taken the rap for one of his subordinates. Why then had he not appealed? "We all know about colonial justice," Maran replied.[34]

If one can believe the press reports, at no point did the defense gain the upper hand in any of these exchanges, and Maran in particular came off badly. Yet the final summations suggest that *Les Continents* had touched a raw nerve. Delmont pointed out, rather patronizingly, that the hapless Fangeat, while officially the defendant, was clearly the marionette of those amoral and dishonest men who were actually running *Les Continents*. It thus behooved everyone to seek out the real force behind the newspaper's lies and calumnies, of which those levied against Diagne were only the latest. And who else loomed as the guilty party than René Maran, the black man who, ever since the publication of *Batouala*, was using all his energies to attack the country that had liberated him? Thanks to his blasphemies, it was the honor and future of France that now stood on trial. Delmont concluded by asking that Fangeat be charged a 10,000FF penalty, which Diagne would pledge to the fund for black soldiers.[35]

To all of this Ernest Charles wittily replied that it really was not necessary to disturb immortal France, when little more was at stake than some imprudent allegations by an inexperienced young journalist. He then came back to the point that Fangeat had made at the very outset: the charges against Diagne were hardly new, having been printed in newspapers much more widely circulated than *Les Continents*; nor was it the first time even that *Les Continents* had attacked Diagne in this manner. Diagne had never previously deigned to dignify such "calumnies" with a court case. The whole affair, in the end, was due to Diagne's desire to diminish Maran's reputation — "une querelle entre deux noirs."[36] The jury, he asked, should acquit Fangeat, given these attenuating circumstances. Delmont's arguments did not persuade the jury. It found for the prosecution on two counts — defamation and defamation against a *fonctionnaire*. Fangeat received a suspended sentence of six months in prison and was fined 1,500FF. He also had to pay Diagne damages of 2,000FF, and five newspapers were to publish the verdict. This verdict surprised no one, since the defendants had made no effort to prove that Diagne had profited from his role in the war. The hefty fines were prohibitive enough to shut down *Les Continents*, which stopped publication several months later.

René Maran: Français Nègre?

The Diagne-Maran confrontation invites analysis on a number of levels. There is, for example, Diagne's and Maran's self-image and self-presentation. Was it concern over his own honor, as well as that of his race, as the influential *Dépêche Coloniale et Maritime* put it, that explained Diagne's actions?[37] What about Maran's? What other factors — local, metropolitan, and international — might account for the dispute? Diagne himself appeared particularly wary of *Les Continents* circulating in West Africa. Why was this so important to him? One can best answer these questions by considering the individual histories of Maran and Diagne, certain debates about the relationship between race, identity, and colonization taking place in France between 1919 and 1924, and the political situation in Senegal.

There can be little doubt that both René Maran and Blaise Diagne considered themselves French, although in each case there was also an important "African" component to their identities. Maran was born in 1887 to Guyanese parents living in Fort de France, Martinique, but his earliest memories were of Equatorial Africa, and then France.[38] His father had chosen to join the colonial service and was posted to Gabon when Maran was only three. René attended elementary school in Gabon, and he then was sent to boarding school in Bordeaux when he turned seven. He did brilliantly in his studies, but also suffered a certain degree of social ostracism because of his race. He, like his father, went on to enter the colonial administration. He, too, was assigned to French Equatorial Africa, where he remained from 1910 to 1923, serving in remote districts, first in Ubangi-Shari, then after 1920 in Chad.

Maran had already begun writing poetry before leaving Bordeaux, and he published two volumes of his poems between 1909 and 1912.[39] He continued writing in Africa, drawing inspiration from his close contact with the Banda people of Ubangi-Shari. This resulted in the novel *Batouala*, the tragic story of a Banda chief facing the loss of his traditional authority under the corrosive influence of French rule. Maran included a preface that decried the abuses of the colonial administration in the colony and called for a policy more worthy of France's republican heritage.[40] Equatorial Africa was among the poorest of French African colonies and had a reputation for attracting the dregs of the colonial service.[41] Many of its peoples were particularly refractory to "pacification," and to the policies of development, or *mise en valeur*, that the French wished to implement. Recruitment of porters was particularly brutal there, especially during the war, and Maran had little choice but to participate in these roundups. Maran's *cri d'alarme* is usually seen as having been fully vindicated by the revelations of André Gide and Albert Londres later that decade.[42] Much more than the novel itself — which won Maran the Goncourt in 1921 — this inflammatory introduction earned its author the collective bile of the colonial establishment.

It is a shame that more has not been written about Maran's years in Africa; Africa would remain at the heart of his creative work as well as of his political concerns for the rest of his life, although he never returned to it. There is a great deal that we do not know about his experiences there, first as a child and then during his coming-of-age as a writer. Clearly, his second period in Africa proved transformative. Maran apparently had many of the typical "French" reactions to bush life — loneliness, alternating fondness for and repulsion toward the "savages" with whom he lived, a search for sexual gratification, and periodic questioning of the legitimacy of the system of which he was a part. As a *nègre* and an intellectual within the administration, however, he also suffered racial discrimination from his white superiors.[43] Discrimination reached its zenith in 1919, when Maran was unfairly found guilty of killing a porter. This was the incident referred to by Diagne; indeed, it was Maran's inability to clear his name in this case that prompted the writing of *Batouala*, and especially its angry preface.[44]

And what was Maran's vision of Africans themselves? Maran approached the continent with curiosity about what was the land of his ancestors, but he had no instinctive identification with it.[45] Whether he had developed a true affinity for the peoples of Ubangi-Shari and Chad by the time he left in 1923 remains an open question. He would continue to write African novels and insisted throughout his life that his best-known work, *Batouala*, was certainly not his best work on the subject. Maran recognized how poorly he had understood the Banda customs, two of which figure at the heart of *Batouala*: a circumcision ritual followed by a "love" dance in which Batouala must suffer the final humiliation of seeing his best friend seduce his favorite wife; and the annual hunt, in which he himself is mortally wounded in the presence of the lovers who are on the point of betraying him. His subsequent novels were driven by a desire to produce a more truthful description of this and the other ethnic groups he encountered (particularly in Chad where he seems to have been happier), without sacrificing his own high literary standards.[46] It is also true that he wrote even more about animals than people in his later African novels. Ironically enough, *Batouala* was heralded at the time and until relatively recently as the first authentic African novel in the French language, one which consciously repudiated the exoticism of the reigning so-called colonial novel and replaced it with a genuinely African sensibility.[47]

Current criticism of *Batouala* is beginning to revise this earlier assessment. Commentators now recognize that both Maran's novel and the popular reaction to it bear witness to a highly charged moment in modern French history, when the representation of Africa was particularly unstable.[48] This moment extended from the end of the war until the mid-1920s and involved not only Maran, but Blaise Diagne as well. It is difficult to overestimate the impact of World War I on the French African empire and official French attitudes toward racial difference. Use of colonial troops, both during the war and afterward in the Rhineland, had raised vociferous protests from the German government, who had dredged up the most vicious racist stereotypes to protest the presence of French Africans. The French government, eager to persuade its citizenry to accept African soldiers, had responded with a propaganda campaign of its own. Africans were no longer portrayed as savages, but as good little brothers fighting for a common *patrie* which made no distinction based on race.[49] This message became all the more important in the early 1920s, given that blacks internationally were beginning for the first time to seriously contest French methods of colonial governance. We have already encountered Blaise Diagne, who by his own account spent the war years fighting for African interests. An impressive number of other groups also made their appearance even before the publication of *Batouala*: Pan-Africanists under the leadership of either W. E. B. Du Bois or Marcus Garvey, claiming that all blacks shared a common oppression and that Africans had to take back their continent; educated Africans and Caribbeans working in France for *la défense de la race noire*; not to mention the new Communist Party calling on proletarians to fight for colonial liberation.

It is only in this larger context that both the decision to award *Batouala* the Goncourt, and the extraordinary outcry against the novel when the prize was announced, can be understood. The entire ordeal changed Maran's life, and it set him on a collision course with Blaise Diagne two years later. On the one hand, most of the positive commentary generated by the book came from the metropole, although even here reviews were very mixed. Those who liked the book noted how different the novel was from run-of-the-mill colonial literature, and how Maran alone had captured the unique qualities of African life.[50] These critics seemed to be responding to the more sympathetic portrayal of Africans current in France since the war. On the other hand, the tidal wave of negative reactions to the book came mostly from the ranks of the colonial press. There were not just bad book reviews. Authorities were quick to identify an entire alternative canon of established colonial writers, not all of whom were hacks. These writers, they claimed, depicted French-African relations much more accurately than Maran. Any one of these authors, these commentators insisted, would have been more deserving of the Goncourt Prize.[51] At the same time, perhaps the most respected Africanist reporting on colonial affairs weighed in the battle and brought the full weight of his scientific authority to bear against Maran. This was the former colonial administrator and renowned ethnographer Maurice Delafosse. Delafosse's most serious accusation was not that Maran had misrepresented the French—Delafosse admitted the constant possibility of abuses—but that Maran had failed adequately to represent Africa.[52] Delafosse would return to the attack later in 1923, when he published his own highly readable reflections on his experiences as a *broussard*, or bush administrator. Included was a reprise of his earlier criticism of Maran, now made even more explicit: no genuine African possibly spoke in the cadences of *Batouala*'s imaginary *nègres*.[53]

Delafosse's criticisms are worth analyzing in more detail, for they seem to have influenced Maran and his subsequent trajectory. Delafosse had always felt a deep sympathy for what he deemed to be the only "authentic" Africa. This was rural Africa, whose complex religious, political, and economic systems, he insisted, had developed differently and at a slower pace than those of the West, but for all their difference still deserved respect. The counterpart to such sympathy was a visceral antipathy for the new westernized elites produced by colonialism. Yet Delafosse was profoundly committed to France's civilizing mission to bring Africans into the modern era. He reconciled these contradictory impulses by arguing that France's role was to preserve the essence of African tradition by working gradually to effect change from within. This strategy could only be successful if the French first took the time to study and understand the rich traditional cultures over which they had assumed responsibility and worked out policies appropriate to each people they encountered. Nothing could be more misguided than to believe in the existence of a universal black civilization. Nor should Caribbean or American blacks think that their own experience of discrimination uniquely qualified them to now represent their *frères noirs* under colonial rule on the African continent.[54] Someday Africans would speak for themselves, but until they did, only those armed with the proper ethnographic knowledge were qualified to lead them forward.[55]

René Maran's *Batouala* was an affront to this vision on many different counts. It offered a singularly disillusioning journey through an Africa whose traditions were already compromised by a corrupt and ignorant colonial administration.[56] Maran's attitude toward these traditions was itself, moreover, deeply ambivalent: he depicted them as barbaric and thus deserving of their fate, and yet he was drawn to them. So much negativity and ambivalence could only annoy Delafosse — given his own confident assessment that traditional Africa was different, but not barbaric; that it was still more or less intact; and that it could best be salvaged by experts like himself. And here we come to yet another offense. Maran was making his rival claims on the basis of no scientific authority whatsoever. His book in Delafosse's view revealed that he had spent his years in Africa sitting on his veranda, rather than getting to know the men he had been sent to govern. The awarding of the Goncourt to *Batouala* marked the final insult, as far as Delafosse was concerned. It created the possibility that the French public would accept Maran's book as true and perhaps mistakenly rally behind this pseudo-spokesman for the continent. Delafosse wished to nip this tendency in the bud before a misguided parliament, swayed by a perhaps well-intentioned but fundamentally misguided universalism à la Maran, chose to bypass the proper technicians of empire and interfere in African affairs directly.

The *Batouala* controversy, including Delafosse's attack, constituted the second transformative experience of René Maran's life. In two very different ways, it set him on a new course that eventually brought him into conflict with Diagne. First, it led Maran to become a political activist and black culturalist. In the wake of the storm he unleashed, Maran left Africa and the colonial administration for good, apparently convinced that it was a viciously flawed but still redeemable system, which he could better help reform from without than from within. In 1923, he moved to Paris, and four years later he married Camille Berthelot, a white French woman who remained devoted to him all her life. Thus began a new and exhilarating, albeit materially difficult, life as a highly visible public intellectual and defender of his race.[57] "His activity, his enlightened intelligence are known. We know the extent of his influence in black circles in France, in America, and in the colonies," the newspaper *Eclair* could already claim in October 1924.[58] He constantly intervened with the colonial minister to call attention to abuses.[59] He also now became a kind of literary ambassador of the New Negro movement and Harlem Renaissance to France, reviewing new works by African Americans in French journals and becoming closely associated with Howard University professor and writer Alain Leroy Locke. Finally, he joined such causes as *Les Continents*, devoted to protecting black interests, without, however, giving up his French identity. The *mouvement noir*, of which *Les Continents* represented the cutting edge in France at this time, still worked within a framework of a French Africa. No one among the small group of Caribbeans and Africans involved was yet calling for anything more than the complete political assimilation of France's colonies.[60] The editors of *Les Continents*, and Maran as one of its chief contributors, understood their mandate as one of forcing France to live up to its traditional commitments as the country of the rights of man. As Maran himself summarized his politics in an interview in October 1924:

> What are the goals I am pursuing? They are as follows: France is a beautiful country and a good mother. Unfortunately for her, she knows practically nothing of the abuses her legitimate sons commit against her adopted children. For a long time, the latter have silently execrated her. They did not know that she did not know. Then came the war. By choice or by force, a number of them came to her help. It was only after this that they began to understand her and love her. My desire therefore is to confront public opinion with all that has been hidden from it. On the other hand, in complete agreement with my fellow blacks from the United States, from Haiti, from Cuba, and from the Antilles, I am attempting to organize a universal confederation of blacks, whose headquarters would be in Paris. For it is only in Paris that blacks of all countries can work joyously, amidst a slightly mocking but friendly curiosity, toward their intellectual freedom, which is the only kind they truly seek.[61]

It is these politics that led Maran to hold Blaise Diagne for contempt because, as he saw it, Diagne belonged to that group of *fils légitimes* who had betrayed the French motherland not just during the war, but more recently.[62]

There is, however, a second and more insidious way in which Maran's Goncourt travails — and Delafosse's response to his prize — affected Maran and also led indirectly to his confrontation with Diagne. At the same time that these experiences turned him into a political activist determined to extend republican liberties to the continent, they also led him to a more positive assessment of Africa — to a vision of the continent which ironically began to look more like Delafosse's and less like the world first evoked in *Batouala*.[63] Maran wrote on past African cultural achievements in *Les Continents* and immediately began his next African novel after his return to Paris.[64] This time he paid much closer attention than he had in *Batouala* to getting the ethnography correct; he contacted his childhood friend, fellow Caribbean and colonial administrator Félix Eboué, for the details that had eluded him the first time round.[65] His ethnographic turn would culminate in the 1931 publication of Maran's own collection of African folktales, which directly addressed Delafosse's work.[66]

All of this suggests that Delafosse's accusations that no African spoke as *Batouala* strongly stung Maran, and that he, in fact, accepted Delafosse's argument that he needed to do more research if he wished successfully to translate Africa to the West. In deferring to Delafosse's ethnographic authority, however, Maran also inherited the latter's notion that "real" Africa was "traditional" Africa, and as such was incapable of defining and defending its own interests before the colonizer. For Maran at least, this meant that assimilated black Frenchmen like himself would have to continue to speak for it and could best determine its needs. But Africa under colonialism, and Senegal in particular, could not be reduced to this archaic — and leaderless — essence. With its right to elect a deputy to parliament, its new boundaries fixed by the French, and its dynamic peanut-led export sector, Senegal was fast developing a modern "national" politics in the 1920s. Here, old elites were hardly dead and gone, as predicted in *Batouala*, and modern elites were emerging with their own conflicting agendas. These groups competed not so much for abstract rights or the recognition of a shared black oppression, but for money and power under the new rules and conditions created by the French administration. These contentious politics were indeed critical of colonialism, but Maran had difficulty recognizing them as such, because they clashed too deeply with the more static Africa that science and his own imagination were now constructing. This inability to see a modern Africa emerging also framed Maran's attack on Diagne in 1924. With this argument in mind, let us now take a closer look at the man defamed by his fellow black radicals, Blaise Diagne.

Blaise Diagne: Sénégalais et Français?

Blaise Diagne found his way to his French identity by following a rather different trajectory than René Maran. He was born on the island of Gorée in 1872, one of the Four Communes of coastal Senegal, which had been French since the seventeenth century. Unlike the rest of Senegal, which the French had only recently conquered and whose rural populations they had placed under a protectorate, the Four Communes had had representation in parliament since 1890. Diagne's community of origin was Lebu, but a Creole family sponsored his education in France. He quickly won a spot in the *service des douanes*, where he served for twenty years in a variety of colonies. He soon made a name for himself as a difficult and contentious civil servant. The issue, apparently, was always the same. Diagne would brook no insult motivated by race. This pattern would characterize his entire career, and it was the cause for his lack of promotion within the colonial service and routine reassignments within it.[67] His remarkable survival is usually attributed to his uncanny political sense and his single-minded pursuit of power, facilitated by the connections he made when he joined the Free Masons in 1900.[68] Indeed, that Diagne took Masonry's ideology of universal brotherhood seriously, and was able to win full acceptance within the lodge's parameters, is a measure of his deep attraction to the idea of a color-blind France, the France of 1789 and 1848.[69] Much of Diagne's subsequent career — and here again the similarities with Maran stand out — was devoted to making France live up to the letter of its revolutionary legacy of racial equality, particularly within the confines of his home colony of Senegal.

In 1914, Diagne returned from a posting in Guadeloupe where he, too, had married a white French woman, to present himself as a candidate for the seat to parliament in the Four Communes. A complete political unknown, he drew together a threefold coalition, including Lebu notables — the dominant ethnic group in the Four Communes, a traditional and predominantly Muslim community deeply unhappy about the loss of their land rights as Dakar expanded; new, urban-based educated elites known as the Young Senegalese — very much a minority but highly nationalist already in 1912; and several independent white traders shut out of the more lucrative markets by the dominant Bordeaux merchant houses. This coalition unseated the conservative incumbent and broke the lock on that seat that the big merchant houses and their St. Louisian Creole allies had held since the late nineteenth century.

Neither the Bordeaux import-export houses nor the local administration missed the revolutionary implications of Diagne's election. Henceforth the *originaires* of Senegal — as the 7,000 mostly illiterate electors out of a total Senegalese population of 1.2 million were known — would have a voice of their own in parliament, an independent power base in Paris which could be used as a counterweight to local French authority. In 1914, war broke out not only between Germany and France, but between Diagne and the French officials in Dakar, although the animosities did not spread to Paris. Diagne's first move was to use the opportunity posed by wartime conscription to resolve a long-standing dispute between the predominantly Muslim inhabitants of the Four Communes of Senegal and the colonial administration. The former insisted that they had been made full citizens of the republic in the early 1890s — with all the privileges and duties that status presumed, including military service in the French rather than the colonial army. The administration replied that no Muslim could be naturalized and recognized only their voting rights. When the chamber of deputies began to consider colonial recruitment, however, Diagne successfully maneuvered through two motions in 1915 and 1916, tying conscription in the Four Communes of Senegal to the recognition of the *originaires'* citizenship. If Africans like himself could legislate in parliament, he argued, they could serve in the same ranks as metropolitan soldiers; and if they could do both, their citizenship had to be recognized. Confronted with the irrefutable logic of France's past assimilationism, the majority of the House enthusiastically concurred.

Three years later, as the French's heavy-handed conscription of soldiers throughout their West African federation led to widespread revolts, Diagne saw a second opportunity to advance his own career and protect the interests of not just the *originaires* of Senegal but all French West Africans. Astute enough to realize that recruitment would occur again in 1918, with or without his cooperation, Diagne struck a hard bargain with Clemenceau. If the latter would name him high commissioner of the republic, with equivalent rank to that of governor-general, and exchange use of force for concrete material incentives for volunteers and conscripts, with the promise of more to come after the war, Diagne would lead the recruitment effort.[70] Historians to date have confirmed Diagne's account of events: force was kept to a minimum and the Africans signed up voluntarily in record numbers.[71] What Diagne did not emphasize was the degree to which his success was linked not just to the promise of future rewards, but to the dramatic impression his "body politics" made. While on tour, Diagne made the most of his rank and uniform, insisting on deference from whites his junior, moving comfortably among his white peers, and saving his handshakes for blacks exclusively. In the words of the Senegalese historian Iba der Thiam, these actions "resonated like a terrible clap of thunder, which was remembered at the time, and which is still proudly remembered today."[72]

Remembered proudly by some, Diagne's participation in recruitment was nevertheless soon denigrated by others—including Maran, of course, in the pages of *Les Continents*—as craven collaboration. This charge, however, tells us more about Maran's newly racialized consciousness in the early 1920s than about Diagne's actual motives in the final year of the war. Although Maran cast Diagne as a *Judas noir*, betraying the republic and his race simultaneously, he can be better understood then and later as a Senegalese and French politician in equal measure. As a politician, Diagne knew that he represented local interests, not a mythic black unity. His nation was both republican France and Senegal, that entity mapped out and controlled by the French, yet dependent on Africans for its day-to-day administration and *mise en valeur*. The challenge was leveraging the maximum number of concessions for Senegal from this very relative position of strength in order to achieve home rule within the French empire as quickly as possible. For Diagne, this meant political equality for all Senegalese within greater France, not autonomy—hence his initial demand for both military service and citizenship for the *originaires*. But it could also mean agreeing to work with the French in exchange for a minimum of influence over policy when continuing to fight them promised to yield nothing at all—hence his willingness in 1918 to become *haut commissaire*.[73]

If Diagne's wartime actions suggested a modern national leader in the making, his postwar trajectory marked another step in this direction. This same trajectory also helps explain why it was that Diagne finally bothered to answer, in 1924, what had apparently become a routine attack on his character by more radicalized blacks in Paris, and why his chosen forum was a trial in the *cours d'assises*. By 1919, Diagne had certainly won himself a coveted place in the limelight in Senegal, in West Africa, and in the metropole. He had emerged, arguably, as the most famous man of color in Europe and thus seemed ideally poised to lead the international movement against colonial oppression shaping up in the 1920s. And, briefly, Diagne appeared to assume this mantle, presiding over the Pan-African congresses held in Paris in 1919 and 1921. Diagne's real energies during these years, however, were directed less at liberating Africa in this forum than at pursuing a single policy of continued assimilation in Paris and Senegal. On the one hand, he broke with Du Bois at the second Pan-African congress, when he rejected the latter's call for African independence in favor of continued European rule.[74] On the other hand, he fought bitterly and protractedly in Dakar and in the corridors of the colonial ministry for a further extension of French citizenship in Senegal, this time to the colony's rural inhabitants. He also demanded equal pay for equal work and that the other colonies of the federation be granted deputies.

Yet the strategy that had worked in the first flush of wartime mobilization would prove disappointingly ineffective in the lean years of postwar reconstruction, when the image of Africa — and France's role there — was changing rapidly. In France, the emergence of the stereotype of the *bon sauvage* and the growth of a more scientific appreciation of African culture had repercussions not only for Maran. These same developments also implicitly marked an ideological shift away from the very assimilation that Diagne was seeking now to expand in rural Senegal in favor of a more limited policy of associating Africans in policy making.[75] As problematic for Diagne, too — albeit for different reasons than for Maran — was the increasing stature of the Africanist Maurice Delafosse in French colonial circles generally. For health reasons, Delafosse by 1919 had left West Africa for good, and both he and his ideas seemed to be everywhere in Paris where Africa was discussed in the early 1920s. Professor at the French colonial school, publicist in the colonial press, internationally recognized Africanist and founder, with Lucien Lévy-Bruhl, Paul Rivet, and Marcel Mauss, of the new Institut d'Ethnologie at the University of Paris, he spent the final years of his life synthesizing his years of African research into a series of more popular volumes that celebrated the need to respect the continent's fundamentally different civilizations.

Given his public visibility, his relativist message, and his strong ties to the colonial administration, Delafosse represented yet another challenge to Diagne and his hopes for more, not less, assimilation. Diagne and Delafosse had already crossed swords in Dakar in 1918, when Delafosse had been one of those who bitterly resisted the final recruiting drive — not, he claimed, because it was led by Diagne, but because Africa had no more to give.[76] The rivalry would continue after the war, as both men jockeyed for the ear of the colonial ministry and for the hearts and minds of the larger French public. A fleeting glimpse of their competing claims and stances is evident in the press coverage of the second Pan-African congress. Thanks to Diagne's presence, the final resolution contained both a recommendation for the betterment of the *race nègre* through massive colonial investment and collaboration and mutual respect between the races, and a ringing endorsement of France's colonial policy to date. Diagne published two editorials in the leading colonial mouthpiece, the *Dépêche Coloniale et Maritime*, within a month after the congress's close. Their purpose was to reassure readers that it was only the "detractors of *la race noire*" who believed that separatism was spreading "its sedition" worldwide, thereby putting French Africa at risk. Such insulting insinuations betrayed a profound ignorance of conditions in Africa and — although Diagne did not say this, it was clearly implied — of his own statesmanship and that of other black elites at the congress in steering delegates to rational and moderate conclusions.[77] In both articles he reaffirmed his loyalty to France and also asserted his unique ability as an African to understand the continent's current evolution.

No sooner had Diagne published these pieces than Delafosse followed up with one of his own, entitled "An Impartial Appreciation of the *Pan-Noir* Congress." Delafosse's was one of two noteworthy articles in the colonial press commenting on the gathering and seeking to reassure its readers about its outcome. Delafosse essentially repeated Diagne's conclusions and then added that the program adopted by the congress was virtually the same one he himself had been recommending for the past thirty years.[78] The second article, by Henri Charpin in the indigenophile *La Revue Indigène*, also applauded Diagne's leadership in denouncing Marcus Garvey, but admonished him that he had not fully understood the real motives behind the slogan "Africa for the Africans": American imperialist designs on Africa. This article ended with an appeal to the minister of the colonies for vigilance and firmness, and for perspicacity on the part of the black deputies who were the living witnesses of the humane liberalism of France's colonial policy.[79]

Also actively involved in the French empire, neither Delafosse nor Charpin unambiguously claimed Diagne as one of their own—despite his exemplary patriotism in endorsing French colonialism in Africa before an international audience. Delafosse implied that Diagne could not bring the impartial gaze to bear on things African that white colonial science could and that Diagne had not said anything at the congress that far-sighted Frenchmen like Delafosse had not already said before him. Charpin likewise asserted his superior analytical skill and bracketed Diagne and Candace off as reflections, not makers or enforcers, of French liberal values. Taken together, these articles subtly undermined the credibility of Diagne as the new spokesman for Africa, while Diagne's original piece had insisted in turn on his unique ability to understand what was happening on the continent. This reflected, of course, the view of the colonial press, and so it should perhaps not surprise us to see French officials, not Diagne, having the last word on Pan-Africanism. But that Diagne had taken the trouble to write in the pages of the leading colonial journal suggests how threatened he felt by this new representation of Africa taking shape in Delafosse's hands, and how crowded the field of those speaking for Africa had become since 1916.

If at least some segments of metropolitan opinion now appeared to respond to Diagne's die-hard republican patriotism with an alternative Africanism of their own, what was the situation in Senegal? Here even more than in Paris, Diagne would find his assimilationism thwarted at every turn, compared to the war years. The local administration continued to consider itself, not the deputy, the more appropriate spokesman for the majority of Senegalese. Most of the colony's inhabitants were peasants and thus absolutely unready in the eyes of French officials for the rights Diagne and his party demanded. Assimilation of any kind, moreover, threatened to destroy governance on the cheap in the countryside, where conservative chiefs had long worked with the French to deliver the labor, taxes, and lucrative flow of peanuts necessary to keep the budget afloat—in exchange for a certain amount of autonomy. This alliance was all the more valuable once it became clear that the colonies could not expect any new investment from the metropole; in the postwar era of inflation, reconstruction, and massive debt, it was the empire which was to jump-start the metropolitan economy by massively increasing its yield. Confronted with the deputy's challenge to substitute messy and unpredictable democratic politics for those of accommodationist chiefs, the local French administration and Bordeaux trading houses worked together — this time with approval from Paris — to hit Diagne where it hurt: they systematically denied employment, loans, and promotions to any Diagnist client, while offering lucrative deals to their own traditional allies.[80]

Given the capital resources at the disposal of the local administration, along with the new metropolitan discourse insisting on respect for African cultures, the French strategy to contain "Diagnism" worked. Worried that his key Lebu constituency's support was wavering, and with elections fast approaching, Diagne chose once again the lesser of two evils. In 1923 he made his peace first with the Bordeaux houses and then with the government general of French West Africa. Yet, as in 1918, the shift was more tactical than substantive. Diagne had not abandoned his goal of Senegalese home rule within greater France. But he would now pursue it by working with, not against, the powerful trading interests and the colonial administration for the rational development of the colony — in exchange for a role in the process. To borrow a phrase from James Searing, the political kingdom — in the form of immediate citizenship for all Senegalese — was deferred but not abandoned, and the future nation's export economy attended to instead.

Diagne's policy reorientation, and the stir it caused in Senegal, go a long way toward explaining why it was in 1924 that Diagne chose to challenge Maran and *Les Continents*. What to Diagne might have looked like the best possible deal given the circumstances, to others clearly smacked of, at best, realpolitik, at worst, opportunism. In May 1924, six months before the alleged libel, Diagne did win reelection to parliament on his new platform; nevertheless, a more radical group espousing Diagne's old war cry — full political rights for all Africans, equal pay for equal work now — had already emerged to challenge the Bordeaux pact.[81] Accused of duplicity not only in Paris but also — and this was new — by his supporters at home, Diagne surely saw the trial as an opportunity to answer all his critics in one blow. Like his stunning tour of West Africa six years earlier, it was political performance at the highest level. The *cour d'assises* guaranteed Diagne a popular audience, full press coverage, and a venue that would show off his masterful oratory to its full advantage. By displaying his powerful connections in Paris, but all the time emphasizing how he had used the needs of the French to promote the interests of all Africans, Diagne reassured those wavering in the Four Communes that he alone among his rivals had the ear—and therefore the influence and access to the resources—of the French. The message for whites as well as the misguided Maran was astutely staged in equal measure: Africans were not all like Batouala, and therefore they should continue to be assimilated. What greater proof of the universality of French civilization than the cultured deputy from Senegal standing before them defending once again their common *patrie*?[82]

Even this thumbnail sketch of our two protagonists suggests an obvious explanation for why Diagne and Maran ended up on opposite sides of a courtroom in 1924. Neither of them questioned his own Frenchness or the right of the French to be in Africa, thanks in part to the extent to which each had profited personally from the nation's (fitfully applied) tradition of color blindness. And both sought to bridge the gap, as they saw it, between the tolerant and truly equal France of the capital, where they lived in the early 1920s, and the France that existed in West and Equatorial Africa, where subjecthood, not citizenship, was the norm, and where a colonial administration fought tooth and nail against the assimilation of any man of color.

But for all their real affinities, their relationships to France, the empire, and Africa in particular were clearly different. As a former administrator turned writer and activist, Maran was responsible only to his own standards of creativity and his conscience. As a displaced French Caribbean, he also yearned for a "home" in Africa, and an identity in Pan-Africanism. His knowledge of Africa, however, was limited to his years there as an official representative of the French *mission civilisatrice*, and it is within the confines of this ideology and its changing image of Africa that he thought and acted as he became politicized in the 1920s. Maran, for example, never questioned that despite having helped to corrupt Africans— especially through wartime recruitment—the French were still the most qualified to lead them to emancipation, principally through education, protection from arbitrary treatment, and civil equality. All true republicans would embrace this stance, and black republicans doubly so.

Diagne viewed matters differently. As an elected representative, the deputy, not surprisingly, had always thought about Senegal's future, and that of Africa in general, in concrete political terms rather than abstract universal ones. For him, the issue was less what the French should be doing to "help" Africans than the kind of deal Africans themselves could cut with the administration to secure tangible concessions in a colonial context. From this perspective, paying the blood tax up front in 1918 and cooperating with the Bordeaux merchants in 1923 had gained the Senegalese critical leverage with the French — and thus constituted eminently justifiable policies. Many of Diagne's constituents apparently agreed with this strategy, since he won such enthusiastic backing after the war, and then again as late as 1923. Maran, however, never even considered the possibility that Diagne truly spoke for any Senegalese. He saw the deputy as a French imperialist who — to borrow a phrase from Du Bois at the time — was "accidentally black," because authentic Africans did not collaborate with the colonizer.[83]

"It is easy to see how history can make you, on the one hand, say, a citizen of Ivory Coast or of Botswana; or on the other hand, say, anglophone or francophone. But what, given all the diversity of the precolonial histories of the peoples of Africa, all the complexities of colonial experience, does it mean to say that someone is African?" so writes the contemporary philosopher Kwame Anthony Appiah — himself of mixed Asante-English heritage, raised in Ghana and now teaching at Princeton.[84] Appiah goes on to point out that to speak of an African identity in the nineteenth century would have been "to give to aery nothing a local habitation and a name."[85] Yet he has no doubt "that now, a century later, an African identity is coming into being" and that it, too, is "a product of history." Appiah sees Du Bois and Senghor as critical players in that history — two men who chose to celebrate Africa rather than give in to its negative stereotypes, but who in the process encouraged the racist notion of an immutable African essence. The case of Maran versus Diagne suggests that the genealogy of an African identity in France is more complex than Appiah allows, and it cautions us not to assume that any African identity forged in the West in the twentieth century is hegemonic, least of all for Africans themselves.

Notes

Earlier versions of this essay were presented at Yale University, Cornell University, and SUNY Binghamton, as well as at meetings of the African Studies Association and the Society for French Historical Studies. I would like to thank the audiences for their stimulating questions and feedback. I am particularly grateful to Christopher Miller, who first brought the trial to my attention, and to Owen White for his close reading of this article. Additional thanks to Robert Nassau, Vicki Caron, Stephen Kaplan, Howard Brown, and Sue Peabody for their critical comments and suggestions.

A word about nomenclature in what follows: in the early 1920s in France, the terms *nègre* and *noir* often appear interchangeably in the black press and those who sympathized with it. *Nègre* in particular seemed not yet to have a fixed connotation. Although white racists in the colonies used the term pejoratively, liberals such as Delafosse, or even Blaise Diagne, readily adopted it as well with no slur intended. In what follows I have reproduced the French term *nègre* where appropriate; otherwise I use the English term *black* to designate the people of African descent whom I discuss.

1   *Les Continents* was founded in June 1924 by the Dahomeyan Kojo Tovalou Houénou Quenum, a French citizen who had organized earlier that same year the Ligue Universelle pour la Défense de la Race Noire (LUDRN). Maran was closely associated with Kojo Tovalou in both enterprises, as were a small number of other Caribbeans and Africans who found themselves in Paris in these years. The ephemeral *Les Continents* and LUDRN (of which *Les Continents* was the organ) were among the first of a number of publications and organizations that promoted the interests of blacks in France in the 1920s. The general line of *Les Continents* was reformist: it hoped that France, particularly under the leadership of Daladier's new Bloc des Gauches, would see the error of its ways and correct colonial abuses. For the history of *Les Continents*, see in particular Philippe Dewitte, *Les mouvements nègres en France, 1919–1939* (Paris: Editions L'Harmattan, 1985), 74–93; J. S. Spiegler, "Aspects of Nationalist Thought among French-Speaking West Africans, 1921–1939" (Ph.D. diss., Oxford University, 1968), chaps. 3 and 4; and J. Ayodele Langley, *Pan-Africanism and Nationalism in West Africa, 1900–1945: A Study in Ideology and Social Classes* (Oxford: Clarendon, 1973), 287–98.

2   Tovalou left Paris in August 1924 to address Marcus Garvey's International Convention of the Negro Peoples of the World in New York as guest of honor. He subsequently toured the United States and then moved back to West Africa in early 1925. According to Spiegler,

articles by Maran dominated *Les Continents'* pages after Tovalou's departure. Spiegler, "Aspects of Nationalist Thought," 74–76.

3 René Maran, *Batouala: Véritable roman nègre* (Paris: A. Michel, 1921).

4 Two notable exceptions were *L'Humanité* (communist) and *Le Canard Enchaîné* (anti-imperial); the latter ran several articles in 1923 exposing the truth about forcible recruitment in West Africa during World War I. Allen Douglas, "Between Racism and Antimilitarism: The *Canard Enchaîné* and France's Colonial Wars of the 1920s," in *Franco-Arab Encounters: Studies in Memory of David C. Gordon*, ed. L. Carl Brown and Matthew S. Gordon (Beirut: American University of Beirut, 1996), 73. *L'Humanité*, 24 and 25 November 1924; *Le Canard Enchaîné*, 26 November 1924. The latter in particular mocked the whole event, asking sarcastically how anyone could doubt French colonial methods or that French subjects in the colonies did not joyously welcome the opportunity to die under French colors.

5 For discussions of this movement, see in addition to Spiegler, "Aspects of Nationalist Thought," Dewitte, *Mouvements nègres*; Langley, *Pan-Africanism*; Claude Liauzu, *Aux origines des tiers-mondismes: Colonisés et anticolonialistes en France, 1919–1935* (Paris: L'Harmattan, 1982); Mar Fall, *Des tirailleurs sénégalais aux . . . blacks: Les Africains noirs en France* (Paris: L'Harmattan, 1986); and Christopher L. Miller, *Nomads and Nationalists: Essays on Francophone African Literature and Culture* (Chicago: University of Chicago Press, 1998), chaps. 1 and 2.

6 See especially Langley, *Pan-Africanism*, 296–300; also Spiegler, "Aspects of Nationalist Thought," 89–90; Dewitte, *Mouvements nègres*, 89–93; as well as N.-S. Russel, "M. Diagne prosecutes *Les Continents*," *Les Continents*, 15 November–1 December 1924, 3.

7 *La Dépêche Coloniale et Maritime*, 26 November 1924. The following account of the trial is based on newspaper reports. The original transcript of the trial, including the *dossier de procédure* and the *débats de l'audience*, burned in a 1974 fire at the archives of the ministry of justice. The ministry of colonies' file on *Les Continents* (ANSOM, SLOTFOM III/dossier 101 [in Aix-en-Provence]) discusses the trial only very briefly. The *arrêt* of the *cour d'assises* can be consulted at the Archives de la Ville de Paris, D1 U8 164. This and all unmarked translations are mine.

8 *Le Quotidien*, 25 November 1924; *Action Française*, 24 November 1924; *La Dépêche Coloniale et Maritime*, 26 November 1924.

9 *La Dépêche Coloniale et Maritime*, 25 November 1924.

10 *Le Petit Parisien*, 25 November 1924.

11 *Les Annales Coloniales*, 25 November 1924.

12 *Le Petit Parisien*, 25 November 1924.

13 *L'Homme Libre*, 24 November 1924.

14 The legislation organizing the recruitment authorized Diagne to make these promises. See "Arrêté promulguant en AOF les décrets du 14 janvier 1918," *Journal Officiel de l'AOF* (1918): 51–52.

15 According to Langley, *Les Continents* was widely circulated in the port cities of Dahomey and appeared elsewhere in West Africa. Langley, *Pan-Africanism*, 294. Articles in *Les Continents* that complained about the colonial administration's illegal banning of the journal also suggest that it did reach West Africa. See, for example, *Les Continents*, 15 July 1924, 1; and 1 November 1924, 3.

16 *Le Petit Parisien*, 25 November 1924; *Le Quotidien*, 25 November 1924.

17 For the criminal side, the state, which was prosecuting the case, was represented by the attorney general, Maître Béguin.

18 The charge of bolshevism was unfounded. Although the defendants called on two communist deputies to testify on their behalf, Maran and his collaborators at *Les Continents* had always distanced themselves from "le péril bolchévique." The government's surveillance files on the newspaper concurred ("Note sur la propagande révolutionnaire intéressant les pays d'outre-mer," 31 May 1924, ANSOM/ SLOTFOM III/dossier 101 [in Aix-en-Provence]). Links between the pan-negro movement and the French Communist Party (PCF) would develop in the mid-1920s, although Maran never changed his hostile views. Spiegler, "Aspects of Nationalist Thought," 26, chap. 4.

19 *Le Quotidien*, 25 November 1924; *Le Journal des Débats*, 26 November 1924.

20 *Le Journal des Débats*, 25 November 1924.

21 Prime minister Poincaré in 1923 reiterated publicly that France was officially color-blind after several racist incidents that summer in Paris involving American tourists and French Africans. On two separate occasions, Americans refused to be seated next to Africans in public places; the second incident involved Kojo Tovalou and led to his founding the LUDRN. Diagne personally interpellated Poincaré on the subject, and the ministry of foreign affairs released a statement warning foreign tourists that they must respect France's customs on this point. *West Africa* 340, 2 (1923): 889. Diagne and Poincaré's exchange of letters can be found in *La Dépêche Coloniale et Maritime* 29 June 1923 and 19–20 August 1923. See also Tyler Stovall, "Colour-Blind France? Colonial Workers during the First World War," *Race and Class* 35, 2 (1993): 33–55.

22 *Le Quotidien*, 25 November 1924; see also *Le Journal des Débats*, 26 November 1924; and *Action Française*, 25 November 1924.

23 *Les Annales Coloniales*, 27 November 1924.

24 N.-S. Russell, "M. Diagne Prosecutes 'Les Continents': Maranism versus Diagnism," *Les Continents*, 15 November–1 December 1924, 3. This accusation was true. In his testimony, Jean Fangeat cited equally defamatory passages that had appeared in the 5 February 1924 edition of *Cri de Paris* and *L'Internationale*; see report of trial in *Les Continents*, 15 November–1 December 1924, 1. Other newspapers also pointed out that these charges were not new. *L'Humanité*, 26 November 1924; *La Dépêche Coloniale et Maritime*, 27 November 1924; and *Action Française*, 26 November 1924. Finally, articles hostile to Diagne had appeared in *Les Continents* from the very beginning. See, for example, "Simple Histoire," *Les Continents*, 15 June 1924, 1; and "La case de l'Oncle Tom," *Les Continents*, 15 June 1924, 2.

25 *Le Temps*, 25 November 1924.

26 *Le Petit Parisien*, 25 November 1924.

27 *Les Continents*, 15 November, 1; 1 December 1924, 1; *Les Annales Coloniales*, 25 November 1924. Inhabitants of the Four Communes were French citizens and thus served under the same conditions as metropolitan soldiers. African subjects in the rest of French West Africa served in the colonial troops as *tirailleurs sénégalais*.

28 *Le Quotidien*, 25 November 1924.

29 Colonel Mangin, a colonial military officer who had served under Archinard in the conquest of the western Sudan, was the driving force behind the creation in 1912 of an African army which could supplement French forces on the battlefields of Europe. *L'Humanité*, 25 November 1924; *Les Annales Coloniales*, 25 November 1924.

30 *L'Homme Libre*, 24 November 1924; *Le Quotidien*, 25 November 1924; see also *Action Française*, 25 November 1924.

31 *Le Petit Parisien*, 25 November 1924; see also *L'Eclair*, 25 November 1924. *Les Continents* had been crusading against the excessive powers of French administrators since its founding. It particularly condemned the exceptional penal code, which applied only to colonial *sujets*, known as the *indigénat*. "La justice à Madagascar," and "La réelection de M. Diagne," *Les Continents*, 15 May 1924, 1 and 3, respectively; "Lettre ouverte au professeur Alain-Leroy Locke," *Les Continents*, 15 June 1924, 1.

32 "Lettre ouverte au professeur Alain-Leroy Locke," *Les Continents*, 1. This was not the first time Maran's earlier conviction had been publicly aired. In the wake of the scandal over *Batouala* winning the Goncourt Prize, the reformist journal *La Revue Indigène* had published the transcript of judgment from 1919 as part of its campaign to discredit the book and its author. See Jean de Lacave, "Chronique des livres," *La Revue Indigène*, July–August 1922, 142–44.

33 *Action Francaise*, 25 November 1924.

34 *Le Petit Parisien*, 25 November 1924. Maran provided a detailed account of these events in his article "Ma condamnation," *Les Continents*, 15 December 1924, 2. According to Maran, it was the gross miscarriage of justice that this case represented that led him to write his polemical preface in *Batouala*.

35 For Delmont's final summation, see *Le Quotidien*, 26 November 1924; *La Dépêche Coloniale et Maritime*, 27 November 1924; and *Annales Coloniales*, 26 November 1924.

36 *Annales Coloniales*, 26 November 1924.

37 *Dépêche Coloniale et Maritime*, 25 November 1924.

38 There is now an extensive literature on Maran. For biographical details, I have relied on Marc Michel, "L'affaire Batouala: René Maran, écrivain anticolonialiste ou écrivain de l'ambiguité?" in *Identités Caraïbes: Actes du 123e congrès des sociétés historiques et scientifiques, section d'histoire moderne et contemporaine, 6–10 avril 1998, Antilles-Guyane*, ed. Pierre Guillaume (Paris, 2001), 77–94; Keith Cameron, *René Maran* (Boston: Twayne, 1985); Femi Ojo-Ade, *René Maran, the Black Frenchman: A Bio-Critical Study* (Washington, D.C.: Three Continents, 1984); John Alfred Dennis, "The René Maran Story: The Life and Times of a Black Frenchman, Colonial Administrator, Novelist, and Social Critic" (Ph.D. diss., Stanford University, 1986); and Eugen Aaron Eaves, "René Maran in Africa: Reflections on the French Colonial Experience" (Ph.D. diss., University of Connecticut, 1977). Also see Jean Marie Abanda-Ndengue, "René Maran et l'Afrique Noire: Colonisateur et humaniste" (Ph.D. diss., Université de Lille, 1984); and *Hommage à René Maran* (Paris: Présence africaine, 1965).

39 René Maran, *La maison du bonheur* (Paris, 1909), and Maran, *La vie intérieure* (Paris: Le Beffroi, 1912).

40 "You build your kingdom on corpses. Whatever you want, whatever you do, you are entrenched in falsehoods. At the mere sight of you, tears well up in people's eyes and they cry out in agony. . . . You are not a candle that lights the flame of knowledge, but a torch that starts a conflagration. You destroy whatever you touch." René Maran, preface to *Batouala*, 11.

41 William B. Cohen, *Rulers of Empire: The French Colonial Service in Africa* (Stanford, Calif.: Hoover Institution Press, 1971), 46; Phyllis M. Martin, "The Violence of Empire," and Ralph Austen and Rita Headrick, "Equatorial Africa under Colonial Rule," both in *History of Central Africa*, vol. 2, *The Colonial Era (1870–1960)* (London: Longman, 1983), 1–26 and 27–94, respectively.

42 André Gide, *Voyage au Congo, suivi de Le retour du Tchad: Carnets de route* (Paris: Gallimard, 1928); Albert Londres, *Terre d'ébène* (Paris: A. Michel, 1929).

43 Michel, "L'affaire Batouala." How common such discrimination was is still unclear. Several hundred Caribbeans served in the French administration in sub-Saharan Africa from 1880 to 1939, but their history remains to be written. For background on these men, see Véronique Hénélon, "Les administrateurs originaires de Guadeloupe, Martinique et Guyane dans les colonies d'Afrique, 1880–1939" (Ph.D. diss., Ecole des Hautes Etudes en Sciences Sociales, Paris, 1997).

44 According to Maran, from January to June 1918, he was given the impossible task of keeping in line hostile, starving, and overworked porters forcibly recruited to carry provisions for the *ravitaillement* effort during the war. Faced with desertion, Maran requested help from his superior, a certain administrator named Bonneveaux. The latter not only refused, but according to Maran, told the Africans under Maran that they did not have to obey him because he was "a negro like them." Deprived of the reinforcements he needed, Maran's white subordinate resorted to beatings. When he was caught, Maran covered for him, went to trial, and was found guilty of "excessive violence against a native." According to Maran, the whole trial was orchestrated by Bonneveaux and was racially motivated. See Maran, "Ma condamnation," 1. Maran was still haunted by the incident as late as 1952. René Maran to André Fraisse, 21 December 1952, ANSOM, 26PA/carton 4/dossier 20 (Aix-en-Provence). For a fuller account of this incident and Maran's relations with his superiors, see Michel, "L'affaire Batouala."

45 Eleni Coundouriotis, *Claiming History: Colonialism, Ethnography, and the Novel* (New York: Columbia University Press, 1998), 21–36; and Ojo-Ade, *René Maran*, chaps. 4–6.

46 Alice Jean Smith, "René Maran's Vision of Africa" (Ph.D. diss., University of Massachusetts, 1978).

47 János Riesz, "Littérature francophone d'Afrique noire: Problèmes d'authenticité et de légitimation," *Französisch Heute* 7, 4 (1985): 278–89; Michel Fabre, "René Maran: Critique de la littérature africaine francophone," *Afrique littéraire et artistique*, 50, 4 (1978): 30–35; see also Léopold Senghor, "René Maran: Précurseur de la négritude," in *Hommage à René Maran*, 9–13; and Abiola Irele, *The African Experience in Literature and Ideology* (Bloomington: Indiana University Press, 1990), 132.

48 Coundouriotis, *Claiming History*, introduction and chap. 1; Hans-Jurgen Lüsebrink, "*Batouala, véritable roman nègre*: La place de René Maran dans la littérature mondiale des années vingt," in *Semper aliquid novi: Littérature comparée et littératures d'Afrique. Mélanges offerts à Albert Gérard*, ed. János Riesz and Alain Ricard (Tübingen: Narr, 1990), 145–53; Iheanachor Egonu, "Le Prix Gon-

court et la 'Querelle Batouala,'" *Research in African Literatures* 2, 4 (1980): 527–45. As part of this reassessment, it is now recognized that the first novel written in French by an African is Ahmadou Mapaté Diagne's *Les trois volontés de Malic* (Paris, 1920).

49 On changing stereotypes after the war, see Dana Hale, "Races on Display: French Representation of the Colonial Native, 1886–1931" (Ph.D. diss., Brandeis University, 1998), chap. 5, and Joe Lunn, *Memoirs of the Maelstrom: A Senegalese Oral History of the First World War* (Portsmouth, N.H.: Heinemann, 1999), chap. 6.

50 This positive reception is discussed briefly by Egonu, "Le Prix Goncourt," 529–31; Dennis, "The René Maran Story," 132–36; Cameron, *René Maran*, 14–16, and Brett Berliner, "The 'Exotic' Black African in the French Social Imagination in the 1920s" (Ph.D. diss., University of Massachusetts, 1999), 102–3. The book was also well received by the colonial press in England and the New Negro movement in America; see *West Africa* 258, 8 (1922): 1661–62; "More about René Maran," *Opportunity* 1, 1 (1923): 30–31; and Alain Locke, "The Colonial Literature of France," *Opportunity* 1, 11 (1923): 331–35.

51 Critics did not just point to other novels. They were inspired to write new works (fiction and nonfiction) that directly contested Maran's vision of Africa by positing a more "authentic" one. The best-known of these were Gaston Joseph's *Koffi, Roman vrai d'un noir* (Paris: Aux editions du Monde nouveau, 1922), J. Blache, *Vrais noirs et vrais blancs d'Afrique au vingtième siècle* (Orleans: Caillette, 1922), and Réné Trautmann, *Au pays de "Batouala": Noirs et blancs en Afrique* (Paris: Payot, 1922). A spate of articles appeared in *Annales Coloniales* under the title "A l'envers de Batouala," signed by "Massamba, boy congolais," who also supposedly represented the views of an authentic African regarding the French and who did not recognize himself in the natives depicted in *Batouala*. See *Annales Coloniales*, 27–28 April, 2–5 May, 8–12 May, and 15–16 May 1922.

52 Maurice Delafosse, "Une oeuvre de haine: 'Batouala,' ou La calomnie," *La Dépêche Coloniale et Maritime*, 26–27 December 1921.

53 Maurice Delafosse, *Broussard, ou Les états d'âme d'un colonial, suivi de ses propos et opinions* (Paris: E. Larose, 1923), 170–74. Delafosse conceded that perhaps his *boys*, as house servants were called, might speak this way, thus underlining his point that "authentic" Africans did not. As János Riesz has pointed out, the quest for authenticity by a wide variety of actors is one of the fascinating themes of this period; see Riesz, "Littérature francophone." As more and more blacks contested colonial rule—Maran, nationalists in Senegal, radicals in Paris—the colonial administration responded by seeking Africans "of their own," whose voices they claimed were the

"most authentic." Africans in the elite French schools, for example, were encouraged to do the ethnography of their own cultures; see on this point François Manchuelle, "Assimilés ou patriotes africains? Naissance du nationalisme culturel en Afrique (1853–1931)," *Cahiers d'Etudes Africaines* 35, 2–3 (1995): 333–68. Looking ahead, the colonial humanists G. Hardy and H. Labouret sought to involve Africans in their new journal *Outre-Mer*, dedicated to colonial ethnology; see Anne Pirou, "Indigénisme, et changement social: Le cas de la revue *Outre-Mer* (1929–1937)," in *L'Africanisme en questions*, ed. Anne Pirou and Emmanuelle Sibeud (Paris: Centre d'etudes africaines, Ecole des hautes etudes en sciences sociales, 1997), 43–70. For more details on the Batouala scandal, which has been much discussed, see Egonu, "Le Prix Goncourt"; Lüsebrink, "Batouala"; Dennis, "The René Maran Story," 136–53; and Berliner, "The 'Black' Exotic," chap. 3.

54 Maurice Delafosse, preface to *Le question des noirs aux États-Unis*, by F. L. Schoell (Paris: Payot, 1923).

55 On Delafosse's career in Africa, see Jean-Loup Amselle and Emmanuelle Sibeud, eds., *Maurice Delafosse: Entre orientalisme et ethnographie, l'itinéraire d'un africaniste, 1870–1926* (Paris: Maisonneuve et Larose, 1998). His ideas on colonization can best be gleaned by reading through his regular columns in the *Dépêche Coloniale et Maritime* from the end of World War I to his premature death in 1926.

56 Coundouriotis, *Claiming History*, 26.

57 Maran's activities and financial worries in these years are well documented in his correspondence with Alain Locke, held in the Moorland Springarn Research Center, Howard University, Washington, D.C.

58 "Paris, capitale des pan-noirs: Ce qu'en pensent MM. Maran et Diagne," *Eclair*, 15 October 1924. This newspaper article referred to Diagne and Maran as the two most visible black men in Paris, and it is clear from other accounts as well that Diagne and Maran moved in overlapping circles. Diagne was good friends with two of the deputies from Guadeloupe and Martinique, Gratien Candace and René Boisneuf; Félix Eboué, a colonial administrator from Guyana, who had been in school with Maran in Bordeaux and remained his close friend, was one link between the world of black deputies and that of the emerging black culturalists. On these connections, see François Manchuelle, "Le rôle des Antillais dans l'apparition du nationalisme culturel en Afrique noire," *Cahiers d'Etudes Africaines* 127, 32–3 (1992): 375–408; John Gaffar LaGuerre, *Enemies of Empire* (St. Augustine, Trinidad: University of the West Indies, 1984), 46–52; Brian Weinstein, *Eboué* (New York: Oxford University Press, 1972).

59 Weinstein, *Eboué*, 80–81, 107; René Maran to Alain Locke, 18 October 1924, Alain Locke Papers, Moorland Springarn Research Center, Howard University, Washington, D.C. Also the letters from Maran to Locke dated 13 October 1926; 1 November 1926; 21 November 1926; 19 April 1927; 7 November 1927; and 23 October 1928.

60 Determining when francophone Africans, as well as Caribbeans with an interest in Africa, began calling for African independence has long interested historians. James Spiegler's dissertation remains the most detailed account of African nationalists in Paris, and he argues that by 1927 a consensus had emerged among the various pan-negro movements that the goal was now political independence. Dewitte argues that radicals in the Union Intercoloniale embraced the idea as early as 1924, under pressure from the Communist Party. Dewitte, *Mouvements nègres*, 104–5. In Africa, in contrast, even the most politically active groups of coastal Senegal and urban Dahomey were not claiming independence in this period. This was due in part to the fact that colonial officials in Africa tried to keep "subversive" journals from circulating there, and in part to the fact that local elites simply had different agendas than many African radicals who found themselves in France, as I shall show in the following.

61 *Eclair*, 15 October 1924.

62 It is interesting to note that criticism of wartime recruitment was one of the dominant themes of Maran's contributions to *Les Continents*. Maran had personally witnessed — indeed participated in — the brutalities associated with wartime recruitment. As a man, he wrote, he understood why Africans rebelled during the war. As a colonial official, he had no choice but to follow orders: "The colonial functionary is not a man. He must silence his heart, and, even when he has had enough, despite everything execute the orders that he has received, because he is paid to do his job of warder [*garde chiourme*], even when it offends his soul and conscience, when he has one." "Ma condamnation," 1. His bad conscience about his own role in perpetuating atrocities perhaps explains the intensity of his antipathy toward Diagne.

63 This is the major conclusion of Alice Smith's dissertation, "René Maran's Vision of Africa." Régis Antoine draws a similar conclusion in his *La littérature franco-antillaise: Haiti, Guadeloupe et Martinique* (Paris: Karthala, 1992), 154–65.

64 Dewitte, *Mouvements nègres*, 79–80.

65 Weinstein, *Eboué*, 70, 120; René Maran to Alain Locke, 23 October 1928, and Maran to Locke, 8 April 1929, Alain Locke Papers, Moorland Springarn Research Center, Howard University, Washington, D.C.

66 René Maran, "Légendes et coutumes nègres de l'Oubangui-Chari," *Les oeuvres libres* 147 (1933): 326. Maran accused Delafosse, among other "specialists," of being too "européenomorphique" — by which he meant they did not sufficiently attempt to "identity with a primitive mentality" [créer une mentalité primitive] so that they could truly penetrate "native life." Ibid., 326–27.

67 For biographical details on Blaise Diagne and his political career generally, see James F. Searing, "Accommodation and Resistance: Chiefs, Muslim Leaders, and Politicians in Colonial Senegal, 1890–1934" (Ph.D. diss., Princeton University, 1985); François Zuccarelli, *La vie politique sénégalaise* (Paris: CHEAM, 1987); G. Wesley Johnson, *The Emergence of Black Politics in Senegal: The Struggle for Power in the Four Communes, 1900–1920* (Stanford, Calif.: Stanford University Press, 1971); Amady Aly Dieng, *Blaise Diagne: Député noir de l'Afrique* (Paris: Editions Chaka, 1990); Charles Cros, ed., *La parole est à M. Diagne, premier homme d'état africain* (Dakar: Maison du livre, 1972); Obeye Diop, ed., *Blaise Diagne: Sa vie, son oeuvre* (Dakar: Nouvelle editions africaines, 1974); Laguerre, *Enemies*; Jean-Louis Domergue, "Blaise Diagne (1872–1934)," *Humanisme: Revue des franc-maçons du grand orient de France* (1994): 56–58; and Fred Zeller, "Blaise Diagne: Premier homme politique sénégalais, franc-maçon, et humaniste," *Humanisme: Revue des franc-maçons du grand orient de France* (1973): 32–39.

68 On Diagne's career in the Free Masons, see Domergue, "Blaise Diagne," and Zeller, "Blaise Diagne."

69 On Diagne's Free Mason connections, see "Discours de M. Fred Zeller, grand maître du grand orient de France," in Diop, *Blaise Diagne*, 23–30.

70 The material incentives the French offered in 1918 were to benefit war veterans mostly. They included 1) exemption of *tirailleurs* and their families from the head tax for the duration of the war; 2) facilitation of naturalization for decorated veterans, provided they renounce their Muslim status; 3) higher enlistment premiums for both volunteers and conscripts; 4) an agricultural school to be created in AOF; 5) the establishment of veterans hospitals; 6) the establishment of a medical school in AOF; 7) privileged access by veterans to certain administrative jobs after the war. Throughout his tour, Diagne also stressed more generous rewards to come after the war.

71 The two most detailed accounts of recruitment in West Africa are Marc Michel, *L'appel à l'Afrique: Contributions et réactions à l'effort de guerre en A.O.F. (1914–1919)* (Paris: Publications de la Sorbonne, 1982), and Lunn, *Memoirs*. Lunn contests Michel's findings on the deployment of African troops, arguing that they were used primarily as shock troops in order to spare French lives by sacrificing African

ones. Lunn, *Memoirs*, chap. 5. But both authors agree on Diagne's success in changing recruitment methods.

72 Thiam, *Sénégal*, 158.

73 Here I'm following loosely the interpretations of Searing, "Accommodation," Lunn, *Memoirs*, and Zuccarelli, *La vie politique*. Unfortunately, Diagne's career in Paris has not been studied systematically. General overviews of his career can be found in Laguerre, *Enemies*, Cros, *Parole*, and "Allocution du docteur Doudou Gueye" in Diop, *Blaise Diagne*, 65–110.

74 For an overview of the Pan-African congresses, see Langley, *Pan-Africanism*, 58–88.

75 Emmanuelle Sibeud, "Les étapes d'un négrologue," in Amselle and Sibeud, *Maurice Delafosse*, 166–90; Louise Delafosse, *Maurice Delafosse: Le Berrichon conquis par l'Afrique* (Paris: Société française d'histoire d'outre-mer, 1976), chap. 9. Delafosse's postwar volumes included *L'âme nègre* (1922), *Les noirs de l'Afrique* (1922), *Les civilisations négro-africaines* (1925), and *Les nègres* (1927).

76 Louise Delafosse, *Maurice Delafosse*, 346–47.

77 *La Dépêche Coloniale et Maritime*, 9 September 1921, and 20 September 1921.

78 Ibid., 6 October 1921.

79 Henri Charpin, "La question noire," *La revue indigène* (1922): 275–85.

80 Searing, "Accommodation," 476–516.

81 Ibid., 517–32.

82 According to Pierre Assouline, this was not the last time Diagne threatened to sue a critic of French abuses in Africa. When Albert Londres published his scathing *Terre d'ébène* in 1929, which first ran as a series of articles in *Le Petit Parisien*, Diagne accused him of treating the voters of the Four Communes as "creeps" [*gnafrons*]. Assouline quotes a passage from the newspaper *Coq Rouge* in which Diagne is reported to have said "but he is the creep, the creep! That Jewish rat with the kinky hair [le gnafron, le gnafron, mais c'est lui! Ce mulot juif aux cheveux crépus]." I thank Owen White for pointing out to me this passage in Assouline. Certainly by the late 1920s, Diagne had lost credibility with most of his constituents and moved even closer to conservative colonial interests in Paris. Pierre Assouline, *Albert Londres: Vie et mort d'un grand reporter, 1884–1932* (Paris: Balland, 1989), 389.

83 "I have walked in Paris with Diagne, who represents Senegal — all Senegal, white and black — in the French Parliament. But Diagne is a Frenchman who is accidentally black." W. E. B. Du Bois, "Worlds of Color," *Foreign Affairs* 3, 3 (1925): 428. Du Bois was not the only black American to follow the trial; for press coverage in the

United States, see Kenneth R. Janken, "African American and Francophone Intellectuals during the Harlem Renaissance," *Historian* 60, 3 (1998): 503–5.

84 Kwame Anthony Appiah, *In My Father's House: Africa in the Philosophy of Culture* (New York: Oxford University Press, 1992), 25.

85 Ibid., 174.

Yaël Simpson Fletcher

Catholics, Communists, and Colonial Subjects

Working-Class Militancy and Racial Difference

in Postwar Marseille

The Catholic intellectual Gustave Thibon praised a 1944 study of Marseille dockers (stevedores) for illuminating the "drama of the proletariat." Thibon describes the proletarian as an alienated worker, "outside the body [of society]; an instrument to be used as needed, rather than an [essential] organ. . . . the emblematic stranger [par excellence l'étranger]."[1] The Mediterranean port for the French empire, Marseille, relied on a labor-intensive daily hire system for the loading and unloading of ships. The figures given by this study show that this "emblematic" stranger was, indeed, often of foreign or colonial origin.[2] With the resumption of harbor activity in the aftermath of the Allied victory, the reconstituted dock workforce continued to draw heavily on immigrant labor. An American visitor at the end of the decade commented that "the heart of the real Marseille is the docks: it is a babel of languages: Frenchmen, Italians, Greeks, Spaniards, Turks, Maltese, Africans, Russians, all rub shoulders there, are all part of its vast army of casual labour, live many of them [*sic*] in national communities herded together in one of the neighbouring slums."[3] These workers were alienated from the French body politic not only by origins, labor status, and location, but also by ideology and militancy.

In this essay I analyze material on Marseille dockers written by three men who worked in the port in the 1940s and 1950s. A Catholic worker-priest, M. R. (Jacques) Loew produced the above-mentioned sociological study of dockers as well as essay collections focusing on his own proselytizing in the city's working-class neighborhoods. Among Loew's admirers was a young Marseille communist, Alfred Pacini. The son of an Italian docker, Pacini in 1996 recorded a memoir of his father's labors and his own struggles as a docker and organizer. A very different perspective is presented in the semiautobiographical 1956 novel of the Senegalese filmmaker and author, Ousmane Sembène. A combination of realism, melodrama, and metaphor, the novel deals with an African writer/worker's attempt to survive on the Marseille docks and in the Parisian literary scene.

This chapter brings these three authors together in order to illuminate the tensions and solidarities of Marseille after the Second World War. All three experienced the backbreaking labor of dockers, the aching poverty of working-class life, and the bitter struggles of the postwar port. Although writing nonfiction, Loew and Pacini, like Sembène, try to make sense of their experiences in the port's all-male multiethnic and multinational workforce in the era of decolonization and the cold war. Although they differ by race, religion, and ideology, the three authors intersect in interesting ways to provide a kaleidoscopic view of race and class relations within a group already marked as outsiders.

La Patrie Ouvrière

The publications of the Catholic worker-priest M. R. (Jacques) Loew present an interesting combination of faith in the human dignity of the dockers and doubts about the possibility of developing a truly religious community among the workers of Marseille. A former lawyer of Protestant background, Loew converted to Catholicism and entered the Dominican order in the late 1930s.[4] He was sent to Marseille in 1941, where he worked as a docker and, with other worker-priests and lay volunteers, established community parishes. In contrast to the typical image of a conservative Catholic priest, Loew was initially sympathetic to the militant communist organizers fighting for workers' rights.[5] An advocate of the church's active participation in the life of the workers, Loew entered the port workforce deliberately, as a way of learning what Marseille was about.[6] His 1944 study, *Les dockers de Marseille*, stands as one of the main sources of information on dockers in wartime Marseille.[7]

At the end of 1942, according to Loew, fewer than half of the almost 5,000 working dockers were French. The majority of the remainder were North African, Italian, Spanish, and Armenian. While supervisors and foremen were required to be French citizens, most were of foreign origin and tended to hire compatriots for their work gangs (generally six to eight men). Loew usually found himself laboring alongside Italians, Spaniards, and "Arabs." He describes Marseille's wharves as a place where "the entire Mediterranean finds itself, a Babel where the most habituated still have a hard time making themselves understood." Loew ranks the Armenians as by far the best workers, and the North Africans as the most willing to accept dirty and unpleasant tasks, like unloading coal.[8] He does not seem to recognize that Armenians, many stateless refugees, had a strong interest in proving their worth, or that North Africans, colonial migrants stranded in Marseille by the war, had few work options. Loew's only mention of an African docker (there were not many at this time) portrays the man as isolated, dreaming of home.[9]

Loew was on a mission to Marseille's proletariat. To be on a mission was not just a turn of speech, but had the literal connotation of being a missionary among non-Christians. After living in working-class neighborhoods for several years, Loew found only a nominal Catholicism, in which " 'I am Christian' meant simply belonging to the white race, of neither Muslim nor Jewish faith, and lack of opposition to the Church." He concludes that "the proletariat is a pagan people with Christian superstitions."[10] While Loew seems to concede here that the French proletariat is by definition white, his use of *pagan people* suggests a savage tribe barely touched by European civilization.

Indeed, Loew tends to exclude the truly non-Catholic (and non-European) from the neighborhood mission community — North Africans (Muslim) and Armenians (Orthodox). Loew's only extended discussion of Muslims in the community takes place in the context of a pending marriage of a young blonde Frenchwoman to a "dark-skinned" Arab bar owner. He expresses concern about the violence of Arab men, although he does allow that the fiancé is an exception. Rather than evangelizing the prospective husband, Loew concentrates on convincing him to raise his children, whether sons or daughters, as Catholics.[11] In discussing the work of several young Frenchwomen in a Catholic welfare center, Loew describes the Armenian community as finally, after three years, showing the potential to "one day yield [*accéder*] to civilization." He characterizes the neighborhood's foreign residents as more of an underclass than a proletariat.[12] As Loew makes clear in another account of his mission activity, his proselytizing to North African, Armenian, and even Spanish Catholic men works through individual contacts he makes working on the docks.[13]

In a 1948 report to his bishop, Loew compares his group's work to that of a Catholic priest well known for his mission in the French Sahara, and the very act of crossing Marseille's main thoroughfare, the Canebière, to "traveling for days and days to reach Cameroon," a French colony in central Africa.[14] He concludes with an extended discussion of a nineteenth-century missionary who succeeds in gaining Chinese converts by "de-Europeanizing" Catholicism, presenting it as perfectly compatible with Chinese national traditions. Loew advocated following the way paved by this missionary: "Sinicize (*Chiniser*) the Catholic Church in China, 'workerize' [it] in Marseille."[15] In this vision, a supranational Catholic faith takes shape only through a transnational alliance of communities of believers. Accordingly, Loew took an increasingly political stance in favor of worker militancy.

Loew develops the notion of a separate worker's homeland, "la patrie ouvrière," with its own culture and values very different from, "even impermeable to,.... our French civilization." For the worker, Loew suggests, benefits such as the regulation of work "came not from France, but from that working class which, by its militants, raised the worker if not from poverty, at least from terrible misery, thanks to a constant and burning struggle that also contributed to his cultural, social, [and] political development."[16] Loew found many positive elements in the culture and values of this proletarian world, a "common patrimony" springing from depths beyond the propaganda of political parties: "The mystique of a new world, just, brotherly, without privileges, a world to construct for tomorrow, the passionate love of the working class, the idea that war in no way concerns the worker . . . the absence of national prejudices, workers' sense of international solidarity, etc., such conceptions common to workers run deeper than Marxism, communism, or anarchism."[17]

Loew's characterization of the Marseille proletariat as a non-Christian people, outside the French nation, enabled him to construct the working-class district as a land of mission, territory for both evangelization and the spread of French civilization. His respect for and engagement with this proletarian *patrie* is certainly reminiscent of the attitude of some Jesuit missionaries to indigenous peoples and cultures. With his talk of the values integral to working-class culture, however favorable, Loew also dehistoricized and depoliticized twentieth-century workers' movements in general, and those of the Marseille dockers in particular. These essentially rhetorical moves allowed Loew to argue that the workers could be convinced that a transcendent Christian love would bring about a better world than international revolution.[18] It remains ambiguous, however, to what degree this multiethnic workforce must accept "French civilization" to become a community of true Catholic believers.

Des Proletaires Ensemble

The son of one of the many Italian immigrants to Marseille, Alfred Pacini, entered the dock workforce as a young man during the postwar reconstruction of the port. In 1996, he published a vivid memoir of his life, *Docker à Marseille*.[19] A union militant from an early age, Pacini never lost faith in the French Communist Party or the Soviet Union. Even the occasional sympathetic portrait of a factory owner or shipping firm manager occurs in the context of the class conflict framing Pacini's narrative. Indeed, in a 1997 interview Pacini clearly stated his continued belief in the cupidity and culpability of the bourgeoisie.[20]

When Pacini signed on as a docker in 1948, he joined a heterogenous labor force united in its common exploitation, but soon to be divided by bitter strikes, red-baiting, and the polarized politics of the cold war era. From his own experience, Pacini gives detailed accounts of the dockers' backbreaking labor, skills, and the organization of their work. A leader in the 1950 and 1953 strikes for better working conditions and against the French colonial war in Vietnam, Pacini suffered the full brunt of employer retaliation and spent many months unemployed. Elected municipal counselor in 1953, he became a force to be reckoned with at the port.

Pacini, as a communist and as the son of Italian immigrants, appreciated the fact that "all the nations of the world" were represented among the Marseille dockers. While conceding that a labor force of immigrants made for a difficult situation, he wrote: "But immigration is also internationalism. . . . it ennobles the profession, just like the solidarity that has always existed in ports. I believe that the mentality of dockers is the same in all the ports of the world, a very strong feeling of solidarity with others, foreigners or not, but not necessarily with the local populations."[21] It is interesting that Pacini sees a natural link between multinational solidarity in local workplace struggles and sympathy with dockers overseas — in communist terms, an "advanced" political consciousness which counters bourgeois forms of national identity (represented by the local populations).

This internationalism was expressed in the 1950 strike which began with dockers refusing to load arms destined for the war in Vietnam (the strike came to include issues of working conditions and wage rates). The authorities and the shipowners responded with repression, the hiring of strikebreakers, and the creation of independent unions. Pacini mentions that the strikebreakers included African workers hired right off the boats.[22] But North Africans constituted the main group of colonial workers among the dockers. In Pacini's narrative, they generally supported the communist Cofédération Genérale du Travail (CGT) union. He carried his electoral campaign to the North African neighborhoods around the rue des Chapeliers, even though most could not vote. As dockers, they formed part of his constituency. He calls them "great guys!" [des gens formidables] and notes the acceptance of Muslim religious practices among the dockers: "When some of the Arabs would go into a corner to kneel at the hour of prayer, we would respect them. It was our manner of not being racist; and this mixture of men — every place was represented at the port — created a very strong feeling of solidarity."[23] It is important to recognize that this recollection was offered in 1996, during a period of heightened xenophobic rhetoric and increased antiracist activity. The expression of solidarity itself took place several years before the beginning of the Algerian war of independence in 1954 and the subsequent demonization of North Africans in France in the mainstream press.[24] Pacini's only comment on the Algerian War is to praise the dockers for their internationalism in refusing to load arms, equating it with the war in Indochina.[25]

The defeat of the 1950 strike left the port workforce riven with tensions and conflicts. Despite speedup as the port mechanized, the continuation of the hated differential shifts (alternating day and night), mandatory overtime, and low pay, strikes no longer shut down the port. The professional dockers, members of the CGT union and veterans of the 1950 conflict, would not work with the new hires, former strikebreakers. Tellingly, in early 1951, a CGT official gave as the most egregious example of overtime "Arabicized [Sidi-lias-a] work teams."[26] Pacini, however, claimed membership in a small group of militants who urged unity in the face of common exploitation, but with little success until the 1960s.[27] He characterizes fights between different ethnic or racial groups in the port as work-related or political disputes, rather than racial conflicts.[28] Pacini's vision of solidarity and internationalism proved more of an ideal than a reflection of reality; it denied the discrimination and prejudice suffered by at least some of the colonial workers on the Marseille docks.

Le Petit Harlem Marseillais

Le docker noir (translated as *The Black Docker*) is the first novel of Senegal's prizewinning author and filmmaker, Ousmane Sembène.[29] Published in 1956, *Le docker noir* is set in Marseille's port district. Somewhat autobiographical, the novel recounts the bitter travails of a black worker who is also a writer. In 1946, Ousmane Sembène had come to Marseille after service in the Free French army. Familiar with labor issues from his youth in the working-class districts of Dakar, Sembène soon became a union militant in the CGT.[30] Ousmane Sembène claims that he was first inspired to write because none of the books in the CGT library's African section, whether by European or African authors, reflected the working-class African reality that he knew.[31]

Le docker noir is set in the bitter aftermath of the 1950 dockers' strike. It tells the story of a young Senegalese man, the Wolof Diaw Falla, who works on the docks of Marseille by day and writes by night. The author's experience as a docker and trade union militant in postwar Marseille obviously informs the book.[32] In this essay, I focus on just one section of the novel, the chronological narrative of Diaw Falla's experience in Marseille. Ousmane Sembène begins this section with a brief history and description of the "little Harlem of Marseille." This reference to the celebrated center of African American cultural life is followed by a paean to the community solidarity of this displaced African "village." Sembène gives an account of the prewar gathering place for African seamen, the place Victor Gelu, the old quarter's destruction by the Nazis during the war, and the subsequent displacement of these seamen to a neighborhood near the railroad station.[33] Sembène lists ethnic groups living in this "meridional microcosm of Africa" — Sarakoles, Susas, Malinkes, Tukulors, Mandiagues, Dyolas, Bambaras, Dahomeens, Martinicans, Moors, and Wolofs — and gives the commonly held (African) stereotype for the characteristics of each group. He describes the Wolofs as a "mélange of all African lineages . . . [with] personalities ranging from calm to volatile," the last characterizing the novel's protaganist Diaw Falla.[34]

This community congregates at the laundry of an African woman ("Maman"), the warm household of a Caribbean immigrant and his French wife, and a welcoming bar run by a French couple.[35] It is a community, however, turned in on itself from unemployment, poverty, and the resulting despair. Sembène uses a gathering to plan a funeral as a forum to present the grievances of the African men. An elderly seaman gives a heartrending account of being refused a pension, and a young man, a veteran of the Battle of the North Atlantic, looks back to wartime solidarity in the face of death: "In those days, there wasn't the difference between skin colors there is today. We called each other 'brother,' sleeping together and sharing the same spoon to eat with. And now, they reject us and call us incompetent! At what point are we Frenchmen? French unity is a dream, not a reality."[36] In this passage, Sembène delineates the links between color consciousness, discrimination, and French national identity. To be French is to be equal and accepted as part of the same family; the recognition of racial difference as significant breaks the familial bonds of brotherhood and effectively bars the black man from claiming a French identity.

An alternative identity, that of a member of the international working class, is presented in one seaman's proposal to go to the union. This suggestion is shot down, however, with the claim that it is the unionized seamen who refuse to share cabins with African seamen. Only one person present, Pipo Alassane, argues that it is the shipowners, not the unions, who are refusing men work, and that furthermore Africans should begin seeing themselves as workers capable of organization.[37] But he does not succeed in rallying the men; they are left with only dreams of home and family for comfort.[38]

In the novel, as in real life, mainly unemployed seamen found work on the docks. Ousmane Sembène vividly portrays the harsh working conditions and tense encounters between strike veterans and newcomers described by Loew and Pacini. Shouting matches degenerate into blows as the two groups interact with "the testiness of wild animals," and the competition with machines forces men to labor at a soul-destroying pace, becoming like robots themselves.[39] Throughout the novel, Diaw Falla claims his identity as an African man, as a black worker, and as a writer. He is driven to distraction by exhaustion and the impossible choice between "two personalities: the docker, who was just an animal being, but who lived and paid his rent, or the intellectual, who could only survive in a climate of rest and freedom of thought."[40] Diaw's dilemma is not just a question of resources, but a question of survival as a man — intellectual life is what differentiates brute from human.

Diaw Falla's identity as an intellectual may set him apart from his workmates, but they, too, have the right to treatment as human beings rather than animals. Protesting unbearable working conditions, Diaw takes the lead in a wildcat strike that unites first his work team of Senegalese, Malagasy, and Arab dockers against the African foreman, and then the dockers of several ships against the boss. New to the role, Diaw asks (in Wolof) the advice of a Senegalese union militant, who urges Diaw to hold firm against the appeals of the French boss. A North African defends Diaw. In this passage, class and ethnic solidarity are articulated together.[41] But the veterans of the 1950 strike do not join in, and Diaw (in the novel), like Pacini (in real life), is blackballed from work on the docks. Here one could see Sembène as arguing the case for those African strikebreakers who work out of necessity — ignorant of labor organization and suspicious of French workers — suffering not just extreme exploitation, but also exclusion from a proletarian *patrie*.

Thibon's "drama of the proletariat" turns out to be about dockers, often reduced to casual labor, trying to maintain their proletarian status as working men. The three authors discussed here clearly saw the need for unity in order to effectively resist exploitation, but even their visions for the future retained the divisions of the port workforce. Despite his own statistics, Loew seemed to have real hope of evangelizing only lapsed French Catholics. Pacini's laudable sentiments of solidarity were based on the assumption of equality within the working class; he collapsed inequality into cultural difference. The only moments of hope in Sembène's novel emerge when solidarities cross racial and ethnic divisions. But his main African characters, even if moored rather than stranded in France, equate a class-conscious, proletarian identity with the French nation from which they are excluded and, in turn, reject. As it turned out, there was only a fleeting moment of solidarity between Catholic and communist, and the realities of religious prejudice and racial difference punctured the idealistic visions of a working-class world united either by Christian love or by internationalism. Whether Senegalese, Malagasy, or Algerian, French citizen or not, the African docker was excluded from both Loew's French civilization and his proletarian *patrie*, and he remained liminal to Pacini's communist vision. But whether strikebreakers, workers, or unemployed, men from Africa and the Maghreb marked an important presence in the port of Marseille, and, as each author indicates, some made the city their home.

Notes

This essay is part of a larger project on labor, race, and gender in postwar France. I am grateful to the University of Cincinnati Charles Phelps Taft Foundation and the University of the South faculty research grants committee for support for travel, research, and writing while engaged in this project. I would also like to thank Joshua Cole, Steve Estes, Gary Gerstle, Gay Gullickson, Tessie Liu, Clare Lyons, Maura O'Connor, Sue Peabody, Catherine Rassiguier, Todd Shepard, Mona Siegel, and the participants of the women's studies seminar at the University of Cincinnati, the undergraduate research seminar at the University of the South, and the Center for Historical Studies seminar at the University of Maryland at College Park for assistance, comments, and suggestions.

1 Gustave Thibon, preface to *Les dockers de Marseille*, by M. R. Loew, 2d ed. (L'Arbresle: Economie et humanisme, 1945), vii. "M. R." stands for Marie Reginald, Loew's name in religion. This and all unmarked translations are mine.

2 Loew, *Les dockers de Marseille*, 45.

3 Maisie Ward, "Père Loew — Catholic Sociologist," in *Mission to the Poorest*, by Jacques Loew, trans. Pamela Carswell (New York: Sheed and Ward, 1950), 7–8.

4 Ronald Matthews, introduction to *The Love We Forget: Lenten T.V. Addresses*, by M. R. Loew, trans. Matthews (Westminster, Md.: Newman Press, 1958), 7.

5 He was also involved with the Catholic sociological journal *Economie et humanisme* founded by his superior, Père Lebret. Ward, "Père Loew — Catholic Sociologist," 5–6. Some of Loew's views on communism and its appeal for workers echo those expressed in the clandestine wartime publication, *Témoignage chrétien*, which indeed had a wide circulation in the Marseille region. See Y. de Montcheuil,

"Communisme," *Courier français du Témoignage chrétien* 5 (1943), reprinted in Rênée Bédarida, *Les armes de l'ésprit: Témoignage chrétien (1941–1944)* (Paris: Editions ouvrières, 1977), 338–40; and ibid., 23–24, 83–84, 101–2. The editor of *Mission to the Poorest*, the 1950 English translation of Loew's *En mission prolétarienne* (Paris: Economie et humanisme, 1946), claimed that this account of the priest's work in Marseille was the most important book in the postwar revival of the French Catholic church. Ward, "Père Loew — Catholic Sociologist," 1.

6 Loew, *En mission prolétarienne*, 13.

7 Loew was able to analyze the makeup of the workforce because every docker had to have a permit from 1940 onward. He found that only 60 percent of the approximately 8,000 dockers were hired on a regular basis. From his own experience, Loew describes how hiring took place twice daily at the different wharves, so that if no daily work became available in the morning, the unemployed docker seeking a place had to return at midday. Loew, *Les dockers de Marseille*, 15–18.

8 Ibid., 2, 10–11, 13, 20–21, table facing 40.

9 Ibid., 12.

10 Loew, *En mission prolétarienne*, 94.

11 Ibid., 41–43.

12 Ibid., 47–49.

13 Jacques Loew, *Journal d'une mission ouvrière, 1941–1959* (Paris: Editions du Cerf, 1959), 351.

14 Ibid., 55, 65–66.

15 The priest was Father Lebbe who learned Chinese and, "searching for the deep roots of the Chinese soul onto which Christianity could be grafted," discovered patriotism and nationalism. Although Father Lebbe was recalled at the insistence of the European consuls, the Pope, who named a number of Chinese priests trained by Lebbe to bishoprics, nevertheless adopted his strategy. Loew, *Journal d'une mission ouvrière*, 74–76, 90–91.

16 Ibid., 81–82, 88–89.

17 Ibid., 84.

18 Ibid., 102–5.

19 Alfred Pacini and Dominique Pons, *Docker à Marseille* (Paris: Payot et Rivages, 1996).

20 "Portrait du docker Alfred Pacini," *Le cercle de minuit*, France 2, 4 June 1997. Available at L'Institut National de l'Audiovisuel à la Bibliothèque Nationale de France (INA), DLT/VIS/19970604/FR2/012:001.

21 Pacini and Pons, *Docker*, 46–47. See also "Portrait du docker."

22 Pacini and Pons, *Docker*, 81.

23 Ibid., 49, 83, 110.

24 While resistant to the idea of complete independence for Algeria, the communist labor press did defend North African workers. For example, in November 1954, the CGT newspaper *La vie ouvrière* published an article criticizing the government's "military operations" in Algeria and calling for solidarity between French and North African workers, both in Algeria and in France. While recognizing the "social and national aspirations" of the "Algerian people," the article places on an equal basis the "protection for the true interests of France" for the "French people." *La vie ouvrière*, 15–22 November 1954, 8.

25 Pacini and Pons, *Docker*, 143. See also "Portrait du docker."

26 Pierre Gagnaire, "Sur le port de Marseille: Assez d'heures supplementaires!" *La vie ouvrière*, 15–21 February 1951, 5.

27 Pacini and Pons, *Docker*, 129.

28 Ibid., 144.

29 Ousmane Sembène's films of conflict in colonial and postindependence Senegal and Mali — *Xala* (1974), *Ceddo* (1976), *Camp de Thiaroye* (1988), and *Guelwaar* (1992), to name just four — have won numerous prizes in Africa, Europe, and the United States, and in 1966, 1971, and 1993, he was recognized for his literary output. *Le soleil*, 17 November 1993, 11. Ousmane Sembène is probably best known in the United States today for his realist novel about the massive 1947–48 strike of railway workers on the Dakar-Niger line, *God's Bits of Wood* (Garden City, N.Y.: Doubleday, 1962)/*Les bouts de bois de Dieu* (Paris: Le livre contemporain, 1960). A Senegalese university professor recently characterized the novelist and filmmaker as "a witness of our century and a militant of one the great causes born of the violent interpenetration of peoples, anticolonialism." Madior Diouf, "Sembène Ousmane: Un militant des grandes causes," *Le soleil*, 18 November 1993.

30 See Brigitte Bertoncello and Sylvie Bredeloup, "A la recherche du docker noir," in *Dockers de la Méditerranée à la Mer du Nord: Des quais et des hommes dans l'histoire*, ed. Jean-Marie Guillon and Robert Mencherini (Aix-en-Provence: Edisud, 1999), 139–51.

31 In this period, Ousmane Sembène periodically went up to Paris to visit with other Africans from the Casamance region, including the writer Birago Diop. Interview (on the occasion of Ousmane Sembène being awarded the 1993 Grand Prix de la République pour les Lettres for his entire literary oeuvre, at age seventy) by Djib Diedhiou, "Cinema littérature: Sembène entre deux passions," *Le soleil*, 17 November 1993. He also had contacts among African students in the Aix-Marseille region. Clara Tsabedze, *African Independence from*

Francophone and Anglophone Voices: A Comparative Study of the Post-independence Novels by Ngugi and Sembène (New York: P. Lang, 1994), 32–33.

32 The novel also has as an unarticulated backdrop the class and racial tensions of wartime Dakar, where the future author came to political consciousness. Bara Diouf, "Ousmane Sembène, ou, L'itinéraire d'un enfant du siècle," *Le soleil*, 17 November 1993.

33 Ousmane Sembène, *Black Docker*, trans. Ros Schwartz (London: Heinemann, 1987), 41; Ousmane Sembène, *Le docker noir* (1956; Paris: Présence Africaine, 1973), 77–78.

34 Sembène, *Black Docker*, 42; *Le docker noir*, 78–79. In the following, I have provided my own translations from the French original.

35 Sembène, *Black Docker*, 12–17, 54–55, 93–104; *Le docker noir*, 33–39, 99–101, 174–90.

36 Sembène, *Black Docker*, 57; *Le docker noir*, 104–6.

37 Sembène, *Black Docker*, 57–59; *Le docker noir*, 106–9.

38 Sembène, *Black Docker*, 64–65; *Le docker noir*, 119.

39 Sembène, *Black Docker*, 69–71, 94–95; *Le docker noir*, 128–29, 173.

40 Sembène, *Black Docker*, 73; *Le docker noir*, 134.

41 Sembène, *Black Docker*, 77–82; *Le docker noir*, 142–49.

Tyler Stovall

From Red Belt to Black Belt

Race, Class, and Urban Marginality in

Twentieth-Century Paris

Several years ago, while attending a conference in Paris, I had an interesting conversation with an African American woman who lived in the city and had come to see my panel on racism in Europe. When she asked what kind of research I did, I told her that I had written a book on the working-class suburbs of Paris, an area commonly known as the Red Belt for its historic tendency to vote communist. She responded to this by saying, "The Red Belt! Well, it's the Black Belt now!"

This brief, offhand remark has remained with me ever since, because it neatly sums up a widely held popular and academic view of the evolution of Paris's outskirts during the twentieth century. Simply put, this view suggests that, whereas during the late nineteenth and first half of the twentieth century the Paris suburbs achieved notoriety for their large working-class, politically radical population, in the last twenty years they have, in contrast, become a central symbol of immigration and racial conflict in France. The spatial margins of the French capital have thus successively come to represent marginalities based first on class, then on race.

The problems of class and race explored in this essay certainly exist in the suburbs of cities other than Paris. The first major riots of the 1980s took place outside Lyons, for example, and the outskirts of Marseille and other major urban areas have also been discussed. However, this essay will concentrate on the suburbs of Paris for a variety of reasons.[1] Not only do they represent by far the biggest suburban region in the country, but the polarity between a bourgeois central city and marginal outskirts is most advanced there. Moreover, the Paris suburbs have far and away the richest and most extensive scholarly studies devoted to them, and in general they have occupied the national imagination much more than those of other cities. Their position just outside the gates of power makes their marginal status all the more striking.

In this essay, I wish to explore this perspective on the contemporary history of the Paris suburbs, considering the ways in which ideas of difference based on both class and race have characterized the area. I will argue that such a view is somewhat simplistic and tends to reify notions of race and class.[2] Instead, one must consider the ways in which the two have interacted in shaping twentieth-century ideas of Paris's suburban frontier. Ultimately, the experience of the Paris suburbs can serve as a model for an understanding of race and class that sees both concepts as dynamic, relational, and constantly evolving. In this context, ideas of race and class constitute a repertoire of alternate approaches to social difference, used in ways that reflect the broader tensions in French society at any given historical moment.[3] Finally, this article wishes to support arguments made by Anne McClintock and others, who refuse to see the concept of the postcolonial as necessarily teleological, something that simply follows the colonial, but rather view it as constituting a complex reordering of social and national identities.[4]

The very concept of the suburb is a relative one; many urban neighborhoods, like London's Chelsea, New York's Greenwich Village, or the Latin Quarter of Paris, which today represent the height of urbanity, were once suburbs. The modern history of Parisian suburbia begins in 1860, with the municipality's annexation of what are today the city's outer arrondissements. From that date until the First World War, various social and economic processes would gradually transform what remained of the Department of the Seine from semirural retreats to appendages of the nation's capital. A number of factors combined to make the Paris suburbs heavily working class. By the beginning of the twentieth century, the Paris area had developed an important industrial sector, complementing the traditional artisanal workshops of neighborhoods like the Faubourg Saint-Antoine. Since the density of Paris's urban fabric offered little room for the largest new factories, and since industries like chemical plants and metalworking frequently produced noxious side effects, heavy industry established itself primarily in the suburbs, producing a ring of industrial towns like Saint-Denis, Boulogne, and Ivry. Rural immigrants to Paris from the provinces often settled in these areas, finding both jobs and housing more easily than in Paris.[5]

At the same time, shortages in low-income housing in Paris itself increasingly pushed unskilled laborers and their families out of the city altogether, especially after the development of suburban mass transit in the late nineteenth century. The suburbanization of the Department of the Seine culminated in the years after the Great War, which intensified both the industrial development and the housing shortage in the Paris area. During the decade after the armistice the population of the suburbs grew by some 700,000, many of the newcomers seeking shelter in cheap housing developments, or *lotissements*, that usually lacked even the most basic urban amenities. The plight of the *mal-lotis*, stuck in muddy suburban plots without utilities, sewers, paved streets, or adequate housing, loomed as one of the great social questions of the 1920s.[6]

The intensification of the suburban crisis after the war coincided with the birth of the French Communist Party (PCF), and the PCF would soon turn the Paris suburbs into one of its areas of greatest strength. Before the founding of the PCF, the French Socialist Party (SFIO) had already laid a strong power base in the suburban Department of the Seine, so that on the Communist Party's emergence in 1920, it inherited a large popular vote there and control of sixteen city halls. However, for several reasons this area soon became far more important to the PCF than it ever had been to the socialists. During the interwar years, the small size of the new party made it especially dependent on solid power bases, and none proved more solid than the Paris suburbs. The area's socioeconomic configuration, strongly working-class and heavily industrial in character, fit the self-image of a consciously proletarian political party. Most significant to the PCF's suburban strength was the *lotissement* issue. Far more than any other political group, the PCF championed the cause of the *mal-lotis*, constantly demanding that the authorities do something to remedy their situation.[7] Thanks in part to this activism, the crisis of the *lotissements* had been largely resolved by the late 1920s. This success created a political base for the PCF that would endure for generations. After the war, the PCF strengthened its hold on the Paris suburbs, becoming the majority party in the region. As the area was transformed from *lotissements* to HLMs (*habitation a loyer modéré*, low-cost housing projects) under the Fourth and Fifth Republics, the area remained strongly communist, its spatial marginality mirroring the social and political isolation of the French working class. National governments might come and go, but the residents of Saint-Denis, Bobigny, Ivry, Vitry, and many other communities could be relied on to cast their ballots for the

PCF. As the saying went, in the Paris suburbs one was born, not made a communist.[8]

In the past twenty years, the position of the Paris suburbs in the French imagination has shifted markedly.[9] Since the mid-1970s, the French have engaged in an anguished debate about immigration and the future of French society. Several factors have shaped this debate. One has been the shift in the ethnic origin of the immigrants coming to France. As recently as 1975, the majority of foreigners in France were Europeans, especially Portuguese, who remain to this day the largest single immigrant group in the country. Since then, however, the relative percentage of Europeans has declined, while that of North Africans has risen sharply, outstripping the former in the 1990s.[10] The nation has also witnessed an increasingly large illegal immigration from sub-Saharan Africa, so that by the end of the twentieth century, the majority of immigrants in France came from outside Europe. This situation has combined with the prolonged economic downturn France has experienced since the mid-1970s, one that has seen the deindustrialization of previously vital regions and has caused chronic unemployment among young people in particular.[11]

These two developments have joined to produce a new cohort of so-called second-generation immigrant youth (a term whose nonsensical character speaks eloquently to the prevailing confusion about race and citizenship in contemporary France).[12] The children of African and North African immigrants, who were usually either born in or grew up in France, are routinely portrayed as delinquents or social misfits, at home neither in France nor in the homelands of their parents. Like the classic colonial stereotype of the métis, or the tragic mulatto, they represent a self-destructive hybrid threat to the racial status quo.[13] To a much greater extent than the descendants of European immigrants, these youth are widely viewed as an inassimilable racial substratum of society. The fact that young people from the French Caribbean, legally French citizens, are typically also considered immigrants underscores the racialized nature of the contemporary immigration debate in France.[14]

As they did in the class conflicts of the early and mid-twentieth century, the suburbs of Paris and of other French cities have assumed center stage in the contentions over immigration and race at the century's end. Starting in the early 1980s, a series of violent clashes between nonwhite youth, whites, and the police shook the suburbs, recalling the American "long hot summers" of a generation earlier. The first major confrontations took place in the Lyonnaise suburbs of Vaulx-en-Velin, Vénissieux, and Villeurbanne during the summer of 1981. In large public housing projects with sizeable North African populations, young people revolted against the heavy police presence there, throwing rocks and burning hundreds of cars.[15] The timing of these revolts was highly significant: right after Mitterand's 1981 victory revealed the decline of the PCF's social and political control of the Red Belt, a new image of dangerous suburbia emerged into the national consciousness. During the 1980s, a series of racially charged attacks against "immigrant youth" prompted popular mobilizations against racism, while conflicts between young people and police multiplied. In the early 1990s a new wave of rioting broke out in Parisian suburbs like Mantes-la-Jolie and Sartrouville. Massively covered in the French media, these upheavals focused national attention on the suburbs as centers of crime, violence, and social problems.[16]

As in the early twentieth century, the Paris suburbs in the 1980s and 1990s came to symbolize political marginality. The socialist victory in 1981 at the head of a broad leftwing coalition brought to an end the Communist Party's political isolation in postwar France, representing a kind of domestication of the traditional outsider's party. During the 1980s and 1990s, the PCF ceded its place as the *enfant maudit* of French politics to the National Front, which burst onto the electoral stage in 1984 by winning 11 percent of the vote in elections to the European Parliament.[17] Although the front's had an electoral base national in scope, journalists and political commentators quickly focused on the party's ability to make political inroads in formerly communist suburbs. This idea of a massive shift from left to right was more than a little sensationalist and not entirely accurate, yet it did have some substance. In the elections of 1993, for example, the National Front won 18.6 percent of the votes in the department of the Seine-Saint Denis, as opposed to 12.4 percent in France as a whole.[18] Many *banlieusards* of non-European heritage responded by joining antiracist political campaigns, most notably SOS-Racisme.[19] Immigration and racial conflict thus emerged as not only a social question, but also as a political issue. Even communist municipalities saw themselves drawn into racial politics, as in 1981, when the communist mayor of Vitry-sur-Seine used a bulldozer to oust African immigrants from squatter housing in his city.

Finally, to a much greater extent than in the interwar years, the suburbs have come to symbolize an alternate French culture, at once marginal and avant-garde. First, the suburbs have become an artistic and creative symbol of marginality. A series of novels, most notably Mehdi Charef's *Le thé au harem d'Archi Ahmed*, have provided socially realistic portraits of suburban life for the benefit of both local residents and national and international audiences who have never set foot in an HLM.[20] Second, the rise of an important school of *banlieue* films, like *Bye-bye* (Karin Dridi, 1997), *Raï* (Thomas Gilou, 1996), and *La haine* (Matthieu Kassovitz, 1996), has had an even greater impact in focusing attention on the plight of the suburbs in general, and nonwhite suburban youth in particular.[21]

While these literary and cinematic genres have used the suburbs as sites of representation, the area's greatest cultural significance arises from its importance to hip-hop music and culture. Rap musicians and groups like Lionel D from Vitry, Suprême NTM from St. Denis, and MC Solaar from Villeneuve St-Georges provide a running musical commentary not just on suburban life, but on the state of France — especially French politics — in general. *Raï* music, the product of North Africans in France, has also at times embraced suburban themes and has frequently originated in the *cités* outside the capital.[22] Like hip-hop musicians in the United States and elsewhere, the rappers of the Paris suburbs represent at the same time the despair of those on the outskirts of society and a consumer product increasingly central to that society.[23] White and middle-class French people who listen to this music can both enjoy its exotic sounds and at the same time appreciate how much worse their own lives could be. Like the colonialist images that permeated French advertising during the late nineteenth and early twentieth centuries, the popularity of suburban rap music denotes both a desire to transgress social norms and an affirmation of the superiority of the dominant culture.[24]

The history of the Paris suburbs during the twentieth century can be viewed, therefore, as a trajectory from Red Belt to Black Belt, that is from a social and political marginality based on social class to one based on race and citizenship. One must consider this trajectory in the context of two broader evolutionary themes, which have often characterized the history of contemporary France. One is the transition from colonialism to postcolonialism, as France has gone from possessing a great colonial empire to undergoing decolonization and the immigration of a large nonwhite population from its former dependencies.[25] From this perspective, the racial split formerly represented by a separate metropole and empire has now been replicated on the territory of the metropole itself, overshadowing previous class distinctions. The other theme is Americanization and modernization, the belief being that as France has become more modern, it has resembled ever more closely its trans-Atlantic ally.[26] In recent years, many French intellectuals have attacked what they perceive as American multiculturalism, arguing that it weakens the unity of the nation and leads to racial conflict.[27] This position often arises from a conviction that race is not a factor in French life, and that attempts to argue the contrary represent erroneous attempts to apply American theoretical perspectives to France. Thus the resistance to considering the role of race in French history and current life, so notable among French scholars, has become intertwined with assertions of French independence from American influence. In this context, the rise of a racialized image of the Paris suburbs suggests that France is nonetheless imitating the postwar American practice of privileging social conflicts based on race over those emphasizing class. To put it bluntly, instead of communists, France now has its own version of African Americans.[28]

In the rest of this essay I would like to challenge this rather cozy pattern, arguing that while not completely erroneous, it tends to oversimplify the Paris suburbs and the realities of both race and class in twentieth-century France. I wish to show how a rereading of suburban life in both the earlier years of the century and the contemporary period can provide a more nuanced view of the Paris suburbs, one that will ultimately contribute to rethinking the interaction of various forms of social difference. The central question therefore becomes not so much reconsidering the Paris suburbs as providing new perspectives on the history of contemporary France.

One consideration has to do with the view of the Paris suburbs in the early twentieth century as a zone of working-class marginality. While this is incontestably true, it is also true that considerations of race played a role in popular perceptions of the Parisian suburbs as well. For some years now, numerous scholars have pointed to the various ways in which European workers in the nineteenth century were characterized by elite groups as a racially separate caste.[29] Moreover, as the work of Arthur de Gobineau makes clear, the rise of modern scientific racism owed more than a little to fears of the proletariat.[30] For the era of industrialization, the close intermingling of notions of race and class calls into question any view of the suburbs that only emphasizes the latter social division. In fact, drawing on perspectives that have dominated the late twentieth century, one could also depict the modern history of the area in terms of changing notions of race.

In the case of Paris, spatial and racial marginality often went hand in hand. The image of suburbanites as barbarians lurking just outside the gates of the civilized city goes back to well before the French Revolution.[31] In the 1850s, Alexandre Privat-d'Anglemont described the Villa des Chiffoniers, a slum on the edge of Paris, as a settlement of exotic savages.[32] Racial ideas of suburban workers continued to surface in the early twentieth century, reinforced by the growing communist presence in the area.[33] During the interwar years, at a time when foreigners from Europe were often characterized in racialized terms, the Paris suburbs became a center of immigration. Jacques Valdour, a royalist observer of working-class life during the 1920s, described the Italian and Eastern European immigrants of the area as "neighboring races" and suggested that they would constitute "a possible cause of troubles and of aggravation of troubles in a weak State."[34]

In particular, commentators in the late nineteenth and early twentieth centuries often drew parallels between the suburbs of Paris and the empire, both constituting marginal and racially different spaces. The fate of the Communards, working-class rebels who attacked the center of Paris only to be first repulsed toward the popular *faubourgs* and then sent into exile in New Caledonia, provide a solid historical example of the kinship between those areas outside the metropolis and those outside the metropole.[35] Much of the French science of *urbanisme* arose first in response to the plight of the suburbs before going on to tackle the challenge of remaking imperial cities. As Gwendolyn Wright has argued, "If the *bidonvilles* [shantytowns] of the colonial cities pointed out the inequalities — and the dangers — of that system, the outskirts of French cities posed a similar, highly visible critique of French republicanism at home."[36] In her recent work on the 1931 colonial exposition, Patricia Morton has demonstrated how the fair's creators decided to locate it outside Paris as a way of addressing the social problems of the suburbs. As one of the main organizers, Hubert Lyautey, put it: "The East of Paris, is this not a region that people say has been won over by Communism? It is interesting to plant our colonial seedlings there in the middle of this working-class world. . . . I am convinced that the Exposition can be a major factor for social peace in this region of Paris."[37] In other words, a demonstration of how the French had civilized the natives abroad could help civilize the savages at home.

One text that illustrates the analogy between suburbs and empire is Pierre Lhande's *Le Christ dans la banlieue* [Christ in the suburbs]. One of the most important sources on interwar working-class life in the Paris suburbs, the book relates the story of the massive evangelical effort mounted by the church to "rechristianize" the workers of the suburbs as a means both of propagating the faith and of fighting communism. In several places the author uses racialized and colonial imagery to explain the strange world of working-class suburbia to his readers. For example, he describes the southern suburb of Malakoff as "a sort of long Indian village extending to Infinity along the Orleans road. One would call it the bush just outside the city, the nude and dusty Orient two steps from the boulevard, whose tall stone houses suddenly stop and bristle before the frail line of superannuated ramparts. Here one world ends and there another begins."[38] He also variously characterizes the suburbs as "a pagan land" and "the Parisian China," emphasizing both its lack of faith and of civilization. Indeed, Lhande goes so far as to label the Zone, the area just outside the city limits, as "la ceinture noire" (the Black Belt), an area peopled with tattooed, degenerate young savages. Most significantly, *Le Christ dans la banlieue* takes the form of a classic missionary account, first relating the initial resistance to Christianity of these exotic inhabitants of a far-off land, then their successful conversion. At one point, for example, Lhande compares the work of one suburban priest (a former missionary in China) to that of Saint François-Xavier among the Japanese.[39]

If the image of interwar suburbia as working-class communities unaffected by racial concerns is not entirely accurate, it is even more true that one cannot consider the Paris suburbs since the 1970s merely as racialized slums. Indeed, much of the scholarly research on the question in France, especially that by social scientists, has been at pains to emphasize the continued working-class character of the capital's suburbs, rejecting the idea that the area's class marginality has been superseded by a racialized one. This rejection has taken two primary forms: 1) studies of historical and contemporary immigration in the suburbs; and 2) the debate over the existence of American-style ghettos in France. A brief consideration of these perspectives should illustrate the different ways in which the French have addressed contemporary interactions of race and class in the Paris suburbs.

In October 1994, a diverse group of French sociologists, historians, geographers, and other scholars took part in a conference on immigration past and present in the Paris suburbs. Held in Saint-Denis at the Université de Paris VIII,[40] itself an interesting symbol of suburban marginality, the meeting wanted to provide some scientific weight to the popular debate about contemporary suburban problems. A year later, Jean-Paul Brunet, organizer of the conference and a leader in suburban research, published the proceedings in a book entitled *Immigration, vie politique, et populisme en banlieue parisienne*. As a statement on the book's cover noted, "Most would agree that the destiny of our society is being played out in the suburbs. Multiform immigration, often still badly integrated and prey to the social ills of drugs and unemployment, the rightist populist temptation that attracts many, difficult living conditions, and explosions of violence, all this has nourished a 'media-feeding frenzy' which has been unfortunately accompanied by a 'scientific deficit.' "[41] In contrast to media stereotypes, therefore, Brunet and company set out to provide a more nuanced, well-informed analysis of the immigration question in the Paris suburbs.[42]

The result is a book that largely ignores questions of race, instead assimilating the recent history of non-European immigrants to earlier patterns of French provincial and European migration. In general, immigration history in France has tended to emphasize class status and regional culture over racial difference, and *Immigration, vie politique, et populisme en banlieue parisienne* proves no exception to this pattern.[43] The volume's seventeen essays survey the history of immigration to the Paris suburbs from the late nineteenth century to the present, concentrating successively on Parisian and provincial migration, European migration, and contemporary non-European immigrants. The collection ends with two different sections on suburban politicization, one concerning the creation of communist power in the area, the second relating the rise of the National Front. The history of nonwhite immigrants in the Paris suburbs thus represents not a break, but rather continuity with the experiences of white immigrants in earlier periods. In his chapter on African families in the metropolitan area, for example, Christian Poiret argues that the marked segregation of Africans arises not just from racial discrimination, but more from the desire of the Africans themselves to create their own ethnic communities, just as other newcomers to the suburbs had done.[44] The authors pay scant attention to the burning question of immigrant youth, source of so much media frenzy. Moreover, for them the idea of the Black Belt refers more to the politics of the National Front than to the new racial composition of suburban Paris. Brunet himself was one of the pioneers of historical research on the interwar suburbs, and he took the lead in conceptualizing them as the Red Belt. His edited volume replicates this earlier historiography and enlarges its focus, applying its emphasis on social class to the nineteenth and twentieth centuries as a whole. In general, French scholarship on the Paris suburbs has rejected the idea of a transition from class to racial marginality, insisting instead on the area's working-class character as the dominant aspect of its identity.

The most notable example of this perspective has been the debate over the existence of ghettos in France. In the early 1990s, in response to riots in Vaulx-en-Velin, Mantes-la Jolie, and elsewhere, French commentators began asking whether or not France was witnessing the rise of U.S.-style ghettos in its suburbs, ghettos characterized by high levels of unemployment, violence, drug use, and, above all, racial segregation.[45] Reporters and suburbanites themselves began routinely referring to the suburbs as "Chicago," "Harlem," or "the Bronx." A special issue of Le Nouvel Observateur in June 1991 asked, "How can we prevent the outskirts of French cities from becoming so many versions of 'the Bronx'?" The June 1992 issue of the journal Esprit devoted several articles to what it labeled "La France de l'exclusion," analyzing the ways in which French suburbs did or did not resemble American slums.[46] The prospect of the ghettoization of French society loomed large during the early 1990s, prompting not only widespread media debates, but also government action. In 1991, the French government passed the loi d'orientation de la ville, which quickly became known as the "antighetto law," in an attempt to prevent the ethnic and racial segregation of suburban housing projects.

Yet most scholars who considered the issue argued against the facile equation of French and American urban slums. First and foremost, several authors observed that French suburbs had nowhere near the level of racial homogeneity often characteristic of African American ghettos, that in fact most continued to house large white, working-class populations. Second, they pointed out that for all the images of suburban violence, the young inhabitants of these areas lagged far behind their American equivalents in terms of access to firearms, not to mention the frequency of violent death. Third, those who reject the French-American ghetto parallel argue that the level of disinvestment and public abandonment of American slum neighborhoods has no parallel in a France that retains a certain commitment to the interventionist state. In a series of articles comparing French suburbs and African American ghettos, sociologist Loïc Wacquant has argued forcefully against this comparison, stating that "to speak of 'the ghetto' in France . . . only makes it more difficult to analyze rigorously both the situation of the black community in the United States and the trajectory of the marginalized populations of the Hexagon's working-class suburbs."[47] Moreover, critiques of the idea of French suburbs as American ghettos have also come from popular culture. The film *La haine* depicts a polyglot suburban world, complete with a racially balanced cast of young antiheroes, a fact routinely commented on by its American viewers. French hip hop also remains firmly multiethnic, with many white and mixed-race performers. As the suburban rap group Suprême NTM proclaimed on its album *Authentik*:

> I am white, he is black
> So take that as an offense
> Because in France the problem has no reason to be
> The United States is not always good to copy
> Multiracial is our society
> So let's work together and create unity.[48]

The argument that the contemporary Paris suburbs continue to represent a working-class slum instead of a racial ghetto is convincing in many respects, yet it does not succeed in demonstrating that race has no place in the area today. In some ways, the ideas outlined above are contradicted, or at least nuanced, by their general context. Whereas the articles in *Immigration, vie politique et populisme en banlieue parisienne* argue strongly for a class interpretation of suburbia, the quotation from the book jacket in contrast touches on most of the racialized stereotypes of the Paris suburbs to attract its readers. Moreover, the book was published not by Presses Universitaires de France or Editions Ouvrières, but by Editions L'Harmattan, France's classic *tiers-mondiste* publishing company. Similarly, the verses from NTM Suprême make the case against the existence of French ghettos by using an avowedly ghettocentric musical form; the United States may not be worth copying socially or politically, but its cultural influence remains incontestable. More generally, although much distinguishes French suburbs from American ghettos, the fact remains that in recent years large segments of French public opinion have seized on the example of the latter as a way of coming to grips with the problems of the former. The rise of a racialized perspective on the Paris suburbs thus constitutes a significant window onto French views of themselves at the end of the century.

But what does this glimpse reveal? I would argue that this racialized image of the Paris suburbs is by no means new, but has important roots going back to the nineteenth century. It has assumed new importance in the last twenty years due to a variety of factors, notably the growth of American cultural influence on France, the economic crisis after the mid-1970s, and the rise of a large nonwhite population in the metropole. Yet ultimately the idea of a transition from Red Belt to Black Belt remains a myth, important less for its veracity than for what it shows about those who create it. The intensity of the anxieties surrounding the Paris suburbs illustrates the increasing importance of urban, and suburban, spaces to French life in general. Only since 1931 have the majority of French people lived in cities, but by the end of the twentieth century, the Paris suburbs alone housed well over 10 percent of the nation's population.[49] Moreover, in France and elsewhere the city has long symbolized citizenship. The relationship of the suburbs to the city, functionally integrated but legally marginal, neatly replicates the relationship between immigrants and citizens in contemporary France.[50]

In considering the recent history of the Paris suburbs, one must view questions of both race and class as crucial to the experience of metropolitan spatial marginality, neither dependent on the other, but both interacting in different ways at different times. The concept of the Paris suburbs as a postcolonial urban space has much merit, but only if one recognizes that they did not neatly assume this identity in 1981, 1960, or even 1945. Rather, the interweaving of colonialism and postcolonialism, like that of race and class, constitutes an important characteristic of French identity in the twentieth century as a whole.

Notes

This essay originally appeared in *Esprit* (fall 2001).

1 See, for example, Colette Pétonnet, *On est tous dans le brouillard: Ethnologie des banlieues* (Paris: Editions Galilée, 1985).

2 The literature on race and class is, of course, enormous and growing every day. Works I have found particularly useful include Michael Omi and Howard Winant, *Racial Formation in the United States:*

From the 1960s to the 1990s (New York: Routledge, 1994); Eric Arnesen, *Waterfront Workers of New Orleans: Race, Class, and Politics, 1863–1923* (New York: Oxford University Press, 1991); Earl Lewis, *In Their Own Interests: Race, Class, and Power in Twentieth-Century Norfolk, Virginia* (Berkeley: University of California Press, 1991); and the work of scholars of "whiteness," particularly David Roediger.

3   Charles Tilly, *The Contentious French* (Cambridge, Mass.: Belknap, 1986).

4   Anne McClintock, *Imperial Leather: Race, Gender, and Sexuality in the Colonial Context* (New York: Routledge, 1995); McClintock, Aamir Mufti, and Ella Shohat, eds., *Dangerous Liaisons: Gender, Nation, and Postcolonial Perspectives* (Minneapolis: University of Minnesota Press, 1997); Gayatri Chakravorty Spivak, *A Critique of Postcolonial Reason: Toward a History of the Vanishing Present* (Cambridge, Mass.: Harvard University Press, 1999).

5   On the development of the Paris suburbs in the late nineteenth century, see Jean Bastié, *La croissance de la banlieue parisienne* (Paris: Presses Universitaires de France, 1964); Louis Chevalier, "La formation de la population parisienne au 19e siècle," *Cahiers de l'Institut national des études démographiques* 10 (1950); René Clozier, *La gare du nord* (Paris: J. B. Baillière, 1940); Maurice Daumas and Jacques Payen, eds., *Evolution de la géographie industrielle de Paris et sa proche banlieue au XIXe siècle* (Paris: Centre de documentation d'histoire des techniques, 1976).

6   Tyler Stovall, *The Rise of the Paris Red Belt* (Berkeley: University of California Press, 1990).

7   Many communist activists themselves lived in *lotissements*.

8   On the Paris Red Belt, see Stovall, *The Rise of the Paris Red Belt*; Jean-Paul Brunet, *Saint-Denis, la ville rouge: Socialisme et communisme en banlieue ouvrière, 1890–1939* (Paris: Hachette, 1980); Annie Fourcaut, *Bobigny: Banlieue rouge* (Paris: Editions Ouvrières, 1986); Jacques Girault, ed., *Ouvriers en banlieue, XIXe-XXe siècle* (Paris: Editions Ouvrières, 1998).

9   On the suburbs since 1980, see Colette Pétonnet, *Espaces habités: Ethnologie des banlieues* (Paris: Editions Galilée, 1982); Gilles Kepel, *Les banlieues d'Islam: Naissance d'une réligion en France* (Paris: Editions du Seuil, 1991); Farid Aichoune, *Nés en banlieue* (Paris: Ramsay, 1991); and Desmond Avery, *Civilisations de La Courneuve: Images brisées d'une cité* (Paris: Editions L'Harmattan, 1987).

10 On postwar immigration to France, see Gérard Noiriel, *Le creuset français: Histoire de l'immigration, XIXe-XXe siècles* (Paris: Editions du Seuil, 1988); James Hollifield, "Immigration and Modern-

ization," in *Searching for the New France*, ed. Hollifield and George Ross (New York: Routledge, 1991); Catherine Wihtol de Wenden, *Les immigrés et la politique: Cent cinquante ans d'évaluation* (Paris: Presses de la Fondation Nationale des Sciences Politiques, 1988); Alec G. Hargreaves, *Immigration, 'Race,' and Ethnicity in Contemporary France* (London: Routledge, 1995).

11 On the industrial and economic decline of France since the early 1970s, see Jean and Jacqueline Fourastié, *D'une France à une autre: Avant et après les trente glorieuses* (Paris: Fayard, 1987); John Tuppen, *France under Recession, 1981–1986* (Albany: State University of New York Press, 1988); Elie Cohen, *L'état brancardier: Politiques du déclin industriel, 1974–1984* (Paris: Calmann-Lévy, 1989); Jean-Pierre Terrail, *Destins ouvriers: La fin d'une classe?* (Paris: Presses Universitaires de France, 1990).

12 Didier Lapeyronnie, "Assimilation, mobilisation et action collective chez les jeunes de la seconde génération de l'immigration maghrébine," *Revue française de sociologie* 28 (1987): 287–318; Maria Llaumett, *Les jeunes d'origine étrangère: De la marginalisation à la participation* (Paris: Editions L'Harmattan, 1984).

13 Anthony Pagden, "Identity Formation in Spanish America," in *Colonial Identity in the Atlantic World, 1500–1800*, ed. Nicholas Canny and Pagden (Princeton, N.J.: Princeton University Press, 1987); Ann L. Stoler, "Sexual Affronts and Racial Frontiers: European Identities and the Cultural Politics of Exclusion in Colonial Southeast Asia," *Comparative Studies in Society and History* 34, 2 (1992): 514–32; Joel Williamson, *New People: Miscegenation and Mulattoes in the United States* (New York: Free Press, 1980); Werner Sollors, *Neither Black nor White yet Both: Thematic Explorations of Interracial Literature* (New York: Oxford University Press, 1997).

14 Alain Anselin, *L'émigration antillaise en France: Du bantoustan au ghetto* (Paris: Editions Anthropos, 1979); Stephanie Condon and Philip Ogden, "Emigration from the French Caribbean: The Origins of an Organized Migration," *International Journal of Urban and Regional Research* 15, 4 (1991): 505–23; Gary Freeman, "Caribbean Migration to Britain and France: From Assimilation to Selection," in *The Caribbean Exodus*, ed. Barry B. Levine (New York: Praeger, 1987), 185–203.

15 Adil Jazouli, *Les années banlieues* (Paris: Editions du Seuil, 1992).

16 "Spécial banlieues: Avant L'incendie," *Le Nouvel Observateur*, 20–26 June 1991; "La France de l'exclusion," *Esprit*, June 1992; Jazouli, *Les années banlieues*; Lapeyronnie, "Assimilation, mobilisation."

17 Peter Fysh and Jim Wolfreys, *The Politics of Racism in France* (New York: St. Martin's, 1998); Françoise Gaspard, *A Small City in France*, trans. Arthur Goldhammer (Cambridge, Mass.: Harvard

University Press, 1995); Jonathan Marcus, *The National Front and French Politics: The Resistible Rise of Jean-Marie Le Pen* (New York: New York University Press, 1995).

18 Henri Rey, "Le Front national en Seine-Saint-Denis: à l'origine d'une implantation électorale réussie," in *Immigration, vie politique et populisme en banlieue parisienne*, ed. Jean-Paul Brunet (Paris: Editions L'Harmattan, 1995), 386.

19 Adil Jazouli, *L'action collective des jeunes maghrébins de France* (Paris: Editions L'Harmattan, 1986); Harlem Désir, *Touche pas à mon pote* (Paris: B. Grasset, 1985); Julia Kristeva, *Lettre ouverte à Harlem Désir* (Paris: Rivages, 1990); Serge Malik, *Histoire secrète de SOS-Racisme* (Paris: A. Michel, 1990).

20 Mehdi Charef, *Le thé au harem d'Archi Ahmed* (Paris: Mercure de France, 1983); Alec G. Hargreaves, *Immigration and Identity in Beur Fiction: Voices from the North African Immigrant Community in France* (New York: Berg, 1997).

21 Carrie Tarr, "French Cinema and Post-colonial Minorities," in *Post-colonial Cultures in France*, ed. Alec G. Hargreaves and Mark McKinney (London: Routledge, 1997), 59–83; Christian Bosséno, "Immigrant Cinema: National Cinema—the Case of Beur Film," in *Popular European Cinema*, ed. Richard Dyer and Ginette Vincendeau (London: Routledge, 1992), 150–66; Dina Sherzer, ed., *Cinema, Colonialism, Postcolonialism: Perspectives from the French and Francophone World* (Austin: University of Texas Press, 1996).

22 Steve Cannon, "Paname City Rapping: B-Boys in the *Banlieues* and Beyond," in Hargreaves and McKinney, *Post-colonial Cultures in France*, 150–66; Hugues Bazin, *La culture hip-hop* (Paris: Desclée de Brouwer, 1995).

23 This is a major theme in the study of American rap music, and, for that matter, of African American culture and history in general. See Trisha Rose, *Black Noise: Rap Music and Black Culture in Contemporary America* (Middletown, Conn.: Wesleyan University Press, 1994).

24 Raymond Bachollet, *Négripub: L'image des noirs dans la publicité depuis un siècle* (Paris: Société des amis de la Bibliothèque Forney, 1987); Jan Nederveen Pieterse, *White on Black: Images of Africa and Blacks in Western Popular Culture* (New Haven, Conn.: Yale University Press, 1992).

25 Kristin Ross, *Fast Cars, Clean Bodies: Decolonization and the Reordering of French Culture* (Cambridge, Mass.: MIT Press, 1995); Raymond F. Betts, *France and Decolonisation, 1900–1960* (London: Macmillan, 1991); Maxim Silverman, *Deconstructing the Nation: Immigration, Racism, and Citizenship in Modern France* (London: Routledge, 1992).

26 Richard F. Kuisel, *Seducing the French: The Dilemma of American-*

ization (Berkeley: University of California Press, 1993); Georges Du-
hamel, *America: The Menace: Scenes from the Life of the Future*,
trans. Charles Miner Thompson (Boston: Houghton Mifflin, 1931);
Jean-Jacques Servan-Schreiber, *The American Challenge*, trans. Ronald Steel (New York: Atheneum, 1968).

27   See Alain Finkielkraut, *The Defeat of the Mind*, trans. Judith Fried-
lander (New York: Columbia University Press, 1995); Julia Kristeva,
Nations without Nationalism, trans. Leon S. Roudiez (New York:
Columbia University Press, 1993); and Emmanuel Todd, *Le destin
des immigrés: Assimilation et ségrégation dans les démocraties occidentales* (Paris: Editions du Seuil, 1994). For a good summary of this
debate, see Jean-Philippe Mathy, *French Resistance: The French-
American Culture Wars* (Minneapolis: University of Minnesota
Press, 2000). An interesting perspective on this debate between universalism and multiculturalism is provided in Michel Wieviorka, ed.,
Une société fragmentée? Le multiculturalisme en débat (Paris: Editions La Découverte, 1997).

28   For examples of works by French scholars that do take race seriously,
see Michel Wieviorka, *La France raciste* (Paris: Editions du Seuil,
1992); Philippe Bataille *Le racisme au travail* (Paris: Editions La
Découverte, 1997); and Fred Constant, *Le multiculturalisme* (Paris:
Flammarion, 2000). See also Tyler Stovall, "Review Article: Histories of Race in France," *French Politics and Society* 18, 3 (fall 2000):
137–42.

29   René Galissot, "Nationalisme français et racisme: A l'encontre
d'idées reçues," *Politique Aujourd'hui* 4 (1984); Etienne Balibar and
Immanuel Wallerstein, *Race, Nation, Classe: Les Identités Ambiguës*
(Paris: Editions La Découverte, 1988); Ann Laura Stoler, *Race and
the Education of Desire: Foucault's History of Sexuality and the
Colonial Order of Things* (Durham, N.C.: Duke University Press,
1995); Richard N. Lebow, *White Britain and Black Ireland: The
Influence of Stereotypes on Colonial Policy* (Philadelphia: Institute
for the Study of Human Issues, 1976).

30   J. Arthur de Gobineau, *Essai sur l'inégalité des races humaines*
([1853] Paris: P. Belfond, 1967); Michael D. Biddis, *Father of Racist
Ideology: The Social and Political Thought of Count Gobineau*
(New York: Weybright and Talley, 1970).

31   John M. Merriman, *The Margins of City Life: Explorations on the
French Urban Frontier, 1815–1851* (New York: Oxford University
Press, 1991); and Bastié, *La croissance de la banlieue parisienne*.

32   Alexandre Privat-d'Anglemout, *Paris inconnu* (Paris: Adolphe De-
lahays, 1861).

33   Wladimir d'Ormesson, *Le problème des lotissements* (Paris, 1928);
Edouard Blanc, *La ceinture rouge* (Paris, 1927).

34 Jacques Valdour, *Ateliers et taudis de la banlieue de Paris* (Paris: Spes, 1923). Valdour also commented disparagingly and at length on non-European suburban immigrants, with whom he lumped the area's Jewish population.

35 Alice Bullard, *Exile to Paradise: Savagery and Civilization in Paris and the South Pacific, 1790–1900* (Stanford, Calif.: Stanford University Press, 2000).

36 Gwendolyn Wright, *The Politics of Design in French Colonial Urbanism* (Chicago: University of Chicago Press, 1991), 34.

37 Hubert Lyautey, quoted in André LeRévérend, *Lyautey* (Paris: Fayard, 1983), 447; Patricia A. Morton, *Hybrid Modernities: Architecture and Representation at the 1931 Colonial Exposition, Paris* (Cambridge, Mass.: MIT Press, 2000); my translation and Lyautey's original capitalization.

38 Pierre Lhande, *Le Christ dans la banlieue: Enquête sur la vie religieuse dans les milieux ouvriers de la banlieue de Paris* (Paris: Plon, 1927), 21; my translation and Lhande's original capitalization.

39 Ibid., 263. See, for example, Francis Audiau, *Souvenirs d'Asie: Inde et Malaisie: Vie d'un prêtre français, missionaire au vingtième siècle* (Paris: Editions L'Harmattan, 1995); André Berthelot, *Hippolyte Bertier (1919–1992), redemptoriste: Premier eveque du Niger en terre d'Islam* (Paris: Editions L'Harmattan, 1997); James Clifford, *Person and Myth: Maurice Leenhardt in the Melanesian World* (Berkeley: University of California Press, 1982).

40 Marie-Louise Azzoug et al., *Vincennes: Ou le désir d'apprendre* (Paris: A. Moreau, 1979); Pierre Merlin, *L'université assassinée: Vincennes, 1968–1980* (Paris: Ramsay, 1980).

41 Brunet, *Immigration, vie politique et populisme*, back book jacket.

42 It is noteworthy that Brunet's book deals only with the suburbs of Paris, not those of Lyons, Marseille, or any other French city. Certainly problems of immigration and race exist in suburban areas outside those of the capital. However, for a variety of reasons, ranging from their sheer size and racial diversity to their prominence as the object of historical and social science research, the Paris suburbs have tended to take center stage in debates about the problems of the *banlieue*.

43 The work of Gérard Noiriel is the most prominent example of this. For an excellent comparative analysis of approaches to immigration history in France and the United States, see Nancy L. Green, *"Le Melting-Pot: Made in America, Produced in France," Journal of American History* 86 (1999): 1188–1208.

44 Christian Poiret, "Ségregation, ethnicisation et politiques territorialisées: Les familles originaires d'Afrique noire en région parisienne," in Brunet, *Immigration, vie politique et populisme*.

45 On this point, see Silverman, *Deconstructing the Nation*, 95–106.

46 See in particular the brief overview article of Patrick Simon, "Banlieues: De la concentration au ghetto," *Esprit* (June 1992). See also the special issue of *Esprit* from February 1991 on the problems of the suburbs.

47 Loïc J. D. Wacquant, "Banlieues françaises et ghetto noir américain: De l'amalgame à la comparaison," *French Politics and Society* 10, 4 (1992): 81–103; my translation. Other articles by Wacquant on this theme include "Pour comprendre la "crise" des banlieues," *French Politics and Society* 13, 4 (1995): 68–81; and "The Comparative Structure and Experience of Urban Exclusion: 'Race,' Class, and Space in Paris and Chicago," in *Poverty, Inequality, and the Future of Social Policy*, ed. Roger Lawson, Katherine McFate, and William Julius Wilson (New York: Russell Sage, 1995).

48 "Je suis blanc, il est noir / Alors prends ça comme une offense / Car en France le problème n'a pas lieu d'exister / Les États-Unis ne sont pas toujours bons à copier / Multiraciale est notre société / Alors bougeons ensemble, et créons l'unité." Quoted in Bernard Loupias, "Les raps pour le dire," *Le Nouvel Observateur*, 20–26 June 1991, 49.

49 Susanna Magri and Christian Topalov, eds., *Villes ouvrières: 1900–1950* (Paris: Editions L'Harmattan, 1989); Maurice Agulhon et al., *Histoire de la France urbaine*, vol. 4, *La ville de l'âge industriel* (Paris: Editions du Seuil, 1983).

50 Rogers Brubaker, *Citizenship and Nationhood in France and Germany* (Cambridge, Mass.: Harvard University Press, 1992); Adrian Favell, *Philosophies of Integration: Immigration and the Idea of Citizenship in France and Britain* (New York: Saint Martin's, 1998); Miriam Feldblum, *Reconstructing Citizenship: The Politics of Nationality Reform and Immigration in Contemporary France* (Albany: State University of New York Press, 1999); and Silverman, *Deconstructing the Nation*.

Notes on Contributors

LEORA AUSLANDER is associate professor of modern European history at the University of Chicago. She is the author of *Taste and Power: Furnishing Modern France* (Berkeley: University of California Press, 1996); "The Everyday of Citizenship: Aesthetics, Affect, and Law in France and Germany, 1890–1933," in *Material Politics: States, Consumers, and Political Cultures*, ed. Martin Daunton and Matthew Hilton (Oxford: Berg, 2001); and " 'Jewish Taste'? Jews, and the Aesthetics of Everyday Life in Paris and Berlin, 1933–1942," in *Histories of Leisure*, ed. Rudy Koshar (Oxford: Berg, 2002). Professor Auslander is currently researching two book-length manuscripts: "Revolutionary Taste: Everyday Life and Politics in England, the United States, and France" and "The Everyday of Citizenship: Aesthetics, Affect, and Law in France and Germany, 1920–1945."

CLAUDE BLANCKAERT is director of research at the Centre National de la Recherche Scientifique (Centre Alexandre Koyré, Paris) and honorary president of the Société Française pour l'Histoire des Sciences de l'Homme. He has published extensively on the history of anthropology, natural history, and the popularization of science. He is editor of *Naissance d'ethnologie? Anthropologie et missions en Amérique, XVIe–XVIIIe siècle* (Paris: Editions du Cerf, 1985); *Des sciences contre l'homme*, 2 vols. (Paris: Autrement, 1993); *Le terrain des sciences humaines: Instructions et enquêtes (XVIIIe–XXe siècle)* (Paris: Editions L'Harmattan, 1996); *Les politiques de l'anthropologie: Discours et pratiques en France (1860–1940)* (Paris: Editions L'Harmattan, 2001); and coeditor of *Julien-Joseph Virey: Naturaliste et anthropologue* (Paris: Vrin, 1988); *Histoire de l'anthropologie: Hommes, idées, moments* (special edition of *Bulletins et mémoires de la Société d'Anthropologie de Paris* 3–4 [1989]); *Le Muséum au premier siècle de son histoire* (Paris: Editions du Muséum, 1997); *Nature, histoire, société: Essais en homage à Jacques Roger* (Paris: Klincksieck, 1995); and *L'histoire des sciences de l'homme: Trajectoire, enjeux et questions vives* (Paris: Editions L'Harmattan, 1999). He has also edited Jacques Roger, *Pour une histoire des sciences à part entière* (Paris: Albin Michel, 1995).

PIERRE H. BOULLE, having recently retired from McGill University, is teaching history there in a postretirement capacity. His publications have focused principally on colonial history and the study of race, including, most recently, the coauthorship of the chapter on "France

Overseas" in volume 3 (1648–1788) of the *Short Oxford History of France*, ed. William Doyle (Oxford: Oxford University Press, 2001), and the article "Race" in *Encyclopedia of the Enlightenment*, ed. Alan Charles Kors (New York: Oxford University Press, 2002). Forthcoming also in 2002 in *Revue française d'histoire d'outre-mer* is an article on the origins of the concept of race in early modern France. He is preparing a book on nonwhite residents in France in the eighteenth century.

ALICE L. CONKLIN is associate professor of history at the University of Rochester. She is the author of *A Mission to Civilize: The Republican Idea of Empire in France and West Africa, 1895–1930* (Stanford, Calif.: Stanford University Press, 1997). Her most recent article is "Civil Society, Science, and Empire in Late Republican France: The Foundation of Paris' Museum of Man," *Osiris* 17 (2002). Professor Conklin is currently coediting a special issue of *French Historical Studies*, with Julia Clancy Smith, on "What Is Colonial History," as well as writing a book on the history of French anthropology in the 1920s, 1930s, and 1940s, tentatively entitled "In the Museum of Man: Ethnographic Liberalism in France, 1920–1945."

FRED CONSTANT is professor of political science and provost of the Université Senghor in Alexandria, Egypt. He has written widely on race, France, and the Caribbean. His books include *La retraite aux flambeaux: Société et politique en Martinique* (Paris: Editions Caribéenes, 1988); *La citoyenneté* (Paris: Montchrestien, 1998); *Le multiculturalisme* (Paris: Flammarion, 2000).

LAURENT DUBOIS is assistant professor of history at Michigan State University. His book, *A Colony of Citizens: Revolution and Slave Emancipation in the French Caribbean, 1787–1804* (Omohundro Institute of Early American History and Culture), is forthcoming from University of North Carolina Press in 2003. He is now working on a narrative history of the Haitian Revolution and, with Richard Turits, a general history of the Caribbean.

YAËL SIMPSON FLETCHER is visiting assistant professor of history at the University of the South. She has published essays in *Memory, Nostalgia, and Identity: Algeria 1800–2000*, ed. Patricia M. E. Lorcin (forthcoming); *Gender, Sexuality, and Colonial Modernities*, ed. Antoinette Burton (New York: Routledge, 1999); *Imperial Cities: Landscape, Display, and Identity*, ed. Felix Driver and David Gilbert (Manchester: Manchester University Press, 1999); and *Domesticating the Empire: Race, Gender, and Family Life in French and Dutch Colonialism, 1830–1962*, ed. Julia Clancy-Smith and Frances Gouda (Charlottesville: University Press of Virginia, 1998). She is completing a book on imperial and transnational identities in interwar Marseilles.

RICHARD FOGARTY recently completed his dissertation in modern French history at the University of California, Santa Barbara and is visiting assistant professor of history at Shippensburg University. He is currently writing a book on the history of colonial soldiers in France during World War I.

JOHN GARRIGUS is professor of history at Jacksonville University. He has published several articles on the free people of color of Saint-Domingue. His book manuscript, provisionally entitled "'Sons of the Same Father': Race, Identity, and Citizenship in Prerevolutionary Saint-Domingue, 1760–1804," is currently under review.

DANA S. HALE is assistant professor of modern European history at Howard University. Her interests include questions of race, colonialism, and representation in modern France. Her most recent publication is "L'indigène mis en scène en France: Entre exposition et exhibition (1880–1931)," in Zoos humains, ed. Nicolas Bancel et al. Professor Hale is currently preparing a manuscript entitled "Races on Display: French Representation of the Colonial 'Native,' 1886–1940."

THOMAS C. HOLT is the James Westfall Thompson Professor of American and African American history at the University of Chicago. His books include Black over White: Negro Political Leadership in South Carolina during Reconstruction (Urbana: University of Illinois Press, 1977); The Problem of Freedom: Race, Labor, and Politics in Jamaica and Britain, 1832–1938 (Baltimore: Johns Hopkins University Press, 1995); and, most recently, The Problem of Race in the Twenty-First Century (Cambridge, Mass.: Harvard University Press, 2000). He is currently working on a general history of the African American people.

PATRICIA M. E. LORCIN is assistant professor of history at Texas Technical University. Her interests center around colonial history and post-colonial studies in modern France. She is the author of Imperial Identities: Stereotyping, Prejudice, and Race in Colonial Algeria (New York: St. Martin's, 1995). Professor Lorcin is currently working on two projects: a monograph on the construction of gender and imperialism in the works of women novelists; and an edited volume on identity, memory, and nostalgia in colonial Algeria.

DENNIS MCENNERNEY is assistant professor of political science at the State University of New York, Oneonta. His interests include political theory, comparative politics, and ideology in twentieth-century France. He is currently writing a study of the problems of resistance and freedom among intellectuals in France after World War II.

MICHAEL A. OSBORNE is associate professor of history at the University of California, Santa Barbara. He is a specialist in the history of the biological sciences in nineteenth-century France, and the author of

Nature, the Exotic, and the Science of French Colonialism (Bloomington: Indiana University Press, 1994). Professor Osborne's current research concerns French tropical medicine, French military medicine, and French environmental history.

LYNN E. PALERMO is assistant professor of French at Susquehanna University. She is completing her dissertation entitled "Modernity and its Discontents: Cultural Debates in Interwar France" and is also working on a study of Louis Aragon and the Anti-Colonial Exposition of 1931.

SUE PEABODY is associate professor of history at Washington State University, Vancouver. Her book *"There Are No Slaves in France": The Political Culture of Race and Slavery in the Ancien Régime* was published by Oxford University Press in 1996. She is currently working on two projects: a comparative study of slaves' suits for freedom in the Atlantic world, and a study of women in the French Caribbean during the period of slavery.

ALYSSA GOLDSTEIN SEPINWALL is assistant professor of history at California State University, San Marcos. Her articles on the Abbé Grégoire have appeared in the *Annales historiques de la Révolution française*, *Revue française d'histoire d'outre-mer*, and the essay collection *The Abbé Grégoire and his World*, ed. Jeremy D. Popkin and Richard H. Popkin (Dordrecht: Kluver Academi Publishers, 2000). She is currently finishing a book manuscript on Grégoire, the French Revolution, and the idea of universalism in France.

TYLER STOVALL is professor of French history at the University of California, Berkeley. He has written several articles on the history of modern France, as well as three books: *The Rise of the Paris Red Belt* (Berkeley: University of California Press, 1990); *Paris Noir: African Americans in the City of Light* (Boston: Houghton-Mifflin, 1996); and *France since the Second World War* (London: Longman, 2002). He is currently working on two projects: a study of consumerism and working-class politics in Paris at the end of World War I; and a study of Caribbean migration to France in the nineteenth and twentieth centuries.

MICHAEL G. VANN is a lecturer in history at Santa Clara University and a specialist on French colonialism in Vietnam. His most recent article is "The Colonial Casbah on the Silver Screen: Using *Pépé le Moko* and *The Battle of Algiers* to Teach Colonialism, Race, and Globalization in French History," *Radical History Review* 83 (2002). Professor Vann is currently working on a study of colonial whiteness in French-ruled Hanoi and is also preparing an edited volume on the new historiography of colonial France.

GARY WILDER is assistant professor of history at Pomona College, specializing in the history of colonialism and race in modern France. He has written several articles, including, most recently, "Framing Greater France," *Journal of Historical Sociology* (forthcoming). Professor Wilder's book *The French Imperial Nation-State: Colonial Humanism, Negritude, and Interwar Political Rationality* is forthcoming from the University of Chicago Press.

Index

Index 383